I0882203

New Facets of Economic Complexity in Modern Financial Markets

The book is motivated by the disruptions introduced by the financial crisis and the many attempts that have followed to propose new ideas and remedies.

Assembling contributions by authors from a variety of backgrounds, this collection illustrates the potentials resulting from the marriage of financial economics, complexity theory and an out-of-equilibrium view of the economic world. Challenging the traditional hypotheses that lie behind financial market functioning, new evidence is provided about the hidden factors fuelling bubbles, the impact of agents' heterogeneity, the importance of endogeneity in the information transmission mechanism, the dynamics of herding, the sources of volatility, the portfolio optimization techniques, the financial innovation and the trend identification in a nonlinear time-series framework.

Presenting the advances made in financial market analysis and putting emphasis on nonlinear dynamics, this book suggests interdisciplinary methodologies for the study of well-known stylized facts and financial abnormalities.

This book was originally published as a special issue of *The European Journal of Finance.*

Catherine Kyrtsou is Professor of MacroFinance in the Department of Economics at the University of Macedonia, Greece and is associated with EconomiX, University of Paris Nanterre. She is also Deputy Director of CAC at the IXXI Institut Rhône-Alpin des Systèmes Complexes in Lyon, France. Her research focuses on money and capital markets, investors' behaviour, financial instability, economic complexity and monetary policy.

Didier Sornette is Professor and Chair of Entrepreneurial Risks at ETH Zurich, Switzerland. He is also Professor at the Swiss Finance Institute and is associated with both the departments of Physics and of Earth Sciences at ETH Zurich. He is the founder of the Financial Crisis Observatory and Systematic Investment Management AG.

Chris Adcock is Professor of Quantitative Finance at SOAS, University of London, UK. His research focuses on portfolio selection and asset pricing theory. He is an advisor to several investment managers and the Founding Editor of *The European Journal of Finance.*

New Facets of Economic Complexity in Modern Financial Markets

Edited by
Catherine Kyrtsou, Didier Sornette and Chris Adcock

Routledge
Taylor & Francis Group
LONDON AND NEW YORK

First published 2019
by Routledge
2 Park Square, Milton Park, Abingdon, Oxon, OX14 4RN

and by Routledge
52 Vanderbilt Avenue, New York, NY 10017

First issued in paperback 2020

Routledge is an imprint of the Taylor & Francis Group, an informa business

British Library Cataloguing-in-Publication Data
A catalogue record for this book is available from the British Library

ISBN 13: 978-0-367-67109-9 (pbk)
ISBN 13: 978-0-367-18829-0 (hbk)

Typeset in Times New Roman
by codeMantra

Publisher's Note
The publisher accepts responsibility for any inconsistencies that may have arisen during the conversion of this book from journal articles to book chapters, namely the inclusion of journal terminology.

Contents

Citation Information

The chapters in this book were originally published in *The European Journal of Finance*, volume 19, issues 5–6 (May–July 2013). When citing this material, please use the original page numbering for each article, as follows:

Introduction

Introduction – New facets of the economic complexity in modern financial markets
Catherine Kyrtsou and Didier Sornette
The European Journal of Finance, volume 19, issues 5–6 (May–July 2013) pp. 337–343

Chapter 1

Diagnostics of rational expectation financial bubbles with stochastic mean-reverting termination times
Li Lin and Didier Sornette
The European Journal of Finance, volume 19, issues 5–6 (May–July 2013) pp. 344–365

Chapter 2

Everything you always wanted to know about log-periodic power laws for bubble modeling but were afraid to ask
Petr Geraskin and Dean Fantazzini
The European Journal of Finance, volume 19, issues 5–6 (May–July 2013) pp. 366–391

Chapter 3

Heterogeneous expectations and exchange rate dynamics
Carl Chiarella, Xue-Zhong He and Min Zheng
The European Journal of Finance, volume 19, issues 5–6 (May–July 2013) pp. 392–419

Chapter 4

Asymmetric returns, gradual bubbles and sudden crashes
Weihong Huang, Huanhuan Zheng and Wai-Mun Chia
The European Journal of Finance, volume 19, issues 5–6 (May–July 2013) pp. 420–437

Chapter 5

Epidemics of rules, rational negligence and market crashes
Kartik Anand, Alan Kirman and Matteo Marsili
The European Journal of Finance, volume 19, issues 5–6 (May–July 2013) pp. 438–447

Chapter 6

A note on institutional hierarchy and volatility in financial markets
S. Alfarano, M. Milaković and M. Raddant
The European Journal of Finance, volume 19, issues 5–6 (May–July 2013) pp. 449–465

Chapter 7

Identifying reference companies using the book-to-market ratio: a minimum spanning tree approach
David Brookfield, Halim Boussabaine and Chen Su
The European Journal of Finance, volume 19, issues 5–6 (May–July 2013) pp. 466–490

Chapter 8

Risk sharing in a financial market with endogenous option prices
Jan Wenzelburger
The European Journal of Finance, volume 19, issues 5–6 (May–July 2013) pp. 491–517

Chapter 9

Performance analysis of a collateralized fund obligation (CFO) equity tranche
Shady Aboul-Enein, Georges Dionne and Nicolas Papageorgiou
The European Journal of Finance, volume 19, issues 5–6 (May–July 2013) pp. 518–553

Chapter 10

Optimal liquidation strategies regularize portfolio selection
Fabio Caccioli, Susanne Still, Matteo Marsili and Imre Kondor
The European Journal of Finance, volume 19, issues 5–6 (May–July 2013) pp. 554–571

Chapter 11

Nonlinear dynamics in economics and finance and unit root testing
Efthymios G. Pavlidis, Ivan Paya, David A. Peel and Costas Siriopoulos
The European Journal of Finance, volume 19, issues 5–6 (May–July 2013) pp. 572–588

Notes on Contributors

Shady Aboul-Enein is a Lecturer in the Department of Finance at the HEC Montréal, Canada. His research focuses on financial markets, security valuation, derivatives and risk management.

Chris Adcock is Professor of Quantitative Finance at SOAS, University of London, UK. His research focuses on portfolio selection and asset pricing theory. He is an advisor to several investment managers and the Founding Editor of *The European Journal of Finance.*

S. Alfarano is Professor in the Department of Economics at the Universitat Jaume I, Castellón de la Plana, Spain. His main areas of research are Computational Economics, Financial Economics and Macroeconomics.

Kartik Anand is an Economist within the Research Centre at the Deutsche Bundesbank. His research interests include topics in banking and sovereign debt.

Halim Boussabaine is Dean of the Faculty of Business and Law at the British University in Dubai, United Arab Emirates. His research integrates various modern management theories and emerging modelling techniques, including artificial intelligence, in order to gain a better understanding of the complexity of management processes.

David Brookfield is Senior Lecturer in Accounting and Finance at the University of Liverpool, UK. His research looks at derivatives pricing, and share price volatility and market reactions.

Fabio Caccioli is a Lecturer in the Department of Computer Science at University College London, UK, where he is a member of the Financial Computing and Analysis Group.

Wai-Mun Chia is Associate Professor of Economics at Nanyang Technological University, Singapore. Her areas of interest include international macroeconomics and cost-benefit analysis.

Carl Chiarella was Emeritus Professor of Quantitative Finance in the School of Finance and Economics at the University of Technology Sydney, Australia. His eminent career was spent working in the fields of quantitative finance, financial economics and macroeconomic dynamics.

Georges Dionne is Professor in the Department of Finance at the HEC Montréal, Canada. His research focuses on risk management, insurance, contract theory, portfolio selection and applied econometrics.

Dean Fantazzini is Chair of Econometrics and Mathematical Methods, and Deputy Head of the Moscow School of Economics, Russia. He specializes in the analysis of time series, financial econometrics and models of multifactor dependence.

Petr Geraskin is based in the Faculty of Economics at the National Research University Higher School of Economics, Moscow, Russia.

Xue-Zhong He is Professor of Finance at University of Technology Sydney, Australia. He is an internationally recognized expert in financial market modelling and nonlinear dynamics in finance and economics.

Weihong Huang is Associate Professor of Economics at Nanyang Technological University, Singapore. He is a leading expert in nonlinear dynamical economics.

Alan Kirman is Professor Emeritus of Economics at the University of Aix-Marseille III and at the Ecole des Hautes Etudes en Sciences Sociales, and is a member of the Institut Universitaire de France.

Imre Kondor is a Fellow at the London Mathematical Laboratory, UK. His current research project is to apply analytic methods borrowed from the theory of disordered systems to the problem of portfolio optimization under various risk measures and regularizers.

Catherine Kyrtsou is Professor of MacroFinance in the Department of Economics at the University of Macedonia, Greece and is associated with EconomiX, University of Paris Nanterre. She is also Deputy Director of CAC at the IXXI Institut Rhône-Alpin des Systèmes Complexes in Lyon, France. Her research focuses on money and capital markets, investors' behaviour, financial instability, economic complexity and monetary policy.

Li Lin currently works in the Business School at the East China University of Science and Technology, conducting research in Financial Engineering, Econometrics and Quantitative Finance Research.

Matteo Marsili is a Research Scientist at the Abdus Salam International Centre for Theoretical Physics, Trieste, Italy.

M. Milaković is Professor of International Economics at the University of Bamberg, Germany. His work focuses on statistical equilibrium economic modelling.

Nicolas Papageorgiou is Professor in the Department of Finance at the HEC Montréal, Canada. His research focuses on fixed income securities, credit risk modelling and alternative investment strategies.

Efthymios G. Pavlidis is Senior Lecturer in the Department of Economics at Lancaster University, Bailrigg, UK, where he works with the Centre for Financial Econometrics, Asset Markets and Monetary Policy.

Ivan Paya is Professor in the Department of Economics at Lancaster University, Bailrigg, UK. His research interests lie in the areas of Applied Macroeconomics, Financial Economics and Time Series Econometrics.

David A. Peel is Professor in the Department of Economics at Lancaster University, Bailrigg, UK. He has published widely on empirical and theoretical issues in macroeconomics, forecasting, applied economics and the economics of decision-making under uncertainty, particularly in gambling markets.

M. Raddant is a Researcher at the Institute for the World Economy, Kiel, Germany. His main research interests include financial markets and complex financial systems.

Costas Siriopoulos is Professor of Finance at the College of Business, Zayed University, Dubai, United Arab Emirates. His research interests include time-series analysis, financial econometrics, market finance, risk analysis and banking regulation.

Didier Sornette is Professor and Chair of Entrepreneurial Risks at ETH Zurich, Switzerland. He is also Professor at the Swiss Finance Institute and is associated with both the departments of Physics and of Earth Sciences at ETH Zurich. He is the founder of the Financial Crisis Observatory and Systematic Investment Management AG.

Susanne Still is Professor of Information and Computer Sciences at the University of Hawai'i, Honolulu, USA. Her research focuses on the physics of computation and optimal information processing, and machine learning applications.

Chen Su is Senior Lecturer in the Business School at Newcastle University, UK, with a research interest in empirical finance and stock market behaviour.

Jan Wenzelburger is Professor of Economics at the University of Liverpool, UK. His main areas of interest are the economics of banking, agent-based finance and theory of expectations formation.

Huanhuan Zheng is Assistant Professor in the Lee Kuan Yew School of Public Policy at the National University of Singapore, with research interests in financial economics, asset pricing and international pricing.

Min Zheng is Associate Professor in the China Institute for Actuarial Science at the Central University of Finance and Economics, Beijing, China.

Introduction – New Facets of the Economic Complexity in Modern Financial Markets

Catherine Kyrtsou and Didier Sornette

Today, much of the applied and theoretical research in finance is influenced by the mainstream view that financial liberalization, global integration, financial innovation, credit creation, increasing market size and liquidity promote growth, improve market stability and positively impact welfare. This view was seemingly supported by the phenomenon dubbed 'the great moderation', characterized by low inflation, reduced financial volatility and smooth sustained GDP growth observed in most developed countries in the last 20 years preceding 2007. The belief was that the above supposedly beneficial processes have led to a genuine taming of the economic beast. However, the emergence of the recent financial crisis, unfolded with the bankruptcy of Lehman Brothers, the occurrence of stock market drawdowns larger than 40%, with the subsequent need for massive bank bailouts as well as the unprecedented monetary actions of the Federal Reserve/European Central Bank, obliged even the firmest believers of 'the great moderation' to reconsider.

As recalled by Merton (1992): 'financial innovation is viewed as the "engine" driving the financial system towards its goal of improving the performance of what economists call the real economy'. Amongst the many examples supporting this stance, we can mention that specialized investment banks emerged in the nineteenth century to evaluate the profitability of railroad companies (Tufano 1997), or that venture capital firms evolved to analyze and fund high-tech entrepreneurs (Gisler, Sornette, and Woodard 2011). According to Michalopoulos, Laeven, and Levine (2009), technological innovation and thus economic growth stops unless financiers continuously innovate. Therefore, financial innovation seems to kill two birds with one stone. It ensures the continuation of technological innovation by providing financial resources to entrepreneurs by credit creation and, therefore, supports economic growth. At the same time, it makes the market more complete by the issuance of new securities that contribute to its greater stability.

When confronted with reality, advocating that financial and technological innovations are inextricably linked leads to a paradox. Indeed, financial innovations in the last 20 years have mainly been concerned with accounting, regulatory and tax arbitrage (Knoll 2008; Smith and Smithson 1990). In recent years, financial innovation has not played its expected role in improving market processes, which should have been to reallocate risk, reduce agency costs and raise liquidity (Finnerty 1992). Among the main constituting factors of financial innovation, such as tax and regulatory arbitrage, classic arbitrage, reduction of the expected costs of financial distress, and increase of corporations' debt capacity (Smith and Smithson 1990), Miller (1992) argues that the exploitation of regulatory inconsistencies has been one of the main drivers of financial innovation, while Stiglitz[1] concludes that 'the people who invented [derivative instruments] have incentives to abuse them'.

Schumpeter (1912) pointed out that the key element of growth was the transfer of capital from old to new and more innovative businesses through the extension of credit via the fractional reserve banking system (FRB) that enables banks to create credit virtually out of nothing, helped in this task by financial innovation. Minsky (1986, 1993) emphasized the importance of credit as a key driver in the banks' pursuit of profit maximization through continuous innovation. His classification of income–debt relations as part of his 'Financial Instability Hypothesis' identifies distinct stages of the economy as it moves from stability to instability. Contrary to equilibrium economics, his qualitative model demonstrated the intrinsically dynamic nature of the economy, driven by various degrees of financing. The contemporary economist Werner (2005), like Schumpeter, emphasizes the FRB system as a key driver of credit and makes an important contribution to understanding the nature of credit by distinguishing between credit that is part of GDP and credit that merely drives up asset prices.

Regarding the actual benefits of financial innovation, Gennaioli, Shleifer, and Vishny (2011) show that, if there is room for financial innovation, new securities tend to be over-issued due to 'local thinking'. Hence, markets for new securities are more fragile. When news about unattended risks catch investors by surprise, they dump the 'false substitutes' and fly to the safety of traditional securities. In their comprehensive analysis of worldwide financial crises, Reinhart and Rogoff (2009) report that 'for the advanced economies during 1800–2008, the picture that emerges is one of serial Banking crises'. In rich as well as poor countries, systemic banking crises are 'typically preceded by asset price bubbles, large capital inflows and credit booms'.

Driven by the aforementioned issues, newly presented tools and techniques provided evidence that standard financial economic approaches can fail to provide realistic interpretations of bubbles and crashes that can be of practical use (Kaizoji and Sornette 2009). Indeed, neither the academic nor professional literature provides a clear consensus for an operational definition of financial bubbles. Moreover, there does not seem to be accepted methodologies for their *ex ante* diagnosis. Instead, the literature reflects a permeating culture that simply assumes that any diagnostic of a bubble's demise is inherently impossible, perhaps taking the efficient market hypothesis too literally. In the same way that financial innovation and credit creation are thought to be critical catalytic elements of economic growth, bubbles may also show a positive Janus face. This can take the form of innovations both in the financial and technological spheres that lead to significant long-term welfare gains (Gisler and Sornette 2009, 2010; Gisler, Sornette, and Woodard 2011). But this does not need to be always the case, especially when the bubbles are seemingly confined to the banking sector.

Financial innovation suffers from another important shortcoming. Indeed, according to financial theory, financial engineers and 'quants' price contingent claims on the basis of the hedging cost of the issued security, that is, under the condition of no-arbitrage. But as recalled by Barberis and Thaler (2003), the absence of arbitrage does not mean that prices are right. No-arbitrage prices are equilibrium prices provided that each asset has an infinitesimal weight in the economy (Connor 1982; Dybvig 1983; Grinblatt and Titman 1983). This assumption is seriously in contradiction with empirical evidence, due to the fat-tailed distribution of financial asset sizes known as Zipf's law (Saichev, Malevergne, and Sornette 2009). This later stylized fact turns out to be instrumental in explaining the cross-section of asset returns (Malevergne, Santa-Clara, and Sornette 2009). In opposition to equilibrium prices, arbitrage prices do not account for the supply and demand of assets and, therefore, neglect the feedback that trading and hedging strategies have on asset prices, which can lead to market instabilities.

In this respect, if Kyle (1985) was the first to account for the feedback of trading practices on market prices, only recently have several empirical and theoretical results shown that such feedback effects can cause dynamic instabilities due to portfolio optimization that increase cross-correlations between assets (Marsili, Raffaelli, and Ponso 2009), or can affect volatility due to heterogeneous beliefs (Zapatero 1998) or options trading (Bhamra and Uppal 2009; Ni, Pearson, and Poteshman 2005; Sircar and Papanicolaou 1998) or even reveal rich macroeconomic dynamics (Kyrtsou and Labys 2006, 2007). This calls for a view of financial markets as dynamical systems made of several entangled interacting components with complex feedback loops (Schweitzer et al. 2009).

In this view, trading strategies can affect the market in important ways. Furthermore, the proliferation of financial instruments, in a model with heterogeneous agents, is found to lead to market instability. Brock et al. (2010) formalized this idea and proved that the introduction of hedging instruments – which is supposed to make the market more complete and hence more stable – may destabilize it in the presence of traders who have heterogeneous expectations and adapt their behavior according to experience-based reinforcement learning. The destabilization becomes more likely as a consequence of the leverage effect of buying more of the risky stock while hedging by shorting the Arrow securities. In addition, the presence of fully rational traders does not always stabilize the financial system. This model does not, however, explain the origin of the market instability. It only states that, if the market is genuinely unstable, the introduction of hedging instruments makes the instability more likely and pronounced.

In a series of papers, Caccioli and Marsili, (2009), Caccioli Marsili, and Vivo (2009) and Marsili (2009) provide a possible answer to the question of the origin of the market instability in relation with the introduction of contingent claims. They identify bifurcations in the dynamic system that describes the financial market when it becomes less incomplete. In this context, the market becomes more unstable as additional Arrow securities are introduced and approaches the ideal situation of completeness. Basically, the intuition is that, as the market becomes less incomplete, the possibility to replicate the same cash flows using different portfolios increases the leverage and enhances the price fluctuations. Hence, according to Haldane and May (2011), once there are enough derivatives to span the space of available states of nature (i.e. when the net supply of derivatives within the system reaches the level necessary to meet the true hedging demand from non-banks), the market can be considered closer to its equilibrium. But as long as there is an incentive to supply new instruments – in the form of a positive premium for trading – banks will continue to expand gross positions, independent of true hedging demand from non-banks. Such trades are essentially redundant, increasing the dimensionality and complexity of the financial network at a cost in terms of stability, with no welfare gain because market completeness has already been achieved. Working differently, Kyrtsou and Malliaris (2009) emphasized the role of the nonlinear underlying dynamics in financial markets that are mainly fed by non-standard and nonlinear trading strategies. Within this framework, it turns out that the incoming news can easily disturb final prices when nonlinearity is at work. Similarly, Harras and Sornette (2011) developed an agent-based model in which the agents are continuously updating their trading strategies to the current market regime as a function of the relative merits of the available public news versus the social influence with respect to their recent predicting performance. It is shown that bubbles and crashes emerge naturally by the amplification of random news by over-learning of boundedly rational agents.

The present volume is clearly motivated by the disruptions introduced by the financial crisis and the many attempts that have followed to propose new ideas and remedies, as briefly summarized above. The volume assembled contributions by authors from a variety of backgrounds, illustrating the potentials resulting from the marriage of financial economics, complexity theory and an out-of-equilibrium view of the economic world.

In the absence of a clear theoretical framework in the literature on what is/are the process/processes of bubble formation, *Lin and Sornette* provide an alternative modeling approach that emphasizes the existence of a critical time at which the bubble bursts. The key innovation is the concept of a stochastic finite-time singularity (FTS). The working hypothesis is built on the interplay between momentum-positive feedback and value-negative feedback investors. Although rational, the presence of heterogeneous expectations about the end time of the bubble can keep alive a speculative bubble via the synchronization problem. The empirical results for four financial markets provide supportive evidence that positive feedback mechanisms are prone to fuel financial bubbles.

In a related conceptual analysis in term of FTS, *Geraskin and Fantazzini* present a comprehensive review of log-periodic power law models for understanding financial bubbles. By means of different diagnostic tools, they investigate the gold dynamics around December 2009. Their findings confirm estimations contained in earlier publications of the aforementioned authors. In this context, it is worthwhile to mention that the presence of FTS dynamics with transient faster-than-exponential growth has recently received support from detailed analyses (Hüsler, Sornette, and Hommes 2012) of controlled laboratory experiments (Heemeijer et al. 2009).

It turns out that heterogeneity in agents' expectations is a determinant factor of bubble dynamics. However, the destabilizing character of heterogeneity has a broader impact. In the race for understanding how exchange rates are determined, the paper by *Chiarella, He, and Zheng* takes the macroeconomic impact of heterogeneity combined with nonlinear attributes into account. Through simulation experiments, it is shown that their model is capable of capturing real stylized facts, such as volatility clustering and multiple regimes, which are very often observed in exchange rate markets.

Huang, Zheng, and Chia present a more stock-market-oriented study emphasizing the role of endogenous heterogeneity. They deviate from the traditional interpretation of a bubble by considering upward movements in prices rather than deviations from fundamentals. The totally deterministic construction of the model allows for long-term dependences and leverage effect in the market prices, pointing out that, even when noise-free mechanisms generate fluctuations, real-life anomalies can still occur.

The inappropriateness of the traditional paradigm, suggesting that exogenous shocks are the sole factors responsible for economic instabilities, has been forced on economists by the pressure of evidence. The extent of the current crisis, which started in 2007, revealed the limits of the assumption that the dynamics of economic systems are naturally converging to a steady state. *Anand, Kirman, and Marsili* draw our attention on this issue. They suggest that many dysfunctions in the credit derivative market can be attributed to the application of specific behavioral rules among the market participants. They show that, in this game, the absence of transparency, as well as the pervading asymmetric information, has contributed the most to push the prices away from their fundamentals.

In line with the heterodox consideration that agents interact so as to promote herding behavior in the market, *Alfarano, Molakovic, and Raddant* show that social interaction can produce non-Gaussian statistical properties that thus rationalize the existence of heavy tails and clustered volatility. It is argued that the interdependence (or herding) between agents' decision processes does not constitute the unique source of financial volatility. The hierarchical structure embodying the socially interacting managers in institutional structures can act additionally as a significant contributing factor.

Besides the behavioral heterogeneity, many other aspects of the complexity of economic systems have emerged throughout the prolonged financial crisis. This has impacted seriously the efficiency of modern asset management and economic policy. Especially, in the presence of unidentified endogenous dynamics, it may be extremely difficult to identify the origin of fat-tail events and risk components. In this context, *Brookfield, Boussabaine, and Su* argue that, within complex economic environments, alternative methodologies such as spanning trees based on cross-sectional correlations can offer significant information that might be capable of supporting investors' strategies. Their empirical findings confirm the working hypothesis of the paper that the book-to-market ratio is a predictive tool for cash flows and subsequent returns.

In the light of theoretical considerations that have been worked out about the traditional capital asset pricing model, which assumes homogenous, totally rational and static investors, *Wenzelburger* incorporates option markets into a class of agent-based models permitting investors to form and update their own beliefs. As he concludes, the inclusion of heterogeneous beliefs makes prices for options to deviate from their arbitrage-free valuations. In addition, short selling of option contracts is shown to increase the volatility of individual wealth. His results appear to be extremely interesting for pension funds, which are prone to use financial derivatives in order to offset risk exposure.

The role of derivatives and their contribution to the high degree of complexity in financial markets has attracted the attention of many researchers in the last few years. Given the complexity of these products, a deep understanding of the securitization process is, therefore, required if we are interested in avoiding the reproduction of inefficiencies. *Aboul-Enein, Dionne, and Papageorgiou* provide a detailed analysis of the factors that might influence the performance of a new category of assets, the Collateralized Fund Obligations (CFOs), which are securitized portfolios of hedge funds. According to their results, the CFOs can create value for the equity tranche investors even during periods of financial distress.

Although the risk of individual assets is a determinant component for the construction of efficient portfolios, their large number can hinder the usefulness of optimization. In their paper, *Caccioli, Still, Marsili, and Kondor* suggest imposing conditions of regularization in the distribution of asset weights in order to address the problem of market impact. This approach tackles the divergent fluctuations that arise in large portfolios. Such regularization scheme can, thus, become a better investment strategy compared with traditional portfolio optimization techniques.

At long last, *Pavlidis, Paya, Peel, and Siriopoulos* perform an analytical study regarding the empirical impression of the above behavioral characteristics as well as market-specific factors into prices. They conclude that, under similar conditions, it is possible to obtain contradictory results, implying the necessity for a continuous update of the set of fitted models and of unit root tests that are usually employed in real-time applications.

Note

1. http://www.economist.com/debate/days/view/471

References

Barberis, N., and R Thaler. 2003. A survey of behavioral finance. Vol. 1, chap. 18. In *Handbook of the economics of finance*, ed. G.M. Constantinides, M. Harris and R.M. Stulz, 1053–128. Amsterdam, The Netherlands: Elsevier.

Bhamra, H.S., and R. Uppal. 2009. The effect of introducing a non-redundant derivative on the volatility of stock-market returns when agents differ in risk aversion. *Review of Financial Studies* 22: 2303–30.

Brock, W.A., C.H. Hommes, and F.O.O. Wagener. 2010. More hedging instruments may destabilize markets. *Journal of Economic Dynamics and Control* 33: 1912–28.

Caccioli, F., and M. Marsili. 2009. Efficiency and stability in complex financial markets. Technical report, The Abdus Salam International Centre for Theoretical Physics, 2009.

Caccioli, F., M. Marsili, and P Vivo. 2009. Eroding market stability by proliferation of financial instruments. *European Physical Journal* B 71: 467–79.

Connor, G. 1982. Asset pricing in factor economies. Doctoral diss., Yale university, New Haven, Connecticut.

Dybvig, P.H. 1983. An explicit bound on individual assets' deviations from APT pricing in a finite economy. *Journal of Financial Economics* 12: 483–96.

Finnerty, J.D. 1992. An overview of corporate securities innovation. *Journal of Applied Corporate Finance* 4: 23–39.

Gennaioli, N., A. Shleifer, and R. Vishny. 2011. *Neglected Risks, Financial Innovation, and Financial Fragility*. Cambridge, MA: NBER.

Gisler, M., and D. Sornette. 2009. Exuberant innovations: The Apollo program. *Society* 46: 55–68.

Gisler, M., and D. Sornette. 2010. Bubbles everywhere in human affairs. In *Modern RISC-societies. Towards a new paradigm for societal evolution*, ed. L. Kajfez-Bogataj, K.H. Müller, I. Svetlik, and N. Tos, 137–53. Wien: Edition echoraum. http://ssrn.com/abstract=1590816

Gisler, M., D. Sornette, and R. Woodard. 2011. Innovation as a social bubble: The example of the human genome project. *Research Policy* 40: 1412–25.

Grinblatt, M., and S. Titman. 1983. Factor pricing in a finite economy. *Journal of Financial Economics* 12: 497–507.

Haldane, A.G., and R.M. May. 2011. Systemic risk in banking ecosystems. *Nature* 469: 351–5.

Harras, G., and D. Sornette. 2011. How to grow a bubble: A model of myopic adapting agents. *Journal of Economic Behavior and Organization* 80: 137–52.

Heemeijer, P., C. Hommes, J. Sonnemans, and J. Tuinstra. 2009. Price stability and volatility in markets with positive and negative expectations feedback: An experimental investigation. *Journal of Economic Dynamics and Control* 33: 1052–72.

Hüsler, A., D. Sornette and C.H. Hommes. 2012. Super-exponential bubbles in lab experiments: Evidence for anchoring over-optimistic expectations on price. ETH Zurich working paper. http://arxiv.org/abs/1205.0635.

Kaizoji, T., and D. Sornette. 2009. *Market bubbles and crashes, the Encyclopedia of Quantitative Finance*. Wiley. http://www.wiley.com//legacy/wileychi/eqf/ (long version at http://arXiv.org/abs/0812.2449).

Knoll, M.S. 2008. The ancient roots of modern financial innovation: The early history of regulatory arbitrage. *Oregon Law Review* 87: 93–116.

Kyle, A.S. 1985. Continuous auctions and insider trading. *Econometrica* 53: 1315–35.

Kyrtsou, C., and W. Labys. 2006. Evidence for chaotic dependences between US inflation and commodity prices. *Journal of Macroeconomics* 28, no. 1: 256–66.

Kyrtsou, C., and W. Labys. 2007. Detecting positive feedback in multivariate time series: The case of metal prices and US inflation. *Physica A* 377, no. 1: 227–9.

Kyrtsou, C., and A. Malliaris. 2009. The impact of information signals on market prices, when agents have non-linear trading rules. *Economic Modelling* 26: 167–76.

Malevergne, Y., P. Santa-Clara, and D. Sornette. 2009. Professor Zipf goes to Wall Street. NBER Working Paper Series w15295, Cambridge, MA. http://www.nber.org/papers/w15295.

Marsili, M. 2009. Spiraling toward market completeness and financial stability. Technical report, The Abdus Salam International Centre for Theoretical Physics, 2009.

Marsili, M., G. Raffaelli, and B. Ponso. 2009. Dynamic instability in generic model of multi-assets markets. *Journal of Economic Dynamics and Control* 33: 1170–81.

Merton, R.C. 1992. Financial innovation and economic performance. *Journal of Applied Corporate Finance* 4: 12–22.

Michalopoulos, S., L.A. Laeven, and R. Levine. 2009. Financial innovation and endogenous growth. NBER Working Paper Series w15356 (2009), Cambridge, MA. http://www.nber.org/papers/w15356.

Miller, M.H. 1992. *Financial innovations and market volatility*. New York: Wiley.

Minsky, H.P. 1986. *Stabilizing an unstable economy*. New Haven: Yale University Press.

Minsky, H.P 1993. The financial instability hypothesis, In *Handbook of Radical Political Economy*, ed. P. Arestis and M. Sawyer. Cheltenham: Edward Elgar (Working paper No. 74. The Jerome Levy Economics Institute of Bard College, New York).

Ni, S.X., N.D. Pearson, and A.M. Poteshman. 2005. Stock price clustering on option expiration dates. *Journal of Financial Economics* 78: 49–87.

Reinhart, C.M., and K.S. Rogoff. 2009. *This time is different: Eight centuries of financial folly*. Princeton: Princeton University Press.

Saichev, A., Y. Malevergne and D. Sornette. 2009. *Theory of Zipf's law and beyond*, Lecture Notes in Economics and Mathematical Systems 632. Heidelberg, Germany: Springer.

Schumpeter, J.A. 1912. *Theorie der wirtschaftlichen Entwicklung*. Leipzig: Duncker und Humblot.

Schweitzer, F., G. Fagiolo, D. Sornette, F. Vega-Redondo, A. Vespignani, and D.R. White. 2009. Economic networks: The new challenges. *Science* 325: 422–4.

Sircar, K.R., and G. Papanicolaou. 1998. General Black-Scholes models accounting for increased market volatility from hedging strategies. *Applied Mathematical Finance* 5: 45–82.

Smith, C.W., and C.W. Smithson. 1990. Financial engineering: An overview, In *The handbook of financial engineering: New financial product innovations, applications, and analyses*, ed. C.W. Smith and C.W. Smithson, 10–12. Pensacola, Florida: Ballinger.

Tufano, P. 1997. Business failure, judicial intervention, and financial innovation: Restructuring US railroads in the nineteenth century. *Business History Review* 71: 1–40.

Werner, R., 2005. The New Paradigm in Macroeconomics: Solving the Riddle of Japanese Macroeconomic Performance. New York: Palgrave Macmillan.

Zapatero, F. 1998. Effects of financial innovations on market volatility when beliefs are heterogeneous. *Journal of Economic Dynamics and Control* 22: 597–626.

Diagnostics of rational expectation financial bubbles with stochastic mean-reverting termination times

Li Lin and Didier Sornette

We propose two rational expectation models of transient financial bubbles with heterogeneous arbitrageurs and positive feedbacks leading to self-reinforcing transient stochastic faster-than-exponential price dynamics. As a result of the nonlinear feedbacks, the termination of a bubble is found to be characterized by a finite-time singularity in the bubble price formation process ending at some potential critical time $\tilde{t}_c$, which follows a mean-reverting stationary dynamics. Because of the heterogeneity of the rational agents' expectations, there is a synchronization problem for the optimal exit times determined by these arbitrageurs, which leads to the survival of the bubble almost all the way to its theoretical end time. The explicit exact analytical solutions of the two models provide nonlinear transformations which allow us to develop novel tests for the presence of bubbles in financial time series. Avoiding the difficult problem of parameter estimation of the stochastic differential equation describing the price dynamics, the derived operational procedures allow us to diagnose bubbles that are in the making and to forecast their termination time. The tests have been performed on four financial markets, the US S&P500 index from 1 February 1980 to 31 October 2008, the US NASDAQ Composite index from 1 January 1980 to 31 July 2008, the Hong Kong Hang Seng index from 1 December 1986 to 30 November 2008 and the US Dow Jones Industrial Average Index from 3 January 1920 to 31 December 1931. Our results suggest the feasibility of advance bubble warning using stochastic models that embody the mechanism of positive feedback.

1. Introduction

Bubbles and crashes in financial markets are of global significance because of their effects on the lives and livelihoods of a majority of the world's population. While pundits and experts alike line up after the fact to claim that a particular bubble was obvious in hindsight, the real-time development of the bubble is often characterized by either a deafening silence or a cacophony of contradictory opinions. Here, we propose two models of financial bubbles, from which we develop the corresponding operational procedures to diagnose bubbles that are in the making and to forecast their termination time. The tests performed on four financial markets, the US S&P500 index from 1 February 1980 to 31 October 2008, the US NASDAQ Composite index from 1 January 1980 to 31 July 2008, the Hong Kong Hang Seng index from 1 December 1986 to 30 November 2008 and the US Dow Jones Industrial Average Index from 3 January 1920 to 31 December 1931, demonstrate the feasibility of advance bubble warning on the major market regimes that were followed by crashes or extended market downturns. The empirical results support the hypothesis that financial bubbles result from positive feedbacks operating on the price and/or on its momentum, leading to faster-than-exponential transients.

These results should be appreciated from the perspective of the present state of art on modeling and detecting bubbles. There is no really satisfactory theory of bubbles, which both encompasses its different possible mechanisms and adheres to reasonable economic principles (no or limited arbitrage, equilibrium or quasi-equilibrium with only transient deviations, bounded rationality). Part of the reason that the literature is still uncertain on even how to define a bubble is that an exponentially growing price can always be argued to result from some fundamental economic factor (Lux and Sornette 2002; Gurkaynak 2008). This is related to the problem that the fundamental price is not directly observable, giving no strong anchor to understand observed prices. Another fundamental difficulty is to go beyond equilibrium to out-of-equilibrium set-ups (Brock 1993; Brock and Hommes 1999; Chiarella, Dieci, and He 2008; Hommes and Wagener 2008).

Two conditions are in general invoked as being necessary for prices to deviate from the fundamental value. First, there must be some degree of irrationality in the market. That is, investors' demand for stocks must be driven by something other than fundamentals, like overconfidence in the future. Second, even if a market has such investors, the general argument is that rational investors will drive prices back to fundamental value. For this *not* to happen, there needs to be some limits on arbitrage. Shleifer and Vishny (1997) provide a description for various limits of arbitrage. With respect to the equity market, clearly the most important impediment to arbitrage are short sales restrictions. Roughly 70% of mutual funds explicitly state (in Securities and Exchange Commission Form N-SAR) that they are not permitted to sell short (Almazan et al. 2004). Seventy-nine percent of equity mutual funds make no use of derivatives whatsoever (either futures or options), suggesting further that funds do not take synthetically short positions (Koski and Pontiff 1999). These figures indicate that the vast majority of funds never take short positions. Then, the argument goes that bubbles can develop because prices reflect mainly the remaining optimistic opinions and not the negative views of pessimistic traders who are already out of the market, and who would take short positions, if given the opportunity.

One important class of theories shows that there can be large movements in asset prices due to the combined effects of heterogeneous beliefs and short-sales constraints. The basic idea finds its root in the original capital asset pricing model theories, in particular, the model of Lintner (1969) of asset prices with investors having heterogeneous beliefs. Lintner and many others after him, show that widely inflated prices can occur (Miller 1977; Harrison and Kreps 1978; Jarrow 1980; Chen, Hong, and Stein 2002; Duffie, Garleanu, and Pedersen 2002; Scheinkman and Xiong 2003). In these models that assume heterogeneous beliefs and short sales restrictions, the asset prices are determined at equilibrium to the extent that they reflect the heterogeneous beliefs about payoffs. But short sales restrictions force the pessimistic investors out of the market, leaving only optimistic investors and thus inflated asset price levels. However, when short sales restrictions no longer bind investors, then prices fall back down. This provides a possible account of the bursting of the Internet bubble that developed in 1998–2000. Many of these models take into account explicitly the relationship between the number of publicly tradable shares of an asset and the propensity for speculative bubbles to form. So far, the theoretical models based on agents with heterogeneous beliefs facing short sales restrictions are considered among the most convincing models to explain the burst of the Internet bubbles.

The role of 'noise traders' in fostering positive feedback trading has been emphasized by a number of models. For instance, DeLong et al. (1990) introduced a model of market bubbles and crashes which exploits this idea of the role of noise traders in the development of bubbles, as a possible mechanism for why asset prices may deviate from the fundamentals over rather long time periods. Their work was followed by a number of behavioral models based on the idea that trend chasing by one class of agents produces momentum in stock prices (Barberis, Shleifer, and Vishny 1998; Daniel, Hirshleifer, and Subrahmanyam 1998; Hong, Kubik, and Stein 2005). An influential empirical evidence on momentum strategies came from the work of Jegadeesh and Titman (1993, 2001), which established that stock returns exhibit momentum behavior at intermediate horizons. Strategies which buy stocks that have performed well in the past and sell stocks that have performed poorly in the past generate significant positive returns over 3- to 12-month holding periods. De Bondt and Thaler (1985) documented long-term reversals in stock returns. Stocks that perform poorly in the past perform better over the next 3– 5 years than stocks that perform well in the past. These findings present a serious challenge to the view that markets are semi-strong-form efficient.

It is important to understand what mechanisms prevent arbitrageurs from removing a bubble as soon as they see one. Abreu and Brunnermeier (2003) have proposed that bubbles continue to grow due to a failure of synchronization of rational traders, so that the later choose to ride rather than arbitrage bubbles. Abreu and Brunnermeier (2003) consider a market where arbitrageurs face synchronization risk and, as a consequence, delay usage of arbitrage opportunities. Rational arbitrageurs are supposed to know that the market will eventually collapse. They know that the bubble will burst as soon as a sufficient number of (rational) traders will sell out. However, the dispersion of rational arbitrageurs' opinions on market timing and the consequent uncertainty on the synchronization of their sell-off are delaying this collapse, allowing the bubble to grow. In this framework, bubbles persist in the short and intermediate terms because short sellers face synchronization risk, that is, uncertainty regarding the timing of the correction. As a result, arbitrageurs who conclude that the arbitrageurs are yet unlikely to trade against the bubble find it optimal to ride the still-growing bubble for a while.

Bhattacharya and Yu (2008) provide a summary of recent efforts to expand on the above concepts, in particular to address the two main questions of (i) the cause(s) of bubbles and crashes and (ii) the possibility to diagnose them *ex ante*. Many financial economists recognize that positive feedbacks and in particular herding is a key factor for the growth of bubbles. Herding can result from a variety of mechanisms, such as anticipation by rational investors of noise traders' strategies (DeLong et al. 1990), agency costs and monetary incentives given to competing fund managers (Dass, Massa, and Patgiri 2008) sometimes leading to the extreme Ponzi schemes, rational imitation in the presence of uncertainty (Roehner and Sornette 2000) and social imitation. The bubble models developed here build strongly on this accepted notion of herding. We refer to Kaizoji and Sornette (2008) for an extensive review complementing this brief survey.

This paper takes its roots in the Johansen–Ledoit–Sornette (JLS) model (Johansen, Sornette, and Ledoit 1999; Johansen, Ledoit, and Sornette 2002) formulated in the Blanchard–Watson framework of rational expectation bubbles (Blanchard 1979; Blanchard and Watson 1982). The JLS model combined a representation of the herding behavior of noise traders controlling a crash hazard rate with the arbitrage response of rational traders on the asset price. One implication of the JLS model is the transient faster-than-exponential acceleration of the price due to the positive feedback associated with the herding behavior of noise traders. This faster-than-exponential pattern can theoretically culminate in a finite-time singularity (FTS), which characterizes the end of the bubble and the time at which the crash is the most probable. Other models have explored further the hypothesis that bubbles can be the result of positive feedbacks and that the dynamical signature of bubbles derives from the interplay between fundamental value investment and more technical analysis. The former can be embodied in nonlinear extensions of the standard financial Black–Scholes model of log-price variations (Corcos et al. 2002; Ide and Sornette 2002; Sornette and Andersen 2002; Andersen and Sornette 2004). The latter requires more significant extensions to account for the competition between inertia between analysis and decisions, positive momentum feedbacks and negative value investment feedbacks (Sornette and Ide 2002). Close to our present formulation, Sornette and Andersen (2002) and Andersen and Sornette (2004) develop a nonlinear generalization of the Black–Scholes process which can be solved analytically. The nonlinear feedback is acting as the effect of price on future growth, according to the view that high prices lead to a wealth effect that drives behavioral investors to invest more aggressively.

The present paper adds to the literature by developing two related models of transient bubbles in which their terminations occur at some potential critical time $\tilde{t}_c$, which follows a mean-reverting stationary process with a fixed unconditional mean T_c. These models provide straightforward ways to determine the potential critical time without confronting the difficult problem of parameter estimation of the stochastic differential equation describing the dynamics of price. In our models, rational arbitrageurs can diagnose bubbles but do not know precisely when they end. These investors are assumed to form rational expectations of the potential critical time but not necessarily of the detailed price process itself, which form a much weaker condition for investors' rationality. Furthermore, we assume that rational arbitrageurs hold consistent expectation for the potential critical time with unbiased errors. Although rational arbitrageurs know that the bubble will burst at its critical time, they cannot make a deterministic prediction of this time and therefore of when other arbitrageurs will sell out, because they have little knowledge about others' belief about the process governing the stochastic critical time $\tilde{t}_c$. Our rational investors continuously update their beliefs on the probable termination of the bubble, according to their observation of the development of the bubble. They exit the market by maximizing their expected payoff, based on their subjective perception of the market bubble risk and the knowledge of the bubble dynamics. Because of the heterogeneity of these rational agents' expectations, there is a synchronization problem between these arbitrageurs, which leads to the survival of the bubble almost all the way to its theoretical end time. In this respect, our model is reminiscent to that of Abreu and Brunnermeier (2003), since the resilience of the bubble results from the lack of synchronization between arbitrageurs on the decision to exit the bubble due to the heterogeneity of their optimal exit times. Our models have the advantage of being quantitatively testable and their concrete implementation provides diagnostics of bubbles in real time series, as we demonstrate below.

The first model, which leads to an FTS in the price dynamics with stochastic critical time is presented in Section 2. This model generalizes Sornette and Andersen's model to allow for a mean reversal dynamics of the bubble end. Section 3 presents a second model leading to a FTS in the momentum price dynamics with stochastic critical time. Both models exemplify the importance of a positive feedback, which is quantified by a unique exponent m. A value of m larger than 1 (respectively, 2) characterize a bubble regime in the first (respectively, second) model. The two models can be solved exactly in explicit analytical forms. These solutions provide nonlinear transformations which allow us to develop novel tests for the presence of bubbles in financial time series. These two classes of tests, one for each bubble model, are developed, respectively, in Sections 4.1 and 4.2 and applied on four financial markets, the US S&P500 index from 1 February 1980 to 31 October 2008, the US NASDAQ Composite index from 1 January 1980 to 31 July 2008, the Hong Kong Hang Seng index from 1 December 1986 to 30 November 2008 and the

US Dow Jones Industrial Average Index from 3 January 1920 to 31 December 1931. Section 5 concludes.

2. First bubble model: FTS in the price dynamics with stochastic critical time

Financial bubbles are often viewed as being characterized by anomalously high growth rates resulting from temporary over-optimistic beliefs in a 'new economy' or in a 'paradigm shift' of the fundamental structure of productivity gains. However, this definition is unsatisfactory because a high growth rate associated with an exponentially growing price can always be justified by some other fundamental valuation models which use higher discount factors and larger dividend growth expectations, or introduce new accounting rules incorporating, for instance, the benefits of real options. This definition also leaves a large ambiguity as to when the bubble is supposed to end, or when a crash might occur.

In contrast, we define a bubble as a transient faster-than-exponential growth of the price, which would end in a FTS in the absence of a crash or change of regime. Such 'super-exponential regime' results from the existence of positive nonlinear feedback mechanisms amplifying past price increases into even faster growth rates. These positive nonlinear feedback mechanisms may be due to a variety of causes, including derivative hedging strategies, portfolio insurance methods or to imitative behaviors of bounded rational arbitrageurs and of noise traders. While herding has largely been documented to be a trait of noise traders, it is actually rational for bounded rational agents to also enter into social imitation, as the collective behavior may reveal information otherwise hidden to the agents. As a result of the nonlinear positive feedbacks, the bubble price becomes less and less coupled to the market fundamentals, and the super-exponential growth of the price makes the market more and more unstable. In this scenario, the end of the bubble conditional in the absence of a crash occurs at a critical time at which the market becomes maximally unstable. The end of the bubble is therefore the time when the crash is the most probable. With or without a crash, the end of the bubble signals the end of the transient super-exponential growth, and the transition to a different regime, with unspecified characteristics.

Here, we assume that sophisticated market participants are indeed aware of the current bubble state, and that they know the price is growing towards its final singularity that will occur at some future random critical time, before which the market may collapse with a finite probability. It should be stressed that a bubble can never persist until the underlying critical time since the infinite profit that would result within a finite time is not compatible with the assumption of a finite money supply. Our bounded rational sophisticated arbitrageurs are able to form unbiased rational expectations of the critical time corresponding to the end of the bubble at which the crash is the most probable. We assume that these sophisticated arbitrageurs enter sequentially into the market, attracted by the potential large gains, given their anticipation of the crash risk quantified by their estimation of the critical end time of the bubble which is formed when they enter the market. Because their anticipations of the bubble demise are heterogeneous, they solve an optimal timing problem with distinct inputs, which leads to different exit strategies. The heterogeneity in their exit strategies is common knowledge among these arbitrageurs, and results in a lack of coordination, ensuring the persistence of the bubble. This *synchronization problem* is analogous to that identified by Abreu and Brunnermeier (2003). However, for Abreu and Brunnermeier, the lack of synchronization stems from the existence of heterogeneous beliefs on the start of the bubble, i.e. arbitrageurs have 'sequential awareness' and do not know whether they have learnt the information on the mispricing early or late relative to other rational arbitrageurs. In contrast, our model emphasizes that the lack of synchronization results from the heterogeneous beliefs concerning future price variation either before or after the end of the bubble. Many reports both in the academic and professional literature state that sophisticated participants like hedge-funds correctly diagnosed the presence of a bubble and actually 'surfed' the bubbles, attracted by the potential large gains. Many reported that the largest uncertainty was how long it would continue its course (Gurkaynak 2008; Sullivan 2009)

Less sophisticated traders investing in the market have little knowledge on the bubble duration and their action add noise which is assumed to have an influence only on the critical time characterizing the end of the bubble, while the super-exponential growth of the price remains robust. In the bubble regime, a well-defined nonlinear exponent characterizes the positive feedbacks at the origin of the bubble. The noisy character of the critical time t_c of the end of the bubble is modeled by an Ornstein–Uhlenbeck process. Intuitively, the price trail resembles the trace of a bug climbing erratically along a hanging curved rope attached to a vibrating support. Such asset price dynamics during the development of a bubble has an explicit and self-consistent economic implication. This robust super-exponential growth of the price that terminates with the FTS allows the sophisticated agents among the population of investors to form a consensus on the termination time of the bubble, which is nothing but the underlying singular point. On the other hand, it is precisely the formation of the consensus that sustains the super-exponential growth regime during the bubble. Whenever a sophisticated arbitrageur does market timing according to the consensus, he will involve himself into the synchronization problem, which supports the bubble and its persistent dynamics.

Specifically, the price dynamics in the bubble regime is assumed to be described by the following stochastic differential equation:

$$\mathrm{d}p = \mu p^m (1 + \theta(p,t))\,\mathrm{d}t + \sigma p^m\,\mathrm{d}W, \tag{1}$$

where the exponent $m > 1$ embodies the positive feedback mechanism, in which a high price p pushes even further the demand so that the return and its volatility tend to be a nonlinear accelerating function of p. When $m > 1$, we will show that the price diverges in finite time. The time at which this divergence occurs is referred to as the critical time $\tilde{t}_c$. As we will see later, the term $\theta(x,t)$ is a time-varying regulator term that governs the behavior of $\tilde{t}_c$, μ is the instantaneous return rate, σ is the volatility of the returns and W is the standard Wiener process. This model recovers the standard Black–Scholes model of the geometric random walk with drift μ and standard deviation σ for $m = 1$ and $\theta = 0$.

Let us consider first the case where $\theta(p,t) = \sigma = 0$, so that expression (1) reduces to $\mathrm{d}p = \mu p^m\,\mathrm{d}t$, whose solution is

$$p = K(t_c - t)^{-\beta}, \tag{2}$$

where $\beta = 1/(m-1)$, $K = (\beta/\mu)^{\beta}$, $t_c = p_0^{-(m-1)}/(m-1)\mu$ and p_0 denotes the price at the start time of the bubble taken to be $t = 0$. Since $\beta > 0$ for $m > 1$, expression (2) exemplifies the existence of a finite-time (or 'movable', Bender and Orszag 1999) singularity of the price that goes to infinity in finite time as $t \to t_c^-$. This pathological behavior is the direct consequence of the positive feedback embodied in the condition $m > 1$.

Motivated by this simple analytical solution, we now consider the more general process (1) and carefully specify $\theta(p,t)$ in order to obtain a price process with stochastic finite-time singularities and an explicit analytical expression. We postulate the following specific form for the process governing $\theta(p,t)$,

$$\theta(p,t) = \alpha\tilde{t}_c(t) + \tfrac{1}{2}m\mu\sigma^2[p(t)]^{m-1}, \tag{3}$$

where

$$d\tilde{t}_c = -\alpha \tilde{t}_c \, dt + \left(\frac{\sigma}{\mu}\right) dW \tag{4}$$

follows an Ornstein–Uhlenbeck process with zero unconditional mean. The Wiener process in Equation (4) is the same as the one in Equation (1). We obtain the following result.

PROPOSITION 1 *Provided that $\theta(p, t)$ follows the process* (3) *with* (4), *the solution of Equation* (1) *can be written under a form similar to Equation* (2) *as follows*:

$$p(t) = K(\tilde{T}_c - t)^{-\beta}, \tag{5}$$

with

$$\beta = \frac{1}{m-1}, \quad K = \left(\frac{\beta}{\mu}\right)^{\beta}, \quad T_c = \frac{\beta}{\mu} p_0^{-1/\beta}, \quad \tilde{T}_c = T_c + \tilde{t}_c. \tag{6}$$

The proof of Proposition (1) is given in Appendix 1.

Note that

$$\mathbb{E}(\tilde{T}_c) = \mathbb{E}(T_c + \tilde{t}_c) = T_c. \tag{7}$$

Thus, T_c given by the third term in Equation (6) is the expected end time of the bubble. This expected end time T_c is the rational expectation consensus on the bubble termination formed by sophisticated arbitrageurs who are observing the stochastic critical time $\tilde{T}_c$ of the bubble demise. The stochastic behavior of $\tilde{T}_c$ expresses that the end of the bubble cannot be known with certainty but is instead a stochastic variable. Each trading day t reveals a different 'actual' critical time $T_c(t) = T_c + t_c(t)$, which is vibrating around its consensus expected value T_c. Actually, Equation (7) precisely reflects the rational expectation financial bubble concept that the financial market as a whole can determine an unbiased estimation of the bubble termination time of bubble. The presence of rational expectation requires that the dynamics of the stochastic $\tilde{T}_c$ should be a mean-reverting stationary process, which is indeed the case as seen from the last term in Equation (6) in which $\tilde{t}_c(t)$ is an Ornstein–Uhlenbeck process (4). Thus, our model is consistent in the sense of rational expectation of the bubble termination time. This is different from the rational expectation of the price formed by each rational arbitrageur in standard rational expectation bubble models.

Our model assumes that there is no coordination mechanism that would ensure the exchange of information among the sophisticated arbitrageurs concerning their expectation of the end of the bubble. The arbitrageurs reveal their private information only upon entering the market. We assume that they do so sequentially, based on their heterogeneous beliefs on the process $\tilde{t}_c$. And the process $\tilde{t}_c$ is an emergent property that results from the aggregation of market beliefs rather than from the action of single arbitrageur. Being aware of the escalating level of the bubble that has not yet burst, each arbitrageur will ride the bubble for a while and identify the best exit strategy according to the maximization of her risk-adjusted return based on her belief.

Let us denote $t_i > 0$ the time at which the i's arbitrageur has entered the market. Being aware of the form (5) of the price dynamics, at each instant t, the rational arbitrageur is aware of her exposition to the risk that a crash might occur in the next instant, conditional on the fact that it has not yet happened, which is quantified by the crash hazard rate $h(t)$. Suppose $1 - \Pi(t)$ denote the probability that the crash will not happen until time t. Given the explosive form (5) of the price dynamics, we assume that the arbitrageur is guessing that the crash hazard rate should be of the same form, that is,

$$h(t) = \frac{\pi(t)}{1 - \Pi(t)} \propto (T_c - t)^{-\beta}, \tag{8}$$

where $\Pi(t)$ is the conditional cumulative distribution function of the bursting date and $\pi(t)$ represents the associated conditional density. T_c denotes the rational expectation consensus on the end of the bubble for each arbitrageur who has entered the market. The exponent β reflects the integrated degree of positive feedback contributed by all traders in the market. The second relationship for Equation (8) embodies that all sophisticated arbitrageurs are fully aware that a bubble is present and that the market may undergo a critical transition at the end of the bubble, embodied by the accelerated power law divergence of the market susceptibility at the critical time, which is then translated into the perception of the singular behavior of the crash hazard rate as formed by the arbitrageurs.

The occurrence of the market collapse is posited to be triggered when a sufficiently large number η of arbitrageurs have exited the market, leading to a large price movement, amplified by the herding of noise traders. Their cumulative effect is accounted for by a postulated percent loss κ associated with the crash, which itself is a random variable. Given such an environment, the date to exit the market for a given rational arbitrageur i determines her best trade strategy according to a risk benefit–cost analysis: the optimal exit time for arbitrager i is the time when her marginal expected gain becomes zero. When this occurs, perceived crash loss risks become larger than expected gains. This condition reads

$$\mathbb{E}^i[(1 - \Pi(t)) \cdot \mathrm{d}p - \pi(t)\,\mathrm{d}t \cdot \kappa p] = 0. \tag{9}$$

The first term $(1 - \Pi(t)) \cdot \mathrm{d}p$ represents each arbitrageur's instantaneous marginal benefit from t to $t + \mathrm{d}t$ provided that the burst of the bubble has not yet happened. The second term $\pi(t)\mathrm{d}t \cdot \kappa p$ is the instantaneous marginal cost each arbitrageur will have to bear when the bubble bursts. After eliminating the term $\mathrm{d}t$, the condition (9) reads

$$(1 - \Pi(t))\mathbb{E}^i(\mu p^m(1 + \theta(p,t))) = \pi(t)\mathbb{E}^i(\kappa p). \tag{10}$$

We can thus state the following:

PROPOSITION 2 *Given a population of heterogeneous arbitrageurs,* (i) *who have different beliefs on the future price variation but* (ii) *who form a consensus on the anticipated critical time T_c and* (iii) *who perceive the crash hazard rate to obey a singular behavior given by expression* (8), *a given arbitrageur i decides to exit the market at the date t_i^{ex} which is the solution of*

$$\frac{\mathbb{E}^i[\mathrm{d}p(\tilde{t}_c, t_i^{\mathrm{ex}})]}{\mathbb{E}^i[\kappa p(\tilde{t}_c, t_i^{\mathrm{ex}})]} = h(t_i^{\mathrm{ex}}) \propto (T_c - t_i^{\mathrm{ex}})^{-\beta}. \tag{11}$$

Although for arbitrary i and j, $\mathbb{E}^i(\tilde{t}_c) = \mathbb{E}^j(\tilde{t}_c) \equiv 0$, since $\mathbb{E}^i(\cdot) \neq \mathbb{E}^j(\cdot)$, we have $\mathbb{E}^i[dp(\tilde{t}_c, t)] \neq \mathbb{E}^j[\mathrm{d}p(\tilde{t}_c, t)]$ and $\mathbb{E}^i[\kappa p(\tilde{t}_c, t)] \neq \mathbb{E}^j[\kappa p(\tilde{t}_c, t)]$. This naturally implies $t_i^{\mathrm{ex}} \neq t_j^{\mathrm{ex}}$. Notwithstanding the fact that the presence of the bubble is common knowledge among all rational arbitrageurs, the absence of synchronization of their market exit allows the bubble to persist and run its course up to a time close to its expected value (7).

For the price process (1) with (3), Equation (11) yields

$$\frac{\mathbb{E}^i(\mu p^m(1+\alpha\tilde{t}_c(t_i^{ex}) + (1/2\mu)m\sigma^2[p(t_i^{ex})]^{m-1}))}{\mathbb{E}^i(\kappa p)} = h(t_i^{ex}) \propto (T_c^* - t_i^{ex})^{-\beta}. \tag{12}$$

This *synchronization problem* is analogous to that identified by Abreu and Brunnermeier (2003), with the important difference that we emphasize that the lack of synchronization results from the heterogeneous beliefs concerning the future price variation.

The corresponding observable logarithmical return for the asset price reads

$$\begin{aligned} r_\tau(t) = \ln p(t+\tau) - \ln p(t) &= -\beta \ln\left(\frac{T_c + \tilde{t}_c(t+\tau) - (t+\tau)}{T_c + \tilde{t}_c(t) - t}\right) \\ &= -\beta \ln\left(1 + \frac{\Delta\tilde{t}_c(t) - \tau}{T_c + \tilde{t}_c(t) - t}\right), \end{aligned} \tag{13}$$

where τ is the time interval between two observations of the price. In the case where T_c is large enough such that $T_c + \tilde{t}_c(t) - t \gg \Delta\tilde{t}_c(t) - \tau$, expression (13) can be approximated by its first-order Taylor expansion:

$$r_\tau(t) = \frac{\beta}{T_c + \tilde{t}_c(t) - t}(\tau - \Delta\tilde{t}_c(t)) = \frac{1}{(m-1)(T_c + \tilde{t}_c(t) - t)}(\tau - \Delta\tilde{t}_c(t)). \tag{14}$$

Therefore, under the condition $m \to 1$ and $T_c + \tilde{t}_c(t) - t \to \infty$, the logarithmical return $r_\tau(t)$ is driven by the change $\Delta\tilde{t}_c(t)$ of the critical time on each trading day. Although $\tilde{t}_c$ follows an Ornstein–Uhlenbeck process, i.e. $\Delta\tilde{t}_c(t) = -\alpha\tilde{t}_c(t) + \varepsilon_t$, the existence of correlation between successive returns will be hardly detectable if α is small enough. Conversely, if $\tilde{t}_c$ follows a unit root process, the logarithmical return $r_\tau(t)$ is only dependent on the realization of the gaussian noise term ε. In this sense, only if T_c is not too far in the future, m is sufficiently larger than 1 and $\tilde{t}_c$ is stationary, can we diagnose the existence of a bubble, characterized by the emergence of a transient super-exponential price growth of the form (5).

3. Second bubble model: FTS in the momentum price dynamics with stochastic critical time

The price process (5) of the first bubble model might appear extreme, in the sense that the price diverges on the approach of the critical time $\tilde{T}_c$ of the end of the bubble. However, such a divergence cannot run its full course in our model due to the divergence of the crash hazard rate which ensures that a crash will occur before. The critical time is thus a ghost-like time, which is out-of-reach, and the price process (5) describes a transient run-up that would diverge only in the hypothetical absence of any arbitrageur. Here, we consider an alternative model in which the price remains always finite but the faster-than-exponential growth associated with the bubble is embodied into the price momentum, i.e. the derivative of the logarithm of the price or logarithmic return.

Defining $y(t) = \ln p(t)$, we assume the following process for $y(t)$:

$$\mathrm{d}y = x(1+\gamma(x,t))\,\mathrm{d}t + \left(\frac{\sigma}{\mu}\right)x\,\mathrm{d}W, \tag{15}$$

$$\mathrm{d}x = \mu x^m(1+\theta(x,t))\,\mathrm{d}t + \sigma x^m\,\mathrm{d}W, \tag{16}$$

where the same Wiener process $W(t)$ acts on both $\mathrm{d}y$ and $\mathrm{d}x$. The process $x(t)$ plays the role of an effective price momentum. To see this, consider the special case $\gamma(x,t) = 0$. Then, expression (15) reduces to $dy = x dt + (\sigma/\mu) x dW$, which shows that $x(t)\, dt = \mathbb{E}[dy]$ and thus $x(t)$ is the average momentum of the price, defined as the instantaneous time derivative of the expected logarithm of the price. The dynamics of the log-price described by Equation (15) with Equation (16) is similar to previous models (Bouchaud and Cont 1998; Farmer 2002; Ide and Sornette 2002; Sornette and Ide 2002), which argued for the presence of some inertia in the price formation process. This inertia is related to the momentum effect (Jegadeesh and Titman 1993, 2001; Carhart 1997; Xue 2003; Cooper, Gutierrez, and Hameed 2004). Intuitively, a price process involving both dy and dx holds if the price variation from today to tomorrow is based in part on decisions using analyses of the price change between yesterday (and possibly earlier times) and today.

In the (unrealistic) deterministic limit $\gamma(x, t) = \theta(x, t) = \sigma = 0$, the two equations (15) and (16) reduce to the deterministic equation

$$\frac{d^2 y}{dt^2} = \mu \left(\frac{dy}{dt}\right)^m, \tag{17}$$

whose solution reads, for $m > 2$,

$$y(t) = A - B(T_c - t)^{1-\beta}, \tag{18}$$

where $\beta = 1/(m-1)$, $T_c = (\beta/\mu)(dp/dt|_{t=t_0})^{-1/\beta}$, $B = (1/(1-\beta))(\mu/\beta)^{-\beta}$ and $A = p(T_c)$. The condition $m > 2$ ensures that $0 < 1 - \beta < 1$. Therefore, the log-price $y(t)$ exhibits a FTS at T_c. But this FTS is of a different type than in the model of the previous section: here, $y(t)$ remains finite at $t = T_c$ and equal to some value $A = p(T_c)$. The singularity is expressed via the divergence of the momentum $x(t) = dy/dt$ which diverges at $t = T_c$. As in the previous model, this FTS embodies the positive feedback mechanism, in which a high price momentum x pushes even further the demand so that the return and its volatility tend to be nonlinear accelerating functions of x. In the previous model, it is the price that provides a feedback on further price moves, rather than the price momentum used here.

Motivated by this simple analytical solution (18), we complement the general process (15) and (16) by specifying $\gamma(x, t)$ and $\theta(p, t)$ in order to obtain analytical solutions with stochastic finite-time singularities in the momentum with finite prices. We postulate the following specific processes:

$$\gamma(x, t) = \alpha \tilde{t}_c(t) + \frac{\sigma^2}{2\mu}[x(t)]^{m-1}, \tag{19}$$

$$\theta(x, t) = \alpha \tilde{t}_c(t) + \tfrac{1}{2} m \mu \sigma^2 [x(t)]^{m-1}, \tag{20}$$

where

$$d\tilde{t}_c = -\alpha \tilde{t}_c dt + \left(\frac{\sigma}{\mu}\right) dW \tag{21}$$

follows an Ornstein–Uhlenbeck process with zero unconditional mean. The Wiener process in Equation (21) is the same as the one in Equations (15) and (16), which reflects that the same series of news or shocks move log-price, momentum and anticipated critical time. We obtain the following result.

PROPOSITION 3 *Provided that $\gamma(x, t)$ and $\theta(p, t)$ follow the processes given, respectively, by Equations* (19) *and* (20), *then the solution of Equations* (15) *and* (16) *for the log-price $y(t) =$*

$\ln p(t)$ *can be written under a form similar to expression* (18) *as follows*:

$$y(t) = A - B(T_c + \tilde{t}_c(t) - t)^{1-\beta}, \tag{22}$$

where

$$\beta = \frac{1}{m-1}, \quad T_c = \frac{\beta}{\mu} x_0^{1/\beta}, \quad x_0 := x(t=0), \quad B = \frac{1}{1-\beta}\left(\frac{\beta}{\mu}\right)^{\beta}, \tag{23}$$

and A is a constant.

The proof of Proposition 3 is given in Appendix 2.

Expression (22) describes a log-price trajectory exhibiting a FTS occurring at an unknown future critical time $T_c + \tilde{t}_c(t)$ which itself follows an Ornstein–Uhlenbeck walk. In the same manner as in the previous model of the preceding section, we assume that there is no coordination mechanism that would ensure the exchange of information among the sophisticated arbitrageurs concerning their expectation of the time $T_c + \tilde{t}_c(t)$ of the end of the bubble. Following step by step the same reasoning as in the previous section, we conclude that Proposition 2 also holds for the present model. Being aware of the escalating level of the bubble that has not yet burst, each arbitrageur will ride the bubble for a while and identify the best exit strategy according to the maximization of her risk-adjusted return based on her belief. Proposition 2 determines that the exit time t_i^{ex} for arbitrageur i is the solution of

$$\frac{\mathbb{E}^i[p(t_i^{\text{ex}})x(t_i^{\text{ex}})(1+\gamma(x(t_i^{\text{ex}}), t_i^{\text{ex}})) + (\sigma^2/2\mu^2)p(t_i^{\text{ex}})[x(t_i^{\text{ex}})]^2]}{\mathbb{E}^i[\kappa p(t_i^{\text{ex}})]} = h(t_i^{\text{ex}}) \propto (T_c - t_i^{\text{ex}})^{-\beta}. \tag{24}$$

The observable logarithmic return for the asset price corresponding to Equation (22) reads

$$r_\tau(t) = y(t+\tau) - y(t) = -B[(T_c + \tilde{t}_c(t+\tau) - (t+\tau))^{1-\beta} - (T_c + \tilde{t}_c(t) - t)^{1-\beta}] \tag{25}$$

$$= -B(T_c + \tilde{t}_c(t) - t)^{1-\beta}\left[\left(1 + \frac{\Delta\tilde{t}_c(t) - \tau}{T_c + \tilde{t}_c(t) - t}\right)^{1-\beta} - 1\right]. \tag{26}$$

For future potential critical times T_c sufficiently far away from the present time t such that $T_c + \tilde{t}_c(t) - t \gg \Delta\tilde{t}_c(t) - \tau$, expression (26) can be simplified into

$$r_\tau(t) = -\frac{(1-\beta)B}{(T_c + \tilde{t}_c(t) - t)^{\beta}}(\Delta\tilde{t}_c(t) - \tau) = \frac{\mu^{-\beta}}{[(m-1)(T_c + \tilde{t}_c(t) - t)]^{\beta}} \cdot (\tau - \Delta\tilde{t}_c(t)). \tag{27}$$

Equation (27) has a structure similar to that of Equation (14). For a weak positive feedback of the momentum on itself ($m \to 2^+$) and when T_c is large enough so that $\mu(T_c + \tilde{t}_c(t) - t)$ is slowly varying, then the logarithmical return r_s is essentially driven by $\Delta\tilde{t}_c(t)$, i.e. the change of critical time disclosed by every trading day is the main stochastic process. The Geometric Brownian Motion (GBM) is then recovered as an approximation in this limit when the correlation of the Orstein–Uhlenbeck process driving the critical time goes to zero.

4. Empirical test of the tow bubble models

We have proposed two models in which a financial bubble is characterized by a transient faster-than-exponential growth culminating into a FTS at some potential critical time. Because both models reduce to a standard GBM in appropriate limits, the diagnostic of a bubble lies in the conjunction of three pieces of evidence that characterize specific deviations from the GBM regime: (i) the reconstructed time series of the critical time $\tilde{t}_c$ should be stationary and thus reject a standard unit-root test; (ii) the critical exponent m should be significant larger than 1, a condition for the existence of the super-exponential regime proposed to characterize bubbles; (iii) the calibrated potential critical date T_c should be close to the end of the time window in which the calibration of the models are made.

4.1 *Construction of alarms from the first model*

Given a financial time series of close prices at the daily scale, our purpose is to develop a procedure using the model of Section 2 to diagnose the presence of bubbles. Suppose we use time windows of N trading days that we slide with a time step of Δ days from the beginning to the end of the available financial time series. The number of such windows is therefore equal to the total number of trading days in the financial time series minus N and divided by Δ. For each window, the purpose is to decide if the model of Section 2 diagnoses an on-going bubble or not and then to compare with the actual subsequent realization of bubble burst that we consider as the validation step.

For each observed window $[t_i - N, t_i]$ ending at t_i, we transform the price time series in that window into a critical time series by inverting expression (5) for $\tilde{T}_{c,i}(t)$:

$$\tilde{T}_{c,i}(t) = \exp\left[\frac{\ln K - \ln p(t)}{\beta}\right] + t, \quad t = t_i - N + 1, \ldots, t_i. \tag{28}$$

The critical time series $\tilde{T}_{c,i}(t)$ is defined over the window i ending at t_i. If the model was exact and no stochastic component was present, and in absence of estimation errors, $\tilde{T}_{c,i}(t)$ would be a constant equal to T_c defined in (6). In the presence of an expected strong stochastic component, we estimate $T_{c,i}$ according to (7) as the arithmetical average of $\tilde{T}_{c,i}(t)$

$$T_{c,i} = \frac{1}{N} \sum_{t=t_i-N+1}^{t_i} \tilde{T}_{c,i}(t). \tag{29}$$

We can then construct $\tilde{t}_{c,i}(t)$ as

$$\tilde{t}_{c,i}(t) = \tilde{T}_{c,i}(t) - T_{c,i}. \tag{30}$$

The transformation (28) from a non-stationary possibly explosive price process $p(t)$ into what should be a stationary time series $\tilde{T}_{c,i}(t)$ in absence of misspecification is a key element of our methodology for bubble detection that avoids the problems documented by Granger and Newbold (1974) and Phillips (1986) resulting from direct calibration of price or log-price time series.

It will not have escaped the attention of the reader that transformation (28) requires the knowledge of the two unknown parameters K and β that specify the bubble process (5). We propose to calibrate these two parameters by applying an optimization procedure as follows, which will be implemented through adopting Taboo search (Cvijomic and Klinowski 1995). Recall that a crucial ingredient of the bubble model is the mean reversal nature of the underlying critical time $\tilde{t}_{c,i}$. This suggest us to apply a unit root test on the reconstructed time series $t_{c,i}(t)$, which has no linear trend by construction, and determine the optimal values K^* and β^* as those that minimize the false positive rate to reject non-stationarity of the time series $\tilde{t}_c$ mistakenly.

We proceed in two steps. We first search in the space of the two parameters $\ln K$ and β and select an elite list of the 10 best candidate pairs $(\ln K, \beta)$ (when they exist) that maximize the probability for an absence of linear trend in the corresponding $\tilde{t}_{c,i}$ time series. This procedure is implemented with the t-test statistic for the coefficient γ_1 in the following regression:

$$t_{c,i} = \gamma_0 + \gamma_1 t, \quad t = t_i - N + 1, \ldots, t_i. \tag{31}$$

The smaller the absolute value of the t-test statistic for γ_1, the larger the probability to accept the existence of a regression towards the mean. Then, for those selected pairs obtained from the first step, we choose the pair $(\ln K^*, \beta^*)$ with the smallest t-test statistic for the Dickey–Fuller unit root test (without intercept) for the corresponding time series $\tilde{t}_{c,i}$. We supplement this procedure with a variance stability test performed on this selected time series $\tilde{t}_{c,i}$ to verify its stationary in the structural sense. This is realized by the F-test at the 90% significance level for the homogeneity of variance between the second half of the $\tilde{t}_{c,i}$ time series and the whole $\tilde{t}_{c,i}$ time series. If we cannot reject the homogeneity of variance, the obtained optimal pair $(\ln K^*, \beta^*)$ from step 2 should be regarded as the calibrated parameter for the model that best 'fit' the data, in the sense of providing the closest approximation to a stationary time series for $\tilde{t}_{c,i}$ given by expression (30), which characterizes the underlying termination of bubbles. From $(\ln K^*, \beta^*)$, the exponent m in Equation (1) can be determined from the two first formula in Equation (6). Recall that the larger m is above 1, the faster is the final growth of the price towards the critical point.

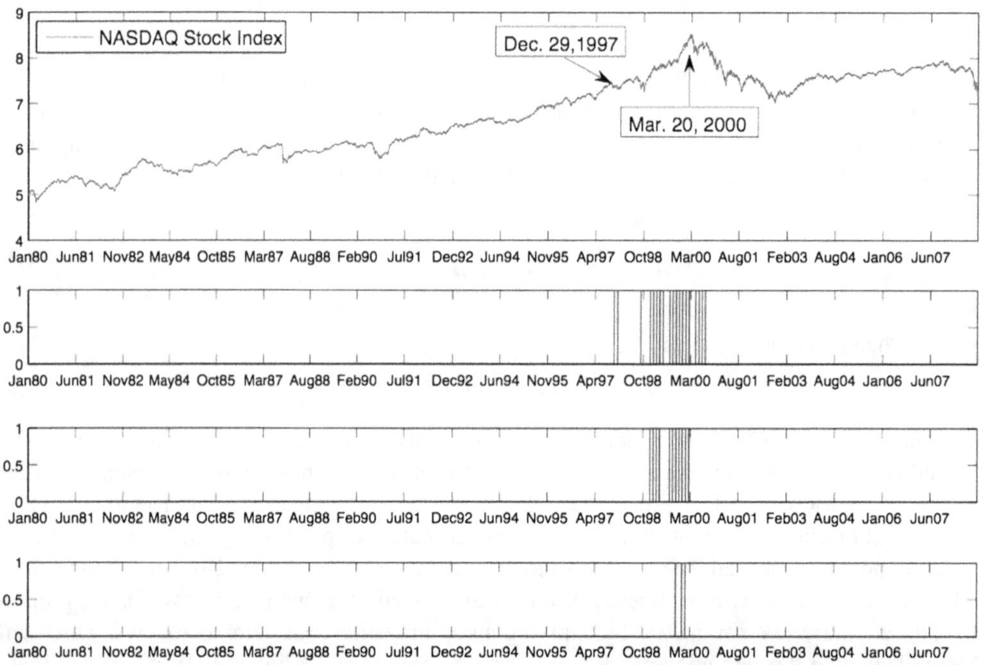

Figure 1. Logarithm of the historical NASDAQ Composite index and corresponding alarms shown in the three lower panels as vertical lines indicating the ends of the windows of 750 trading days in which our procedure using the first bubble model of Section 2 flags a diagnostic for the presence of bubble. The three lower panels correspond to alarms for which $T_{c,i} - t_i < 750$, $T_{c,i} - t_i < 500$ and $T_{c,i} - t_i < 250$, from top to bottom. By definition, the set of alarms of the lowest panel is included in the set of alarms of the middle panel which is itself included in the set of alarms of the upper panel. The exponents m found for the upper panel corresponding to $T_{c,i} - t_i < 750$ have a mean of 2.30 with a standard deviation of 0.46.

For a given window i, a diagnostic for the presence of bubble is flagged and an alarm is declared when

(i) The time series $\tilde{t}_{c,i}$ associated with the optimal pairs ($\ln K^*, \beta^*$) rejects the unit-root test at the 95% significance level,
(ii) $\beta^* > 0$ such that $m > 1$ (signature of a positive feedback on price) and
(iii) the distance $S_{c,i} \equiv T_{c,i} - t_i$ to the critical point is smaller than 750 days, i.e. the estimated critical time of bubble is not too distant in the future. When condition (i) is not satisfied, $S_{c,i}$ is actually a spurious critical time distance, even if it is small.

Figures 1–4 depict all the bubble alarms obtained by applying this procedure to four major stock indices, the US S&P500 index from 1 February 1980 to 31 October 2008, the US NASDAQ Composite index from 1 January 1980 to 31 July 2008, the Hong Kong Hang Seng index from 1 December 1986 to 30 November 2008 and the US Dow Jones Industrial Average Index from 3 January 1920 to 31 December 1931.[1]. An alarm is indicated by a vertical line positioned on the last day t_i of the corresponding window that passes the three criteria (i)–(iii). We refine the diagnostic by presenting three alarm levels, corresponding, respectively, to $S_{c,i} < 750$, $S_{c,i} < 500$ and $S_{c,i} < 250$: the closer the estimated termination of the bubble, the stronger should be the evidence for the bubble as a faster-than-exponential growth. Another indication is the existence of clustering of the alarms. If indeed a bubble is developing, it should be diagnosed repeatedly by several successive windows.

Our bubble diagnostic procedure is novel. It is thus instructive to apply it to time series generated by a known benchmark process without bubbles but that possesses the other main stylized facts

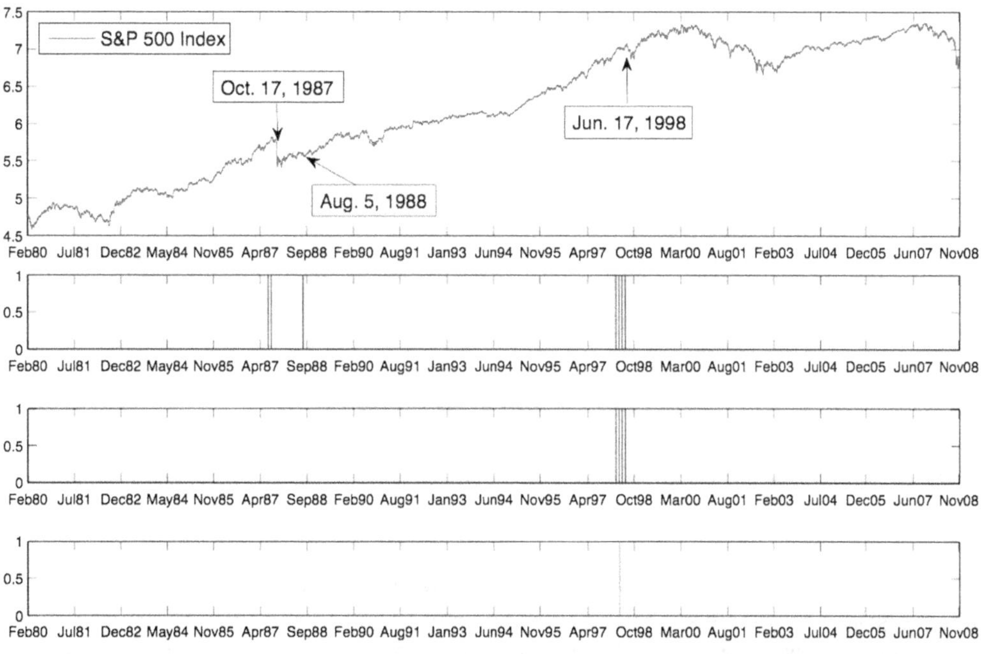

Figure 2. Same as Figure 1 for the S&P500 stock index. The exponents m found for the upper panel corresponding to $T_{c,i} - t_i < 750$ have a mean of 2.38 with a standard deviation of 0.32.

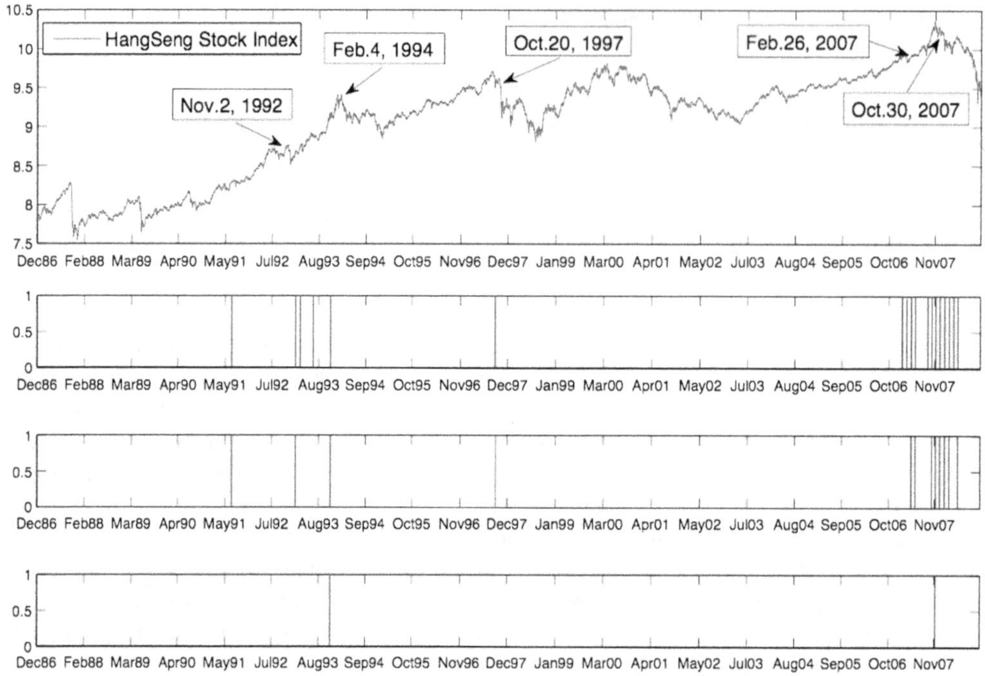

Figure 3. Same as Figure 1 for the Heng Seng index of Hong Kong and corresponding alarms shown in the three lower panels as vertical lines indicating the ends of the windows of 500 trading days. The exponents m found for the upper panel corresponding to $T_{c,i} - t_i < 750$ have a mean of 2.54 with a standard deviation of 0.37.

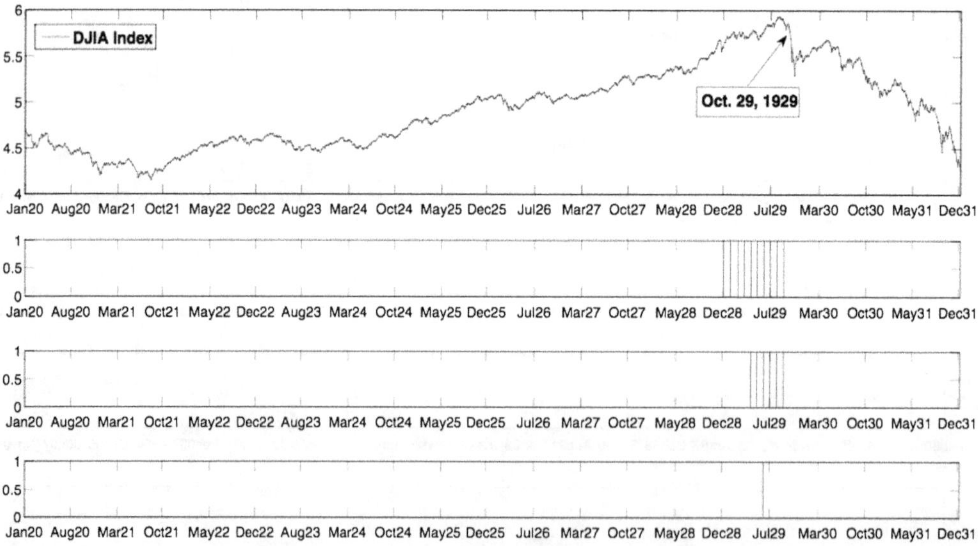

Figure 4. Same as Figure 1 for the Dow Jones Industrial Average index and corresponding alarms shown in the three lower panels as vertical lines indicating the ends of the windows of 750 trading days. The exponents m found for the upper panel corresponding to $T_{c,i} - t_i < 750$ have a mean of 2.35 with a standard deviation of 0.23.

characterizing financial time series. This provides a useful information of the false alarm rate (for the diagnostic of bubbles) for such a benchmark. We thus generated 1000 GARCH(1,1) time series with parameters estimated from the S&P500 index from 3 January 1985 to 30 September 1987 at the daily time scale. Out of these 1000 benchmark time series, we find only 43 among them that fulfill our criteria for the triggering of a bubble alarm with $S_c < 750$. This implies a probability of errors of type I error smaller than 5% for the bubble ending with 'Black Monday' shown in Figure 2. Out of 1000 GARCH-generated time series which parameters fitting the S&P500 index from 28 April 1995 to 16 April 1998, we find that only 22 of them meet our criteria for $S_c < 250$, which again indicates that the alarms flagged in 1998 have also a rate of false positives smaller that 5%.

4.2 *Construction of alarms from the second model*

Similarly to the procedure described in Section 4.1, we transform a given price time series in a given window i of N successive trading days into what should be a stationary time series of underlying critical times, supposing that the bubble price series is indeed described by the bubble model of Section 3 in which positive feedback is implemented through the momentum instead of

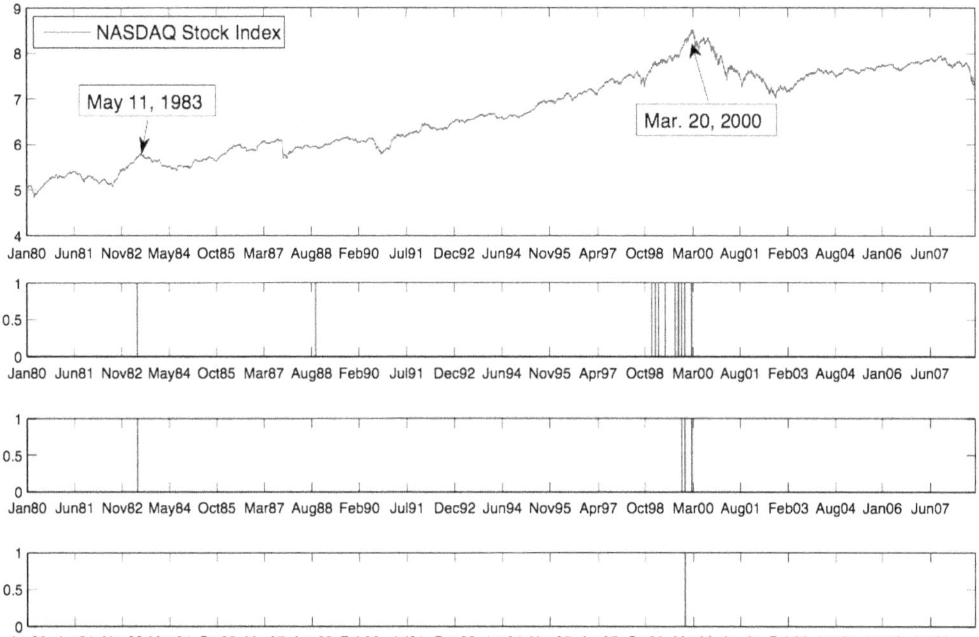

Figure 5. Logarithm of the historical NASDAQ Composite index and corresponding alarms shown in the three lower panels as vertical lines indicating the ends of the windows of 750 trading days in which our procedure using the second bubble model of Section 3 flags a diagnostic for the presence of bubble. The three lower panels correspond to alarms for which $T_{c,i} - t_i < 250$, $T_{c,i} - t_i < 90$ and $T_{c,i} - t_i < 50$, from top to bottom. from top to bottom. By definition, the set of alarms of the lowest panel is included in the set of alarms of the middle panel which is itself included in the set of alarms of the upper panel.The exponent m corresponding to the alarm in the lowest panel is 2.30.

the price. Inverting expression (22), we get, similarly to expression (28),

$$\tilde{T}_{c,i}(t) = \left(\frac{A - \ln p(t)}{B}\right)^{1/(1-\beta)} + t, \quad t = t_i - N + 1, \ldots, t_N. \tag{32}$$

The critical time series $\tilde{T}_{c,i}(t)$ is defined within window i ending at t_i. If the model was exact and no stochastic component was present, and in absence of estimation errors, $\tilde{T}_{c,i}(t)$ would be a constant equal to T_c defined in Equation (23). The expected potential critical time $T_{c,i}$ of a bubble, if any, is then estimated by expression (29) and the fluctuations around $T_{c,i}$ are described by $\tilde{t}_{c,i}(t)$ defined by Equation (30).

As for the first bubble model, the transformation (32) requires the determination of parameters in advance, here the triplet (A, B, β). For this, we proceed exactly as in the previous subsection, with t-test for the regression coefficient γ_1 in Equation (31) applied to the time series $\tilde{t}_{c,i}(t)$, followed by the selection of the best triplet (A^*, B^*, β^*) that minimize the t-test statistic of Dickey–Fuller unit-root test to $\tilde{t}_{c,i}(t)$ to make it as stationary as possible. The search of the additional parameter A is performed in an interval bound from above by $2 * \max_{t_1 \le t \le t_N} \ln p(t)$. Then, for a given window i, a diagnostic for the presence of bubble is flagged and an alarm is declared when

(i) The time series $\tilde{t}_c$ resulting from the optimal triplet (A^*, B^*, β^*) can reject the unit-root test at the 95% significance level;
(ii) $0 < \beta^* < 1$ such that $m > 2$ (the signature of a positive feedback in the momentum price dynamics model) and
(iii) $S_{c,i} = T_{c,i} - t_i < 250$, i.e. the estimated distance to the critical time ought to be small enough.

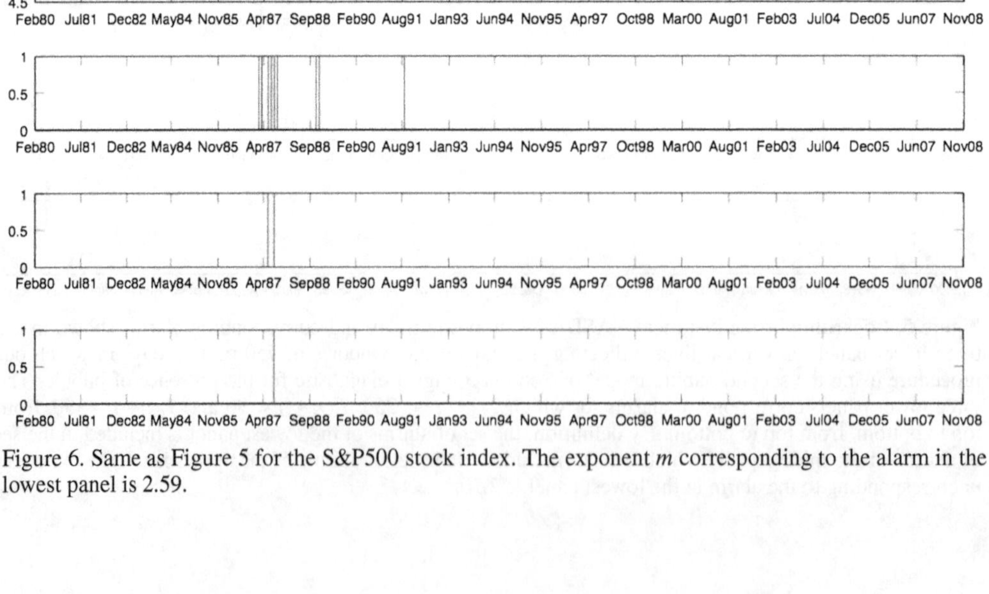

Figure 6. Same as Figure 5 for the S&P500 stock index. The exponent m corresponding to the alarm in the lowest panel is 2.59.

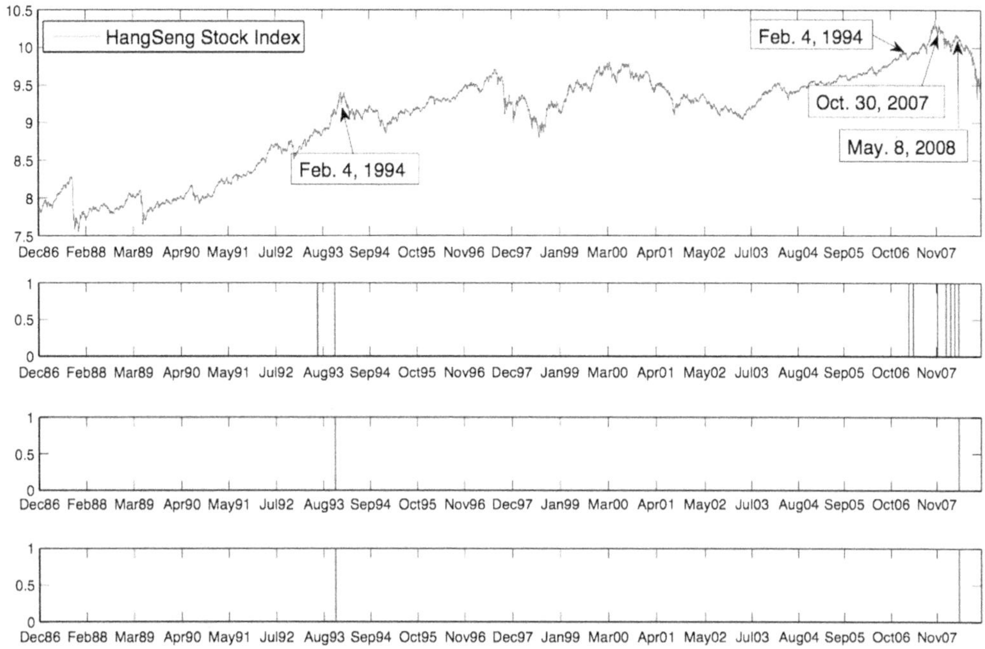

Figure 7. Same as Figure 5 for the Heng Seng index of Hong Kong and corresponding alarms shown in the three lower panels as vertical lines indicating the ends of the windows of 500 trading days. The exponents m corresponding to the two alarms in the lowest panel are, respectively, 2.23 and 2.13.

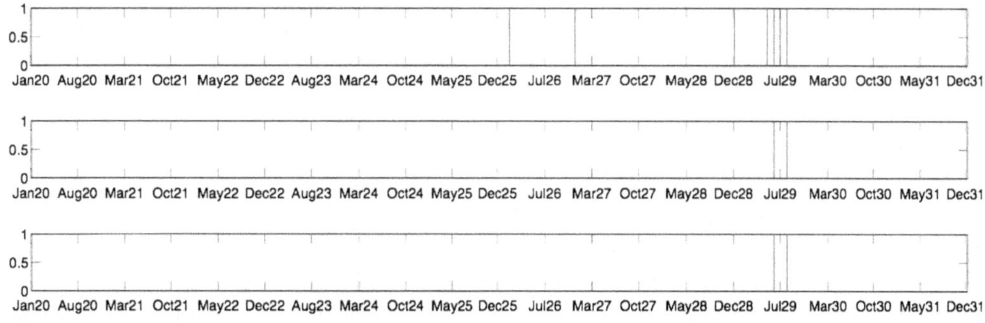

Figure 8. Same as Figure 5 for the S&P500 stock index. The exponents m corresponding to the two alarms in the lowest panel are, respectively, 3.74 and 3.06.

Figures 5–8, respectively, depict all the bubble alarms obtained by applying the above procedure to the same four major stock indices studied in the previous subsection. The lengths of the sliding windows are the same as for the first model, that is, $N = 750$ for US stock index and $N = 500$ for Hong Kong stock index. Similarly, we consider three refinement levels for the bubble diagnostic, with $S_{c,i} < 250$, $S_{c,i} < 90$ and $S_{c,i} < 50$. Note that the condition $S_{c,i} < 50$ is much more stringent than its counterpart, i.e. for the shorter level $S_{c,i} < 250$ in the first bubble model. This is due to the fact that a FTS occurring in the price momentum is a weaker singularity that a FTS occurring in the price itself. The signal for a bubble is expected to be weaker, and only detected quite close to the critical time.

We also perform tests with GARCH-generated synthetic time series in order to estimate the false positive rate for alarms with the second model. Out of 1000 synthetic time series generated with the GARCH(1,1) model fitted to the NASDAQ index from 17 March 1997 to 6 March 2000, only 35 series (respectively, 29 series) generated alarms with $S_{c,i} < 90$ ($S_{c,i} < 50$) (and passing conditions (i) and (ii). We thus conclude that the rate of false positives is smaller that 5%.

5. Concluding remarks

We have developed two rational expectation models of financial bubbles with heterogeneous rational arbitrageurs. Two key ingredients characterize these models: (i) the existence of a positive feedback quantified by a nonlinear power-law dependence of price growth as a function of either price or momentum; (ii) the stochastic mean-reversion dynamics of the termination time of the bubble. The first model characterizes a bubble as a faster-than-exponential accelerating stochastic price ending in a FTS at a stochastic critical time. The second model views a bubble as a regime characterized by an accelerating momentum ending at a FTS, also with at a stochastic critical time. This second model has the additional feature of taking into account the existence of some inertia in the price formation process, which is related to the momentum effect.

In these two models, the heterogeneous arbitrageurs exhibit distinct perception for the rising risk of a crash as the bubble develops. Each arbitrageur is assumed to know the price formation process and to determine her exit time so as to maximize her expected gain. The resulting distribution of exit times lead to a synchronization problem, preventing arbitraging of the bubble and allowing it to continue its course up to close to its potential critical time.

The explicit analytical solutions of the two models allow us to propose nonlinear transformations of the price time series into stochastic critical time series. The qualification of a bubble regime then boils down to characterize the nature of the transformed stochastic critical time series, thereby avoiding the difficult problem of parameter estimation of the stochastic differential equation describing the price dynamics. We develop an operational procedure that qualifies the existence of a running bubble (i) if the critical time series is found to reject a standard unit-root test at a high confidence level, (ii) if the exponent m of the nonlinear power law characterizing the positive feedback is sufficient large and (iii) if the expected critical time is not too distant from the time of the analysis.

The two procedures derived from the two bubble models have been applied to four financial markets, the US S&P500 index from 1 February 1980 to 31 October 2008, the US NASDAQ Composite index from 1 January 1980 to 31 July 2008, the Hong Kong Hang Seng index from 1 December 1986 to 30 November 2008 and the US Dow Jones Industrial Average Index from 3 January 1920 to 31 December 1931. Specificall, we have developed criteria to flag an alarm for the presence of a bubble, that we validate by determining if the diagnosed bubble is followed by a crash in short order. Remarkably, we find that the major known crashes over these periods are correctly identified with few false alarms. The method using the second bubble model in terms of an FTS of the price momentum seems to be more reliable with fewer false alarms and a better detection of the two principal bubbles phases characterizing the last 30 years or so. This is further confirmed by the application of our method to the bubble developing in the 1920s that ended in the well-known crash on 'Black Tuesday' in 1929. In this later case, we find again that model 2 provides a refinement and more precise diagnostic of the impending bubble end. Except for one false alarm in 1927, the alarms generated by model 2 give two strongest alarms ($t_c - t_{end} < 50$ days) for the bubble end. Compared with model 1, model 2 improves the precision of warning since it generates the strongest alarm about 2 months before the big crash (generated in 26 August 1929) while the most important alarms ($t_c - t_{end} < 250$ days) of model 1 are generated about 3 months (in 27 July 1929) before the big crash.

These results suggest the feasibility of advance bubble warning using stochastic models that embody the mechanism of positive feedback.

Note

1. We choose sliding windows of length $N = 750$ for the US stock market and $N = 500$ for the Hong Kong stock market. The reduced size for the Hong Kong market is required due to the larger frequency of bubbles found in that market, so as to avoid overlaps of bubbles in a same window that would confuse our procedure.

References

Abreu, D., and M. K. Brunnermeier. 2003. Bubbles and crashes. *Econometrica* 71, no. 1: 173–204.

Almazan, A., K.C. Brown, M. Carlson, and D. A. Chapman. 2004. Why constrain your mutual fund manager? *Journal of Financial Economics* 73, 289–321.

Andersen, J. V., and D. Sornette. 2004. Fearless versus fearful speculative financial bubbles. *Physica A* 337, nos. 3–4: 565–85.

Barberis, N., A. Shleifer, and R. Vishny. 1998. A model of investor sentiment. *Journal of Financial Economics* 49, no. 3: 307–43.

Bender, C., and S. Orszag. 1999. *Advanced mathematical methods for scientists and engineers: Asymptotic methods and perturbation theory*. Heidelberg: Springer.

Bhattacharya, U., and X. Yu. 2008. The causes and consequences of recent financial market bubbles: An introduction. *Review of Financial Studies* 21, no. 1: 3–10.

Blanchard, O. J. 1979. Speculative bubbles, crashes and rational expectations. *Economics Letters* 3, 387–389.

Blanchard, O., and M. Watson. 1982. Bubbles, rational expectations and speculative markets. In *Crisis in economic and financial structure: Bubbles, Bursts and Shocks*, ed. P. Wachtel, 295–316. Lexington: Heath and Company.

Bouchaud, J.-P., and R. Cont. 1998. A Langevin approach to stock market fluctuations and crashes. *European Physical Journal B* 6, 543–50.

Brock, W. 1993. Pathways to randomness in the economy: emergent nonlinearity and chaos in economics and finance. *Estudios Economicos* 8, no. 1: 3–55.

Brock, W., and C. Hommes. 1999. Rational animal spirits. In *The theory of markets*, ed. P.J.J. Herings and G. van der Laan, 109–137. Amsterdam: North-Holland.

Carhart, M. 1997. On persistence in mutual fund performance. *The Journal of Finance* 52, no. 1: 57–82.

Chen, J., H. Hong, and J.C. Stein. 2002. Breadth of ownership and stock returns. *Journal of Financial Economics* 66: 171–205.

Chiarella, C., R. Dieci, and X.-Z. He. 2008. Heterogeneity, market mechanisms, and asset price dynamics Research Paper 231, Quantitative Finance Research Center, University of Technology Sydney, September 2008.

Cooper, M. J., R. Gutierrez, and A. Hameed. 2004. Market states and momentum. *The Journal of Finance* 59, no. 3: 1345–65.

Corcos, A., J.-P. Eckmann, A. Malaspinas, Y. Malevergne, and D. Sornette. 2002. Imitation and contrarian behavior: hyperbolic bubbles, crashes and chaos. *Quantitative Finance* 2: 264–81.

Cvijomic, D., and J. Klinowski. 1995. Taboo search: An approach to the multiple minima problem. *Science* 267: 664–66.

Daniel, K., D. Hirshleifer, and A. Subrahmanyam. 1998. Investor psychology and security market under- and overreactions. *Journal of Finance* 53, 1839–85.

Dass, N., M. Massa, and R. Patgiri. 2008. Mutual funds and bubbles: The surprising role of contractual incentives. *Review of Financial Studies* 21, no. 1: 51–99.

De Bondt, W. M., and R. Thaler. 1985. Does the stock market overreact? *Journal of Finance* 40: 793–805.

DeLong, J. B., A. Shleifer, L.H. Summers, and R.J. Waldmann. 1990. Noise trader risk in financial markets. *Journal of Political Economy* 98, no. 4: 703–38.

Duffie, D., N. Garleanu, and L.H. Pedersen. 2002. Securities lending, shorting, and pricing. *Journal of Financial Economics* 66: 307–39.

Farmer, J. 2002. Market force, ecology and evolution. *Industrial and Corporate Change* 11, no. 5: 895–953.

Granger, C., and P. Newbold. 1974. Spurious regressions in econometrics. *Journal of Econometrics* 2: 111–20.

Gurkaynak, R. S. 2008. Econometric tests of asset price bubbles: taking stock. *Journal of Economic Surveys* 22, no. 1: 166–86.

Harrison, M., and D. Kreps. 1978. Speculative investor behavior in a stock market with heterogeneous expectations. *Quarterly Journal of Economics* 92: 323–36.

Hommes, C., and T. Wagener. 2008. Complex evolutionary systems in behavioral finance. In *Handbook of financial markets: Dynamics and evolution* (Tinbergen Institute Discussion Paper TI 2008-054/1, CeNDEF, School of Economics, University of Amsterdam), eds. T. Hens and K. Schenk-Hoppe. New York: Academic Press.

Hong, H., J.D. Kubik, and J.C. Stein. 2005. Thy neighbor's portfolio: Word-of-mouth effects in the holdings and trades of money managers. *Journal of Finance*, 2801–24.

Ide, K., and D. Sornette. 2002. Oscillatory finite-time singularities in finance, population and rupture. *Physica A* 307, nos. 1–2: 63–106.

Jarrow, R. 1980. Heterogeneous expectations, restrictions on short sales, and equilibrium asset prices. *Journal of Finance* 35: 1105–13.

Jegadeesh, N., and S. Titman. 1993. Returns to buying winners and selling losers: Implications for stock market efficiency. *The Journal of Finance* 48, no. 1: 65–91.

Jegadeesh, N., and S. Titman. 2001. Profitability of momentum strategies: An evaluation of alternative explanations. *Journal of Finance* 54: 699–720.

Johansen, A., O. Ledoit, and D. Sornette. 2000. Crashes as critical points. *International Journal of Teoretical and Applied Finance* 3: 219–55.

Johansen, A., D. Sornette, and O. Ledoit. 1999. Predicting financial crashes using discrete scale invariance. *Journal of Risk* 1, no. 4: 5–32.

Kaizoji, T., and D. Sornette. 2008. Market bubbles and crashes. *The Encyclopedia of Quantitative Finance* (http://arXiv.org/abs/0812.2449). New York: Wiley.

Koski, J., and J. Pontiff. 1999. How are derivatives used? Evidence from the mutual fund industry. *Journal of Finance* 54, no. 2: 791–816.

Lintner, J., 1969. The aggregation of investors' diverse judgments and preferences in purely competitive security markets. *Journal of Financial and Quantitative Analysis* 4: 347–400.

Lux, T., and D. Sornette. 2002. On rational bubbles and fat tails. *Journal of Money, Credit and Banking, Part 1* 34, no. 2: 589–610.

Miller, E. 1977. Risk, uncertainty and divergence of opinion. *Journal of Finance* 32: 1151–68.

Phillips, P. 1986. Understanding spurious regressions in econometrics. *Journal of Econometrics* 31: 311–40.

Roehner, B. M., and D. Sornette. 2000. "Thermometers" of speculative frenzy. *The European Physical Journal B-Condensed Matter* 16, no. 4: 729–39.

Scheinkman, J., and W. Xiong. 2003. Overconfidence and speculative bubbles. *Journal of Political Economy* 111: 1183–219.

Shleifer, A., and R. Vishny. 1997. Limits of arbitrage. *Journal of Finance* 52: 35–55.

Sornette, D., and J.V. Andersen. 2002. A nonlinear super-exponential rational model of speculative financial bubbles. *International Journal of Modern Physics C* 13, no. 2: 171–88.

Sornette, D., and K. Ide. 2002. Theory of self-similar oscillatory finite-time singularities in finance, population and rupture. *International Journal of Modern Physics C* 14, no. 3: 267–75.

Sullivan, R. Summer 2009. Taming global village risk ii: Understanding and mitigating bubbles. *Journal of Portfolio Management* 35, no. 4: 131–41.

Xue, H. 2003. Identifying factors within the apt: A new approach. AFA 2004 San Diego Meetings, Available at SSRN: http://ssrn.com/abstract=462561 or DOI: 10.2139/ssrn.462561.

Appendix 1. Proof of Proposition 1

Proof Let $n = m - 1$ and $z = p^{-n}$. Employing Itö lemma for Equation (1), we have

$$dz = \frac{\partial z}{\partial p} dp + \frac{1}{2} \frac{\partial^2 p}{\partial p^2} (dp)^2 \tag{A1}$$

$$= -np^{-m}(\mu p^m [1 + \theta(p,t)]\, dt + \sigma p^m\, dW) - \frac{1}{2} n(-n-1) p^{-m-1} \sigma^2 p^{2m}\, dt \tag{A2}$$

$$= -n\mu(1 + \theta(p,t) - \frac{1}{2}(n+1)\sigma^2 \mu p^{m-1})\, dt + n\sigma\, dW. \tag{A3}$$

Recalling that $\theta(p,t) = \alpha \tilde{t}_c + \frac{1}{2} m\mu\sigma^2 p^{m-1}$, the previous expression can be simplified into

$$dz = -n\mu dt + n\mu \left(-\alpha \tilde{t}_c dt + \frac{\sigma}{\mu} dW \right) \tag{A4}$$

$$= -n\mu\, dt + n\mu\, d\tilde{t}_c. \tag{A5}$$

Integrating both sides of the above equation and with $x(t=0) = p_0^{-n}$, we obtain

$$p = (n\mu)^{-1/n} [T_c + \tilde{t}_c - t]^{-1/n}, \quad T_c = \frac{p_0^{-n}}{n\mu}. \tag{A6}$$

Replacing n by $1/\beta$, this reproduces the solution (5).

Appendix 2. Proof of Proposition 3

Proof We now check that Equation (22) is the solution of the SDEs (15) and (16). For this, we apply Itö lemma on equation (22) by regarding $\ln p_t$ as a function of $\tilde{t}_c$. This leads to

$$d \ln p = \frac{\partial \ln p}{\partial t} dt + \frac{\partial \ln p}{\partial \tilde{t}_c} d\tilde{t}_c + \frac{1}{2} \frac{\partial^2 \ln p}{\partial \tilde{t}_c^2} (d\tilde{t}_c)^2 \tag{A7}$$

$$= (1-\beta) B (T_c + \tilde{t}_c - t)^{-\beta}\, dt - (1-\beta) B (T_c + \tilde{t}_c - t)^{-\beta}\, d\tilde{t}_c \tag{A8}$$

$$+ \frac{1}{2} \beta (1-\beta) B (T_c + \tilde{t}_c - t)^{-\beta-1} \left(\frac{\sigma}{\mu} \right)^2 dt. \tag{A9}$$

Taking into account that $B = (1/(1-\beta))(\beta/\mu)^\beta$ and let Z represent $(\beta/\mu)^\beta [T_c + \tilde{t}_c - t]^{-\beta}$, the above expression can be rewritten as

$$d \ln p = Z \left[1 + \alpha \tilde{t}_c + \frac{1}{2} \left(\frac{\sigma^2}{\mu} \right) Z^{1/\beta} \right] dt + Z \left(\frac{\sigma}{\mu} \right) dW. \tag{A10}$$

On the other hand, it is easy to see that Z is the solution of (16) in the light of Proposition 1, which leads to $Z = x$. Furthermore, we note that $\alpha \tilde{t}_c + (\sigma^2/2\mu) Z^{1/\beta}$ is nothing but $\gamma(Z, t)$. Therefore $\ln p_t$ given by (22) satisfies both Equations (15) and (16).

Everything you always wanted to know about log-periodic power laws for bubble modeling but were afraid to ask

Petr Geraskin and Dean Fantazzini

Sornette, Johansen, and Bouchaud (1996), Sornette and Johansen (1997), Johansen, Ledoit, and Sornette (2000) and Sornette (2003a) proposed that, prior to crashes, the mean function of a stock index price time series is characterized by a power law decorated with log-periodic oscillations, leading to a critical point that describes the beginning of the market crash. This article reviews the original log-periodic power law model for financial bubble modeling and discusses early criticism and recent generalizations proposed to answer these remarks. We show how to fit these models with alternative methodologies, together with diagnostic tests and graphical tools, to diagnose financial bubbles in the making in real time. An application of this methodology to the gold bubble which burst in December 2009 is then presented.

1. Introduction

Detecting a financial bubble and predicting when it will end have become of crucial importance, given the series of financial bubbles that led to the current 'Second Great Contraction', using the definition given by Reinhart and Rogoff (2009). As noted by Sornette (2009), Sornette and Woodard (2010), Kaizoji and Sornette (in press), Sornette, Woodard, and Zhou (2009) and Fantazzini (2010a, 2010b), the global financial crisis that had started in 2007 can be considered an example of how the bursting of a bubble can be dealt with by creating new bubbles. This consideration, which is not new in the financial literature (see e.g. Sornette and Woodard 2010 and references therein), was indirectly confirmed by Lou Jiwei, the Chairman of the $298 billion sovereign wealth fund named China Investment Corporation, which was created in 2007 with the goal to manage an important part of the People's Republic of China's foreign exchange reserves. On 28 August 2009, Lou told reporters on the sidelines of a forum organized by the Washington-based Brookings Institution and the Chinese 'Economists 50 Forum', a Beijing think-tank, that 'both China and America are addressing bubbles by creating more bubbles and we're just taking advantage of that. So we can't lose.' Moreover, Lou also added that 'CIC was building a broad investment portfolio that includes products designed to generate both alpha and beta; to hedge against both inflation and deflation; and to provide guaranteed returns in the event of a new crisis' (see Xin and Zhou Wheatley 2009 for more details). The previous comments clearly point out how important it is to have tools able to detect bubbles in the making.

Unfortunately, there is no consensus in the economic literature on what a bubble is: Gürkaynak (2008) surveyed a large set of econometric tests of asset price bubbles and found that for each paper that finds evidence of bubbles, there is another one that fits the data equally well without allowing for a bubble, so that it is not possible to distinguish bubbles from time-varying fundamentals. A similar situation can also be found in the professional literature: for example, Alan Greenspan stated on 30 August 2002 that '...We, at the Federal Reserve ... recognized that, despite our suspicions, it was very difficult to definitively identify a bubble until after the fact, that is, when its bursting confirmed its existence.' (Greenspan 2002) So, is this a lost cause? Absolutely not.

A model which has quickly gained a lot of attention among financial practitioners and in the physics academic literature due to the many successful predictions is the so-called *log-periodic power law* (LPPL) approach proposed by Sornette, Johansen, and Bouchaud (1996), Sornette and Johansen (1997), Johansen, Ledoit, and Sornette (2000) and Sornette (2003a, 2003b). The Johansen–Ledoit–Sornette (JLS) model assumes the presence of two types of agents in the market: a group of traders with rational expectations and a second group of so-called noise traders, that is, irrational agents with herding behavior. The idea of the JLS model comes from statistical physics and it shares many elements with a model introduced by Ising for explaining ferromagnetism (see e.g. Goldenfeld 1992). According to this model, traders are organized into networks and can have only two states: buy or sell. In addition, their trading actions depend on the decisions of other traders and on external influences. Due to these interactions, agents can form groups with self-similar behavior which can lead the market to a bubble situation, which can be considered a situation of 'order' compared with the 'disorder' of normal market conditions. Another important feature introduced in this model is the positive feedbacks which are generated by the increasing risk and the agents' interactions, so that a bubble can be a self-sustained process.

Many examples of calibrations of financial bubbles with LPPLs were reported by Sornette (2003a), who suggested that the LPPL model provides a good starting point to detect bubbles and forecast their most probable end. Johansen and Sornette (2004) identified the most extreme cumulative losses (i.e. drawdowns) in a large set of financial assets and showed that they belong to a probability density distribution, which is distinct from the distribution of the 99% of the smaller drawdowns which represent the normal market regime. Moreover, they showed that for two-thirds of these extreme drawdowns, the market prices followed a super-exponential behavior prior to their occurrences, as confirmed by a calibration of an LPPL model. These particular drawdowns (or outliers) are called 'dragon kings' in Sornette (2009). Interestingly, this approach allowed to diagnose bubbles *ex ante*, as shown in a series of real-life tests (see Zhou and Sornette 2003, 2006, 2008, 2009, Sornette and Zhou 2006, Sornette, Woodard, and Zhou 2008). Furthermore, it is currently being used at the Financial Crisis Observatory, which is a scientific platform set up at the ETH – Zurich, aimed at 'testing and quantifying rigorously the hypothesis that financial markets exhibit a degree of inefficiency and a potential for predictability, especially during regimes when bubbles develop', (Financial Crisis Observatory website).

The goal of this article is to present an easy-to-use and self-contained guide for bubble modeling and detecting with LPPLs, which contains all the sufficient steps to derive the main models in this growing and interesting field of the literature, and discuss the important aspects for practitioners and researchers.

The rest of the paper is organized as follows. Section 2 reviews the original JLS model with the main steps required for its derivation. Section 3 discusses the early criticism to this approach and recent generalizations proposed to answer these remarks. Section 4 discusses how to fit LPPL models, by presenting three estimation methodologies: the original two-step nonlinear optimization proposed by Johansen, Ledoit, and Sornette (2000), the genetic algorithm (GA) approach proposed by Jacobsson (2009) and the two-step/three-step maximum-likelihood (ML) approach proposed by Fantazzini (2010a). Section 5 is devoted to the diagnosis of bubbles in the making by using a set of different techniques. We describe diagnostic tests based on the LPPL fitting residuals and diagnostic tests based on rational expectation models with stochastic mean-reverting termination times, as well as graphical tools useful for capturing bubble development and for understanding whether a crash is in sight or not. Section 6 presents a detailed empirical application devoted to the burst of the gold bubble in December 2009, while Section 7 briefly concludes.

2. The original LPPL model

Johansen, Ledoit, and Sornette (2000) considered an ideal market with no dividends and where interest rates, risk aversion and market liquidity constraints are ignored. Therefore, the fundamental value for an asset is $p(t) = 0$, so any positive value of $p(t)$ represents a bubble. In general, $p(t)$ can be viewed as the price in excess of the fundamental value of an asset. In this framework, there are two types of agents: first, a group of rational agents who are identical in their preferences and characteristics, and so they can be substituted with a single representative agent, and second, a group of irrational agents whose herding behavior leads to the development of a financial bubble. When this tendency develops till a certain critical value, a large proportion of agents will then assume the same short position, thus causing a crash. A financial crash is not a certain event in this model, but it is characterized by a probability distribution: as a consequence, it is rational for financial agents to continue investing, because the risk for the crash to happen is compensated by the positive return generated by the financial bubble and there exists a small probability for the bubble to disappear smoothly, without the occurrence of a crash.

The key variable to model the price behavior before a crash is the crash hazard rate $h(t)$, that is, the probability per unit of time that the crash will take place, given that it has not yet occurred. The hazard rate $h(t)$ quantifies the probability that a great number of agents will assume the same sell position simultaneously, a position that the market will not be able to satisfy unless the prices decrease substantially. We remark that a strong collective answer (as it is the case for a crash) is not necessarily the consequence of one elaborated internal mechanism of global coordination in this model, but it can appear starting from imitative local micro-interactions, which are then transmitted by the market resulting in a macroscopic effect. In this regard, Johansen, Ledoit, and Sornette (2000) first discussed a macroscopic 'mean field' approach and then turned to a more microscopic approach.

2.1 *Macroscopic modeling*

According to the mean field theory from Statistical Mechanics (Stanley 1971, Goldenfeld 1992), a simple way for describing an imitative process is to assume that the hazard rate $h(t)$ can be described by the following equation:

$$\frac{\mathrm{d}h}{\mathrm{d}t} = Ch^{\delta}, \tag{1}$$

where $C > 0$ is a constant and $\delta > 1$ represents the average number of interactions among traders minus one. Thus, it follows that an amplification of interactions increases the hazard rate. If we integrate Equation (1), we have

$$h(t) = \left(\frac{h_0}{t_c - t}\right)^{\alpha}, \quad \alpha = \frac{1}{\delta - 1}, \tag{2}$$

where t_c is the critical time determined by the initial conditions at some origin of time. It can be shown that the condition $\delta > 1$ (and consequently $\alpha > 0$) is crucial to obtain a growth of $h(t)$ as $t \to t_c$ and, therefore, a critical point in finite time. Moreover, the condition that $\alpha < 1$ is required for the price not to diverge at t_c. Rewriting these condition for δ, we have that $2 < \delta < \infty$, that is, an agent should be connected at least with two agents.

Another important feature of this approach is the possibility of self-fulfilling crisis, which is a concept recently proposed to explain the recession in the 1990s in seven countries (Argentina, Indonesia, Hong Kong, Malaysia, Mexico, South Korea and Thailand) (see Krugman 1998, Sornette 2003a). It is suggested that the loss of investors' confidence caused a self-fulfilling process in these countries and thus led to severe recessions. This feedback process can be modeled by using the previous mean field approach:

$$\frac{\mathrm{d}h}{\mathrm{d}t} = Dp^{\mu}, \quad \mu > 0, \tag{3}$$

where D is a positive constant. The underlying idea is that the lack of confidence quantified by the hazard rate increases when the market price departs from its fundamental value. Therefore, the price has to increase to compensate the increasing risk.

2.2 *Microscopic modeling*

Johansen, Ledoit, and Sornette (2000) and Sornette (2003a) assumed that the group of irrational agents are connected into a network. Each agent is indexed by a integer number $i = 1, \ldots, I$ and $N(i)$ represents the number of agents who are directly connected to agent i in the network. Johansen, Ledoit, and Sornette (2000) assumed that each agent can have only two possible states s_i: 'buy' ($s_i = +1$) or 'sell' ($s_i = -1$). Johansen, Ledoit, and Sornette (2000) supposed that the state of agent i is determined by the following Markov process:

$$s_i = \operatorname{sign}\left(K \sum_{k \in N(i)} s_j + \sigma \varepsilon_i\right), \tag{4}$$

where the sign function $\operatorname{sign}(x)$ is equal to +1 if $x > 0$ and to -1 if $x < 0$, K is a positive constant and ε_i is an i.i.d. standard normal random variable. In this model, K governs the tendency of imitation among traders, while σ governs their idiosyncratic behavior. If K increases, the order in the network increases as well, while the reverse is true when σ increases. If order wins, the agents will imitate their close neighbors and their imitation will spread all over the network, thus causing a crash.[1] More specifically and in analogy with the Ising model, there exists a critical point K_c that determines the separation between the different regimes: when $K < K_c$, the disorder reigns and the sensibility to a small global influence is low. When the imitation force K grows approaching K_c, a hierarchy of groups of agents acting collectively and with the same position is formed. As a consequence, the market becomes extremely sensitive to small global disturbances.

Finally, for a larger imitation force so that $K > K_c$, the tendency of imitation is so intense that there exists a strong predominance of one state/position among agents.

A physical quantity that represents the degree of a system sensitivity to an external perturbation (or general global influence) is the so-called *susceptibility* of the system. This quantity describes the probability that a large group of agents will have the same state, given the existent external influences in the network. Let us assume the existence of a term G which measures the global influence and add it to Equation (4):

$$s_i = \text{sign}\left(K \sum_{k \in N(i)} s_j + \sigma \varepsilon_i + G \right). \tag{5}$$

If we define the average state of the market as $M = (1/I) \sum_{i=1}^{I} s_i$, for $G = 0$, we have $E[M] = 0$ by symmetry. For $G > 0$, we have $M > 0$, while for $G < 0$, $M < 0$. Thus, it follows that $E[M] \times G \geq 0$. The susceptibility of the system is then defined as $\chi = \mathrm{d}E[M]/\mathrm{d}G|_{G=0}$. In general, the susceptibility has three possible interpretations: first, it measures the sensitivity of M to a small change in the global influence. Secondly, it is (a constant times) the variance of M around its zero expectation, caused by idiosyncratic shocks ε_i. Finally, if we consider two agents and we force one to be in a certain state, the impact that our intervention will have on the second agent will be proportional to the susceptibility.

2.3 *Price dynamics and derivation of the JLS model*

As anticipated previously, the rational agent considered by Johansen, Ledoit, and Sornette (2000) is risk neutral and has rational expectations. Thus, the asset price $p(t)$ follows a martingale process, that is, $E_t[p(t')] = p(t)$, $\forall t' > t$, where $E_t[\cdot]$ represents the conditional expectation, given all information available up to time t. In the case of market equilibrium, the previous equality is a necessary condition for no arbitrage.

Considering that there exists a non-zero probability for the crash to happen, we can define a jump process j which is equal to zero before crash and one after the occurrence of the crash at time t_c. Since t_c is unknown, it is described by a stochastic variable with a probability density function $q(t)$, a cumulative distribution function $Q(t)$ and a hazard rate given by $h(t) = q(t)/[1 - Q(t)]$, which is the probability per unit of time of the crash taking place in the next instant, given that it has not yet occurred. Assuming for simplicity that the price falls during a crash by a fixed percentage $k \in (0, 1)$, the asset price dynamics is given by

$$\begin{aligned} \mathrm{d}p &= \mu(t)p(t)\mathrm{d}t - kp(t)\mathrm{d}j \\ \Rightarrow E[\mathrm{d}p] &= \mu(t)p(t)\mathrm{d}t - kp(t)[P(\mathrm{d}j = 0) \times (\mathrm{d}j = 0) + P(\mathrm{d}j = 1) \times (\mathrm{d}j = 1)] \\ &= \mu(t)p(t)\mathrm{d}t - kp(t)[0 + h(t)\mathrm{d}t] = \mu(t)p(t)\mathrm{d}t - kp(t)h(t)\mathrm{d}t. \end{aligned} \tag{6}$$

The no-arbitrage condition and rational expectations together imply that $E[\mathrm{d}p] = 0$, so that $\mu(t)p(t)\mathrm{d}t - kp(t)h(t)\mathrm{d}t = 0$, which yields $\mu(t) = kh(t)$. Substituting the last equality into Equation (6), we obtain the differential equation defining the price dynamics before the occurrence of the crash given by $\mathrm{d}(\ln p(t)) = kh(t)$, whose solution is

$$\ln\left[\frac{p(t)}{p(t_0)}\right] = \kappa \int_{t_0}^{t} h(t')\,\mathrm{d}t'. \tag{7}$$

The idea is that the higher the probability of the crash is, the faster the price should grow to compensate investors for the increased risk of a crash in the market (see also Blanchard 1979). At this point, Johansen, Ledoit, and Sornette (2000) employed the result that a system of variables close to a critical point can be described by a *power law* and the susceptibility of the system diverges as follows:

$$\chi \approx A(K_c - K)^{-\gamma}, \tag{8}$$

where A is a positive constant and $\gamma > 0$ is called the critical exponent of the susceptibility (equal to $7/4$ for the two-dimensional Ising model). Unfortunately, the two-dimensional Ising model considers only investors interconnected in an uniform way, while in real markets, some agents can be more connected than others. Modern financial markets are constituted by a collection of interacting investors, which differ substantially in size, going from the individual investors until the large pension funds. Furthermore, all investors in the world are organized inside a network (family, friends, work, etc.), within which they locally influence each other. A more appropriate representation for the current structure of financial markets is given by a *hierarchical diamond lattice*, which was used by Johansen, Ledoit, and Sornette (2000) to develop a model of rational imitation. This structure can be described as follows: first, consider two agents linked to each other, so that we have one link and two agents. Secondly, substitute this link with four new links forming a diamond: the two original agents are now situated in the two diametrically opposite vertices, whereas the two other vertices are occupied by two new traders. Thirdly, for each one of these four links, substitute them with four new links, forming a diamond in the same way. If we repeat this operation an arbitrary number of times, we will get a hierarchical diamond lattice. As a result, after n iterations, there will be $N = (2/3) * (2 + 4^n)$ agents and $L = 4^n$ links among them. For example, the last generated agents will have only two links and the initial agents will have 2^n neighbors, while the others will have an intermediate number of neighbors in between. A version of this model was solved by Derrida, De Seze, and Itzykson (1983). The basic properties are similar to those of the rational imitation model using the bi-dimensional network. The only crucial difference is that the critical exponent γ of the susceptibility in Equation (8) can be a complex number. Therefore, the general solution is given by

$$\begin{aligned} \chi &\approx \mathrm{Re}[A_0(K_c - K)^{-\gamma} + A_1(K_c - K)^{-\gamma + i\omega} + \cdots] \\ &\approx A_0'(K_c - K)^{-\gamma} + A_1'(K_c - K)^{-\gamma} \cos[\omega \ln(K_c - K) + \psi] + \cdots, \end{aligned} \tag{9}$$

where A_0, A_1 and ω are real numbers and $\mathrm{Re}[\cdot]$ represents the real part of a complex number. The power law in Equation (9) is now corrected by oscillations called 'log-periodic', because they are periodic in the logarithm of the variable $(K_c - K)$, and $\omega/2$ is their log frequency. These oscillations are accelerating since their frequency explodes as it reaches the critical time. Considering this mechanism, Johansen, Ledoit, and Sornette (2000) assumed that the crash hazard rates behave in a similar way to the susceptibility in the neighborhood of a critical point. Therefore, using Equation (9) and considering a hierarchical lattice for the financial market, the hazard rate has the following behavior:

$$h(t) \approx B_0(t_c - t)^{-\alpha} + B_1(t_c - t)^{-\alpha} \cos[\omega \ln(t_c - t) + \psi']. \tag{10}$$

This behavior of the hazard rate shows that the risk of a crash per unit of time, given that it has not yet occurred, increases drastically when the interactions among investors become sufficiently strong. However, this acceleration is interrupted and superimposed with an accelerating sequence of phases where the risk decreases, which is represented by the log-periodic oscillations. Applying Equation (10) to Equation (7), we get the following evolution for the asset price before a crash:

$$\ln[p(t)] \approx \ln[p(c)] - \frac{\kappa}{\beta}\{B_0(t_c - t)^\beta + B_1(t_c - t)^\beta \cos[\omega \ln(t_c - t) + \phi]\}, \tag{11}$$

which can be rewritten in a more suitable form for fitting a financial time series as follows:

$$\ln[p(t)] \approx A + B(t_c - t)^\beta\{1 + C\cos[\omega \ln(t_c - t) + \phi]\}, \tag{12}$$

where $A > 0$ is the value of $[\ln p(t_c)]$ at the critical time, $B < 0$ is the increase in $[\ln p(t)]$ over the time unit before the crash if C were to be close to zero, $C \neq 0$ is the proportional magnitude of the oscillations around the exponential growth, $0 < \beta < 1$ should be positive to ensure a finite price at the critical time t_c of the bubble and quantifies the power law acceleration of prices, and ω is the frequency of the oscillations during the bubble, while $0 < \phi < 2\pi$ is a phase parameter. Expression (12), which is known as the LPPL, is the fundamental equation that describes the temporal growth of prices before a crash and it has been proposed in different forms in various papers (e.g. Sornette 2003a, Lin, Ren, and Sornette 2009 and references therein). We remark that A, B, C and ϕ are just units distributions of betas and omegas, as described in Sornette and Johansen (2001) and Johansen (2003), and do not carry any structural information.

3. Criticism and recent generalizations

3.1 *Criticism*

The most important and detailed criticism against the LPPL approach was put forward by Chang and Feigenbaum (2006), who tested the mechanism underlying the LPPL using Bayesian methods applied to the time series of returns (see also Laloux et al. 1999 for additional criticism and the reply given by Johansen 2002). By comparing marginal likelihoods, they showed that a null hypothesis model without log-periodical structure outperforms the JLS model. And if the JLS model was true, they found that parameter estimates obtained by curve fitting have a small posterior probability. As a consequence, they suggested to abandon the class of models in which the LPPL structure is revealed through the expected return trajectory. These problems are due to the fact that the JLS model considers a deterministic time-varying drift decorated by a non-stationary stochastic random walk component: the latter component has a variance which increases over time, so that the deterministic trajectory moves away from the observable price path and model estimation with prices is no more consistent. Therefore, Chang and Feigenbaum (2006) considered the time series of returns instead of prices and resorted to Bayesian methods to simplify the analysis of a complicated time-series model like the JLS model (see Bernardo and Smith 1994 or Koop 2003 for an introduction to Bayesian theory). The benchmark model in Chang and Feigenbaum (2006) is represented by the Black-Scholes model, whose logarithmic returns are given by

$$r_i \sim N(\mu(t_i - t_{i-1}), \sigma^2(t_i - t_{i-1})), \tag{13}$$

where $r_i = q_i - q_{i-1}$ and q_i is the log of the price. The drift μ is drawn from the prior distribution $N(\mu_r, \sigma_r)$, while the variance σ^2 is specified in terms of its inverse $\tau = 1/\sigma^2$, known as the precision, which is higher the more precisely the random variable is known. The precision is drawn from the prior distribution $\tau \sim \Gamma(\alpha_\tau, \beta_\tau)$. The alternative hypothesis model proposed by Chang and Feigenbaum (2006) is the LPPL model with a constant drift μ in the mean function (which was not included in the original JLS model):

$$r_i \sim N(\mu(t_i - t_{i-1}) + \Delta H_{i,i-1}, \sigma^2(t_i - t_{i-1})),$$

$$\text{where} \quad \Delta H_{i,i-1} = B(t_c - t_{i-1})^\beta \left[1 + \frac{C}{\sqrt{1+(\omega/\beta)^2}} \cos(\omega \ln(t_c - t_{i-1}) + \phi)\right] \\ - B(t_c - t_i)^\beta \left[1 + \frac{C}{\sqrt{1+(\omega/\beta)^2}} \cos(\omega \ln(t_c - t_i) + \phi)\right]. \tag{14}$$

The LPPL model is characterized by the parameter vector $\xi = (A, B, C, \beta, \omega, \phi, t_c)$, and these parameters are drawn independently from the following prior distributions:

$$A \sim N(\mu_A, \sigma_A), \quad B \sim \Gamma(\alpha_B, \beta_B), \quad C \sim U(0,1), \quad \beta \sim B(\alpha_\beta, \beta_\beta),$$
$$\omega \sim \Gamma(\alpha_\omega, \beta_\omega), \quad \phi \sim U(0, 2\pi), \quad t_c - t_N \sim \Gamma(\alpha_{t_c}, \beta_{t_c}),$$

where Γ, B and U denote the gamma distribution, beta distribution and uniform distribution, respectively. Given the independence among prior distributions, the prior density for this model is simply given by the product of all marginal priors, while the probability data density for q_i is

$$f(q_i|q_{i-1}, \theta_{\text{LPPL}}; \text{LPPL}) = \sqrt{\frac{\tau}{2\pi(t_i - t_{i-1})}} \exp\left[-\frac{\tau(q_i - q_{i-1} - \mu(t_i - t_{i-1}) - \Delta H_{i,i-1})^2}{2(t_i - t_{i-1})}\right]$$

so that the likelihood function for the observed data Q is given by

$$f(Q|\theta_{\text{LPPL}}; \text{LPPL}) = \prod_{i=1}^{N} f(q_i|q_{i-1}, \theta_{\text{LPPL}}; \text{LPPL}).$$

Finally, the log marginal likelihood necessary for the computation of the Bayes factor is given by

$$\mathcal{L} = \ln\left(\int_\Theta f(Q|\theta_{\text{LPPL}}; \text{LPPL}) \varphi(\theta_{\text{LPPL}}; \text{LPPL})\, d\theta_{\text{LPPL}}\right),$$

which can be computed with Monte-Carlo methods and a large number of sampling values.

By using relatively diffuse priors with large variances in order to encompass the true values of the parameters, Chang and Feigenbaum (2006) found that the marginal likelihoods remain basically the same, whether they consider the LPPL specification in the mean function or only the drift term μ. This result remains robust to a change of prior distributions and they showed that the null hypothesis outperforms the JLS model in terms of marginal likelihood with different sets of priors.

Apart from the problem with weakly informative prior densities (see e.g. Bauwens, Lubrano, and Richard 2000) for a discussion, Lin, Ren, and Sornette (2009) pointed out that the Bayes approach to hypothesis testing assumes that some kind of ergodicity on a single data sample applies and that this sample has to be of sufficiently large size (which is not always the case). Clearly, this has to be tested and is far from being trivial. Furthermore, it is known that LPPL models can have likelihoods with several local maxima (see Jacobsson 2009) for a recent review, and the Bayes approach aims to solve this problem by integration, that is, by smoothing. However, for small to medium sample sizes, the smoothing in the marginal likelihoods can be harmful, particularly in the case of poor priors, and can decrease the number of local maxima at the price of a loss of efficiency. This may explain why the null hypothesis model with no log-periodic components showed a better result than the LPPL model.

3.2 *The generalized LPPL model with mean-reverting residuals*

The work by Chang and Feigenbaum (2006) represented the most important challenge to the original JLS model, and this is why it prompted a response by Sornette and his co-authors in 2009. Lin, Ren, and Sornette (2009) proposed a generalization of the original model which wants to make the process consistent with direct price calibration. As we have reported in the previous sections, the original JLS model has a random walk component with increasing variance, which makes direct estimation with prices inconsistent, as well as causes the lack of power of Bayesian methods, as shown by Lin, Ren, and Sornette (2009). Instead, the 'volatility-confined LPPL model' proposed by Lin, Ren, and Sornette (2009) combines a mean-reverting volatility process together with a stochastic conditional return which represents the continuous reassessments of investors' beliefs for future returns. As a consequence, the daily logarithmic returns are no longer described by a deterministic drift decorated by a Gaussian-distributed white noise, and the expected returns become stochastic.

Using the standard framework of rational expectations, Lin, Ren, and Sornette (2009) assumed that the price dynamics during a bubble is governed by the following process:

$$\frac{\mathrm{d}I}{I} = \mu(t)\mathrm{d}t + \sigma_Y \mathrm{d}Y + \sigma_W \mathrm{d}W - \kappa \mathrm{d}j,$$

$$\mathrm{d}Y = -\alpha Y \mathrm{d}t + \mathrm{d}W,$$

where I is the stock price index or the price of a generic asset, W is the standard Wiener process, $\mu(t)$ is a time-varying drift characteristic of a bubble regime and j is equal to zero before the crash and one afterwards, while κ represents the percentage by which the asset price falls during a crash. When $0 < \alpha < 1$, Y denotes an Ornstein–Uhlenbeck process, so that $\mathrm{d}Y$ and Y are both stationary, and the volatility remains bounded till the crash. This property guarantees that direct estimation with prices is consistent. We remark that if $\alpha = 0$, we retrieve the original JLS model. The corresponding model in discrete time is given by

$$\ln I_{i+1} - \ln I_i = \mu_i + \sigma_Y (Y_{i+1} - Y_i) + \sigma_W \varepsilon_i - \kappa \Delta j_i, \tag{15}$$

$$Y_{i+1} = (1-\alpha) Y_i + \varepsilon_i, \quad \varepsilon_i \sim N(0,1). \tag{16}$$

Using the theory of the stochastic discount factor (SDF), complete markets and no arbitrage, Lin, Ren, and Sornette (2009) showed that the asset log returns follow this process:

$$\ln I_{i+1} = \ln I_i + \Delta H_{i,i-1} - \alpha(\ln I_i - H_i) + u_i, \tag{17}$$

where $\Delta H_{i,i-1}$ is given by expression (14) and u_i is a Gaussian white noise, while the conditional probability distribution for the logarithmic returns is given by

$$r_{i+1} = \ln I_{i+1} - \ln I_i \sim N(\Delta H_{i+1,i} - \alpha(\ln I_i - H_i), \sigma_u^2 (t_{i+1} - t_i)). \tag{18}$$

Differently from the original JLS model, the additional term $-\alpha(\ln I_i - H_i)$ ensures that the log price fluctuates around the LPPL trajectory H_t, thus guaranteeing the consistency of direct estimation with prices.

Lin, Ren, and Sornette (2009) remarked that the previous model based on rational expectation separates rather artificially the noise traders and the rational investors. Moreover, even though the rational investors cannot make profit on average, rational agents endowed with different preferences may, in principle, arbitrage the risk-neutral agents. Therefore, assuming that rational investors have homogeneous preferences is rather restrictive. Nevertheless, Lin, Ren, and Sornette (2009) showed that the previous results can be obtained by using a complete different approach, which considers the theory of the so-called *behavioral SDF*, where the price movements follow the dynamics of the *market sentiment* (see Shefrin 2005) for a textbook treatment of the behavioral approach to asset pricing. We refer to Lin, Ren, and Sornette (2009) for more details about this alternative approach.

3.3 *Other generalizations: the log-periodic AR(1)–GARCH(1,1) model*

While the original LPPL specification can model the long-range dynamics of price movements, nevertheless it is unable to consider the short-term market dynamics, thus showing residual terms which can be strongly autocorrelated and heteroskedastic. As a consequence, Gazola et al. (2008) proposed the following AR(1)–GARCH(1,1) log-periodic model:

$$\begin{aligned}
I_i &= A + B(t_c - t_i)^\beta + C(t_c - t_i)^\beta \cos[w \ln(t_c - t_i) + \phi] + u_i, \\
u_i &= \rho u_{i-1} + \eta_i, \\
\eta_i &= \sigma_i \varepsilon_i, \quad \varepsilon_i \sim N(0,1), \\
\sigma_i^2 &= \alpha_0 + \alpha_1 \eta_{i-1}^2 + \alpha_2 \sigma_{i-1}^2,
\end{aligned} \tag{19}$$

where ε_i is a standard white noise term satisfying $E[\varepsilon_i] = 0$ and $E[\varepsilon_i^2] = 1$, whereas the conditional variance σ_i^2 follows a GARCH(1,1) process. Under the normality assumption for the error term ε_i, the ML estimator for the parameter vector $\mathbf{\Pi} = [A, B, C, t_c, \beta, w, \phi, \rho, \alpha_0, \alpha_1, \alpha_2]$ is obtained through the numerical maximization of the log-likelihood:

$$\ln L(\Theta) = -\frac{1}{2}(N-1)\ln(2\pi) - \frac{1}{2}\sum_{i=2}^{N} \ln \sigma_i^2 - \frac{1}{2}\sum_{i=2}^{N} \frac{\eta_i^2}{\sigma_i^2}. \tag{20}$$

In order to improve the optimization procedure, each parameter of the log-periodic model (19) denoted by θ and defined in a restricted interval denoted by $[a, b]$ can be re-parameterized according to the following monotonic transformation:

$$\theta = b\frac{\exp(\tilde{\theta})}{1+\exp(\tilde{\theta})} + a\left(1 - \frac{\exp(\tilde{\theta})}{1+\exp(\tilde{\theta})}\right). \tag{21}$$

This monotonic transformation turns the original estimation problem over a restricted space of solutions into an unrestricted problem, which eases estimation particularly when poor starting values are chosen. In this case, the delta method can be used to compute the standard errors of the estimate. We remind that the delta method is used to compute an estimator for the variance of functions of estimators and the corresponding confidence bands. Let $\hat{V}[\tilde{\theta}]$ be the estimated variance–covariance matrix of $\tilde{\theta}$, then, by using the delta method, a variance–covariance matrix for a general nonlinear transformation $g(\tilde{\theta})$ is given by (see Hayashi 2000 for more details)

$$\hat{V}[g(\tilde{\theta})] = \frac{\partial g(\tilde{\theta})}{\partial \tilde{\theta}'} \hat{V}[\tilde{\theta}] \frac{\partial g(\tilde{\theta})}{\partial \tilde{\theta}}' .$$

Gazola et al. (2008) used a two-step procedure to choose the starting values for the numerical maximization of Equation (20):

(1) the starting values for the set of parameters $\Phi = [A, B, C, t_c, \beta, w, \phi]$ are retrieved from the estimation of the original LPPL model (12);
(2) the starting values for the set of parameters $[\rho, \alpha_0, \alpha_1, \alpha_2]$ of the short-term stochastic component u_i are obtained by estimating an AR(1)–GARCH(1,1) model on the residuals $\hat{u}_i$ from the original LPPL model (12).

4. How to fit LPPL models?

Estimating LPPL models, in general, has never been easy due to the frequent presence of many local minima of the cost function where the minimization algorithm can get trapped. However, some recent developments have considerably simplified the estimation process.

4.1 *The original two-step nonlinear optimization*

Johansen, Ledoit, and Sornette (2000) noted that noisy data, relatively small samples and a large number of parameters make the estimation of LPPL models rather difficult. Therefore, they proposed to reduce the number of free parameters by slaving the three linear parameters and computing them from the estimated nonlinear parameters.

More specifically, if we rewrite the original LPPL model as follows:

$$y_i = A + B(t_c - t_i)^\beta + C(t_c - t_i)^\beta \cos(\omega \ln(t_c - t_i) + \phi) \tag{22}$$

or more compactly as

$$y_i = A + Bf_i + Cg_i,$$

where

$$y_i = \ln I_i \text{ or } I_i, \quad f_i = (t_c - t_i)^\beta$$
$$g_i = (t_c - t_i)^\beta \cos(\omega \ln(t_c - t_i) + \phi),$$

then it is straightforward to see that the linear parameters A, B and C can be obtained analytically by using ordinary least squares:

$$\begin{pmatrix} \sum_{i=1}^N y_i \\ \sum_{i=1}^N y_i f_i \\ \sum_{i=1}^N y_i g_i \end{pmatrix} = \begin{pmatrix} N & \sum_{i=1}^N f_i & \sum_{i=1}^N g_i \\ \sum_{i=1}^N f_i & \sum_{i=1}^N f_i^2 & \sum_{i=1}^N f_i g_i \\ \sum_{i=1}^N g_i & \sum_{i=1}^N f_i g_i & \sum_{i=1}^N g_i^2 \end{pmatrix} \begin{pmatrix} A \\ B \\ C \end{pmatrix} . \tag{23}$$

We can write the previous system compactly by using matrix notation:

$$\mathbf{X}'\mathbf{y} = (\mathbf{X}'\mathbf{X})\mathbf{b}, \quad \text{where } \mathbf{X} = \begin{pmatrix} 1 & f_1 & g_1 \\ \vdots & \vdots & \vdots \\ 1 & f_N & g_N \end{pmatrix}, \quad \mathbf{b} = \begin{pmatrix} A \\ B \\ C \end{pmatrix} \tag{24}$$

so that

$$\hat{\mathbf{b}} = (\mathbf{X}'\mathbf{X})\mathbf{X}'\mathbf{y}, \tag{25}$$

and we have only four free parameters to estimate (see also Jacobsson 2009 for a similar derivation). We remark that this simplification can also be seen as an example of concentrated ML.

The estimation procedure consists of two steps:

(1) Use the so-called *Taboo search* (Cvijović and Klinowski 1995) to find 10 candidate solutions, where only the cases with $B < 0$, $0 < \beta < 1$ and $t_c > t_i$ (if a bubble) are considered (see also Sornette and Johansen 2001). However, alternative grid searches can also be considered. Recently, Lin, Ren, and Sornette (2009) have imposed stronger restrictions, by considering $0.1 < \beta < 0.9$ and $6 \leq \omega \leq 15$ so that the log-periodic oscillations are neither too fast (to avoid fitting noise) nor too slow (otherwise they would provide a contribution to the trend), and $|C| < 1$ to ensure that the hazard rate $h(t)$ remains always positive.[2]

(2) Each of these 10 solutions is then used as the starting value in a Levenberg–Marquardt nonlinear least squares algorithm. The solution with the minimum sum of squares between the fitted model and the observations is taken as the final solution.

4.2 *Genetic algorithms*

The GA is an algorithm inspired by Darwin's 'survival of the fittest idea', and its theory was developed by John Holland in 1975. The GA is a computer simulation that aims to mimic the natural selection in biological systems, which is governed by four phases: a *selection mechanism*, a *breeding mechanism*, a *mutation mechanism* and a *culling mechanism*. The GA does not require the computation of any gradient or curvature and it does not need the cost function to be smooth or continuous.

The use of GA to estimate LPPL models has been proposed by Jacobsson (2009) following the GA methodology proposed by Gulsten, Smith, and Tate (1995). Similarly Johansen, Ledoit, and Sornette (2000), Jacobsson (2009) reduced the number of free parameters to four, by 'slaving' the three linear parameters A, B and C, which are computed by using Equation (25). Her procedure consists of four steps:

(1) *Selection mechanism: Generating the initial population.* Each member of the 'financial' population is represented by a vector of the four nonlinear coefficients t_c, ϕ, ω and β. The members of the initial population are randomly drawn from a uniform distribution with a pre-specified range, and for each member, the residual sum of squares is calculated. Jacobsson (2009) considered an initial population of 50 members (i.e. 50 parameter vectors).

(2) *Breeding mechanism.* The 25 members with the best value of the cost function are selected from the population to be included in the breeding program. An offspring is then generated by randomly drawing two parents, without replacement, and taking the arithmetic mean of

them. Jacobsson (2009) repeated this procedure 25 times, and each pair of parents is drawn randomly with replacement, so that one parent can generate an offspring with another parent (. . .therefore, betrayals are allowed!).

(3) *Mutation mechanism*. Genetic mutations in nature play a key role in the evolution of a species, since they may increase its probability of survival, as well as introduce less favorable characteristics. In our framework, mutations perturb the previous solutions to allow new regions of the search space to be explored, so that premature convergence in local minima can be avoided.

The mutation process is implemented by computing the statistical range ($\theta_{\max} - \theta_{\min}$) for each parameter in the population. The range for each parameter is then multiplied with a factor $\pm k$, to obtain the perturbation variable ε, which is uniformly distributed over the interval [$-k \times$ (parameter range), $k \times$ (parameter range)]. Jacobsson (2009) considered $k = 2$. Twenty-five members are then drawn randomly, without replacement, from the initial population of 50 computed in the first step. Each selected member is then mutated by adding an exclusive vector of random perturbations for every parameter. Therefore, the mutation mechanism allows to compensate the problem of an inaccurate guess for the initial intervals in the solution space.

(4) *Culling mechanism*. Jacobsson (2009) merged the members generated by mutation and breeding into the population, so that a total of 100 solutions is present (50 old, 25 offsprings and 25 mutations). All of the 100 solutions are ranked according to their cost function in ascending order, and the 50 best solutions are culled and live on into the next generation. The rest is deleted.

The previous algorithm is then iterated a certain number of times till a desired termination criterion is met. Similar to the second step of the optimization process used by Johansen, Ledoit, and Sornette (2000) and described in Section 4.1, Jacobsson (2009) further refined the parameters estimated with the GA by using them as starting values for the Nelder–Mead simplex method, also known as the downhill simplex method.

4.3 *The two-step/three-step ML approach*

Fantazzini (2010a) found that estimating LPPL models for ‘anti-bubbles’ was much easier than estimating LPPL models for bubbles: an anti-bubble is symmetric to a bubble and represents a situation when the market peaks at a critical time t_c and then decreases following a power law with decelerating log-periodic oscillations (see Johansen and Sornette 1999; Johansen and Sornette 2000; Zhou and Sornette 2005; Fantazzini 2010b for more details). Furthermore, estimating models with log prices was much simpler than estimating models with prices in levels, and in the latter case, a much more careful choice of the starting values had to be made.

In this regard, we have already seen that the original LPPL model has a stochastic random walk component with increasing variance, so that the deterministic pattern moves away from the observable price path. Therefore, the idea given by Fantazzini (2010a) is to reverse the original times series in order to minimize the effect of the non-stationary component during the estimation process. The same idea can also be of help in the case of models with stationary error terms, like the one proposed by Lin, Ren, and Sornette (2009): a time series with strongly autocorrelated error terms is almost undistinguishable from a non-stationary process in small-to-medium-sized samples (see e.g. Stock 1994; Ng and Perron 2001; Stock and Watson 2002 for a discussion of this hotly debated issue in the econometric literature). Figure 1 shows a simulated LPPL model with AR(1) error terms and 1000 observations, as well as its reverse.

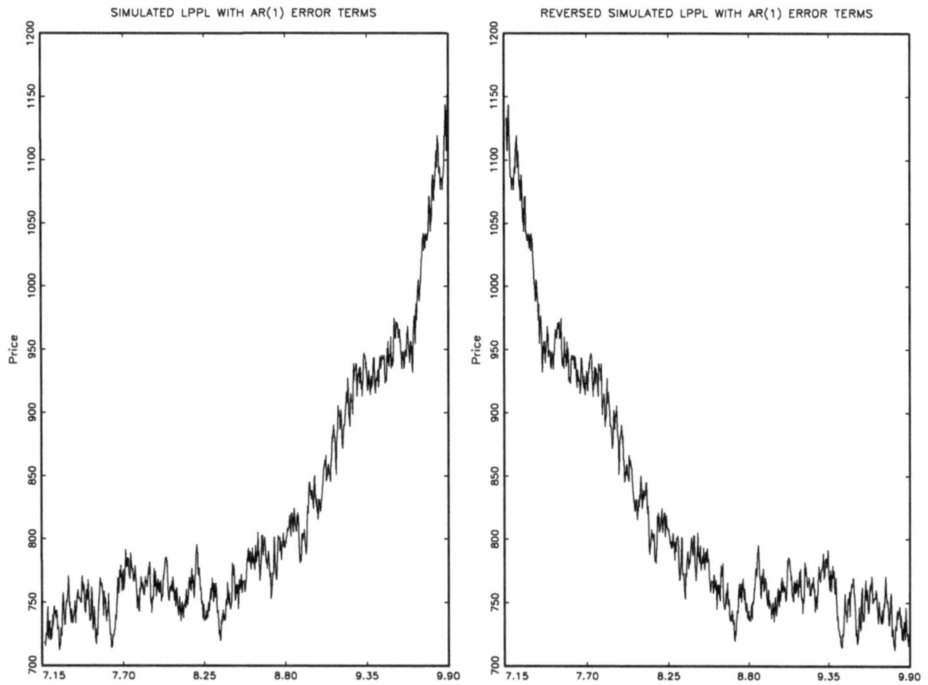

Figure 1. Simulated LPPL with AR(1) error terms and its reverse. Parameters: $A = 7.16$, $B = -0.43$, $C = 0.035$, $\beta = 0.35$, $\omega = 4.15$, $\phi = 2.07$, $t_c = 9.92$, $\rho = 0.88$, $\alpha_0 = 0.00007$.

The two-step ML approach used in Fantazzini (2010a) to estimate LPPL models for financial bubbles, also allowing for an AR(1)–GARCH(1,1) model in the error terms as in Equation (19), is given below:

(1) Reverse the original time series and estimate the LPPL for the case of an anti-bubble by using the BFGS (Broyden, Fletcher, Goldfarb, Shanno) algorithm, together with a cubic or quadratic step length method (STEPBT) (see e.g. Dennis and Schnabel 1983).
(2) Keeping fixed the LPPL parameters $\hat{\Phi} = [\hat{A}, \hat{B}, \hat{C}, \hat{t}_c, \hat{\beta}, \hat{\omega}, \hat{\phi}]$ computed in the first stage, estimate the parameters of the short-term stochastic component $[\rho, \alpha_0, \alpha_1, \alpha_2]$.

In case of poor starting values, or when the bubble has just started forming (Jiang et al. 2010 and Sornette 2003a remarked that a bubble cannot be diagnosed more than one year in advance of the crash), the numerical computation can be further eased by considering one additional step. The three-step ML approach used in Fantazzini (2010a) is described below:

(1) Reverse the original time series and then consider the first temporal observation as if it was the date of the crash, that is, set $t_c = t_1$. Estimate the remaining LPPL parameters $[A, B, C, \beta, \omega, \phi]$ for the case of an anti-bubble by using the BFGS (Broyden, Fletcher, Goldfarb, Shanno) algorithm, together with a cubic or quadratic step length method (STEPBT).
(2) Use the estimated parameters in the previous step as *starting values* for estimating all the LPPL parameters by using again the reversed times series.

(3) Keeping fixed the LPPL parameters $\hat{\Phi} = [\hat{A}, \hat{B}, \hat{C}, \hat{t}_c, \hat{\beta}, \hat{\omega}, \hat{\phi}]$ computed in the second stage, estimate the parameters of the short-term stochastic component $[\rho, \alpha_0, \alpha_1, \alpha_2]$.

Being a multi-stage estimation process, the asymptotic efficiency is lower than that of the one-step full ML estimation. However, the dramatic improvement in numerical convergence and the improved efficiency in small-to-medium-sized samples more than justify the multi-step procedure. An (unreported) simulation study confirms the benefits of this procedure in small-to-medium data sets.

5. Diagnosing bubbles in the making

The main method that we have considered so far to detect financial bubbles is by fitting an LPPL model to a price series. However, in order to reduce the possibility of false alarms, it is good practice to implement a battery of tests, so that a prediction must pass all tests to be considered worthy (see e.g. Sornette and Johansen 2001; Jiang et al. 2010).

5.1 *Diagnostic tests based on the LPPL fitting residuals*

We have seen in Section 3.2 that Lin, Ren, and Sornette (2009) proposed a model for financial bubbles where the LPPL fitting residuals follow a mean-reverting Ornstein–Uhlenbeck process. This implies that the corresponding residuals follow an AR(1) process and we can test this hypothesis by using unit-root test.

Lin, Ren, and Sornette (2009) used Phillips–Perron and augmented Dickey–Fuller (ADF) unit-root tests, where the null hypothesis H_0 is the presence of a unit root. Unfortunately, a well-known shortcoming of the previous two unit-root tests is their low power when the underlying data-generating process is an AR(1) process with a coefficient close to one. Therefore, we suggest to also consider the test proposed by Kwiatkowski et al. (1992), where the null hypothesis is a stationary process. Considering the null hypothesis of a stationary process and the alternative of a unit root allows us to follow a conservative testing strategy: if we reject the null hypothesis, we can be confident that the series has indeed a unit root; but if the results of the previous two tests indicate a unit root while the result of the KPSS test indicates a stationary process, one should be very cautious and opt for the latter result.

The KPSS test is implemented in the most common statistical and econometric software (see e.g. Griffiths, Hill, and Lim 2008) for applications with Eviews as well as the Eviews User's Guide (version 5 or higher) and Pfaff (2008) for a description of unit-root tests in R, together with the many routines written for Gauss and Matlab, which can be found on the web.

5.2 *Diagnostic tests based on rational expectation models with stochastic mean-reverting termination times*

Lin and Sornette (2009) proposed two models of transient bubbles in which their termination dates occur at some potential critical time $\tilde{t}_c$, which follows a stationary process with a unconditional mean T_c. The main advantage of these models is the possibility of computing the potential critical time without the need to estimate the complex stochastic differential equation describing the underlying price dynamics. Interestingly, the rational arbitrageurs discussed in Lin and Sornette (2009) can detect bubbles, but they cannot make a deterministic forecast because they have little knowledge about the other arbitrageurs' beliefs about the process governing the stochastic critical time $\tilde{t}_c$. The heterogeneity of the rational agents' expectations determines a synchronization problem among these arbitrageurs, thus allowing the financial bubble to survive till its theoretical end time (see also Abreu and Brunnermeier 2003 for a similar model). Moreover, the two models proposed by Lin and Sornette (2009) can be tested and they allow us to diagnose financial bubbles in the making in real time. Besides, both models highlight the importance of positive feedback, that is, when a high price pushes even further the demand so that the return and its volatility tend to be a nonlinear accelerating function of the price. This positive feedback mechanism is quantified by a unique exponent m, which is larger than 1 (respectively, 2 for the second model) when we are in a bubble regime.

5.2.1 A test based on a finite-time singularity in the price dynamics with stochastic critical time
The first model proposed by Lin and Sornette (2009) views a bubble as a faster-than-exponential accelerating stochastic price, which leads to a finite-time singularity in the price dynamics at a stochastic critical time. They showed in their Proposition 1 that the price dynamics in a bubble regime follows this process:

$$p(t) = K(\tilde{T}_c - t)^{-\beta},$$
$$\beta = \frac{1}{m-1}, \quad K = \left(\frac{\beta}{\mu}\right)^{\beta}, \quad T_c = \frac{\beta}{\mu} p_0^{-1/\beta}, \quad \tilde{T}_c = T_c + \tilde{t}_c, \tag{26}$$

where μ is the instantaneous return rate and p_0 denotes the price at the start time of the bubble at $t = 0$, while the critical time $\tilde{t}_c$ follows an Ornstein–Uhlenbeck process with zero unconditional mean (see Lin and Sornette 2009 for the full derivation of the model). The last property provides that the end of the bubble cannot be forecasted with certainty but it is a stochastic variable, while the time T_c can be interpreted as the consensus forecast formed by rational arbitrageurs of the stochastic critical time $\tilde{T}_c$. In fact, we have that

$$E[\tilde{T}_c] = E[T_c + \tilde{t}_c] = T_c. \tag{27}$$

In order to build a diagnostic test for financial bubbles, Lin and Sornette (2009) inverted Equation (26) to obtain an expression for the critical time series $\tilde{T}_{c,i}$:

$$\tilde{T}_{c,i}(t) = \frac{1}{K}\frac{1}{[p(t)]^{1/\beta}} + t, \quad t = t_i - 749, \ldots, t_i, \tag{28}$$

where $\tilde{T}_{c,i}$ is defined over the time window i ending at time t_i, and they considered time windows of 750 trading days that slide with a time step of 25 days from the beginning to the end of the available financial time series. We remark that $p(t)$ is known, while the parameters K and β have to be estimated. The previous inversion aims to transform a non-stationary possibly explosive price process $p(t)$ into what should be a stationary time series $\tilde{T}_{c,i}$ in the absence of misspecification. Therefore, we can then estimate T_c according to Equation (27) by using the arithmetic average of $\tilde{T}_{c,i}(t)$:

$$T_{c,i} = \frac{1}{750}\sum_{i=1}^{750} \tilde{T}_{c,i}(t) \tag{29}$$

so that the fluctuations $\tilde{t}_{c,i}(t)$ can be computed as

$$\tilde{t}_{c,i}(t) = \tilde{T}_{c,i}(t) - T_{c,i}. \tag{30}$$

The first test proposed by Lin and Sornette (2009) consists of the following two steps:

(1) Perform a bivariate grid search over the parameter space of K and β to find the 10 best pairs (K, β) such that the resulting time series $\tilde{t}_{c,i}(t)$ given by Equation (30) rejects a standard unit-root test of non-stationarity at the 99.5% significance level. Lin and Sornette (2009) employed the ADF test, but the addition of the KPSS test would be advisable. Needless to say, only a subset of the windows will reject the null hypothesis of a unit root (for the ADF test) or will not reject the null of stationarity (for the KPSS test).
(2) If there are time windows for which there are selected pairs (K, β) according to the previous step, select the pair with the smallest variance for its corresponding time series $\tilde{t}_{c,i}(t)$. This gives the optimal pair K_i^* and β_i^* which provides the closest approximation to a stationary time series for $\tilde{t}_{c,i}(t)$ given by Equation (30). For a given window i, an alarm is declared when
   - $\beta^* > 0$, which yields $m > 1$;
   - $T_{c,i} - t_i < 750$, which implies that the termination time of the bubble is not too far. Lin and Sornette (2009) also considered two additional alarm levels: $T_{c,i} - t_i < 500$ and $T_{c,i} - t_i < 250$.

The idea of the last step is that the closer we are to the end of the financial bubble, the stronger should be the evidence for the bubble as a faster-than-exponential growth, and the alarms should be diagnosed repeatedly by several successive windows.

5.2.2 *A test based on a finite-time singularity in the momentum price dynamics with stochastic critical time*

The main disadvantage of the previous model is that the price diverges when approaching the critical time $\tilde{T}_c$ at the end of the bubble. Therefore, Lin and Sornette (2009) considered a second model where the price remains always finite and a bubble is a regime characterized by an accelerating momentum ending at a finite-time singularity with a stochastic critical time. They showed in their Proposition 3 that the log price $y(t) = \ln p(t)$ in a bubble regime follows this process:

$$y(t) = A - B(T_c + \tilde{t}_c(t) - t)^{1-\beta},$$

$$\beta = \frac{1}{m-1}, \quad T_c = \frac{\beta}{\mu} x_0^{1/\beta}, \quad x_0 := x(t=0), \quad B = \frac{1}{1-\beta}\left(\frac{\beta}{\mu}\right)^{\beta}, \quad \tilde{T}_c = T_c + \tilde{t}_c, \tag{31}$$

where μ is the instantaneous return rate, A is a constant and $x(t) = \mathrm{d}y/\mathrm{d}t$ denotes the effective price momentum, that is, the instantaneous time derivative of the logarithm of the price, while the critical time $\tilde{t}_c$ follows an Ornstein–Uhlenbeck process with zero unconditional mean (see Lin and Sornette 2009 for the full derivation of this model). In the second model, it is the high price momentum x which pushes the demand higher, so that the return and its volatility become nonlinear accelerating functions. Instead, in the first model, it is the price that provides a positive feedback on future prices, rather than the price momentum.

Using a procedure similar to Equation (28) to transform a non-stationary possibly explosive log-price process $y(t)$ into a stationary time series $\tilde{T}_{c,i}$, Lin and Sornette (2009) inverted Equation (31) to obtain an expression for the critical time series $\tilde{T}_{c,i}$:

$$\tilde{T}_{c,i}(t) = \left(\frac{A - \ln p(t)}{B}\right)^{1/(1-\beta)} + t, \quad t = t_i - 899, \ldots, t_i, \tag{32}$$

where $\tilde{T}_{c,i}$ is defined over the time window i ending at time t_i, and they considered time windows of 900 trading days that slide with a time step of 25 days from the beginning to the end of the available financial time series. We can then estimate $T_{c,i}$ according to Equation (29) by computing the arithmetic average of $\tilde{T}_{c,i}(t)$ (with 750 replaced by 900), whereas the fluctuations $\tilde{t}_{c,i}(t)$ around $T_{c,i}$ can be computed by using Equation (30). Similar to the first model, we remark that $p(t)$ is known, while the parameters A, B and β have to be estimated.

The second test proposed by Lin and Sornette (2009) consists of the following two steps:

(1) Perform a trivariate grid search over the parameter space of A, B and β to find the 10 best triplets (A, B, β) such that the resulting time series $\tilde{t}_{c,i}(t)$ given by Equation (30) rejects a standard unit-root test of non-stationarity at the 99.5% significance level. Lin and Sornette (2009) employed the ADF test, but again the addition of the KPSS test would be advisable.
(2) If there are time windows for which there are selected triplets (A, B, β) according to the previous step, select the pair with the smallest variance for its corresponding time series $\tilde{t}_{c,i}(t)$. This gives the optimal triplet A_i^*, B_i^* and β_i^* which provides the closest approximation to a stationary time series for $\tilde{t}_{c,i}(t)$ given by Equation (30). For a given window i, an alarm is declared when
   - $0 < \beta_i^* < 0$, which yields $m > 2$ and is called *level 1* filter. Lin and Sornette (2009) also considered two additional alarm levels: $m > 2.5$ (*level 2*) and $m > 3$ (*level 3*);
   - $-25 \le T_{c,i} - t_i \le 50$.

The stronger upper bound on $T_{c,i} - t_i$ stems from the fact that the finite-time singularity in the price momentum is a weaker singularity which can only be observed only close to the critical time. The lower bound of −25 days is due to the fact that the analysis is performed in sliding windows with a time step of 25 days. Using a data set covering the last 30 years of the SP500 index, the NASDAQ composite index and the Hong Kong Hang Seng index, Lin and Sornette (2009) found that the second diagnostic method was more reliable and with fewer false alarms than the first method analyzed in Section 5.2.1.

5.3 *Graphical tools: the crash lock-in plot*

Fantazzini (2010a) proposed a graphical tool that proved to be useful to track the development of a bubble and to understand whether a possible crash is in sight or at least a bubble deflation. The idea is to plot on the horizontal axis the *date of the last observation in the estimation sample* and on the vertical axis the *estimated crash date* $\hat{t}_c$ computed by fitting the LPPL to the data: if a change in the stock market regime is approaching, then the recursively estimated $\hat{t}_c$ should

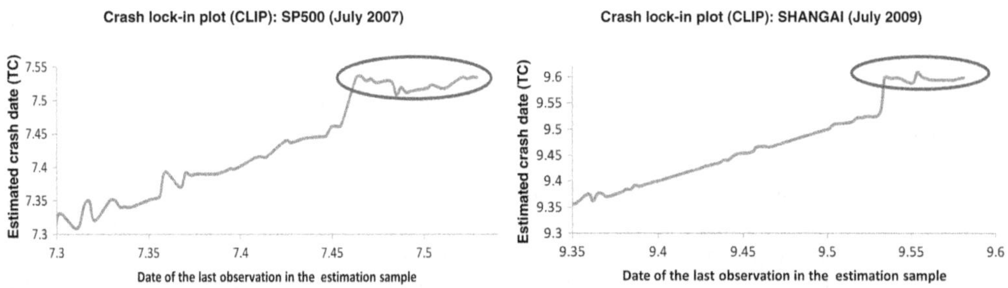

Figure 2. CLIPs for the SP500 and Shanghai composite index.

stabilize around a constant value close to the critical time. Fantazzini (2010a) called such a plot the crash lock-in plot (CLIP).

This idea can be easily justified theoretically by resorting to the models proposed by Lin and Sornette (2009), in which the critical time $\tilde{T}_c$ follows an Ornstein–Uhlenbeck process.

We report in Figure 2 the CLIPs for the Chinese Shanghai Composite Index in July 2009, a case which was analyzed in detail in Bastiaensen et al. (2009) and Jiang et al. (2010), and for the SP500 in July 2007, with these being the peak of the market in the decade. We used data spanning from the global minima till one day before the market peak.

6. An application: the burst of the gold bubble in December 2009

The gold market peaked on 2 December 2009, hitting the record high at $1216.75 an ounce in Europe, and then started falling on 4 December 2009, losing more than 10% in two weeks. The main concerns cited to be behind this bubble were the future prospects for a weak dollar as well as inflationary fears (see e.g. Mogi 2009; White 2009). However, there were also some worried calls about the possibility of a gold bubble: the prestigious magazine *Fortune* wrote on 12 October 2009 that '...Signs of gold fever are everywhere...' but '...amid the buying frenzy and after a decade-long run-up that has seen the price quadruple, is gold still a smart investment? The simple answer: Wherever the price of gold is headed in the long term, several market watchers say the fundamentals indicate that gold is poised to fall' (Cendrowski 2009). Interestingly, on the day the gold price peaked, that is, 2 December 2009, Hu Xiaolian, a vice-governor at the People's Bank of China, told reporters in Taipei that '...gold prices are currently high and markets should be careful of a potential asset bubble forming...', see the original report by Tung (2009). The gold price, starting from 12 November 2008 (which represents the global minima over a three-year span) till the end of January 2010 is reported in Figure 3. This figure also reports the 'Search Volume Index' by Google Trends, which computes how many searches have been done for the term 'Gold Price' on Google over time.[3]

The 'Search Volume Index' is an interesting tool because it allows us to get some insights as to when the bubble started: looking at Figure 3, we can see that a massive interest around gold started to build during the year 2008, just before the price minima in November 2008. Therefore, we expect that a possible LPPL model can be fitted using data starting from the year 2008.

6.1 *LPPL fitting with varying window sizes*

Jiang et al. (2010) tested the stability of LPPL estimation parameters by varying the size of the estimation samples and adopting the strategy of fixing one endpoint and varying the other one (see also Sornette and Johansen 2001). By sampling many intervals as well as by using bootstrap techniques, they obtained probabilistic predictions on the time intervals in which a given bubble may end and lead to a new market regime (which may not necessarily be a crash, but also a transition to a plateau or a slower decay). Following their example, we fit the logarithm of the gold price by using the LPPL Equation (22) in *shrinking windows* and in *expanding windows*. The shrinking windows have a fixed end date $t_2 = 1$ December 2009, while the starting date t_1 increases from 12 November 2008 to 17 August 2009 in steps of 5 (trading) days. The expanding windows have a fixed starting date $t_1 = 12$ November 2008, while the end date t_2 increases from 17 August 2009 to 1 December 2009 in steps of 5 (trading) days.

Given the stochastic nature of the initial parameter selection and the noisy nature of the underlying generating processes, we employed four estimation algorithms: the original Taboo Search

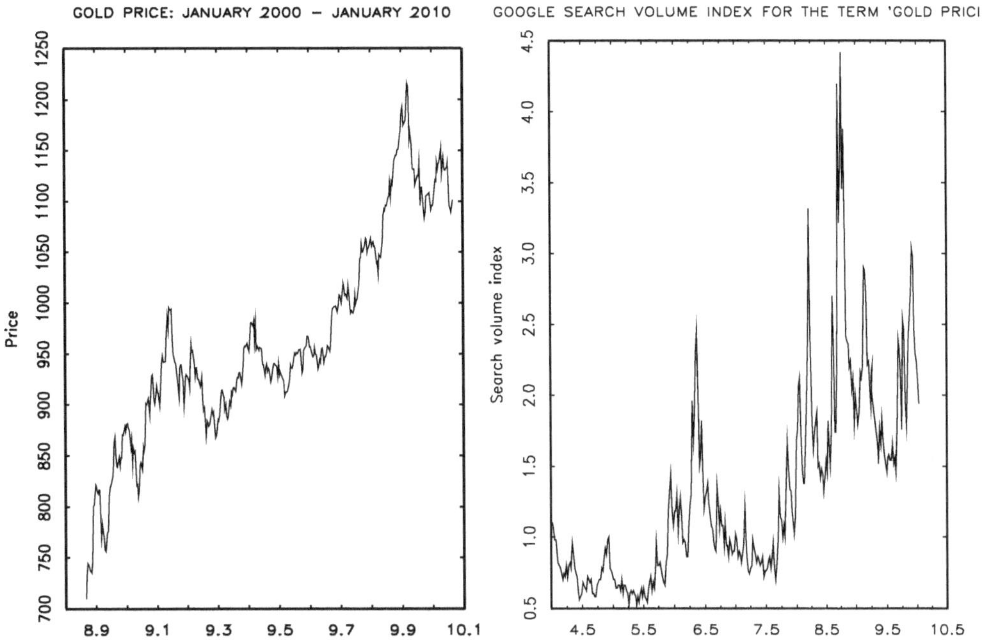

Figure 3. Gold price and `Google` search volume index. Time t converted in units of 1 year.

algorithm proposed by Cvijović and Klinowski (1995), the two-step nonlinear optimization proposed by Johansen, Ledoit, and Sornette (2000), and the pure random search (PRS) and the three-step ML approach proposed by Fantazzini (2010a).[4]. The estimation results are then filtered by the following LPPL conditions, which were also used in Jiang et al. (2010) for the case of Chinese bubbles: $\hat{t}_c > t_2$, $B < 0$ and $0 < \beta < 1$. The selected $\hat{t}_c$ are then used to compute the 20%/80% and 5%/95% quantile range of values of the crash dates, which are reported in Figure 4: the left plot shows the ranges which are obtained by considering the filtered results from all four estimation methods, whereas the right plot shows the ranges obtained by considering only the two-step nonlinear optimization and the three-step ML approach.

As expected, the original Taboo Search and the PRS are very inefficient methods compared with the competing two-step and three-step approaches and deliver very large quantile ranges. Nevertheless, the two medians $\hat{t}_c$, equal to 11 December 2009 for the left plot and 5 December 2009 for the right plot, are very close to the actual market peak date, which is 2 December 2009 (i.e. 9.9206 when converted in units of one year). Moreover, if we consider only the most efficient methods, the 20%/80% quantile interval is rather close and precise and diagnoses that the critical time t_c for the end of the bubble and the change of market regime lies in the time sample 3 December 2009–11 December 2009 (the market started to fall on 4 December 2009).

6.2 *Diagnostic tests based on the LPPL fitting residuals*

We discussed in Section 3.2 that Lin, Ren, and Sornette (2009) proposed a model for financial bubbles where the LPPL fitting residuals follow a mean-reverting Ornstein–Uhlenbeck process. Therefore, the corresponding residuals should follow a stationary AR(1) process and this hypothesis can be tested by using unit-root tests. We employed ADF and KPSS tests: a rejection of the

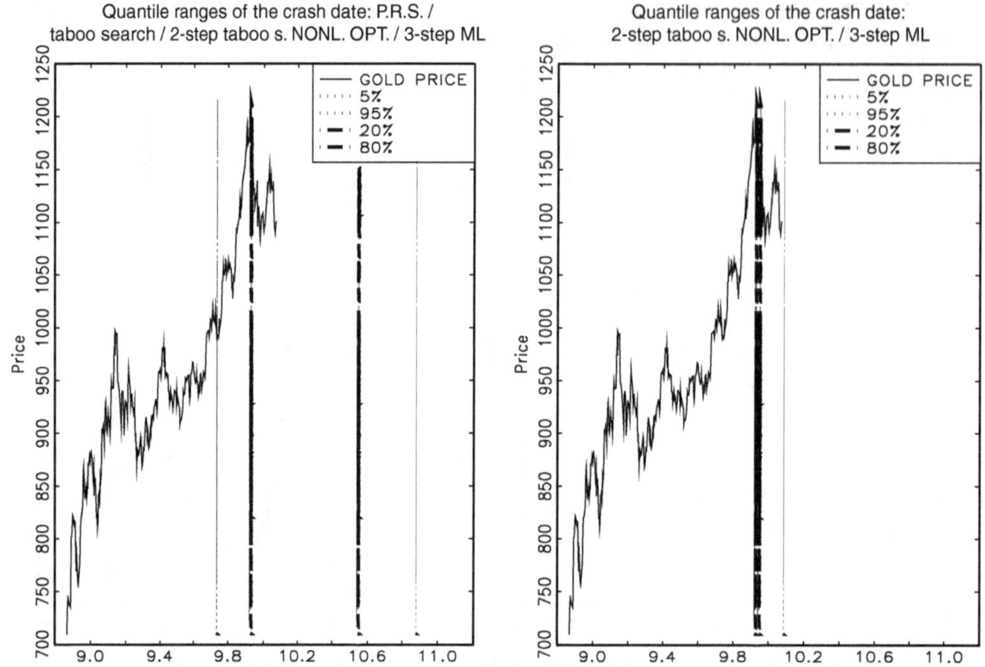

Figure 4. Quantile ranges of the crash date.

null hypothesis in the first test, together with a failure to reject the null in the second test, indicates that the residuals are stationary and thus compatible with an O–U process.

We used the residuals resulting from the previous estimation windows and numerical algorithms, that is, 48 shrinking windows, 19 expanding windows and four estimation methods, which give a total of 268 calibrations. The fraction P_{LPPL} of these different windows that met the LPPL conditions was equal to $P_{\mathrm{LPPL}} = 60.1\%$. The conditional probability that, out of the fraction P_{LPPL} of windows that satisfied the LPPL conditions, the null hypothesis of non-stationarity was rejected for the residuals was equal to $P_{\mathrm{Stat.Res.|LPPL}} = 100\%$ when using the ADF test at the probability level $\alpha = 0.001$. As for the KPSS test, the null of stationarity was not rejected at the 10% level or higher in all cases which satisfied the LPPL conditions. Therefore, this empirical evidence is comparable with the results reported by Jiang et al. (2010) for the case of the 2005–2007 and 2008–2009 Chinese stock market bubbles.

6.3 *Diagnostic tests based on rational expectation models with stochastic mean-reverting termination times*

We employed the two diagnostics proposed by Lin and Sornette (2009) to detect the presence of a bubble (and reviewed in Section 5.2) in the gold price time series, from 12 November 2008 to 1 December 2009. As discussed previously, we considered both the ADF and KPSS unit-root tests. Moreover, we also used time windows of 500 and 250 trading days to compute the critical time series $\tilde{T}_{c,i}$ in Equations (28)–(29) and Equation (32), together with the original 750 trading days for the first diagnostic and 900 for the second one. The rationale for this choice is that a long time span may include data which are not observed during a bubble regime but during a

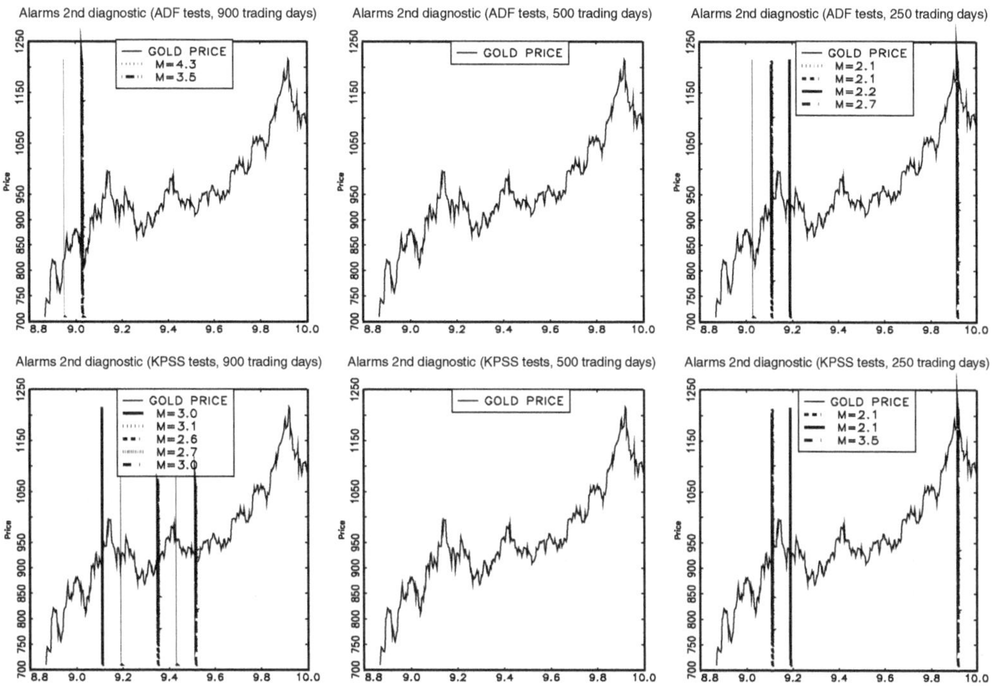

Figure 5. Logarithm of the gold price and corresponding alarms as vertical lines indicating the ends of the windows of T trading days, in which the second diagnostic flags an alarm for the presence of a bubble. The value of the exponent m for each alarm is reported in the legend.

standard geometric Brownian motion regime (or other regimes). Of course, reducing the time window implies a loss of efficiency.

Interestingly, the first procedure did not flag any alarm for the presence of a bubble, whereas the second one flagged three series of alarms close to three important price falls (Figure 5): the first group of alarms was centered around the local market peak on 20 February 2009 when gold reached the value of \$995.3 an ounce, very close to the important psychological barrier of \$1000, and after two days, it started falling, losing more than 10% in two weeks. The second group of alarms was centered around the local market peak on 2 June 2009 when gold reached the value of \$982.9, and after two days, it started falling, losing more than 5% in a week. Finally, the third group of alarms was centered around the global market peak on 2 December 2009 when gold reached the value of \$1216 an ounce.

This empirical evidence seems to suggest that the KPSS test provides more precise alarms than the ADF test, which is not a surprise, given the well-known limitations of the latter test. Moreover, a time window of 250 observations delivers more reliable flags for the presence of a bubble (or imminent price falls) than longer time spans, with it being more robust to market regime changes. However, a time window of 900 observations still provides useful information.

6.4 *CLIPs for the gold bubble*

The CLIP plots on the horizontal axis the date of the last observation in the estimation sample and on the vertical axis the estimated crash date $\hat{t}_c$ computed by fitting the LPPL to the data.

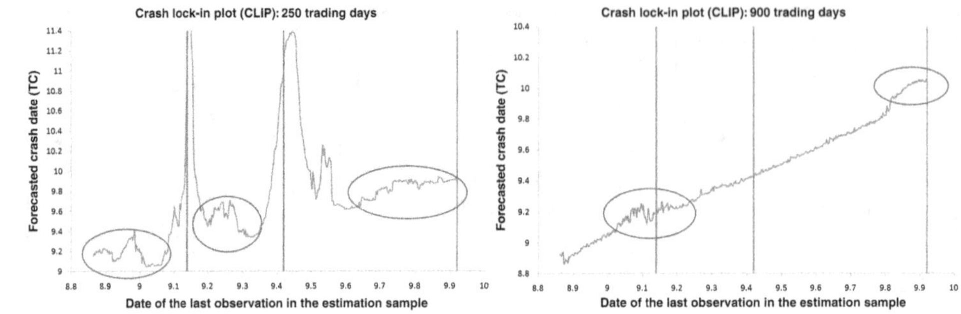

Figure 6. CLIPs for the gold price series. The three vertical lines correspond to the two local market peaks on 20 December 2009 and 2 June 2009 and to the global market peak on 2 December 2009, respectively.

Following the previous empirical evidence as well as the one reported in Lin and Sornette (2009) and Fantazzini (2010a), we computed the CLIP by fitting the data with two rolling estimation windows of 900 and 250 days and by using the simple average of the estimated $\hat{t}_c$ resulting from the four estimation algorithms discussed in Section 6.1. We used data spanning from 12 November 2008 till 1 day before the global market peak on 2 December 2009. The two CLIPs are shown in Figure 6.

Not surprisingly, the indications provided by the two CLIPs are rather similar to those provided by the second diagnostic test proposed by Lin and Sornette (2009) discussed in the previous section: the recursive forecasted crash dates computed with time windows of 250 trading days stabilize around three constant values which are very close to the dates corresponding to the two local market peaks on 20 February 2009 and 2 June 2009 and to the global market peak on 2 December 2009. The indications from the second CLIP computed with time windows of 900 trading days are somewhat weaker, but confirm the previous alarms. As expected, the estimates computed with smaller time spans are more noisy than those computed with longer time spans.

7. Conclusions

We presented an easy-to-use and self-contained guide for modeling and detecting financial bubbles with LPPLs, which contains the sufficient steps to derive the main models and discusses the important aspects for practitioners and researchers. We reviewed the original JLS model and we discussed early criticism to this approach and recent generalizations proposed to answer these remarks. Moreover, we described three different estimation methodologies which can be employed to estimate LPPL models. We then examined the issue of diagnosing bubbles in the making by using a set of different techniques, that is, by considering diagnostic tests based on the LPPL fitting residuals and diagnostic tests based on rational expectation models with stochastic mean-reverting termination times, as well as graphical tools useful for capturing bubble development and for understanding whether a crash is in sight or not. We finally presented a detailed empirical application devoted to the burst of the gold bubble in December 2009, which highlighted how a series of different diagnostics flagged an alarm for the presence of a bubble before prices started to fall.

Notes

1. In the context of the alignment of atomic spins to create magnetization, this model represented by Equation (4) is identical to the so-called two-dimensional *Ising model* which was solved explicitly by Onsager (1944), and where the disorder parameter is represented by the temperature of the system.
2. The lower bound on ω is rather strong, given that Sornette (2003a) found that $\omega = 6.36 \pm 1.56$ by using a large collection of empirical evidence. Moreover, the recent work about Chinese market bubbles by Jiang et al. (2010) considers only the former set of conditions.
3. See http://www.google.com/intl/en/trends/about.html for more details. In this case, the time span starts from 2004, which is the first year available for this analysis.
4. Similar to Cvijović and Klinowski (1995), we found that GA has a performance in between Taboo Search and PRS. However, even though PRS is computationally inefficient, it has the benefit to potentially visit regions of the parameter space that sometimes are not visited by the previous algorithms. This is why we consider it in our analysis in the place of GA.

References

Abreu, D., and M.K. Brunnermeier. 2003. Bubbles and crashes. *Econometrica* 71, no. 1: 173–204.

Bastiaensen, K., P. Cauwels, D. Sornette, R. Woodard, and W.X. Zhou. 2009. The Chinese equity bubble: ready to burst. http://arxiv.org/abs/0907.1827.

Bauwens, L., M. Lubrano, and J.F. Richard. 2000. *Bayesian inference in dynamic econometric models*. New York: OUP.

Bernardo, J.M., and A.F.M. Smith. 1994. *Bayesian theory*. New York: Wiley.

Blanchard, O.J. 1979. Speculative bubbles, crashes and rational expectations. *Economics Letters* 3, no. 4: 387–89.

Cendrowski, S. 2009. Beware the gold bubble. http://money.cnn.com/2009/10/06/pf/gold_investing_bubble.fortune/index.htm.

Chang, G., and J. Feigenbaum. 2006. A Bayesian analysis of log-periodic precursors to financial crashes. *Quantitative Finance* 6, no. 1: 15–36.

Cvijović, D., and J. Klinowski. 1995. Taboo search – an approach to the multiple minima problem. *Science* 267, no. 5: 664–6.

Dennis, Jr., J.E., and R.B. Schnabel. 1983. *Numerical methods for unconstrained optimization and nonlinear equations*. Englewood Cliffs, NJ: Prentice-Hall.

Derrida, B., L. De Seze, and C. Itzykson. 1983. Fractal structure of zeros in hierarchical models. *Journal of Statistical Physics* 33, no. 3: 559–69.

Fantazzini, D. 2010a. Modelling bubbles and anti-bubbles in bear markets: a medium-term trading analysis. In *Handbook of trading*, ed. G. Gregoriou, 365–88. New York: McGraw-Hill.

Fantazzini, D. 2010b. Modelling and forecasting the global financial crisis: initial findings using heteroskedastic log-periodic models. *Economics Bulletin* 30, no. 3: 1833–41.

Financial Crisis Observatory website. http://www.er.ethz.ch/fco.

Gazola, L., C. Fernandes, A. Pizzinga, and R. Riera. 2008. The log-periodic-AR(1)-GARCH(1,1) model for financial crashes. *The European Physical Journal B* 61, no. 3: 355–62.

Goldenfeld, N. 1992. *Lectures on phase transitions and the renormalization group*. Reading, MA: Addison-Wesley.

Greenspan, Alan. 2002. Remarks by Chairman Alan Greenspan at a symposium sponsored by the Federal Reserve Bank of Kansas City, Jackson Hole, Wyoming, 30 August.

Griffiths, W.E., R. Hill, and G.C. Lim. 2008. *Using EViews for principles of econometrics*. 3rd edn. Hoboken, NJ: Wiley.

Gulsten, M., E.A. Smith, and D.M. Tate. 1995. A genetic algorithm approach to curve fitting. *International Journal of Production Research* 33, no. 7: 1911–23.

Gürkaynak, R. 2008. Econometric tests of asset price bubbles: taking stock. *Journal of Economic Surveys* 22, no. 1: 166–86.

Hayashi, F. 2000. *Econometrics*. Princeton, NJ: PUP.

Jacobsson, E. 2009. How to predict crashes in financial markets with the log-periodic power law. Master diss., Department of Mathematical Statistics, Stockholm University.

Jiang, Z.Q., W.H. Zhou, D. Sornette, R. Woodard, K. Bastiaensen, and P. Cauwels. 2010. Bubble diagnosis and prediction of the 2005–2007 and 2008–2009 Chinese stock market bubbles. *Journal of Economic Behavior and Organization* 74: 149–62. http://arxiv.org/abs/0909.1007.

Johansen, A. 2002. Comment on 'Are financial crashes predictable?'. *Europhysics Letters* 60, no. 5: 809–10.

Johansen, A. 2003. Characterization of large price variations in financial markets. *Physica A* 324, no. 1: 157–66.

Johansen, A., O. Ledoit, and D. Sornette. 2000. Crashes as critical points. *International Journal of Theoretical and Applied Finance* 3, no. 2: 219–55.

Johansen, A., and D. Sornette. 1999. Financial anti-bubbles: log-periodicity in gold and Nikkei collapses. *International Journal of Modern Physics C* 10, no. 4: 563–75.

Johansen, A., and D. Sornette. 2000. Evaluation of the quantitative prediction of a trend reversal on the Japanese stock market in 1999. *International Journal of Modern Physics C* 11, no. 2: 359–64.

Johansen, A., and D. Sornette. 2004. Endogenous versus exogenous crashes in financial markets. In *Contemporary Issues in International Finance*. Nova Science Publishers. Reprinted as Shocks, crashes and bubbles in financial markets. *Brussels Economic Review (Cahiers economiques de Bruxelles)* 49, no. 3/4, Special Issue on Nonlinear Analysis, 2006.

Kaizoji, T., and D. Sornette. In press. Market bubbles and crashes. In *Encyclopedia of quantitative finance*. Wiley. http://www.wiley.com//legacy/wileychi/eqf/ (long version available at http://arXiv.org/abs/0812.2449).

Koop, G. 2003. *Bayesian econometrics*. Chichester: Wiley.

Krugman, P. 1998. The confidence game, how Washington worsened Asia's crash. *The New Republic*, 5 October.

Kwiatkowski, D., P. Phillips, P. Schmidt, and Y. Shin. 1992. Testing the null hypothesis of stationary against the alternative of a unit root. *Journal of Econometrics* 54, nos. 1–3: 159–78.

Laloux, L., M. Potters, R. Cont, J.P Aguilar, and J.P. Bouchaud. 1999. Are financial crashes predictable? *Europhysics Letters* 45, no. 1: 1–5.

Lin, L., R.E. Ren, and D. Sornette. In press. A consistent model of explosive financial bubbles with mean-reversing residuals. *Quantitative Finance*. http://arxiv.org/abs/0905.0128 and http://papers.ssrn.com/abstract=1407574.

Lin, L., and D. Sornette. 2009. Diagnostics of rational expectation financial bubbles with stochastic mean-reverting termination times. ETH working paper. http://arxiv.org/abs/0911.1921.

Mogi, C. 2009. Gold hits record high as dollar sets new lows. *Reuters*, 26 November. http://www.reuters.com/article/goldMktRpt/idUSSP7486520091126.

Ng, S., and P. Perron. 2001. Lag length selection and the construction of unit root tests with good size and power. *Econometrica* 69, no. 6: 1519–54.

Onsager, L. 1944. Crystal statistics. A two-dimensional model with an order-disorder transition. *Physics Review* 65, nos. 3–4: 117–49.

Pfaff, B. 2008. *Analysis of integrated and cointegrated time series with R*. New York: Wiley.

Reinhart, C., and K. Rogoff. 2009. *This time is different: eight centuries of financial folly*. Princeton, NJ: PUP.

Shefrin. H. 2005. *A behavioral approach to asset pricing*. Academic Press Advanced Finance Series. Burlington, VT: Academic Press.

Sornette, D. 2003a. *Why stock markets crash (critical events in complex financial systems)*. Princeton, NJ: PUP.

Sornette, D. 2003b. Critical market crashes. *Physics Reports* 378, no. 1: 1–98.

Sornette, D. 2009. Dragon-kings, black swans and the prediction of crises. *International Journal of Terraspace Science and Engineering* 2, no. 1: 1–18.

Sornette, D., and A. Johansen. 1997. Large financial crashes. *Physica A* 245, nos. 3–4: 411–22.

Sornette, D., and A. Johansen. 2001. Significance of log-periodic precursors to financial crashes. *Quantitative Finance* 1, no. 4: 452–71.

Sornette, D., A. Johansen, and J.P. Bouchaud. 1996. Stock market crashes, precursors and replicas. *Journal de Physique I* 6, no. 1: 167–75.

Sornette, D., and R. Woodard. 2010. Financial bubbles, real estate bubbles, derivative bubbles, and the financial and economic crisis. In *'Proceedings of APFA7 (Applications of Physics in Financial Analysis)', New approaches to the analysis of large-scale business and economic data*, ed. Misako Takayasu, Tsutomu Watanabe, and Hideki Takayasu. Springer. http://www.thic-apfa7.com/en/htm/index.html, http://arxiv.org/abs/0905.0220, http://web.sg.ethz.ch/wps/CCSS-09–00003/, and http://papers.ssrn.com/sol3/papers.cfm?abstract_id=1407608.

Sornette, D., R. Woodard, and W.X. Zhou. 2008. The 2006–2008 oil bubble and beyond. ETH Zurich preprint. http://arXiv.org/abs/0806.1170.

Sornette, D., R. Woodard, and W.X. Zhou. 2009. The 2006–2008 oil bubble: evidence of speculation, and prediction. *Physica A* 388, no. 8: 1571–76.

Sornette, D., and W.X. Zhou. 2006. Predictability of large future changes in major financial indices. *International Journal of Forecasting* 22, no. 1: 153–68.

Stanley, H.E. 1971. *Introduction to phase transitions and critical phenomena*. New York: OUP.

Stock, J.H. 1994. Unit roots, structural breaks and trends. In *Handbook of econometrics*, ed. R.F. Engle and D.L. McFadden, vol. 4, chap. 46, 2740–831. Amsterdam: Elsevier.

Stock, J.H., and M.W. Watson. 2002. *Introduction to econometrics*. Addison Wesley.

Tung, R. 2009. China c.Bank: Gold prices high, warns of bubble. *Reuters*, 2 December. http://www.reuters.com/article/idUSTPU00193020091202.

White, G. 2009. Golden times for precious metals but pick carefully. *The Daily Telegraph*, 8 September. http://www.telegraph.co.uk/finance/markets/questor/6156983/Golden-times-for-precious-metals-but-pick-carefully.html.

Zhou, W.X., and D. Sornette. 2003. 2000–2003 Real estate bubble in the UK but not in the USA. *Physica A* 329, nos. 1–2: 249–63.

Zhou, W.X., and D. Sornette. 2005. Testing the stability of the 2000–2003 US stock market antibubble. *Physica A* 348: 428–52.

Zhou, W.X., and D. Sornette. 2006. Is there a real-estate bubble in the US? *Physica A* 361, no. 1: 297–308.

Zhou, W.X., and D. Sornette. 2008. Analysis of the real estate market in Las Vegas: bubble, seasonal patterns, and prediction of the CSW indexes. *Physica A* 387, no. 1: 243–60.

Zhou, W.X., and D. Sornette. 2009. A case study of speculative financial bubbles in the South African stock market 2003–2006. *Physica A* 388, no. 1: 869–80.

Zhou, Xin and Alan Wheatley (2009) China's CIC wealth fund muscles up as markets recover. Reuters, Beijing, 28 August. http://www.reuters.com/article/cusir/idUSTRE57S0D420090829.

Heterogeneous expectations and exchange rate dynamics

Carl Chiarella, Xue-Zhong He and Min Zheng

This article presents a continuous-time model of exchange rates not only relying on macroeconomic factors but also having an investor heterogeneity component. The driving macroeconomic factor is the domestic–foreign interest rate differential, while the investor heterogeneity is described by the expectations of boundedly rational portfolio managers who use a weighted average of the expectations of fundamentalists and chartists. Within this framework, the different roles of the macroeconomic factor and investor heterogeneity in the determination of the exchange rate are examined explicitly. We show that this simple model generates very complicated market behaviour, including the existence of multiple steady-state equilibria, deviations of the market exchange rate from the fundamental one and market fluctuations. Numerical simulation of the corresponding stochastic version of the model shows that the model is able to generate typical time series and volatility clustering patterns observed in exchange rate markets.

1. Introduction

In the traditional macro-structure paradigm that underpins the influential rational expectations Dornbusch (1976) model, exchange rate determination is based on macroeconomic fundamental factors, in particular, on interest rates and monetary policy. However, many empirical studies of exchange rates have shown that there are often large movements in exchange rates that are apparently unexplained by macroeconomic fundamental factors. Sometimes, the market exchange rate can deviate from its fundamental equilibrium and stabilise at some non-fundamental levels for quite long periods of time. In particular, Meese and Rogoff (1983) showed that a random walk model outperforms standard open economy macroeconomic models in explaining exchange rate movements. The weak explanatory power of macroeconomic factors on the exchange rate is referred to as the exchange rate puzzle or anomaly (Lyons 2001). Over the last two decades, an increasing number of anomalies and puzzles have been uncovered in empirical research. These anomalies or puzzles include, for example, (i) the 'disconnect' puzzle, referring to the fact that exchange rates appear to be disconnected from their underlying fundamental factors most of the time (Williamson 1985), (ii) the 'excess volatility' puzzle, whereby the volatility of exchange rates by far exceeds the volatility of their underlying economic variables (Baxter and Stockman 1989; Flood and Rose 1995) and (iii) the stylised facts, referring to the non-normality, fat tails and power-law behaviour of exchange rate returns (Lux 1998, 2009; Lux and Marchesi 2001; LeBaron 2006).

We refer to De Grauwe and Grimaldi (2006) for more discussion of these empirical anomalies. The foregoing comments suggest that explanations of exchange rate movements based solely on macroeconomic fundamental factors are unsatisfactory. As a result, the attention of researchers has moved away from the examination simply of macroeconomic factors towards that taking into account the structure of the foreign exchange, in particular, by considering the heterogeneity and bounded rationality of investors.

Empirical literature on survey data, in particular, Ito (1990), Allen and Taylor (1990), Taylor and Allen (1992), Menkhoff (1998), Chinn and Frankel (2002) and more recently Menkhoff and Taylor (2007), provide evidence of heterogeneity and bounded rationality of the investors in exchange rate markets. These studies show the widespread influence of foreign exchange fundamental analysts who base their predictions on macroeconomic fundamental factors and technical analysts who base their predictions purely on the identification of supposedly recurring patterns in exchange rate movements. So models seeking to explain exchange rate movements should incorporate both of these elements.

Over the last two decades, the literature on models of heterogeneous agents who are boundedly rational in speculative markets has developed rapidly. In order to explain the US dollar's behaviour in the 1980s, Frankel and Froot (1986) considered an exchange rate model with three classes of agents: fundamentalists who believe the Dornbusch overshooting model, chartists who believe that the exchange rate follows a random walk and portfolio managers who form their expectations as a weighted average of the predictions of the fundamentalists and chartists. The framework of Frankel and Froot departs from the rational expectations orthodoxy, by virtue of the fact that the three types of agents are boundedly rational rather than fully rational. They found that the portfolio managers learn more slowly about the model than they change it by revising a linear combination of chartist and fundamentalist views they incorporate in their own forecasts, which leads to the take-off of bubbles. In addition, the fundamental equilibrium of the model may not be stable and the exchange rate may stabilise around a value that is far from the fundamental equilibrium. Recently, some exchange rate models that study jointly the dynamics of speculative and macroeconomic forces and other exchange rate models that solely focus on the behaviour of speculators have been developed (Westerhoff 2003; Westerhoff and Reitz 2003; Reitz and Taylor 2008; Westerhoff 2009). These models are able to mimic the dynamics of foreign exchange markets and provide some policy implications such as central bank intervention. From the prospective of asset pricing, by incorporating bounded rationality and heterogeneity, various heterogeneous agent models have successfully explained many types of features (such as market booms and crashes and long deviations of the market price from the fundamental price), the stylised facts (such as skewness, kurtosis, volatility clustering and fat tails of returns) and various power laws (such as the long memory in return volatility) observed in financial markets. We refer the reader to Hommes (2006), Hommes and Wagener (2009), LeBaron (2006), Chiarella, Dieci and He (2009) and Westerhoff (2009) for surveys of the recent developments in this literature.

This article seeks to revisit the Dornbusch overshooting mechanism in light of the understanding that macroeconomic factors alone are not the drivers of exchange rate movements. We present a continuous-time model of exchange rate dynamics containing both macroeconomic and investor heterogeneity elements. The macroeconomic fundamental factor is determined by the domestic-foreign interest rate differential, while the investor heterogeneity is characterised by the expectations of the portfolio managers. From Frankel and Froot (1986, 1990a, 1990b), we borrow the idea that the expectations of the portfolio managers are a function of the weighted average of the expectations of fundamentalists and chartists. However, unlike in Frankel and Froot (1986), this function is nonlinear instead of being linear, with the nonlinearity being due to the cautiousness of the portfolio managers as weighted expectations take extreme values. The incorporation of fundamentalists and chartists allows for the bounded rationality of the heterogeneous investors rather than for the full rationality that is usually proposed and that creates an 'infinite regress' problem, as argued in De Grauwe and Grimaldi (2006). Within our framework, we are able to examine explicitly the different roles of the macroeconomic fundamental factor and investor heterogeneity in the determination of the exchange rate. By the introduction of cautiousness into the expectations of the portfolio managers, we provide a channel for the market exchange rate to deviate from and fluctuate around the fundamental exchange rate. It is this channel which is missing from the current literature and which turns out to play a very important role in the stability of non-fundamental equilibrium exchange rates and the complicated exchange rate behaviour observed in exchange rate markets. We show that the long-run convergence of the fundamental equilibrium exchange rate is related to the macroeconomic fundamental factors and the persistent fluctuations are due to the heterogeneity of the investors. Numerical simulations of the stochastic version of the model show that the model is able to generate the broad features of typical time series behaviour and volatility clustering observed in exchange rate markets.

The article is organised as follows. In Section 2, we lay out an exchange rate model with nonlinear heterogeneous beliefs in a continuous-time framework. Based on this model, in Section 3, the existence of fundamental and non-fundamental steady states is analysed. In Section 4, the stability of the fundamental steady state is analysed based on three types of market expectations, those of the fundamentalists, of the chartists and then of a weighted average of both groups. The conditions and mechanisms under which the exchange rate deviates from its fundamental value are highlighted. In Section 5, we consider the effect of market noise and Markov switching of the weighting process on the exchange rate market. Some conclusions are given in Section 6. Proofs of some technical results are given in the appendices.

2. The model

The classical Dornbusch (1976) model, which incorporates perfect myopic foresight in predicting exchange rate changes, displays a saddle-point structure. Under the rational expectation assumption of the Dornbusch model, any unanticipated discrete jump in money supply leads to an immediate discrete jump in the exchange rate and the magnitude of this jump is assumed to be precisely that necessary to move the system from its present state onto the stable arm of the saddle point associated with the new equilibrium (see Gray and Turnovsky 1979 for a very elegant and detailed discussion of this issue). This is the underlying factor behind the well-known overshooting of the exchange rate, which was the important idea introduced by the Dornbusch model.

The model we develop modifies the Dornbusch model by incorporating macroeconomic fundamental factors and the market activity of heterogeneous investors. This means that the market exchange rate is determined not only by the macroeconomic fundamental factors, such as the interest rate differential, but also by the activities of portfolio managers in the market who aggregate in a certain way the expectations of fundamentalists and chartists. More precisely, consider an exchange rate market populated by many portfolio managers who use a weighted average of the expectations of fundamentalists and chartists as specified below. The following notation is used throughout this article:

R^*: the foreign (nominal) rate of interest, taken to be exogenous;
R: the domestic (nominal) interest rate;

X^{m}, X^{f} and X^{c}: the expected rate of exchange depreciation by the portfolio managers, fundamentalists and chartists, respectively;
E: the logarithm of the current exchange rate, measured in units of domestic currency per unit of foreign currency;
P: the logarithm of the domestic price level;
M: the logarithm of the domestic nominal money supply, taken to be exogenous;
Y: the logarithm of the domestic real output, taken to be exogenous.

The fundamentalists believe that the depreciation of the spot rate should regress to the fundamental value, which is determined by the interest rate parity condition. Specifically, the expected rate of exchange depreciation of the fundamentalists, X^{f}, is assumed to follow

$$\dot{X}^{f} = \beta_{f}(R - R^{*} - X^{f}), \tag{1}$$

where $\beta_{f} > 0$ is a constant. Equation (1) states that the expectations of the fundamentalists of the rate of exchange depreciation X^{f} form a mean-reverting process to the nominal interest rate differential $R - R^{*}$, with β_{f} measuring the speed of adjustment of the mean-reverting process. In the special case where the speed of the adjustment of the fundamentalists is infinite, $\beta_{f} = \infty$, it follows from $(1/\beta_{f})\dot{X}^{f} = R - R^{*} - X^{f}$ that $R - R^{*} = X^{f}$, which is the interest rate parity condition.

In contrast, the chartists use some technical methods to attempt to discover the trend of the market exchange rate. Here, we assume that they believe that the change in the log-exchange rate (LER) follows a weighted average of past changes of the LER,[1] that is,

$$\dot{X}^{c} = \beta_{c}(\dot{E} - X^{c}), \tag{2}$$

where $\beta_{c} > 0$ measures the speed of adjustment of the chartists to the change in the LER or their rate of extrapolation to the LER trend. In the special case where the speed of the adjustment of the chartists is infinite, $\beta_{c} = \infty$, it follows from $(1/\beta_{c})\dot{X}^{c} = (\dot{E} - X^{c})$ that $X^{c} = \dot{E}$, that is, the chartists would have a perfect foresight expectation.[2]

The portfolio managers are the investors who actually buy and sell foreign assets in the market. Their decision is based on an aggregate of the expectations of the fundamentalists and chartists of the change in the LER. We could think of the portfolio managers as being in a large financial institution that employs groups of fundamental analysts and groups who engage in technical analysis of market data. The role of the managers is to blend these two sources of information in some fashion. We assume that they do this by taking a weighted average of the expectations of the fundamentalists and chartists, so that the expected rate of exchange depreciation of the portfolio managers is given by

$$X^{m} = H((1 - \omega)X^{f} + \omega X^{c}), \quad \omega \in [0, 1], \tag{3}$$

where ω and $1 - \omega$ represent the market fractions that the portfolio managers attach to the expectations of the chartists and fundamentalists, respectively, and $H(\cdot)$ is a function of the expectations mix that is nonlinear due to the cautiousness of the portfolio managers and is discussed further below.

Exchange rate determination

A general model of LER adjustment is assumed to be of the form

$$\dot{E} = X^{m} + Z, \tag{4}$$

where X^{m} is the expected rate of exchange depreciation of the portfolio managers defined by Equation (3) and Z represents some macroeconomic fundamental factor, which here is assumed to be determined by the nominal interest rate differential, so that

$$Z = \beta_{\mathrm{R}}(R^* - R), \tag{5}$$

where $\beta_{\mathrm{R}} > 0$ is a constant, measuring the impact of the fundamental factor on the exchange depreciation in the market. In order to remain within the spirit of the original Dornbusch model, we assume that the interest rate differential is the main driver of exchange rate variation in the macroeconomic fundamental factor. Of course, other macro fundamental factors could also be included in Z, but we take Equation (5) for simplicity.

The first term on the right-hand side of Equation (4), as in Frankel and Froot (1986), can be thought of as capturing the speculative factors in the market. Here, these come from a nonlinear combination of heterogeneous expectations, described by Equation (3). The function $H(x) = \mu h(x)$, where $\mu > 0$ is a constant scaling factor and $h(\cdot)$ is a nonlinear function satisfying[3]

$$h(0) = 0, \quad h'(0) = 1, \quad \lim_{x \to \pm\infty} h'(x) = 0, \quad \text{and} \quad h''(x)x < 0 \quad \text{for } x \neq 0. \tag{6}$$

Thus, the function H is an S-shaped function and is illustrated in Figure 1 for different scaling factors. Note that $\mu = H'(0) = \max_x H'(x)$ measures the weight that the portfolio managers put on the expectations of the fundamentalists and chartists when their expected rates of exchange depreciation are near zero.

Intuitively, when the deviation of the exchange rate from the fundamental equilibrium increases, the impact of the macroeconomic fundamental factor dominates the bounded nonlinear function in Equation (4) so that the exchange rate is mean-reverting to the fundamental equilibrium, as will be demonstrated later. The function H captures the cautiousness of the portfolio managers with regard to the speculative elements in the market. That is, portfolio managers are more confident in the aggregate expected rate of depreciation of the fundamentalists and chartists when it is small and become less confident or more cautious as it becomes larger in absolute value. For example, when the macroeconomic fundamental factor dominates the market, the portfolio managers downplay the aggregate expectation either when the chartists expect a large change by extrapolating strongly the LER trend or when the fundamentalists expect a large exchange rate depreciation from the mean-reverting process to the nominal interest rate differential. However,

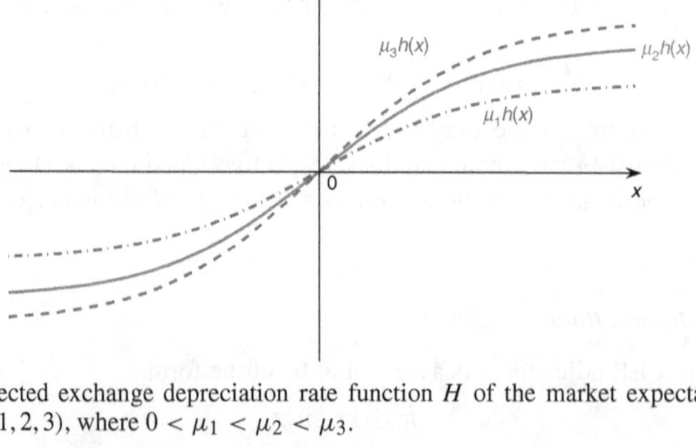

Figure 1. The expected exchange depreciation rate function H of the market expectation with different parameter μ_i $(i = 1, 2, 3)$, where $0 < \mu_1 < \mu_2 < \mu_3$.

when the macroeconomic fundamental factor becomes less dominant, the portfolio managers react strongly to the aggregate expectation. The implications and significance of this choice with respect to current exchange rate models will be discussed later in this section.

Relation to earlier literature

We now discuss in some detail further motivation behind our model and its relationship to the Dornbusch (1976) model, the Gray and Turnovsky (1979) (GT hereafter) model and the Frankel and Froot (1986) (FF hereafter) model. First, the stabilising mechanism of the macro fundamental factor measured by the interest rate differential in our model is largely motivated by the GT model. To overcome the saddle-point problem of the Dornbusch model and stabilise the exchange rate at its fundamental equilibrium, GT suggested an extension of the perfect myopic foresight mechanism in the Dornbusch model that makes LER adjustment sluggish, namely

$$\dot{E} = \gamma[R^* - R + X] = \gamma X + \gamma(R^* - R) \tag{7}$$

for some $\gamma > 0$. Equation (7) should be contrasted with Equation (4). Instead of the linear homogeneous market expectation (the first term in Equation (7)), we incorporate the nonlinear function H of the expectations of the portfolio managers due to their cautiousness. It turns out that this extension introduces a mechanism that can generate non-fundamental equilibria.

Second, the rate of change in the spot exchange rate expected by the fundamentalists X^{f} in the FF model is given by $X^{\mathrm{f}} = \theta(\bar{E} - E)$, where $\bar{E}$ is the logarithm of the long-run equilibrium exchange rate and θ is the speed of regression of E to $\bar{E}$. In our model, the rate of exchange depreciation expected by the fundamentalists X^{f} is assumed to follow a mean-reverting process to the nominal interest rate differential $R - R^*$, which corresponds to the interest rate parity condition. There are several implications resulting from this difference: (i) The long-run equilibrium $\bar{E}$ in the FF model, which is unknown to the investors in general, is specifically linked to the interest rate differential in our model. In some exchange rate markets, there may be no unique long-run equilibrium exchange rate or the exchange rate may shift among different equilibrium levels from time to time because of changing economic conditions, in particular, interest rates. (ii) Equation (1) describes a sluggish adjustment in the rate of exchange depreciation expected by the fundamentalists. If there were no chartists and the speed of the adjustment of the fundamentalists were infinite, then as we have shown, Equation (1) would lead to the well-known interest rate parity condition assumed in the Dornbusch model.

Third, the exchange rate expected by the chartists in the FF model is assumed to follow a random walk, which is equivalent to assuming that the rate of exchange depreciation expected by the chartists is zero, that is, $X^{\mathrm{c}} = 0$, rather than the conventional assumption that the chartists form their expectations from historical exchange rates. Instead, in our model, the expected depreciation rate by the chartists is a geometrically weighted average of the historical changes in the LER with higher weight on the more recent changes. Intuitively, this is consistent with what we observe in financial market practice and survey literature in which geometrically weighted trends are used by practitioners (see e.g. the survey by Chiarella, Dieci, and He 2009).

Fourth, in the FF model, in order to characterise the temporary 'bubble' in the exchange rate, the weight that the portfolio managers put on the fundamentalist expectation is assumed to be time dependent and so is written[4] ϖ_t and evolves according to $\Delta\varpi_t = \delta(\hat{\varpi}_{t-1} - \varpi_{t-1})$, where $0 \leq \delta \leq 1$ measures the speed of adaptation and $\hat{\varpi}_{t-1}$ is defined as the weight given to the fundamentalist view, computed *ex post*, that would have perfectly predicted the realised change in the previous period. By assuming a random walk process for the exchange rate expected by the chartists, $\hat{\varpi}_{t-1}$

is given by $\Delta E_t = \hat{\varpi}_{t-1}\theta(\bar{E} - E_{t-1})$. Hence, the change in weights that the portfolio managers give to the fundamentalists' view is determined by $\Delta\varpi_t = \delta[\Delta E_t/(\theta(\bar{E} - E_{t-1})) - \varpi_{t-1}]$. This specification is based on the assumption of the knowledge of the long-run equilibrium of LER $\bar{E}$. As we have discussed in the previous point, when $\bar{E}$ is unknown to the investors, or there is no long-run equilibrium, or the exchange rate shifts among several different equilibrium levels from time to time, choosing $\hat{\varpi}_{t-1}$ as the weight that would have perfectly predicted the realised change in the spot rate would be difficult, if not impossible. In our model, by choosing the weight ϖ as a parameter, we examine how changes in ϖ lead to different exchange rate dynamics.[5] For the deterministic model, the parameter ϖ is a constant and its effect on the exchange rate dynamics will be examined by stability and bifurcation theory in Sections 3 and 4. For the stochastic version of the model, it is a random variable and its effect will be analysed by simulation in Section 5.

Fifth, in the FF model, the LER itself is assumed to follow $E_t = c\varpi_t X^{\mathrm{f}} + Z_t$, where c is the semi-elasticity of money demand with respect to the alternative rate of return and Z_t represents other contemporaneous determinants, which is defined by $Z_t = (D_t - F_t) - b(R_t - R^*)$, where D_t and F_t are the log of supply of domestic and foreign assets, respectively. By assuming that the actual rate of depreciation is given by

$$\dot{E}_t = \nu(\bar{E} - E_t) \tag{8}$$

with some constant $\nu > 0$, a two-dimensional differential equation system for (E_t, ϖ_t) is constructed in the FF model. In our model, rather than assuming (8), we model the change in the LER $\dot{E}(t)$ directly by assuming that it follows Equation (4). This approach has the following advantages: (i) When the LER is solely driven by the expected depreciation rate, we would have $\dot{E} = X^{\mathrm{m}}$, leading to perfect myopic foresight in predicting LER changes. In addition, if there were no chartists, the speed of adjustment of the fundamentalists were infinite and the function H were linear, then we would obtain $\dot{E} = X^{\mathrm{m}} = X^{\mathrm{f}} = R - R^*$, which corresponds to the interest rate parity condition. (ii) When the LER is solely driven by the macro fundamental factor $Z(t)$, which depends on the interest rate differential $R - R^*$, the nominal interest rate differential should be positively related to the appreciation of the exchange rate. This is because if $R > R^*$, the domestic interest rate exceeds the foreign one, there will be a tendency for capital inflow, leading to a depreciation of the foreign currency. The adjustment is reversed if $R < R^*$. As we will see from the discussion in the following section, the combination of the speculative and fundamental factors in Equation (4) can essentially provide a mechanism that generates multiple equilibrium exchange rates under certain conditions as well as an endogenous mechanism for fluctuation between them.

The complete model

In summary, substituting Equations (3) and (5) into Equation (4), the dynamics of the spot LER are determined by

$$\dot{E} = H((1 - \omega)X^{\mathrm{f}} + \omega X^{\mathrm{c}}) + \beta_{\mathrm{R}}(R^* - R). \tag{9}$$

The domestic interest rate is determined by the nominal quantity of money, the real income and the goods price via[6]

$$\alpha_1 Y - \alpha_2 R = M - P, \quad \text{where} \quad \alpha_1, \alpha_2 > 0. \tag{10}$$

However, for the goods price, we adopt the specification in the original Dornbusch model and assume that it follows a sluggish adjustment process according to which the rate of the log-domestic price adjusts to excess demand. The excess demand is assumed to be a decreasing function of the output and domestic nominal interest rate and an increasing function of the relative price $E - P$. More specifically,

$$\dot{P} = \rho[\beta_0 - \beta_1 Y - \beta_2 R + \beta_3(E - P)], \tag{11}$$

where $\rho > 0, \beta_1 \in (0, 1), \beta_2 > 0, \beta_3 > 0$ and β_0 is a shift parameter.

To sum up, the model of exchange rate, price and the heterogeneous expectations becomes

$$\begin{aligned} \dot{E} &= H((1-\omega)X^{\mathrm{f}} + \omega X^{\mathrm{c}}) + \beta_{\mathrm{R}}(R^* - R), \\ \dot{P} &= \rho[\beta_0 - \beta_1 Y - \beta_2 R + \beta_3(E - P)], \\ \dot{X}^{\mathrm{f}} &= \beta_{\mathrm{f}}(R - R^* - X^{\mathrm{f}}), \\ \dot{X}^{\mathrm{c}} &= \beta_{\mathrm{c}}(\dot{E} - X^{\mathrm{c}}), \end{aligned} \tag{12}$$

with $R = (\alpha_1 Y - M + P)/\alpha_2$ and R^* is given. With a constant R^*, system (12) is a four-dimensional deterministic dynamical system.

Several models in the literature can be recovered from the model (12) under the assumption that the rate of exchange depreciation function expected by the portfolio managers is linear instead of being nonlinear. First, the classical Dornbusch model can be recovered if, under the conditions $\mu = H'(0) = \beta_R + 1$ and $H(x) = \mu x$, we assume either $\omega = 0$ (zero weight on the chartist expectation) and $\beta_{\mathrm{f}} = \infty$ (the speed of adjustment of the fundamentalists becomes infinite) or $\omega = 1$ (zero weight on the fundamentalist expectation) and $\beta_{\mathrm{c}} = \infty$ (the chartists extrapolate infinitely rapidly). Second, by choosing $\omega = 1, \beta_{\mathrm{c}} = \infty, H(x) = \gamma x$ and $\beta_{\mathrm{R}} = \gamma$, our model (12) yields the Gray and Turnovsky (1979) model with sluggish adjustment in the exchange rate.

In the following two sections, we examine the existence of multiple equilibria and their stability. By introducing market noise and a Markov switching process into the weighting parameter of the heterogeneous expectations, we establish a stochastic version of the deterministic system (12) in Section 5. The analysis of the dynamics of the deterministic system provides some insights into the dynamics of the stochastic model.

3. Existence of multiple equilibria

The evolution of the system (12) describing the dynamics of the LER depends on the characteristics of its steady states, which encapsulate the long-run behaviour of the system. In this section, we examine the existence of equilibria. In particular, we provide conditions for the existence of multiple steady states. The long-run behaviour of the system will be analysed in the following section.

Let $\mathcal{S} := (\bar{E}, \bar{P}, \bar{X}^{\mathrm{f}}, \bar{X}^{\mathrm{c}})$ be a steady state of the system (12). Then, $\mathcal{S}$ satisfies

$$\bar{E} = \frac{1}{\beta_3}[-\beta_0 + \beta_1 Y + \beta_2 \bar{R} + \beta_3 \bar{P}], \tag{13a}$$

$$\bar{P} = M - \alpha_1 Y + \alpha_2(R^* + \bar{X}^{\mathrm{f}}), \tag{13b}$$

$$\beta_{\mathrm{R}}\bar{X}^{\mathrm{f}} = H((1-\omega)\bar{X}^{\mathrm{f}}), \tag{13c}$$

$$\bar{X}^{\mathrm{c}} = 0, \tag{13d}$$

where $\bar{R} = R^* + \bar{X}^{\mathrm{f}}$ satisfies the interest rate parity condition. Obviously, $\bar{X}^{\mathrm{f}} = 0$ is always a solution of Equation (13c). In this case, the corresponding steady state is given by $\mathcal{S}_0 := (E^*, P^*, 0, 0)$

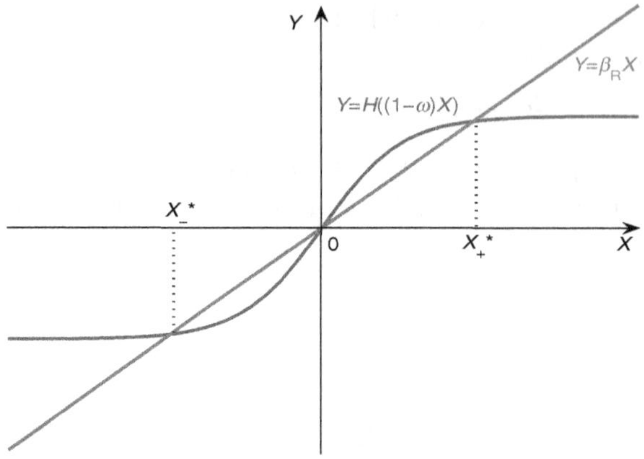

Figure 2. The three solutions of $H((1-\omega)X) = \beta_R X$ for $\mu(1-\omega) > \beta_R$.

and the zero interest rate parity condition holds, that is, $\bar{R} - R^* = 0$, where E^* and P^* are defined in Equation (14) below. This steady state corresponds to the classical equilibrium of the exchange rate in the Dornbusch (1976) model and hence we call $\mathcal{S}_0 = (E^*, P^*, 0, 0)$ the *fundamental steady state*.

When $\mu(1-\omega) > \beta_R$, Equation (13c) has two other solutions, $\bar{X}^f = X_{\pm}^*$, satisfying $X_-^* < 0 < X_+^*$, the graphical determination of which is illustrated in Figure 2. The condition $\mu(1-\omega) > \beta_R$ can be interpreted as either the portfolio managers giving a higher weight (relatively) to the expectations of the fundamentalists or that they are having a greater impact relative to the macro-environment factor. In this case, the system (12) has both the fundamental equilibrium and other non-fundamental equilibria. At $\bar{X}^f = X_{\pm}^*$, the non-zero interest rate parity condition holds, that is, $X_{\pm}^* = \bar{R}_{\pm} - R^* \neq 0$. At the same time, the steady states corresponding to $\bar{X}^f = X_{\pm}^*$ are given by $\mathcal{S}_{\pm} := (\bar{E}, \bar{P}, \bar{X}^f, \bar{X}^c) = (\bar{E}_{\pm}, \bar{P}_{\pm}, X_{\pm}^*, 0)$ with $\bar{E}_{\pm} = E^* + (\beta_2/\beta_3 + \alpha_2)X_{\pm}^*$ and $\bar{P}_{\pm} = P^* + \alpha_2 X_{\pm}^*$. Because of the deviation of the LER from the fundamental level E^* and the corresponding interest rate differential away from zero, we call $\mathcal{S}_{\pm}$ *non-fundamental steady states* of the system. Summarising the above analysis, we obtain the following result on the existence of steady states.

Theorem 3.1 *For given R^*, let*

$$P^* = M - \alpha_1 Y + \alpha_2 R^*, \quad E^* = \frac{1}{\beta_3}[-\beta_0 + \beta_1 Y + \beta_2 R^* + \beta_3 P^*]. \tag{14}$$

Then,

(1) *the fundamental steady state $\mathcal{S}_0 = (E^*, P^*, 0, 0)$ is always a steady state of the system* (12);
(2) *if $\mu(1-\omega) > \beta_R$, then the system* (12) *has another two non-fundamental steady states $\mathcal{S}_{\pm} = (\bar{E}_{\pm}, \bar{P}_{\pm}, \bar{X}_{\pm}^f, \bar{X}_{\pm}^c) = (E^* + (\alpha_2 + \beta_2/\beta_3)X_{\pm}^*, P^* + \alpha_2 X_{\pm}^*, X_{\pm}^*, 0)$ in which $X_{\pm}^*$ are the non-zero roots of $\beta_R X^* = H((1-\omega)X^*)$.*

It is interesting to see that the condition for the existence of the non-fundamental steady states is independent of the adjustment rate of the expectations of the fundamentalists and chartists, as measured by β_f and β_c, respectively. Rather the condition depends on the relation among the strength of the portfolio managers' response (μ), the weight ascribed to the fundamentalists

$(1-\omega)$ and the strength of the macroeconomic fundamental factor (β_R). Note that both $\bar{P}_{\pm}$ and $\bar{E}_{\pm}$ increase as $X^*_{\pm}$ increases. The levels of $X^*_{\pm}$ depend on not only μ and ω but also on β_R. As β_R increases, $X^*_{\pm}$ and hence the non-fundamental equilibrium levels decrease. Note that when β_R increases to $\mu(1-\omega)$, $X^*_{\pm}$ converge to 0 and the corresponding two non-fundamental steady states $\mathcal{S}_{\pm}$ converge to the fundamental steady state $\mathcal{S}_0$. In contrast, an increase in μ leads the non-fundamental steady states $\mathcal{S}_{\pm}$ to move further away from the fundamental steady state $\mathcal{S}_0$. More discussion about the economic intuition of Theorem 3.1 will be given in the following section.

4. Stability of the exchange rate market

To better understand the dynamic evolution of the system (12), we need to analyse the local stability and bifurcations of the fundamental equilibrium $\mathcal{S}_0 = (E^*, P^*, 0, 0)$, which is characterised by the following result.

Theorem 4.1 *For the system* (12), *the fundamental steady state* $\mathcal{S}_0$ *is locally asymptotically stable* (*LAS*) *if and only if*

$$d_1 > 0, \quad d_2 > 0, \quad d_4 > 0, \quad \Delta_4 > 0, \tag{15}$$

where

$$\begin{aligned}
d_1 &:= \beta_c(1-\mu\omega) + \beta_f + \beta_p,\\
d_2 &:= \beta_c(1-\mu\omega)(\beta_f + \beta_p) + \beta_p\beta_f + \beta_e\beta_R,\\
d_3 &:= \beta_p\beta_c\beta_f(1-\mu\omega) + \beta_e\beta_R\beta_c + \beta_e\beta_f(\beta_R - \mu + \mu\omega),\\
d_4 &:= \beta_e\beta_c\beta_f(\beta_R - \mu + \mu\omega),\\
\Delta_4 &:= d_1d_2d_3 - d_1^2d_4 - d_3^2,
\end{aligned} \tag{16}$$

with

$$\beta_p := \rho\left(\beta_3 + \frac{\beta_2}{\alpha_2}\right)(>0), \quad \beta_e := \frac{\rho\beta_3}{\alpha_2}(>0). \tag{17}$$

The conditions (15) are obtained by application of the Routh–Hurwitz theorem to the dynamical system (12) as explained in Appendix 1. When the conditions (15) are not satisfied, the fundamental steady state $\mathcal{S}_0$ becomes unstable and the system (12) exhibits complex dynamics through different types of bifurcations. In particular, on the manifold $d_4 = 0$, there is at least one zero eigenvalue. At $d_4 \lessapprox 0$, it follows from Theorem 3.1 that the system (12) has two additional non-fundamental steady states $\mathcal{S}_{\pm}$. Hence, at $d_4 \lessapprox 0$, the system (12) diverges from the fundamental steady state and numerical simulations show that the system converges locally to one of the non-fundamental steady states $\mathcal{S}_{\pm}$, depending on the initial conditions. In nonlinear dynamical systems theory (Kuznetsov 2004), this phenomenon is referred to as a *pitchfork bifurcation* and consequently $d_4 = 0$ is called a *pitchfork boundary*. On the manifold $\Delta_4 = 0$, there is a pair of conjugate imaginary eigenvalues. This means that the fundamental steady state $\mathcal{S}_0$ loses its stability and, in its neighbourhood, a stable limit cycle can emerge. This phenomenon is referred to as a *Hopf bifurcation* and consequently Δ_4 is called a *Hopf manifold* or *Hopf boundary*.

Given the complexity of the stability conditions and the difficulty of saying very much in the general case, we consider three special cases in detail in the following in order to gain some insights

Table 1. Parameter values.

M	Y	R^*	ρ	β_0	β_1	β_2	β_3	α_1	α_2	γ
3.5	2	0.01	0.25	2.1	0.5	1	0.5	0.5	4	10

into the dynamical behaviour of the general case. These three cases help us to understand the different roles played by the different expectation mechanisms in the dynamics of the system (12), including the stability and dynamical behaviour resulting from the instability of the fundamental equilibrium. The portfolio managers put all the weight on either the fundamentalist or the chartist expectations in the first two cases or on both in the third case. The first two cases include the classical Dornbusch (1976) model and the Gray and Turnovsky (1979) model as special situations. The analysis in the first two special cases provides some helpful insights into the understanding of the third general case.

In the subsequent analysis, we shall illustrate many of our points with numerical simulations, for which, unless stated otherwise, we take the parameter set in Table 1 and set $H(x) = \mu h(x)$, where $h(x) = \tanh(\gamma x)/\gamma$, and the other parameters will be specified later.

4.1 *The model with fundamentalist expectations*

We first consider the case of $\omega = 0$, that is, the portfolio managers put all the weight on the expectations of the fundamentalists. In this case, the system (12) reduces to the three-dimensional system

$$
\begin{aligned}
\dot{E} &= H(X^{\mathrm{f}}) + \beta_{\mathrm{R}}\left(R^* - \frac{\alpha_1 Y - M}{\alpha_2} - \frac{P}{\alpha_2}\right),\\
\dot{P} &= \rho\left[\beta_0 - \beta_1 Y - \beta_2\left(\frac{\alpha_1 Y - M}{\alpha_2} + \frac{P}{\alpha_2}\right) + \beta_3(E - P)\right],\\
\dot{X}^{\mathrm{f}} &= \beta_{\mathrm{f}}\left(\frac{\alpha_1 Y - M}{\alpha_2} + \frac{P}{\alpha_2} - R^* - X^{\mathrm{f}}\right).
\end{aligned}
\tag{18}
$$

Concerning the dynamical behaviour of the system (18), we obtain the following result.

Theorem 4.2 *For the system* (18),

(i) *if* $\beta_{\mathrm{R}} > \mu$, *then the fundamental steady state* $\mathcal{S}_0 = (E^*, P^*, 0)$ *of Equation* (18) *is LAS*;
(ii) *at* $\beta_{\mathrm{R}} = \mu$, *the fundamental steady state* $\mathcal{S}_0$ *undergoes a pitchfork bifurcation*;
(iii) *if* $\beta_{\mathrm{R}} < \mu$, *then the fundamental steady state* $\mathcal{S}_0$ *is unstable and the two non-fundamental steady states* $\mathcal{S}_\pm = (E^* + (\beta_2/\beta_3 + \alpha_2)X_\pm^*, P^* + \alpha_2 X_\pm^*, X_\pm^*)$ *of Equation* (18) *exist and are LAS, where* $X_\pm^*$ *satisfy* $H(X_\pm^*) = \beta_{\mathrm{R}} X_\pm^*$ *and* $X_\pm^* \neq 0$.

The proof of Theorem 4.2 is given in Appendix 1. The stability/instability of the fundamental equilibrium $\mathcal{S}_0$ and its pitchfork bifurcation boundary are plotted in Figure 3 in $(\mu, \beta_{\mathrm{R}})$ parameter space. The economic implications of Theorem 4.2 are far more significant than are apparent at first glance, and we elaborate on them in the following discussion.

First, the stabilising effect of the fundamental equilibrium due to the sluggish exchange rate adjustment considered in Gray and Turnovsky (1979) is also present in our model. As we have

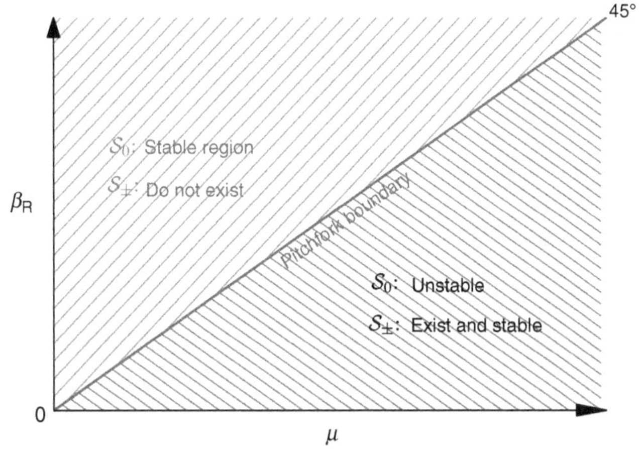

Figure 3. Parameter regions of the stable and unstable fundamental steady states in (μ, β_R) space and the corresponding pitchfork bifurcation boundary.

mentioned earlier, when $\beta_f = \infty$, the expected depreciation rate by the fundamentalists X^f in Equation (18) is equal to the nominal interest rate differential $X^f = R - R^*$ and consequently (18) simplifies to the two-dimensional system

$$\dot{E} = H(R - R^*) + \beta_R(R^* - R), \tag{19a}$$

$$\dot{P} = \rho[\beta_0 - \beta_1 Y - \beta_2 R + \beta_3(E - P)], \tag{19b}$$

with $R = (\alpha_1 Y - M + P)/\alpha_2$. The characteristic polynomial of the fundamental steady-state equilibrium (E^*, P^*) is given by $p(\lambda) = \lambda^2 + \beta_p\lambda + \beta_e(\beta_R - \mu)$ and the corresponding two eigenvalues λ_1 and λ_2 satisfy $\lambda_1 + \lambda_2 = -\beta_p < 0$ and $\lambda_1\lambda_2 = \beta_e(\beta_R - \mu)$. So, when the macro fundamental factor dominates the speculative factor due to the expectations of the fundamentalists in the sense that $\beta_R > \mu$, the fundamental steady-state equilibrium (E^*, P^*) is stable as illustrated in Figure 4(a).

Second, when the macro fundamental factor is dominated by the speculative factor of the expectations of the fundamentalists, that is, $\beta_R < \mu$, the fundamental equilibrium (E^*, P^*) becomes a saddle point, see Figure 4(c), which corresponds to the Dornbusch saddle-point case discussed in Gray and Turnovsky (1979). In particular, if we take $\mu = \beta_R + 1 (> \beta_R)$ and $H(x) = \mu x$, then Equation (19) reduces to

$$\dot{E} = R - R^*, \tag{20a}$$

$$\dot{P} = \rho[\beta_0 - \beta_1 Y - \beta_2 R + \beta_3(E - P)], \tag{20b}$$

which is the classical Dornbusch model. However, due to the introduction of the nonlinear S-shaped expectation function for the portfolio managers, the saddle-point instability of the fundamental equilibrium leads the exchange rate to stabilise at one of the two non-fundamental equilibria, depending on the initial market conditions, as illustrated in Figure 4(b). Thus, the emergence of the two non-fundamental steady states avoids the explosive outcome for the dynamics implied by the saddle-point instability without imposing the instantaneous (and unexplained) jump in the exchange rate to place the system on a stable arm of the saddle.

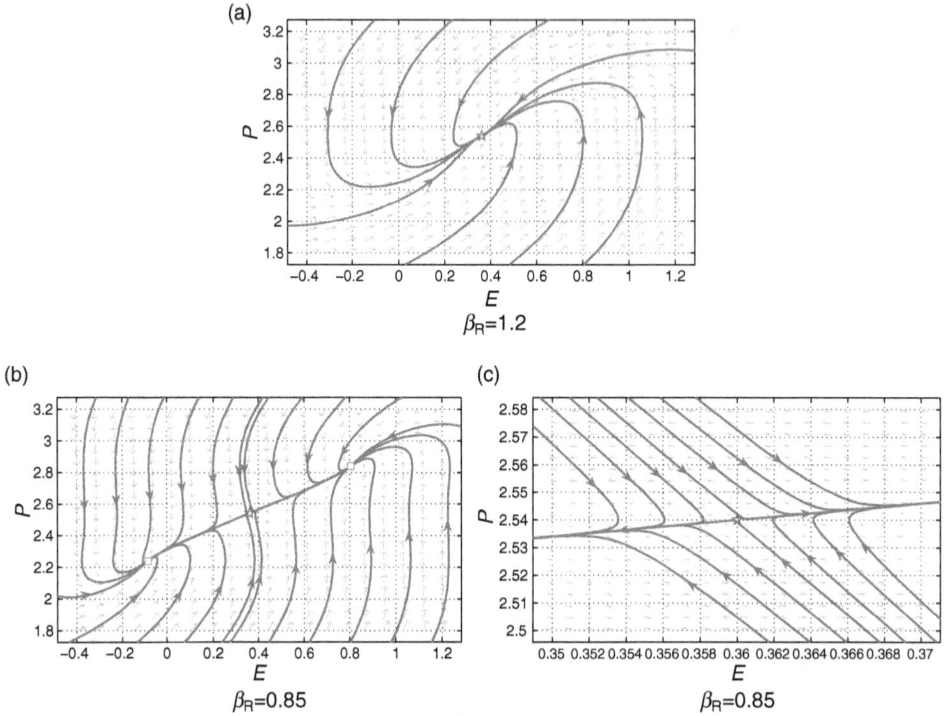

Figure 4. The phase plots of (E, P) and the stability analysis when $\beta_{\mathrm{f}} = \infty$ and $\mu = 1$. (a) When $\beta_{\mathrm{R}} > \mu$, there is a unique and stable fundamental equilibrium (E^*, P^*); (b) when $\beta_{\mathrm{R}} < \mu$, the fundamental equilibrium (E^*, P^*) becomes unstable and two locally stable non-fundamental steady states appear; (c) result obtained by looking at the picture in (b) very locally and seeing just the saddle-point nature of the unstable equilibrium. The star ($\star$) denotes (E^*, P^*) and the squares ($\square$) denote the non-fundamental equilibria.

The economic intuition of the above implications is as follows. Consider the special case with $\beta_{\mathrm{R}} \to 0$ in Equation (19) (so that $\beta_{\mathrm{R}} < \mu$). When $X^{\mathrm{f}} = R - R^* > 0$, the rate of exchange depreciation expected by the fundamentalists is positive, leading to a higher LER E and hence a higher log-price P, which in turn pushes the expected rate of exchange depreciation to be even higher. Consequently, the fundamental steady state becomes unstable. However, since the portfolio managers become more cautious as the expected rate of exchange depreciation becomes larger (reflected in their nonlinear S-shaped function H of the expected depreciation rate), the system does not explode but rather converges to one of the two non-fundamental steady- state equilibria $\mathcal{S}_{\pm} = (\bar{E}_{\pm}, \bar{P}_{\pm}) = (E^* + (\beta_2/\beta_3 + \alpha_2)X^*_{\pm}, P^* + \alpha_2 X^*_{\pm})$, where $X^*_{\pm}$ satisfy the non-zero interest rate parity condition, that is, $X^*_{\pm} = \bar{R}_{\pm} - R^* \neq 0$, and $H(X^*_{\pm}) = \beta_{\mathrm{R}} X^*_{\pm}$.

For the general case with $\beta_{\mathrm{f}} > 0$, phenomena similar to those displayed in Figure 4 occur, and the appearance of two locally stable non-fundamental steady-state equilibria corresponds to the occurrence of a pitchfork bifurcation at the fundamental equilibrium. Figure 5(a) shows a bifurcation plot of the LER with respect to the parameter β_{R} for $\beta_{\mathrm{f}} = 0.8$. For the given value $\mu = 1$, it shows that a pitchfork bifurcation occurs at $\beta_{\mathrm{R}} = \mu = 1$. For $\beta_{\mathrm{R}} > \mu$, the fundamental steady state is stable, but for $\beta_{\mathrm{R}} < \mu$, it is unstable and two locally stable non-fundamental steady states appear. Figure 5(b) shows the dynamics for the LER when $\beta_{\mathrm{R}} = 0.85 < \mu = 1$. For different initial values for E_0, it shows that $E \to \bar{E}_+$ or $E \to \bar{E}_-$ as time increases.

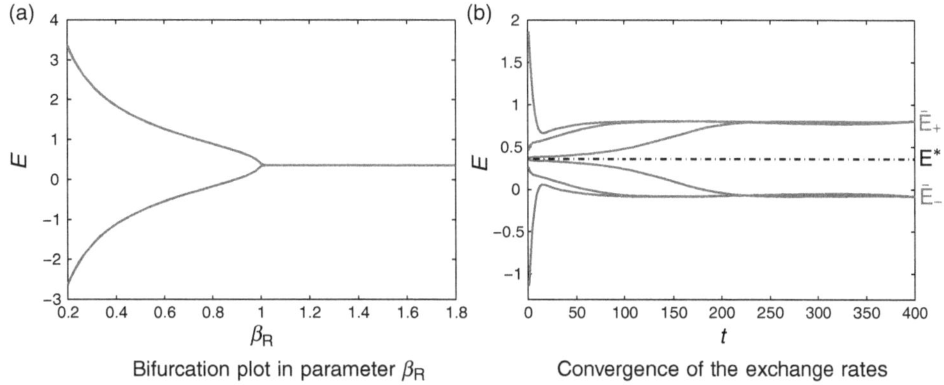

Figure 5. (a) The bifurcation plot of the LER with respect to the parameter β_R and pitchfork bifurcation when $0.8 = \beta_f < \infty$ and $\mu = 1$ as in Figure 4, and (b) the evolution of the LER $E(t)$ from different initial values when $\beta_R = 0.85(< \beta_R^* = \mu)$.

In summary, the Dornbusch model and its various extensions have played an important role in the development of the exchange rate literature. It is very interesting to see how the simple model (18) retains the basic idea of the Dornbusch model and can also generate a number of new desirable features. The original Dornbusch model had some notable shortcomings.

First, the stability of exchange rate markets is achievable only when agents adopt rational expectations and so there is no room for the bounded rationality uncovered in the literature survey cited earlier. Also, speculative activity, which plays a very important role (in fact, it is a much bigger component of exchange rate transactions than those based on 'real' factors) in exchange rate markets, is missing. In the model presented here, this stability can be achieved as a result of interaction of speculation and the macro fundamental factor. Second, if we do believe that in exchange rate markets, there exist steady-state equilibria, our result shows that there may exist multiple stable equilibria. Depending on the market conditions, the exchange rate can stabilise at different steady-state equilibrium levels and changing conditions can cause the exchange rate to shift among different equilibrium levels. Third, interest rate parity holds at all the three steady-state equilibria in our model, even when the interest rate differential $R - R^*$ is not zero. In the Dornbusch model, the unique steady state in which the interest rate parity condition holds is the one with no interest rate differential. As far as we are aware, this is the first result on the dynamics of the interest rate parity condition that allows the interest rate differential to be non-zero.

4.2 *The model with chartist expectations*

We now consider the second special case of $\omega = 1$. That is, the expectations of the portfolio managers depend solely on the expectations of the chartists, which follow a sluggish adjustment to a geometric average of the historical changes in the LER. In this case, the system (12) reduces to the three-dimensional system

$$\dot{E} = H(X^c) + \beta_R\left(R^* - \frac{\alpha_1 Y - M}{\alpha_2} - \frac{P}{\alpha_2}\right), \tag{21a}$$

$$\dot{P} = \rho\left[\beta_0 - \beta_1 Y - \beta_2\left(\frac{\alpha_1 Y - M}{\alpha_2}\right) + \beta_3 E - \left(\frac{\beta_2}{\alpha_2} + \beta_3\right)P)\right], \tag{21b}$$

$$\dot{X}^{\mathrm{c}} = \beta_{\mathrm{c}}\left(H(X^{\mathrm{c}}) + \beta_{\mathrm{R}}\left(R^* - \frac{\alpha_1 Y - M}{\alpha_2} - \frac{P}{\alpha_2}\right) - X^{\mathrm{c}}\right). \tag{21c}$$

Since $\omega = 1$ and $\beta_{\mathrm{R}} > 0$, the condition $(1-\omega)\mu > \beta_{\mathrm{R}}$ is not satisfied in this case. It then follows from Theorem 3.1 that the fundamental equilibrium $\mathcal{S}_0 = (\bar{E}, \bar{P}, \bar{X^{\mathrm{c}}}) = (E^*, P^*, 0)$ is the unique steady state of the system (21) at which $\bar{R} = R^*$. With regard to the stability of the steady state and its bifurcation, we have the following result.

Theorem 4.3 *For the system* (21), *let*

$$\beta_{\mathrm{R}}^* := \frac{\beta_{\mathrm{p}}^2(1-\mu)(2-\mu+2\sqrt{1-\mu})}{\mu^2\beta_{\mathrm{e}}}, \quad \beta_{\mathrm{c}}^{\pm} := \frac{-b_2 \pm \sqrt{b_2^2 - 4b_1b_3}}{2b_1},$$

where $b_1 := \beta_{\mathrm{p}}(1-\mu)^2$, $b_2 := \beta_{\mathrm{p}}^2(1-\mu) - \beta_{\mathrm{e}}\mu\beta_R$, *and* $b_3 := \beta_{\mathrm{e}}\beta_{\mathrm{p}}\beta_{\mathrm{R}}$.

(i) *For* $0 < \mu < 1$,
- $\mathcal{S}_0$ *is LAS if either (i)* $\beta_{\mathrm{R}} < \beta_{\mathrm{R}}^*$, *or (ii)* $\beta_{\mathrm{R}} > \beta_{\mathrm{R}}^*$ *and* $0 < \beta_{\mathrm{c}} < \beta_{\mathrm{c}}^-$, *or (iii)* $\beta_{\mathrm{R}} > \beta_{\mathrm{R}}^*$ *and* $\beta_{\mathrm{c}} > \beta_{\mathrm{c}}^+$;
- $\mathcal{S}_0$ *is unstable for* $\beta_{\mathrm{R}} > \beta_{\mathrm{R}}^*$ *and* $\beta_{\mathrm{c}}^- < \beta_{\mathrm{c}} < \beta_{\mathrm{c}}^+$;
- *if* $\beta_{\mathrm{R}} > \beta_{\mathrm{R}}^*$, $\mathcal{S}_0$ *undergoes Hopf bifurcations at* $\beta_{\mathrm{c}} = \beta_{\mathrm{c}}^{\pm}$.

(ii) *For* $\mu = 1$, $\mathcal{S}_0$ *is LAS when* $0 < \beta_{\mathrm{c}} < \beta_{\mathrm{p}}$, *unstable when* $\beta_{\mathrm{c}} > \beta_{\mathrm{p}}$, *and undergoes a Hopf bifurcation at* $\beta_{\mathrm{c}} = \beta_{\mathrm{p}}$.

(iii) *For* $\mu > 1$, $\mathcal{S}_0$ *is LAS when* $0 < \beta_{\mathrm{c}} < \beta_{\mathrm{c}}^-$, *unstable when* $\beta_{\mathrm{c}} > \beta_{\mathrm{c}}^-$, *and undergoes a Hopf bifurcation at* $\beta_{\mathrm{c}} = \beta_{\mathrm{c}}^-$.

Depending on the balance between the macro fundamental factor and the chartist expectations, Theorem 4.3 provides a very interesting result about the stability of the fundamental steady state $\mathcal{S}_0$ and periodic oscillations[7] of the market around the steady state when it becomes unstable. In the following discussion, we focus on the economic intuition of the different possible situations.

For the case of $\mu = 1$, from Theorem 4.3(ii), the stability of $\mathcal{S}_0$ depends on the balance between β_{c} and β_{p}. Given that $\beta_{\mathrm{p}} = \rho(\beta_2/\alpha_2 + \beta_3) > 0$ (see Equation (17)), it follows from Equation (21b) that β_{p} measures the speed of the convergence of the log-price level P to an equilibrium. Obviously, β_{c} measures the speed of the convergence of the expected depreciation rate of the chartists X^{c} to the instantaneous depreciation rate $\dot{E}$ in the market, or the weight on the latest change in the LER when forming the expected depreciation rate by the chartists. Intuitively, on the one hand, when $\beta_{\mathrm{p}} > \beta_{\mathrm{c}}$, that is, the speed of the convergence of the log-price P is faster than that of X^{c}, the extrapolation of the expected depreciation rate from the chartists is weak and its impact is not so significant. Consequently, the market converges to its fundamental steady state. On the other hand, when $\beta_{\mathrm{p}} < \beta_{\mathrm{c}}$, that is, the speed of the convergence of the log-price P is slower than that of X^{c}, any change in the exchange rate and the price is extrapolated quickly by the chartists, which in turn feeds back into the market and generates instability. For instance, if the initial values (E, P) are above the steady-state levels (E^*, P^*) and X^{c} starts near zero, the system leads to a high interest rate R. For given R^*, this leads to a negative change in the LER. Then, the extrapolation of the expected depreciation from the chartists will very quickly push the LER even lower and bring it further below E^*. This low LER will push the log-price P down below P^*. Because of the slow convergence in the log-price P, this trend will continue and the LER will continue to drift down below E^* until the moment at which the impact of the extrapolation from the chartists becomes

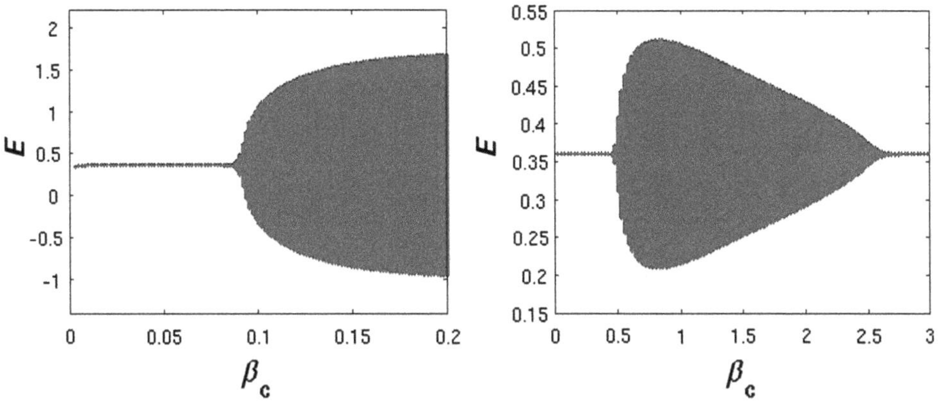

Figure 6. The bifurcation plots of the LER with respect to the parameter β_c for $\beta_R = 10$ and (a) $\mu = 2 > 1$ and (b) $0.5 = \mu < 1$ when $\omega = 1$.

less significant for large X^c due to the cautious reaction of the portfolio managers (reflected in their S-shaped extrapolation function). Then, the price moves back and a reverse cycle starts. Consequently, the fundamental steady state becomes unstable and a periodic fluctuation around the steady state appears.

For the case of $\mu > 1$, a similar intuition applies. The only difference here is that, because of higher weight μ from the expectations of the portfolio managers, the impact of the extrapolation from the chartists becomes even stronger. To maintain the stability of the fundamental steady state, a lower extrapolation coefficient β_c from the chartists is required to be bounded above by β_c^-, satisfying $\beta_c^- < \beta_p$. For $\mu \geq 1$, Figure 6(a) shows the bifurcation of the LER E in terms of the parameter β_c, which clearly indicates the stability of the fundamental steady state for the LER when β_c is small and the stable periodic orbits induced by the Hopf bifurcation when β_c is large.

For the case of $\mu < 1$, the economic intuition we can obtain from our results seems very limited. In general, the fundamental coefficient β_R plays a stabilising role, while the extrapolation activity on the expected depreciation rate from the chartists destabilises the market. For example, in the cases of $\beta_R < \beta_R^*$, and $\beta_R > \beta_R^*$ and $\beta_c < \beta_c^-$, the fundamental steady state is stable. Note that when $\beta_R > \beta_R^*$, a balance between the macro fundamental factor (β_R) and the extrapolation of the chartists (β_c) is necessary to achieve the stability of the fundamental steady state, and this is the source of the condition $\beta_c < \beta_c^-$. For the case that $\beta_R > \beta_R^*$ and $\beta_c^- < \beta_c < \beta_c^+$, a strong tendency to convergence (measured by β_R) could generate a trend which would be extrapolated by the chartists (measured by β_c), pushing the market from one extreme to the other, even though the market does not react actively to the chartist expectation (since $\mu < 1$). However, the condition $\beta_c > \beta_c^+$ is unexpected and it does not follow this intuition. One possible explanation is that a higher β_c indicates that more weight is given to the most recent changes, meaning that the chartists move closer to the perfect foresight limit when forming their expectations. This could help to stabilise the fundamental steady state. In any case, our analysis indicates how a simple expectation scheme like the geometrically weighted average of the historical changes in the LER can generate very complicated dynamics. For $\mu < 1$, Figure 6(b) demonstrates the bifurcation of the LER E in terms of the parameter β_c, which clearly indicates the stability of the steady state for the LER when β_c is either small or large, and the appearance of stable periodic orbits induced by the Hopf bifurcations when β_c is in the intermediate region determined by β_c^- and β_c^+.

The results and discussions for these two special cases illustrate explicitly the different roles played by different expectations of the fundamentalists and chartists and the different ways that the exchange rate dynamics are generated through different types of bifurcations. An understanding of this difference provides insight into the exchange rate dynamics when the expectations of the portfolio managers are formed as a weighted average of the expectations of the fundamentalists and chartists, to which we turn in the following subsection.

4.3 *The model with the expectations of the fundamentalists and chartists*

We now consider the general case when the expectations of the portfolio managers are formed from a weighted average of the heterogeneous expectations of the fundamentalists and chartists. From Sections 4.1 and 4.2, we have seen that different expectation schemes lead to different market behaviour when the fundamental equilibrium loses its stability.

We now examine how such a mixture of the expectation schemes influences the market exchange rate. Intuitively, we expect to see the types of behaviour induced by both pitchfork and Hopf bifurcations when the fundamental steady state loses its stability. Depending on the dominance of the two schemes, the system may display one type of behaviour rather than the other type. Indeed, our analysis below confirms this intuition. To simplify the mathematical exposition, we consider two simplified cases which shed light on the general case. The first case explores the different dynamics induced by the change of the weighting parameter ω, while the second case demonstrates the stability property when the heterogeneous expectations are balanced in a certain sense. We examine the first case in detail here and relegate the second case to Appendix 2.

In the first case, in order to explore the different dynamics induced by the change of the weighting parameter ω, we assume that the speeds of adjustment of both the fundamentalists and chartists to their beliefs are the same, that is, $\beta_f = \beta_c$, and the intensity of the adjustment of the portfolio managers on their expected depreciation rate is unity, that is, $\mu = 1$. By an application of Theorem 4.1, we obtain the following theorem that provides a result on the stability of the fundamental equilibrium and market behaviour when it loses its stability.

Theorem 4.4 *For the system* (12), *assume* $\beta_p < \beta_f = \beta_c$, *and* $\mu = 1$. *Let* $\phi := \beta_f = \beta_c$ *and*

$$\omega^* = 1 + \frac{\beta_p^2 + \beta_e(\beta_R + 1) - \sqrt{(\beta_p^2 - \beta_e(1+\beta_R))^2 + 4\beta_p\beta_e(\beta_p + \phi\beta_R)}}{2\beta_p\phi}.$$

(a) *If* $\beta_R \leq 1$, *then* $1 - \beta_R < \omega^* < 1$ *and the fundamental equilibrium* S_0 (*i*) *is unstable for* $0 < \omega < 1 - \beta_R$; (*ii*) *undergoes a pitchfork bifurcation at* $\omega = 1 - \beta_R$; (*iii*) *is stable for* $1 - \beta_R < \omega < \omega^*$; (*iv*) *undergoes a Hopf bifurcation at* $\omega = \omega^*$; (*v*) *is unstable for* $\omega^* < \omega < 1$.

(b) *If* $\beta_R > 1$, *then* $0 < \omega^* < 1$ *and the fundamental equilibrium* S_0 (*i*) *is stable for* $0 < \omega < \omega^*$; (*ii*) *undergoes a Hopf bifurcation at* $\omega = \omega^*$; (*iii*) *is unstable for* $\omega^* < \omega < 1$.

It is interesting to see from Theorem 4.4 how changes in the weight ω lead to different market behaviour. The result confirms the intuition induced from our analysis in the previous two special cases. However, the nature of the exact connection to the two special cases $\omega = 0$ and $\omega = 1$, as well as the question as to whether a weighted average of the two expectation schemes can

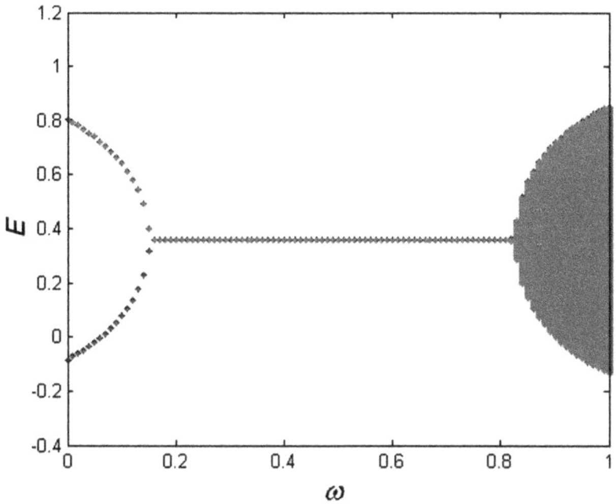

Figure 7. The bifurcation of the LER E in terms of the parameter $\omega \in (0, 1)$ for $\mu = 1$, $\beta_R = 0.85$, $\beta_f = 0.8$ and $\beta_c = 0.8$. The fundamental steady state undergoes a pitchfork bifurcation at $\omega = 1 - \beta_R = 0.15$ and a Hopf bifurcation at $\omega = \omega^* = 0.8286$.

stabilise an otherwise unstable fundamental steady state, is what we shall be concerned with in the following discussion.

On the one hand, when $\omega = 0$ and $\beta_R < 1 = \mu$, it follows from Theorem 4.2 that $\mathcal{S}_0$ is unstable and undergoes a pitchfork bifurcation at $\beta_R = \mu = 1$. By taking the limiting case of $\omega \to 0$, we have from Theorem 4.4 that a pitchfork bifurcation occurs as $\beta_R \to 1(= \mu)$ and consequently we obtain the exact same result as in the case of $\omega = 0$. On the other hand, when $\omega = 1$, $\beta_p < \phi = \beta_c$, it follows from Theorem 4.3(ii) that $\mathcal{S}_0$ is unstable, which is implied by Theorem 4.4. In this way, we see how the results of Theorems 4.2 and 4.3 are consistent with those of Theorem 4.4.

For $0 < \omega < 1$, the stability and the induced bifurcations based on Theorem 4.4 are illustrated by the bifurcation plot of the LER E in terms of the parameter ω in Figure 7 for the indicated set of parameters. Two things are clearly indicated by this figure. First, it shows different types of bifurcations when the market expectation is dominated by either one of the expectation schemes. When $\mathcal{S}_0$ loses its stability for $\omega < 1 - \beta_R$, the expectations of the fundamentalists are responsible for the induced pitchfork bifurcation, while the expectations of the chartists are responsible for the induced Hopf bifurcation when $\omega > \omega^*$. Second, a mixture of the two expectations can stabilise an otherwise unstable steady state $\mathcal{S}_0$ when $\omega \in (1 - \beta_R, \omega^*)$. This stabilising effect of combining different types of expectations is also shared by asset pricing models with heterogeneous beliefs (Chiarella and He 2002).

We now extend our analysis to the stabilising effect of the combined expectation schemes further when two of the key parameters β_R and ϕ change. First, recall that the parameter β_R measures the strength of the macro fundamental factor related to the interest rate differential. Note that the pitchfork boundary $\omega = 1 - \beta_R$ is monotonically decreasing in β_R. This means that a larger β_R results in a higher weight put by the portfolio managers on the fundamentalist expectation, which in turn can stabilise the fundamental steady state $\mathcal{S}_0$. Second, for the Hopf bifurcation boundary $\omega = \omega^*$, we can show that $-1 < \mathrm{d}\omega^*/\mathrm{d}\beta_R < 0$ for $\beta_R > 0$, implying that the Hopf boundary ω^* also decreases as β_R increases. This is clearly demonstrated in Figure 8(a), in which the stability region and bifurcation boundaries are plotted in the (β_R, ω) parameter space.

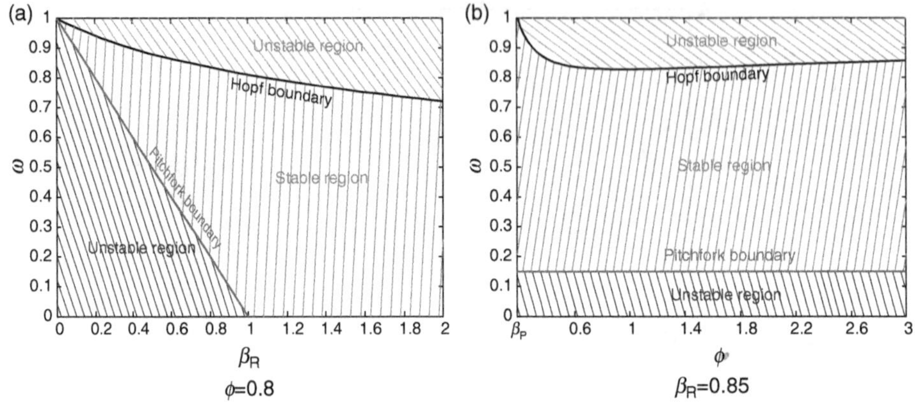

Figure 8. Stability regions and bifurcation boundaries (a) in the (β_R, ω) plane and (b) in the (ϕ, ω) plane. Here, $\beta_f = \beta_c = \phi$, $\mu = 1$ and $\beta_p < \phi$.

Therefore, as the strength $\beta_R \in (0, 1]$ of the macro fundamental factor increases, the stability interval $\omega \in (1 - \beta_R, \omega^*)$ shifts to the left. In other words, the stability region of the fundamental equilibrium in the weighting parameter ω is enlarged. One can also see that the fundamental steady state can be stabilised by either increasing ω from below or decreasing ω from above, meaning that a balanced combination of the two expectations can stabilise the fundamental steady state. In addition, for fixed $\beta_R > 1$, the fundamental steady state is destabilised by increasing ω further, leading to periodic fluctuations around the steady state induced by a Hopf bifurcation.

The other parameter $\phi = \beta_f = \beta_c$ measures the speed of adjustment of the expectations of the fundamentalists and chartists. Obviously, changing ϕ does not change the pitchfork bifurcation boundary. However, for the Hopf bifurcation boundary $\omega = \omega^*$, we can show that there exists a ϕ^* such that ω^* is monotonically decreasing for $\phi < \phi^*$ and increasing for $\phi > \phi^*$. This feature is illustrated by the bifurcation boundaries in Figure 8(b) in the parameter space of (ϕ, ω) for the chosen set of parameters. We see that for high ω (in fact, ω near to 0.85), as ϕ increases from β_p, the fundamental steady state is stable initially, then becomes unstable through a Hopf bifurcation, and finally becomes stable again through a second Hopf bifurcation. This result is consistent with what we observed in the case of $\omega = 1$ in Figure 6(b).

For the second case when $\omega = 0.5$ and $\beta_f \neq \beta_c$, a stability analysis is given in Appendix 2, the result of which can be summarised as follows. When the portfolio managers weight the expectations of the fundamentalists and chartists equally, the stability of the fundamental equilibrium can be affected by the balance between the speeds of the mean-reversion of the fundamentalists and the extrapolation of the chartists. When the portfolio managers react weakly to the expectations of the fundamentalists and chartists, the impact of the fundamentalists and chartists on the exchange rate is limited even if they are very active in forming their expectations. In contrast, if the portfolio managers dominate the market, the fundamental equilibrium becomes unstable and the active behaviour of the fundamentalists and chartists will accelerate the frequency of the market fluctuation due to the Hopf bifurcation. Therefore, the combination of the reaction of the portfolio managers to the heterogeneous expectations and the activities of the fundamentalists and chartists is an important factor in determining the evolution of the market exchange rate.

5. A stochastic version of the model

The model analysed in the previous sections is entirely deterministic. However, in the real exchange rate market, there always exist some noise factors which have an important influence on the exchange rate dynamics. For example, fundamental noise (by which we mean noise in the underlying economic processes determining the fundamental value of the exchange rate) or market noise (this can best be thought of as noise impinging on the market due perhaps to the arrival of news events causing stochastic shifts in demand and supply– so-called noise traders could be incorporated under this rubric) or both. For simplicity, we focus on the case of market noise only. To capture this effect, the first equation in (12) is replaced by the stochastic differential equation

$$\mathrm{d}E = [H((1-\omega)X^{\mathrm{f}} + \omega X^{\mathrm{c}}) + \beta(R^* - R)]\,\mathrm{d}t + \sigma_{\mathrm{E}}\,\mathrm{d}W_{\mathrm{E}}, \tag{22}$$

where W_{E} is a Wiener process on a probability space $(\Omega, \mathcal{F}, \mathcal{P})$ with zero drift and unit variance per unit time and $\sigma_{\mathrm{E}} > 0$ measures the intensity of the market noise.

In addition, in order to capture the different dynamics induced by the change in the weighting parameter in the deterministic model, the market fraction of the fundamentalists or chartists ($1-\omega$ or ω) will not be treated as constant but allowed to randomly change.[8] Based on the analysis for the deterministic model in the previous sections, we see that changes in ω lead to the existence of three types of dynamics with a stable fundamental steady state (Case $\mathcal{F}$), two stable non-fundamental steady states (Case $\mathcal{P}$) and a stable limit cycle (Case $\mathcal{H}$) (Figure 7). To allow for all three types of behaviour, the market fraction ω is assumed to follow a simple discrete random choice process satisfying

$$\mathrm{d}\omega_t = (\xi - \omega_{t-})\,\mathrm{d}N_t, \tag{23}$$

where N_t is a compound Poisson process with jump intensity λ. The process (23) can be rewritten as

$$\omega_{t+} = \begin{cases} \xi & \text{with prob. } \lambda\,\mathrm{d}t + o(\mathrm{d}t), \\ \omega_{t-} & \text{with prob. } 1 - \lambda\,\mathrm{d}t + o(\mathrm{d}t). \end{cases}$$

This means that when $\mathrm{d}N_t = 0$, the market fraction remains at the original level ω_{t-}, while when $\mathrm{d}N_t = 1$, the market fraction $\omega_{t+} = \xi$ follows a Markov chain with three discrete states $\{\omega_{\mathcal{P}}, \omega_{\mathcal{F}}, \omega_{\mathcal{H}}\}$ and the transition probability matrix $\mathbf{P}$. The three states correspond to the three particular values of market dynamics in the cases $\mathcal{P}$, $\mathcal{F}$ and $\mathcal{H}$, respectively. Hence, the system (12) can be modified to the stochastic differential system

$$\begin{aligned}
\mathrm{d}E &= [H((1-\omega_t)X^{\mathrm{f}} + \omega_t X^{\mathrm{c}}) + \beta_{\mathrm{R}}(R^* - R)]\,\mathrm{d}t + \sigma_{\mathrm{E}}\,\mathrm{d}W_{\mathrm{E}}, \\
\mathrm{d}P &= \rho[\beta_0 - \beta_1 Y - \beta_2 R + \beta_3(E - P)]\,\mathrm{d}t, \\
\mathrm{d}X^{\mathrm{f}} &= \beta_{\mathrm{f}}(R - R^* - X^{\mathrm{f}})\,\mathrm{d}t, \\
\mathrm{d}X^{\mathrm{c}} &= \beta_{\mathrm{c}}\{[H((1-\omega_t)X^{\mathrm{f}} + \omega_t X^{\mathrm{c}}) + \beta_{\mathrm{R}}(R^* - R) - X^{\mathrm{c}}]\,\mathrm{d}t + \sigma_{\mathrm{E}}\,\mathrm{d}W_{\mathrm{E}}\}, \\
\mathrm{d}\omega_t &= (\xi - \omega_{t-})\,\mathrm{d}N_t,
\end{aligned} \tag{24}$$

where $R = (\alpha_1 Y - M + P)/\alpha_2$. The system (24) implies that when the exchange rate reacts to the noise factors, the chartists simultaneously adapt their belief to changes in the market. The fundamentalists rather focus on the fundamental information of the nominal interest rate differential, and they are not very sensitive to the immediate adjustments in the exchange rate.

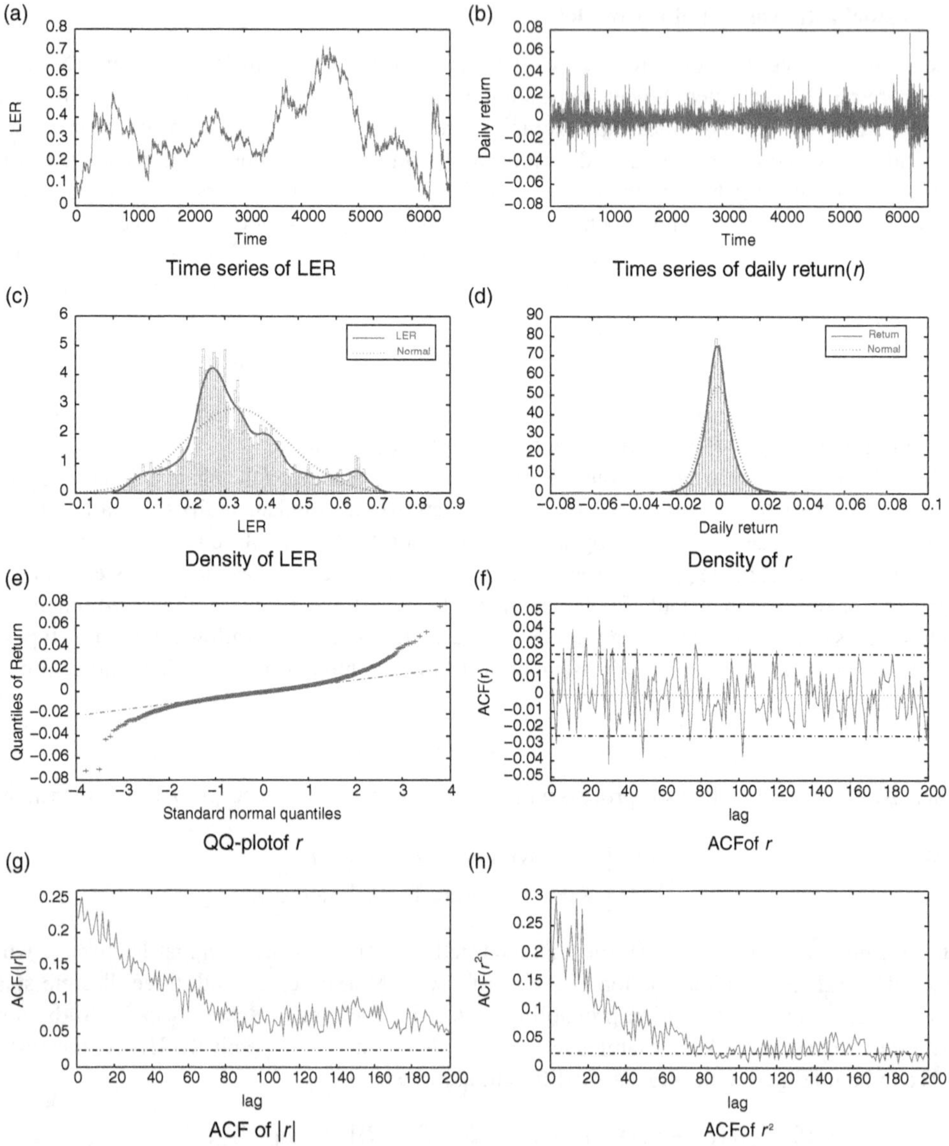

Figure 9. Statistical analysis of the exchange rate daily data between the Australian dollar and the US dollar from 12 December 1983 to 31 December 2009.

5.1 *Empirical evidence*

As mentioned in the introduction, a great deal of empirical research has uncovered many puzzles or anomalies in exchange rate markets, for example, disconnection from fundamental factors, excess volatility, volatility clustering and fat tails. As a benchmark, we use daily Australian–US exchange rate market data coming from the Reserve Bank of Australia from 12 December 1983 to 31 December 2009. The exchange rate is measured by the amount of AUD for 1 unit of USD. In total, there are 6577 daily exchange rate observations. Figure 9(a) shows the time series of the real

LER We observe that the AUD fluctuates a great deal over the years 1985–1986, 2000–2001 and 2006–2009 (the first 800, the 3500–4500 and the 5500–6577 data points) and is relatively stable over the rest of the time period. The corresponding distribution of the LER in Figure 9(c) displays two peaks, one high peak near 0.25 and one low peak near 0.65. The returns of the exchange rate in Figure 9(b) show the switching between high volatility and low volatility that is typical of many financial return time series. Also, the density distribution of the returns in Figure 9(d) and (e) is not normal, having very fat tails. The absolute and squared returns in Figure 9(f)–(h) display rapidly decreasing positive ACs, but the return itself has insignificant ACs.

5.2 *Stochastic simulations of the model and statistical analysis*

For our stochastic model (24), we regard ω as the bifurcation parameter. Let $\mu = 1$, $\beta_R = 0.85$, $\beta_f = 0.8$ and $\beta_c = 0.8$ as in Figure 7. Then, we know from Section 4.3 that $\omega^*_{\mathcal{P}} = 0.15$ and $\omega^*_{\mathcal{H}} \approx 0.8286$ are the pitchfork and Hopf bifurcation points of the fundamental steady state, respectively. That is, when $\omega < \omega^*_{\mathcal{P}}$ (e.g. $\omega = 0.10$), the fundamental steady state is unstable and two non-fundamental steady states appear (Case $\mathcal{P}$). When $\omega > \omega^*_{\mathcal{H}}$ (e.g. $\omega = 0.85$), the fundamental steady state is unstable and a stable limit cycle exists (Case $\mathcal{H}$). When $\omega^*_{\mathcal{P}} < \omega < \omega^*_{\mathcal{H}}$ (e.g. $\omega = 0.25$), the fundamental steady state is stable (Case $\mathcal{F}$).

To examine the effect of random disturbance on the deterministic dynamics, we assume that the random market fraction ω satisfies (23) in which ξ follows a Markov chain with three states $\{0.10, 0.25, 0.85\}$. These three states correspond to the three typical dynamical regions that the analysis described in Section 4 has shown that the model displays, namely Cases $\mathcal{P}$, $\mathcal{F}$ and $\mathcal{H}$, respectively. The transition probability matrix among the different states is assumed to be given by

$$\mathbf{P} = \begin{array}{c} \\ \end{array} \begin{array}{c} \quad\mathcal{P} \quad\;\; \mathcal{F} \quad\;\; \mathcal{H} \\ \begin{pmatrix} 0.9 & 0.1 & 0 \\ 0.25 & 0.4 & 0.35 \\ 0 & 0.95 & 0.05 \end{pmatrix} \end{array} \begin{array}{c} \\ \mathcal{P} \\ \mathcal{F} \\ \mathcal{H} \end{array} .$$

The principle behind this choice is that the weights are not allowed to have extreme jumps, say, from $\omega = 0.10$ to $\omega = 0.85$, without going through $\omega = 0.25$. The size of the noises is given by $\sigma_E = 0.0158$ per trading period and $\lambda = 0.05$ (meaning that, on average, there is one jump for every 20 trading periods). Figure 10 displays the time series and statistical characteristics based on the system (24).

Figure 10(a) shows a typical time series of the LER and Figure 10(b) shows the corresponding return series. They display persistent deviation of the market exchange rate from the (constant) fundamental exchange rate and irregular switching between phases of low volatility with returns close to zero and phases of high volatility. This is because the weight between the fundamentalists and chartists changes stochastically, as illustrated in Figure 11. For different weights, the exchange rate has different stability properties. When $\omega = 0.25$, the fundamental exchange rate converges to the fundamental steady-state equilibrium and the corresponding time series shows such a converging tendency. However, when $\omega = 0.10$, the fundamental equilibrium is unstable and another two non-fundamental steady states co-exist. In this case, the time series undergoes a deviation from the fundamental equilibrium. When $\omega = 0.85$, there is a stable limit cycle around the unstable fundamental equilibrium for the deterministic model and the time series shows a fluctuation around the fundamental equilibrium level. Not surprisingly, adding the dynamical noise to the system destroys the regularity of the exchange rate around the (non-)fundamental steady state or the cycle and leads to an irregular switching between phases of low volatility

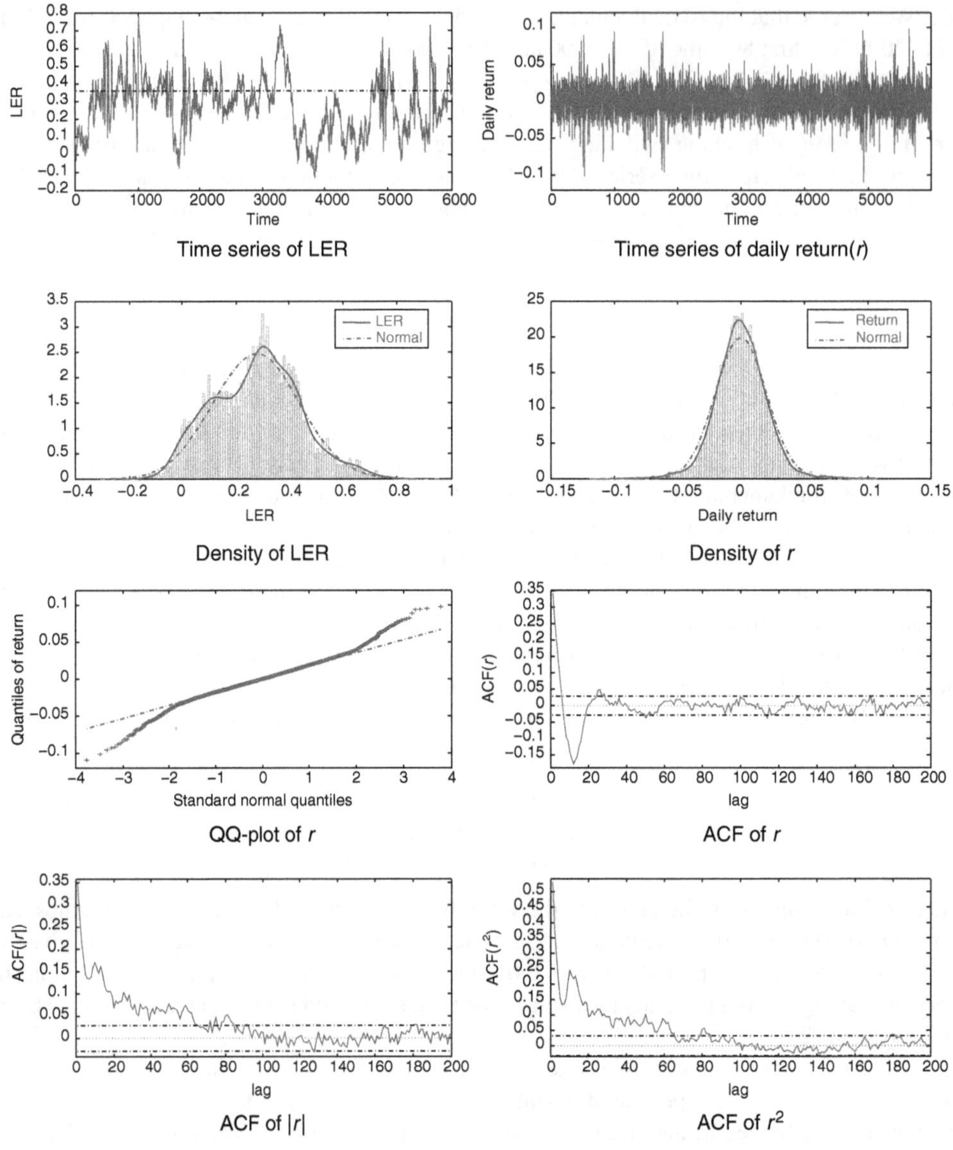

Figure 10. Statistical analysis of the simulation results.

(where the fundamental equilibrium is stable) and phases of high volatility (where the fundamental equilibrium is unstable) and of deviation from the underlying fundamental equilibrium most of the time. Furthermore, the density of the LER is bimodal as observed in Figure 10(c) and the return of the exchange rate in Figure 10(b) shows volatility clustering. In addition, the absolute and squared returns in Figure 10(g) and (h) display strong positive autocorrelations (ACs), but the ACs of the return in Figure 10(f) are insignificant (except the first few time lags). The distribution of the exchange rate returns in Figure 10(d) and (e) is non-normal with fat tails. These effects correspond to most of the stylised facts observed in exchange rate markets.

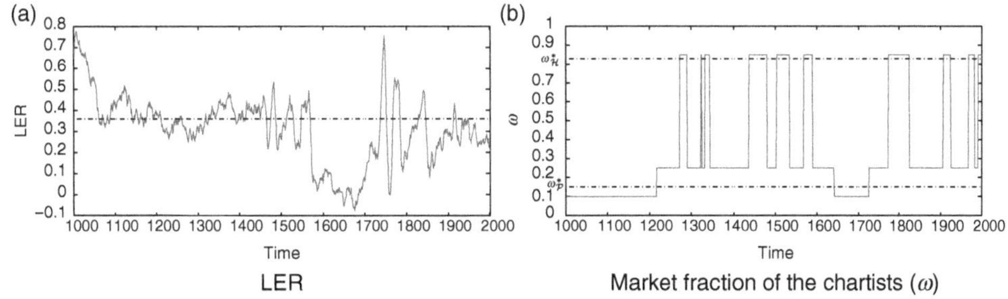

Figure 11. Time series of the LER and the market fraction of the chartists from Time 1000 to Time 2000.

Comparing the characteristics in Figures 9 and 10, we can see that our simple heterogeneous expectations model can replicate the broad features of realistic time series and some stylised facts in exchange rate markets, for example, deviation from fundamental factors, bimodal density of LER, volatility clustering and fat tails for returns. The AC patterns also show the broad tendencies of those observed in the actual times series, but clearly these are not as satisfactory. Overall, our results indicate that heterogeneous beliefs in exchange rate markets can potentially explain the puzzles and anomalies of exchange rates to a certain extent and the interaction between the fundamentalists and chartists is a potential source of the mechanism generating some of those characteristics.

6. Conclusion

Motivated by the challenges faced by traditional macroeconomic exchange rate models in explaining an increasing number of anomalies and puzzles uncovered in empirical research and empirical evidence that many popular technical trading strategies are used in exchange markets, this paper extends the classical Dornbusch exchange rate model with homogeneous expectation to incorporate heterogeneous beliefs and bounded rationality into a dynamical model of exchange rates in a continuous-time framework.

Essentially, the heterogeneity is characterised by the expectations of the portfolio managers, which are a weighted average of the expectations of the fundamentalists and chartists, and the bounded rationality is characterised by the different information of the heterogeneous investors and the S-shaped expectation function of the portfolio managers. The model not only inherits the classical saddle-point instability of the Dornbusch model and the stabilising effect of the sluggish adjustment in exchange rates of the Gray and Turnovsky model, but also introduces many new desirable features. These include the stability of the fundamental equilibrium, the existence and stability of non-fundamental equilibria and different exchange rate dynamics induced by different types of bifurcations.

The analysis of the model highlights the different roles played by the macro fundamental factor and the combination of the heterogeneous expectations. In general, the macro fundamental factor is a stabilising force in the market, while the speculative activities from the fundamentalists and chartists can destabilise the fundamental equilibrium of the exchange rate. In particular, the macro fundamental factor can stabilise an otherwise unstable market when the macro fundamental factor dominates speculative expectations. When the market fundamental equilibrium is unstable, the fundamentalist expectation tends to cause the exchange rate to deviate from the fundamental towards a non-fundamental equilibrium level characterised by a pitchfork bifurcation, while the chartist expectation causes the exchange rate to fluctuate periodically around the fundamental equilibrium characterised by a Hopf bifurcation. This difference is clearly demonstrated in two special cases where the expectations of the portfolio managers follow the view of either the fundamentalists or the chartists. In the general case, when the expectations of the portfolio managers are a weighted average of the heterogeneous expectations, the exchange rate displays a mixture of these two different features dominated by either one of the expectation schemes. Also, a mixture of the two schemes can stabilise an otherwise unstable fundamental steady state and this stabilising effect of combining different types of expectations is also shared by asset pricing models with heterogeneous beliefs. In addition, it is shown that the balance between the macro fundamental factor and the expectations of the portfolio managers is an important factor in determining the exchange rate market evolution.

For the corresponding stochastic model, noise processes are introduced through the market noise in terms of the change in the LER (Equation (22)) and the random switching of the weights of the two heterogeneous expectations (Equation (23)). Numerical simulations show that our simple heterogeneous expectations model can replicate typical time series and some stylised facts observed in exchange rate markets, including deviation from fundamental factors, bimodal density, volatility clustering and fat tails.

Here, in order to focus just on the underlying mechanism driving the exchange rate, namely the different stability regimes, we have simply relied on stochastic switching between the various strategies. The next step is to adopt some of the more sophisticated switching mechanisms introduced in the literature such as that of Brock and Hommes (1997, 1998) involving switching populations or that of Lux (1997) involving transition probabilities. Incorporation of such switching mechanisms should lead to better realism in the generated time series; however, we leave this task to further research.

Acknowledgements

An earlier version of this article was presented at the 2008 SNDE (San Francisco) and CEF 2008 (Paris) conferences and seminars at UTS and Deakin University. Financial support from the Australian Research Council (ARC) under a Discovery Grant (DP0773776) and a Faculty Research Grant at UTS is gratefully acknowledged. We would like to thank the editor of this special issue, Didier Sornette, and a referee for their helpful comments and valuable suggestions. The usual caveat applies.

Notes

1. If we use $dE(s)$ to represent the instantaneous LER change at time s in the continuous-time case, we can define $X^c(t) = \beta_c \int_{-\infty}^{t} e^{-\beta_c(t-s)}\, dE(s)$, which is a declining weighted average of past LER changes, then this can be rewritten as Equation (2). In the discrete-time case, we can define $X^c_{t+\Delta t} = \beta_c(E_{t+\Delta t} - E_t) + (1 - \beta_c)X^c_t$, which leads to Equation (2) in the limit as $\Delta t \to 0$.
2. The perfect foresight case was also discussed by Gray and Turnovsky (1979) within the framework of the Dornbusch (1976) model.
3. The choice of this functional form is also motivated by the literature (such as Chiarella, Dieci and Gardini 2002) on heterogeneous agent asset pricing models.
4. In our model, we use $1 - \omega$ to represent the market fraction of the fundamentalists in place of the ϖ_t of the FF model.
5. Ideally, in line with what is done in the recent heterogeneous agent asset pricing literature, the weight should be time dependent (ϖ_t) and the market would have a systematic way to determine ϖ_t based on a certain fitness function. We refer to De Grauwe and Grimaldi (2005a, 2005b, 2006) for a discussion of heterogeneous agent exchange rate models in this spirit within the discrete-time framework.
6. As in the Dornbusch model, Equation (10) is obtained by taking the logarithm of the money market equilibrium condition $\mathbb{M}/\mathbb{P} = \mathbb{Y}^{\alpha_1} \exp(-\alpha_2 R)$, where $\mathbb{M} = \exp(M)$, $\mathbb{P} = \exp(P)$ and $\mathbb{Y} = \exp(Y)$.

7. The stability of the periodic solution induced by the Hopf bifurcation depends on the nonlinearity of the H function. It is difficult to obtain precise mathematical conditions for our model, but numerical simulations indicate that the periodic solution is stable, as demonstrated in the bifurcation plots in Figure 6.
8. Another mechanism for changing weights could be based on some fitness measure, which has been widely used in asset pricing models with heterogeneous beliefs following Brock and Hommes (1998) and De Grauwe and Grimaldi (2006) in exchange rate markets.

References

Allen, H., and M.P. Taylor. 1990. Charts, noise and fundamentals in the London foreign exchange market. *The Economic Journal* 100, no. 400: 49–59.

Baxter, M., and A. Stockman. 1989. Business cycles and the exchange rate regime: Some international evidence. *Journal of Monetary Economics* 23, no. 3: 377–400.

Brock, W., and C. Hommes. 1997. A rational route to randomness. *Econometrica* 65, no. 5: 1059–95.

Brock, W., and C. Hommes. 1998. Heterogeneous beliefs and routes to chaos in a simple asset pricing model. *Journal of Economic Dynamics and Control* 22, nos. 8–9: 1235–74.

Chiarella, C., R. Dieci, and L. Gardini. 2002. Speculative behaviour and complex asset price dynamics: A global analysis. *Journal of Economic Behavior and Organization* 49, no. 2: 173–97.

Chiarella, C., R. Dieci, and X. He. 2009. Heterogeneity, market mechanisms and asset price dynamics. In *Handbook of financial markets: Dynamics and evolution*, eds. T. Hens and K.R. Schenk-Hoppé, 277–344. Amsterdam: North-Holland.

Chiarella, C., and X. He. 2002. Heterogeneous beliefs, risk and learning in a simple asset pricing model. *Computational Economics* 19, no.1: 95– 132.

Chinn, M.D., and J.A. Frankel. 2002. Survey data on exchange rate expectations: More currencies, more horizons, more tests. In *Monetary policy, capital flows and exchange rates: Essays in honour of Maxwell Fry*, eds. D.G. Dickinson and W.A. Allen, 145–67, Chapter 9. London: Routledge.

De Grauwe, P., and M. Grimaldi. 2005a. Heterogeneity of agents and the exchange rate: A nonlinear approach. In *Exchange rate economics: Where do we stand?* ed. P. De Grauwe, 125–67. Cambridge: MIT Press.

De Grauwe, P., and M. Grimaldi. 2005b. Heterogeneity of agents, transactions costs and the exchange rate. *Journal of Economic Dynamics and Control* 29, no. 4: 691–719.

De Grauwe, P., and M. Grimaldi. 2006. Exchange rate puzzles. A tale of switching attractors. *European Economic Review* 50, no. 1: 1–33.

Dornbusch, R. 1976. Expectations and exchange rate dynamics. *Journal of Political Economy* 84, no. 6: 1161–76.

Flood, R., and A. Rose. 1995. Fixing exchange rates: A virtual quest for fundamentals. *Journal of Monetary Economics* 36, no. 1: 3–37.

Frankel, J.A., and K.A. Froot. 1986. Understanding the US dollar in the eighties: The expectations of chartists and fundamentalists. Special issue, *The Economic Record*: 24–38.

Frankel, J.A., and K.A. Froot. 1990a. Chartists, fundamentalists and the demand for dollars. In *Private behaviour and government policy in interdependent economies*, eds. A.S. Courakis and M.P. Taylor, 73–126. New York: Oxford University Press.

Frankel, J.A., and K.A. Froot. 1990b. The rationality of the foreign exchange rate. chartists, fundamentalists and trading in the foreign exchange market. *American Economic Review* 80, no. 2: 181–5 (AEA papers and proceedings).

Gray, M.R., and S.J. Turnovsky. 1979. The stability of exchange rate dynamics under perfect myopic foresight. *International Economic Review* 20, no. 3: 643–60.

Hommes, C. 2006. Heterogeneous agent models in economics and finance. In *Handbook of computational economics, Vol. 2: Agent-based computational economics*, eds. L. Tesfatsion and K.L. Judd, 1109–86, Amsterdam: North-Holland.

Hommes, C., and F. Wagener. 2009. Complex evolutionary systems in behavioral finance. In *Handbook of financial markets: dynamics and evolution*, eds. T. Hens and K. Schenk-Hoppé, 217–76. Amsterdam: North-Holland.

Ito, T. 1990. Foreign exchange rate expectations: Micro survey data. *American Economic Review* 80, no. 3: 434–49.

Kuznetsov, Y.A. 2004. *Elements of applied bifurcation theory*. 3rd edn. New York: Springer.

LeBaron, B. 2006. Agent-based computational finance. In *Handbook of computational economics, Vol. 2: Agent-based computational economics*, eds. L. Tesfatsion and K.L. Judd, 1187–233. Amsterdam: North-Holland.

Lux, T. 1997. Time variation of second moments from a noise trader/infection model. *Journal of Economic Dynamics and Control* 22, no. 1: 1–38.

Lux, T. 1998. The socio-economic dynamics of speculative markets: Interacting agents, chaos, and fat tails of return distributions. *Journal of Economic Behavior and Organization* 33, no. 2: 142–65.
Lux, T. 2009. Stochastic behavioural asset pricing and stylized facts. In *Handbook of financial markets: Dynamics and evolution*, eds. T. Hens and K.R. Schenk-Hoppé, 161–215. Amsterdam: North-Holland.
Lux, T., and M. Marchesi. 2001. Volatility clustering in financial markets: A micro-simulation of interacting agents. *International Journal of Theoretical and Applied Finance* 3, no. 4: 675–702.
Lyons, R. 2001. *The microstructure approach to exchange rates*. Cambridge: MIT Press.
Meese, R., and K. Rogoff. 1983. Empirical exchange rate models of the seventies: Do they fit out of sample? *Journal of International Economics* 14, nos. 1–2: 3–24.
Menkhoff, L. 1998. The noise trading approach-questionnaire evidence from foreign exchange. *Journal of International Money and Finance* 17, no. 3: 547–64.
Menkhoff, L., and M. Taylor. 2007. The obstinate passion of foreign exchange professionals: Technical analysis. *Journal of Economic Literature* 45, no. 4: 936–72.
Reitz, S., and M. Taylor. 2008. The coordination channel of foreign exchange intervention: A nonlinear microstructure analysis. *European Economic Review* 52, no. 1: 55–76.
Taylor, M.P., and H. Allen. 1992. The use of technical analysis in the foreign exchange market. *Journal of International Money and Finance* 11, no. 3: 304–14.
Westerhoff, F. 2003. Expectations driven distortions in the foreign exchange market. *Journal of Economic Behavior and Organization* 51, no. 3: 389–412.
Westerhoff, F. 2009. Exchange rate dynamics: A nonlinear survey. In *Handbook of research on complexity*, ed. J.B. Rosser Jr., 287–325, Cheltenham: Edward Elgar.
Westerhoff, F., and S. Reitz, 2003. Nonlinearities and cyclical behavior: The role of chartists and fundamentalists. *Studies in Nonlinear Dynamics and Econometrics* 7, no. 4: article no. 3.
Williamson, J. 1985. *The exchange rate system*. vol. 5. Washington, DC: Institute for International Economics.
Zadeh, L.A., and C.A. Desoer. 1963. *Linear system theory: The state space approach*. McGraw-Hill Series in System Science, New York: McGraw-Hill.

Appendix 1. Proofs

Proof of Theorem 4.1 At the fundamental steady state, the corresponding Jacobian matrix is given by

$$A = \begin{pmatrix} 0 & -\frac{\beta_R}{\alpha_2} & \mu(1-\omega) & \mu\omega \\ \rho\beta_3 & -\rho\left(\beta_3 + \frac{\beta_2}{\alpha_2}\right) & 0 & 0 \\ 0 & \frac{\beta_f}{\alpha_2} & -\beta_f & 0 \\ 0 & -\frac{\beta_R\beta_c}{\alpha_2} & \beta_c\mu(1-\omega) & \beta_c(\mu\omega - 1) \end{pmatrix},$$

the characteristic equation of which has the form

$$p(x) := x^4 + d_1x^3 + d_2x^2 + d_3x + d_4 = 0, \tag{A1}$$

where d_i $(i = 1, \ldots, 4)$ are defined in Equation (16). Applying the Routh–Hurwitz theorem (see Zadeh and Desoer 1963), we obtain the result on the stability of the fundamental steady state. □

By the Routh-Hurwitz criterion, Theorems 4.2–4.4 can be proven. Here, we just give the proof of Theorem 4.2 as an example.

Proof of Theorem 4.2 For the system (18), the characteristic equation of the fundamental steady state $\mathcal{S}_0$ becomes

$$p(x) = x^3 + a_{01}x^2 + a_{02}x + a_{03}, \tag{A2}$$

where

$$a_{01} := \beta_f + \beta_p, \quad a_{02} := \beta_p\beta_f + \beta_e\beta_R, \quad a_{03} := \beta_e\beta_f(\beta_R - \mu).$$

Let $\Delta_{03} := a_{01}a_{02} - a_{03} = \beta_p\beta_f^2 + \beta_p^2\beta_f + \beta_p\beta_e\beta_R + \beta_e\mu\beta_f$, then $\mathcal{S}_0$ is LAS if and only if (Here the conditions (A3) are equivalent to Equation (15) under $\omega = 0$ and especially, $a_{03} = 0$ corresponds to $d_4 = 0$ and $\Delta_{03} = 0$ corresponds to $\Delta_4 = 0$.)

$$a_{01} > 0, \quad a_{03} > 0, \quad \Delta_{03} > 0. \tag{A3}$$

It is obvious that a_{01} and Δ_{03} are always positive and the fundamental steady-state loses its stability only at $a_{03} = 0$, that is, $\beta_R = \mu$. At $\beta_R < \mu$, two non-fundamental steady states $\mathcal{S}_\pm = (E^* + (\beta_2/\beta_3 + \alpha_2)X_\pm^*, P^* + \alpha_2 X_\pm^*, X_\pm^*)$ appear, where $X_\pm^*$ satisfy $H(X_\pm^*) = \beta_R X_\pm^*, X_\pm^* \neq 0$ and $H'(X_\pm^*) < \beta_R$, that is to say a pitchfork bifurcation occurs. At the non-fundamental steady states $\mathcal{S}_\pm$, their stability properties are determined by the eigenvalues that are the solutions of

$$\tilde{p}(y) = y^3 + \tilde{a}_{01}y^2 + \tilde{a}_{02}y + \tilde{a}_{03},$$

where

$$\tilde{a}_{01} := \beta_f + \beta_p, \quad \tilde{a}_{02} := \beta_p\beta_f + \beta_e\beta_R, \quad \tilde{a}_{03} := \beta_e\beta_f(\beta_R - H'(X_\pm^*)),$$

and $\tilde{\Delta}_{03} := \tilde{a}_{01}\tilde{a}_{02} - \tilde{a}_{03}$. Since $\tilde{a}_{0i}$ $(i = 1, 2, 3)$ and $\tilde{\Delta}_{03}$ are all positive, $\tilde{p}(y) = 0$ only has negative eigenvalues, that is, $\mathcal{S}_\pm$ is LAS. □

Appendix 2. The stability analysis of Case 2: $\omega = 0.5$ and $\beta_f \neq \beta_c$ in Section 4.3

In this case, the stability of the fundamental equilibrium is determined by the balance between the expectations of the fundamentalists and chartists. This is characterised by the sign change of the discriminants d_i $(i = 1, 2, 4)$ given in Equation (16), and $\Delta_4 = c_0\beta_c^3 + c_1\beta_c^2 + c_2\beta_c + c_3$, where

$$c_0 = \frac{(2-\mu)^2}{8}[(2-\mu)\beta_p\beta_f^2 + ((2-\mu)\beta_p^2 + \beta_e\mu)\beta_f + 2\beta_p\beta_e\beta_R],$$

$$c_3 = \frac{(2\beta_p\beta_f^2 + (\beta_e\mu + 2\beta_p^2)\beta_f + 2\beta_p\beta_e\beta_R)(2\beta_R - \mu)\beta_f\beta_e}{4},$$

and c_1, c_2 are also some polynomials, and at $\mu = 2$, $c_1 = -\beta_e^2\beta_R^2 < 0$. As before, $d_4 = 0$ and $\Delta_4 = 0$ correspond to the pitchfork and Hopf bifurcation boundaries, respectively. Note that the changes in both β_f and β_c do not affect the sign of $d_4 = \beta_e\beta_c\beta_f(\beta_R - \mu/2)$. Hence, we assume $d_4 > 0$, that is, $\mu < 2\beta_R$, and hence $c_3 > 0$. Thus, we only need to focus on the sign change of Δ_4. At $\beta_c = 0$, $\Delta_4 > 0$ but Δ_4 changes as β_f and β_c increase.

(i) For $\mu < 2$ and $\beta_f > 0$, we have $c_0 > 0$. Note that $\lim_{\beta_c \to +\infty} \Delta_4 = +\infty$, that is to say that there exists $\beta_c^* \geq 0$ which depends on β_f such that $\Delta_4 > 0$ for $\beta_c > \beta_c^*$. Correspondingly, the fundamental steady-state equilibrium $\mathcal{S}_0$ is stable for $\beta_c > \beta_c^*$ and $\mu < \min\{2, 2\beta_R\}$.
(ii) For $\mu = 2$, $c_0 = 0$ and $c_1 < 0$. So, for any $\beta_f > 0$, there exists $\beta_c^* = \beta_c^*(\beta_f) > 0$ such that $\Delta_4 < 0$ for $\beta_c > \beta_c^*$. Correspondingly, the fundamental steady-state equilibrium $\mathcal{S}_0$ is unstable for $\beta_c > \beta_c^*$ and $\mu = 2$.
(iii) For $\mu > 2$, there exist $\beta_f^* > 0$ such that when $\beta_f > \beta_f^*$, $c_0 < 0$. At the same time, $\lim_{\beta_c \to +\infty} \Delta_4 = -\infty$, that is to say that there exists $\beta_c^* = \beta_c^*(\beta_f) > 0$ such that since $\beta_c > \beta_c^*$, it follows that $\Delta_4 < 0$. Correspondingly, the fundamental steady-state equilibrium $\mathcal{S}_0$ is unstable for $\beta_f > \beta_f^*$ and $\beta_c > \beta_c^*$ and $2 < \mu < 2\beta_R$.

Essentially, the local stability of the fundamental equilibrium is determined by the sign of Δ_4. When the intensity of the adjustment of the portfolio managers on the weighted depreciation rate of the fundamentalists and chartists is comparatively weak (so that $\mu < \min\{2, 2\beta_R\}$), a strong extrapolation from the chartists (so that $\beta_c > \beta_c^* = \beta_c^*(\beta_f)$ for any given speed of the mean-reversion of the fundamentalists) can locally stabilise the fundamental equilibrium. In contrast, if the portfolio managers dominate the market (so that $\mu \geq 2$), the fundamental equilibrium becomes unstable and the active behaviour of the fundamentalists and chartists will accelerate the frequency of the market fluctuation due to the Hopf bifurcation.

Asymmetric returns, gradual bubbles and sudden crashes

Weihong Huang, Huanhuan Zheng and Wai-Mun Chia

By applying the deterministic heterogenous agent model developed by Huang et al. [Financial crises and interacting heterogeneous agents. *Journal of Economic Dynamics and Control* 34, no. 6: 1105–22], this paper examines the phenomena of asymmetric returns, gradual bubbles and sudden crashes. It shows that (i) returns are asymmetric because the most positive returns initiated by fundamentalist are attenuated by the selling force of chartists, while the most negative return initiated by chartists is hardly affected by the buying force of fundamentalists; (ii) bubbles arise gradually while crashes happen suddenly as the upward price movements are counterbalanced while the downward movements are enhanced by fundamentalists. It also shows for the first time that deterministic dynamic model can simultaneously generate a wide range of stylized facts common across financial markets, including those hardly duplicated by current heterogeneous agent models, such as long-range dependence.

1. Introduction

It has been documented that the aggregate financial market returns, such as returns of the stock market index, are asymmetric. In other words, the largest possible upward return movement is smaller than the absolute magnitude of the largest drawdown, that is, $\max(r_t, 0) < |\min(r_t, 0)|$ (Cont 2001; Hong and Stein 2003). For example, during the past decades (January 1900–January 2010), the most positive monthly return of the Dow Jones Industry Average Indices (DJIA) was 34% in April 1933, the scale which was not comparable with the most negative return of −37% in September 1931. Even though the understanding on return asymmetry is important for risk management, a satisfactory economic explanation is still lacking. Among many agent-based models as surveyed by Chen, Chang, and Du (2009) only a few are capable of duplicating such characteristic.[1] Another interesting observation of the financial time series is that price bubbles appear gradually while price crashes suddenly (Veldkamp 2005). For example, it took 5 years for the recent price bubble to reach the top (the DJIA rise from 7591.93 in September 2002 to the peak 13,930.01 in October 2007), but it took less than 2 years for the bubble to burst bringing the DJIA down to a level (7062.93 in February 2009) which was much lower than the bottom of the bubble. Simple modelling of human learning and adaption enables agent-based models to reproduce bubbles and crashes,[2] which are generally ascribed to the interaction of heterogeneous investors.[3] Nevertheless, only a few studies are found to address the ubiquitous feature of 'gradual' bubbles and 'sudden' crashes.

The goal of this paper is to generate the phenomena of asymmetric returns, gradual bubbles and sudden crashes, and to explain these central qualitative attributes. Ideally, if one were to build a mathematical model based on economic forces that can duplicate such facts, it should have shed some light on these issues. However, as these phenomena are sporadic, the chance of duplicating such facts without capturing the essential fundamental factors is not impossible. For precaution, we first verify the solidity of the model by checking whether it could duplicate the most documented and frequently observed stylized facts that are common across financial markets. If the model succeeds in doing so, relying on it for origins of these sporadic phenomena shall be more convincing.

What are the most intensively discussed stylized facts that characterize the commonality of financial markets? Empirical studies consistently show that the financial time series of prices are random and non-stationary (or possess a unit root), which is in line with the efficient market hypothesis, under which prices instantly and correctly adjust to reflect new information, making arbitrage impossible. However, recent empirical evidence suggests that the financial time series of returns are predictable to some extent (Carhart 1997; Avramov 2002), which challenges the idea that returns are random as implied by the market efficiency hypothesis. Some argue that a certain degree of predicability may be necessary to reward investors for bearing certain dynamic risks and for gathering and processing information. Others suggest that returns may not fully reflect rational evaluations and investors could be boundedly rational. Motivated by these considerations, various models and techniques have been proposed to address return predicability-related issues, in an attempt to beat the market. Despite the controversy on how future returns relate to historical returns, there are several well-recognized findings. First, the distribution of returns is not Gaussian. Instead, it is characterized by fat tails, with extreme returns appearing more frequently than what are predicted by Gaussian distribution. Second, there are positive autocorrelations in absolute and square returns, resulting from the volatility clustering, with periods of quiescence and turbulence cluster together. It means that large (small) return fluctuations are followed by large (small) fluctuations. Even though there is a lack of serial autocorrelation in raw returns, the volatility clustering suggests that past returns are informative for future returns and such relationship is non-linear. Third, returns exhibit an unusually high degree of persistence or long-range dependence – their autocorrelation functions (ACFs) decay slowly as a power of lags. Fourth, most measures of the volatility are negatively correlated with past returns, which is called leverage effect.

Rich literature has contributed to the identifications (Pagan 1996; Cont 2001) and duplications of these stylized facts, in particular, the characteristics of fat tails and volatility clustering in returns (Lux and Marchesi 1999, 2000; Challet, Marsili, and Zhang 2001; He and Li 2007, 2008; Kirchler and Huber 2007; Shimokawa, Suzuki, and Misawa 2007). Agent-based models have been quite successful in the latter. Some of them even shed light on the origins of the stylized facts (Kyrtsou and Terraza 2002; Alfarano, Lux, and Wagner 2008). While for early models, a close fit to some of the statistical features is developed at the expense of a bad fit to others (Cont 2001), some recent models do demonstrate the capability of reproducing many stylized facts simultaneously (Shimokawa, Suzuki, and Misawa 2007). Nevertheless, most models that fit into the real data rely crucially on a somewhat unrealistic modelling of the noise term[4] ($p_t = f(p_{t-1}) + \varepsilon_t$, $\varepsilon_t \backsim N(0, \sigma^2)$, $f(p_{t-1})$ is a function of p_{t-1}). Amilon (2008) shows that if the normally distributed noise is replaced with a more proper stochastic process ($p_t = f(p_{t-1}) + p_{t-1}\varepsilon_t$), even though the model could generate some stylized facts, the fit is generally poor. Removing the noise term ($p_t = f(p_{t-1})$) would render the model too simple to capture the dynamics of real markets and fail to demonstrate stylized facts. One may infer from these findings that stylized facts essentially arise from exogenous shocks. There is no doubt that these models provide excellent dynamic mechanisms that convert random shocks into price patterns. They, however, leave the question that why some properties arise in the absence of external shocks, unexplored. How do random shocks generate consistent stylized facts across markets and over time?

If the internal dynamics play the fundamental role in determining the financial market characteristics while randomness only serves as a trigger (see, e.g. Farmer and Joshi 2002; Sornette 2004), stylized facts that are common across various financial markets over decades ought to be endogenous, arising from the internal price dynamics. In other words, exogenous shocks shall be able to shape stylized facts of different magnitudes but not their fundamental characteristics. To show this, one shall disentangle the impact of exogenous shocks in replicating stylized facts. The safest choice is to exclude external noise terms and stochastic processes of any forms. This is, however, at the cost of fitness into real data as demonstrated by Amilon (2008). Nevertheless if a purely deterministic model is capable of reproducing a variety of stylized facts, one shall extrapolate it to capture some, if not all, essential of the complex market dynamics.

The structure of the paper is organized as follows. Section 2 reviews the model developed in Huang, Zheng, and Chia (2010). In the deterministic model, interacting heterogeneous agents keep updating their forecasts for future price and switch to trading strategy that they believe to outperform the others. Section 3 examines the statistical properties of the simulated data. It shows that even without the noise term and stochastic process of any forms, the simulated data match with the well-documented statistical features that characterize the financial time series. Specifically, we find that the simulated returns demonstrate features such as fat tails, volatility clustering, long-range dependence and leverage effect. In particular, we find that large returns follow a power low distribution with an exponent of three. After verifying the solidity of the model, Section 4 analyses the underlying mechanisms of asymmetric returns as well as gradual bubbles and sudden crashes. Section 5 concludes.

2. Model

We outline the deterministic heterogeneous agent model in this section and refer the reader to Huang, Zheng, and Chia (2010) for full details. This model is closely related to the framework of Day and Huang (1990), Gennotte and Leland (1990), Lux and Marchesi (1999), Lux and Marchesi (2000), Brock and Hommes (1998) and Tramontana, Westerhoff, and Gardini (2010).

There are two types of investors distinguished by their beliefs, fundamentalists (α-investor) and chartists (β-investor). Denote p_t as the price per share of risky asset in period t. Following Farmer and Joshi (2002) and many others, the price impact function is defined by

$$p_{t+1} = p_t + \gamma D_t, \tag{1}$$

where γ measures the price impact and D_t is the aggregate market excess demand for risky asset weighted by market power. Note that the price in Equation (1) refers to the real price instead of log price, the relative price change or return is not proportional to the excess demand. Instead, a given excess demand has a larger impact on return when the price is lower.[5]

The excess demand D_t is given by

$$D_t = \frac{(n_{\alpha,t}x_{\alpha,t} + n_{\beta,t}x_{\beta,t})}{(a_{\alpha,t}x_{\alpha,t} + a_{\beta,t}x_{\beta,t})}, \tag{2}$$

where $n_{i,t}$ represents the number of shares purchased by investor i, $x_{i,t}$ is the number of i-investors and a_i is the degree of risk tolerance for i-investors for $i \in \{\alpha, \beta\}$. $a_{\alpha,t}x_{\alpha,t} + a_{\beta,t}x_{\beta,t}$, the sum of the whole market's weighted risk tolerances, measures the total market power.

2.1 *Adaptive beliefs and demand function*

Let r be the interest rate of risk-free asset which is completely elastic. Given mean variance preference in expected return, $n_{i,t}$ is given by

$$n_{i,t} = \frac{E_{i,t}(p_{t+1}|\Omega_t) - (1+r)p_t}{a_i V_{i,t}(p_{t+1}|\Omega_t)}. \tag{3}$$

where $\Omega_t = \{p_t, p_{t-1}, \ldots p_0\}$ is the public information set available at period t, $E_i(p_{t+1}|\Omega_t)$ and $V_i(p_{t+1}|\Omega_t)$ are the expected price and price variance in the next period.

Fundamentalists hold both price expectation and variance expectation constant over time, that is,

$$E_\alpha(p_{t+1}|\Omega_t) \equiv \bar{p}_\alpha \quad \text{and} \quad V_\alpha(p_{t+1}|\Omega_t) \equiv \sigma_\alpha^2, \tag{4}$$

where the price expectation $\bar{p}_\alpha$ is the long-term fundamental value of the risky asset, to which they believe the price would eventually converge to. They buy low and sell high with the cut-off point $\bar{p}_\alpha$.

Chartists update their price expectation every period but hold constant expected price variance:

$$E_\beta(p_{t+1}|\Omega_t) = p_t + \tau \cdot (p_t - \bar{p}_{\beta,t}) \quad \text{and} \quad V_\beta(p_{t+1}|\Omega_t) \equiv \sigma_\beta^2, \tag{5}$$

where $\bar{p}_{\beta,t}$ is the short-term estimate of the 'fundamental value' and $\tau \in (0, 1)$ measures chartists' sensitivity to past estimation bias (Day and Huang 1990; Westerhoff 2003a).

How do chartists update $\bar{p}_{\beta,t}$? Divide the price domain $\mathbb{P} = [p_{\min}, p_{\max}]$ equally into n mutually exclusive regimes such that

$$\mathbb{P} = \cup_{j=1}^{n} \mathbb{P}_j = [0, \lambda) \cup [\lambda, 2\lambda) \cup \cdots \cup [(n-1)\lambda, n\lambda],$$

where $j\lambda$ ($j = 1, 2 \ldots, n$) represents psychological threshold corresponding to different support (resistance) level in the chartist analysis. When p_t is observed, chartists extrapolate $\bar{p}_{\beta,t}$ to be in the middle of the trading window that p_t falls into, that is,

$$\bar{p}_{\beta,t} = \left(\left\lfloor \frac{p_t}{\lambda} \right\rfloor + \left\lceil \frac{p_t}{\lambda} \right\rceil \right) \cdot \frac{\lambda}{2} \quad \text{if } p_t \in [\bar{p}_{j-1}, \bar{p}_j), \; j = 1, 2 \ldots, n, \tag{6}$$

where $\lfloor p_t/\lambda \rfloor = \bar{p}_{j-1}$ and $\bar{p}_j = \lceil p_t/\lambda \rceil$ are the two threshold prices that enclose the regime j. The price is expected to go up (down) if $p_t > \bar{p}_{\beta,t}$ ($p_t < \bar{p}_{\beta,t}$).[6]

Substituting Equations (4) and (5) into Equation (3) yields the demand function for both types of investors:

$$\begin{aligned} n_{\alpha,t} &= \frac{\bar{p}_\alpha - (1+r)p_t}{a_\alpha \sigma_\alpha^2}, \\ n_{\beta,t} &= \frac{\tau \cdot (p_t - \bar{p}_{\beta,t}) - rp_t}{a_\beta \sigma_\beta^2}, \end{aligned} \tag{7}$$

where $\bar{p}_{\beta,t}$ is given by Equation (6).

2.2 *Interaction and the Market Fraction Index*

Forward-looking investors update their strategies according to a fitness measure – the discounted expected profit per share, π, given by

$$\pi_{i,t} = s_{i,t} \cdot \theta_{i,t}, \quad i \in \{\alpha, \beta\}.$$

s is the discount factor and θ, the expected profit per share before discounting, is defined as follows:

$$\begin{aligned} \theta_{\alpha,t} &= |\bar{p}_\alpha - (1+r)p_t| - \frac{C}{s(p_t)}, \\ \theta_{\beta,t} &= |\tau \cdot (p_t - \bar{p}_{\beta,t}) - rp_t|, \end{aligned} \tag{8}$$

where C is the information cost. $s_{\beta,t}$ is set equal to 1 (see Lux and Marchesi 1999), as chartists realize capital gains or loss immediately. $s_{\alpha,t} = (\bar{p}_\alpha - p_t)^2/3\bar{p}_\alpha^2$ indicates that the farther the price deviates from its value, the more likely it is going to reverse, and therefore the greater the discount factor is.

Let $\eta_{i,t}$ be the market fraction of investors in group i. Its update follows the discrete choice probability (Brock and Hommes 1998)

$$\eta_{i,t}(p_t) = \frac{x_i(p_t)}{\sum_k x_k(p_t)} = \frac{\exp(\rho\pi_{i,t}(p_t))}{\sum_k \exp(\rho\pi_{k,t}(p_t))}, \tag{9}$$

where ρ is the intensity of choice that measures the speed of switching to a different trading strategy. $\eta_{i,t}$ is increasing with $\pi_{i,t}$, suggesting that investors cluster to strategy that generates higher discounted expected profit.

The market fraction index m_t is the difference in market fraction between fundamentalists and chartists:

$$\begin{aligned} m_t = \eta_{\alpha,t}(p_t) - \eta_{\beta,t}(p_t) &= \tanh\left[\frac{\rho}{2} \cdot (\pi_{\alpha,t} - \pi_{\beta,t})\right], \\ &= \tanh\left\{\frac{\rho}{2} \cdot [|\bar{p}_\alpha - (1+r)p_t| - C - |\bar{p}_\alpha - (1+r)p_t|]\right\}. \end{aligned} \tag{10}$$

$m_t \in [-1, 1]$ is positive (negative) when $\pi_{\alpha,t} > \pi_{\beta,t}$ ($\pi_{\alpha,t} < \pi_{\beta,t}$), indicating that the group with superdiscounted expected profit dominates the market in terms of the number of investors.

2.3 *The complete price dynamics*

Dividing the numerator and denominator of Equation (2) by $(x_{\alpha,t} + x_{\beta,t})$ yields:

$$D_t = \frac{(n_{\alpha,t}\eta_{\alpha,t} + n_{\beta,t}\eta_{\beta,t})}{(a_\alpha\eta_{\alpha,t} + a_\beta\eta_{\beta,t})}. \tag{11}$$

Let $a_\beta = \delta a_\alpha$, where $\delta > 0$ is a parameter that measures the relative risk tolerance of chartists against fundamentalists. Substituting $\eta_{\alpha,t} = (1+m_t)/2$, $\eta_{\beta,t} = (1-m_t)/2$, Equations (7), (10) and (11) into Equation (1) gives rise to the complete price dynamics

$$p_{t+1} = p_t + \gamma\frac{\sigma_\beta^2(1+m_t)[\bar{p}_\alpha - (1+r)p_t] + \sigma_\alpha^2\delta(1-m_t)[\tau \cdot (p_t - \bar{p}_{\beta,t}) - rp_t]}{\sigma_\alpha^2\sigma_\beta^2[(1+\delta) + (1-\delta)m_t]}, \tag{12}$$

where $\bar{p}_{\beta,t}$, m_t are non-linear functions of p_t, given in Equation (6) and (10), respectively.

3. Statistical properties of simulated data

In this section, we check the fitness of the model in capturing the essential of the complex dynamics by showing its capacity to generate the well-documented stylized facts described in Section 1. Besides testing the non-stationarity of prices that supports the market efficiency,[7] we also verify various forms of predicability in returns that cannot be explained by the efficient market hypothesis, such as volatility clustering, long-range dependence and leverage effect. Without loss of generality, we simulate the price series using a set of parameters: $p_0 = 85 - 0.01\sqrt{2}, \bar{p}_\alpha = 50$, $\gamma = 2.16 + 0.01\sqrt{2}$, $\delta = 10.12 - 0.01\sqrt{2}$, $\tau = 0.5$, $r = 10^{-5}$, $\rho = 0.9$, $C = 5$, $\lambda = 11.17871$ and $\sigma_\alpha^2 = \sigma_\beta^2 = 1$. The compounded single-period return of the asset from $t-1$ to t is defined as $r_t = \log(p_t) - \log(p_{t-1})$. We could have changed certain parameters to better capture some stylized facts, however, to maintain the consistency of analysis and further support the solidity of the model, we maintain the same set of simulated data throughought the paper.

Before moving to financial econometric tests, we present an overview of the simulated prices and returns in Figure 1. It is observed that (i) the price goes up and down with occasional bubbles and crashes but without any trend or pattern and (ii) the return moves around zero and appears to cluster. The summary statistics in Table 1 confirm that the average return is zero. Note that the most positive return is 0.279, the magnitude of which is smaller than the most negative return of −0.311.

3.1 *Non-stationary prices and stationary returns*

Literature has consistently shown that the time series of asset prices are not stationary but that the returns are. Despite the robust evidence in the finance literature, heterogeneous agent models

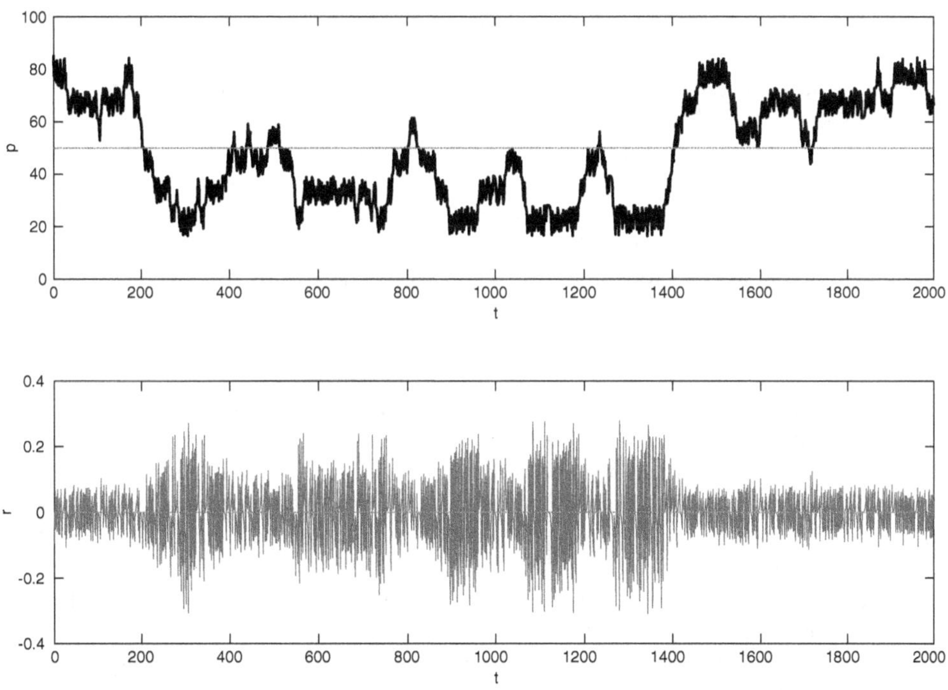

Figure 1. The time series of prices (top) and returns (bottom).

Table 1. Summary statistics of prices and returns.

Sample	Mean	SD	Min	Max	N
p_t	47.53	19.097	16.445	84.986	2001
r_t	0.000	0.099	−0.311	0.279	2000

Table 2. Unit root test.

Series	ADF(6)	MacKinnon p-value	R^2	N
p_t	−2.304	0.171	0.116	1994
$\ln(p_t)$	−2.498	0.116	0.146	1994
r_t	−20.37	0.000	0.664	1993
Notes				
Significance level		1%	5%	10%
ADF critical value		−3.43	−2.86	−2.57

tend to ignore these properties in prices and returns with a few exceptions, such as Lux and Marchesi (2000) and Alfarano, Lux, and Wagner (2008). We test the existence of a unit root (non-stationarity) using the augmented Dickey–Fuller (ADF):

$$\Delta y_t = a_0 + by_{t-1} + \sum_{i=1}^{i=q} c_i \Delta y_{t-i} + \epsilon_t,$$

where $y_t \in \{p_t, \log(p_t), r_t\}$ and q is the number of lags, which is set to be 6 according to the information criteria and the law of parsimony.

Table 2 presents the estimation results. The ADF for price and log price series are −2.304 and −2.498, respectively, which are significantly greater than the critical value at 10% significance level. The corresponding MacKinnon p-values for price and log price series are 0.171 and 0.116 individually, suggesting that one cannot reject the hypothesis of a unit root process for either series even at a significance level of 10%. In the return series, the ADF test significantly rejects the hypothesis of non-stationarity at the 1% significance level. The simulated data match with the stylized facts. There is a unit root process in prices but not in returns.

3.2 *Fat tails*

The summary statistics of returns in upper part of Table 3 further support the presence of fat tails: kurtosis (the fourth moments) is 3.328, which is greater than the benchmark value when returns are normally distributed. It suggests that returns are not normally distributed but exhibit fat tails, with extreme returns appearing more frequently than what are predicted by the normal distribution. The skewness (the third moment) of returns is negative, meaning that price falls in greater scales than it rises on average.

Skewness and kurtosis are however ambiguous in measuring the characteristics of fat tails. As a complement to see how heavy the tail is, we estimate the tail index. First, the return series are sorted into descending order so that $r^{(1)} > r^{(2)} \cdots > r^{(N)}$. Assuming Pareto-type tail in the density, we have $\Pr(R \geqslant r) = kr^{-h}$, where k is a parameter and h is the tail index, with a lower value corresponding to a fatter tail. Conditioning upon the $\varphi\%$ upper tail that includes the j

Table 3. Fat tails.

Sample	Skewness	Kurtosis	Mean	SD	N
A: Skewness and kurtosis					
r_t	−0.082	3.328	0	0.099	2000
B: Hill estimator of the tail index					
$\varphi\%$	10%	5%			
h	3.054	4.533			

($= \lfloor \varphi\% * N \rfloor$) largest observations, the Hill (1975) estimator is given by

$$\hat{h} = \frac{1}{[\sum_{i=1}^{i=j} \ln(r^{(i)})/j - \ln r^{(j)}]}.$$

For the upper 10% and 5% tails, the Hill estimator shown in lower part of Table 3 falls into [2, 6], a range reported consistently in current literature (see Cont 2001).

Since the accuracy of Hill estimator largely depends on the number of observations that are within the specified tail, we have to be cautious about the selection of percentiles. To see whether 10% or 5% is a better choice in calculating the tail index, we run a robustness check using the method of Mandelbrot (1997), by representing the sample moments as a function of the sample size. If the tail index h is larger than the moment of order c, the moment of order c exists and settles down around a finite value. Figure 2 illustrates that the behaviour of skewness (moment of order three) and kurtosis (moment of order four) corresponds to the sample size. As observed, while the skewness or the third moment stabilizes at a negative value as the sample size increases, the kurtosis or the fourth moment shows no such stability. The results are in favour of a choice of

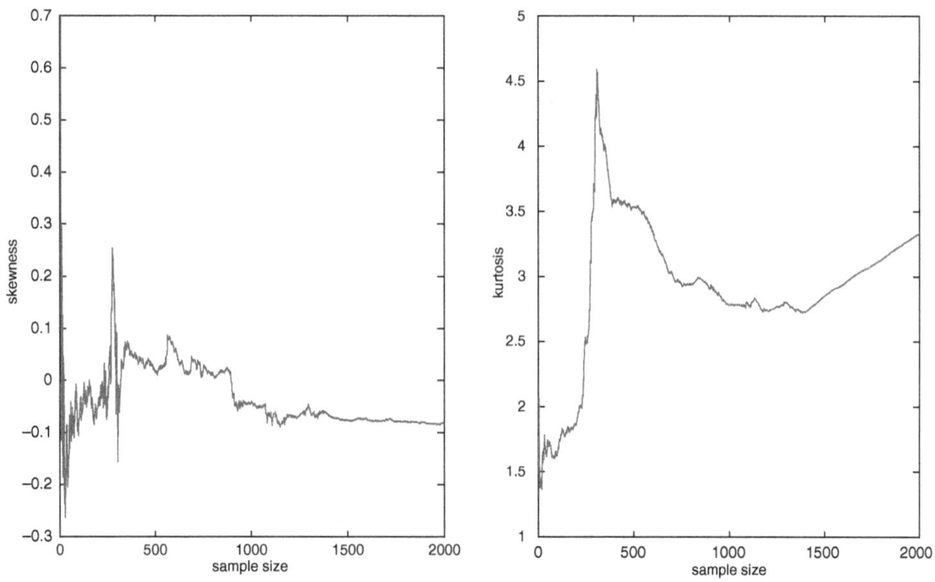

Figure 2. Skewness and kurtosis as a function of sample size.

10% tail and a Hill estimator of around 3. This is in line with the cubic-law distribution of returns (see Gabaix et al. 2003).

3.3 *Volatility clustering*

Except for very small trading time scales, ACF of returns are insignificant. The absence of linear correlation does not imply independence of returns. In fact, non-linear functions of returns, such as absolute or square returns, are significantly autocorrelated. Such correlation is positive and persistent, which is a quantitative feature of volatility clustering, with periods of quiescence and turbulence cluster together. Panel A of Figure 3 demonstrates such properties: while the ACF of raw returns decays quickly to 0, the ACF of absolute returns is relatively large and persistent even after 100 lags. Note that the ACF of the raw returns at the lag 1 and 2 is −0.28 and −0.13, respectively, the similar statistics at lag 3 diminishes to 0.01 and then fluctuates around 0 with small magnitude. The magnitude of ACFs of absolute returns remains significantly different from 0 over the 100 lags. The slow decay in the ACFs of absolute returns is a characteristic (but not a sufficient condition) of a long memory process.

The plot of the ACFs against the number of lags is however ambiguous in measuring the decaying characteristics of volatility clustering. As a quantitative complement, exponent of power laws is proposed to measure how fast the ACF of absolute returns decays

$$\mathrm{corr}(|r_{t+q}|, |r_t|) \simeq \frac{\varsigma}{q^d},$$

where q is the number of lags, ς is a parameter and d is the exponent, with a smaller value corresponding to slower decay.

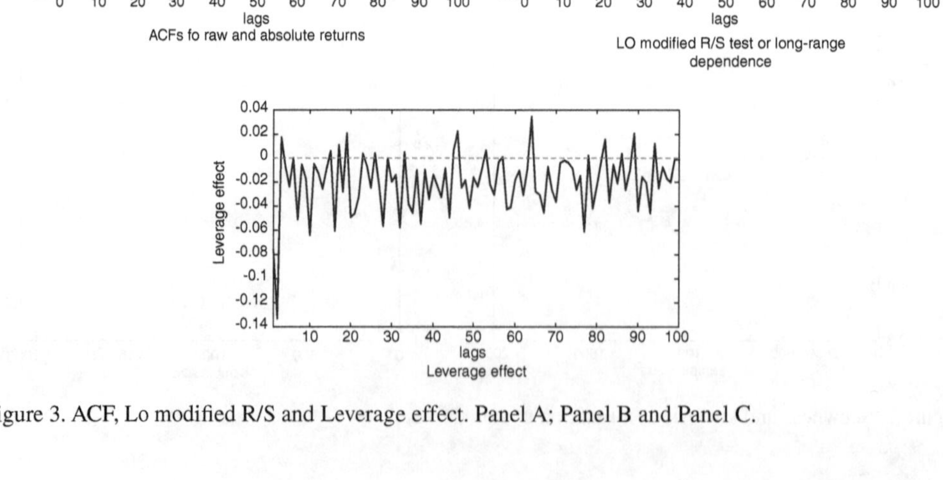

Figure 3. ACF, Lo modified R/S and Leverage effect. Panel A; Panel B and Panel C.

Table 4. NLS estimation of ACF.

Coefficient	t-Statistics	R^2	Root MSE	
ς	0.604	14.35	0.9134	0.065
d	0.325	14.38		

Non-linear least-square (NLS) estimation (Table 4) shows that the ACF of absolute returns decays with an exponent $d = 0.325$, which matches with the real markets that typically have an exponent falling in the range of $(0.2, 0.4)$. It loosely suggests the presence of 'long-range dependence', which is to be discussed in detail later.

3.4 *Long-range dependence*

r_t is said to have long-range dependence if its ACF fades away as a power of the lag:

$$\operatorname{corr}(r_t, r_{t+q}) \backsim \frac{L(q)}{q^{1-2\tilde{d}}}, \quad 0 < \tilde{d} < \frac{1}{2} \quad \text{as } q \to \infty,$$

where $L(q)$ is any slowly varying function at infinity, i.e. verifies $\forall a > 0$, $L(aq)/L(q) \to 1$ as the number of lags $q \to \infty$. Long-range dependent time series exhibits an unusually high degree of persistence even at the lowest frequencies, which is thought to be a common phenomenon in financial variables.

To complement a comprehensive analysis of long-range dependence, we test the hypothesis of no long-range dependence in r_t using Lo-modified range over standard deviation or R/S statistic (also called re-scaled range), which is robust to short-range dependence (Lo 1991).[8] The Lo-modified R/S statistic over n observations, denoted by Q_n, is defined by

$$Q_n \equiv \frac{1}{\hat{\sigma}_n(q)} \left[\max_{1 \leq k \leq n} \sum_{j=1}^{j=k} (r_j - \bar{r}_n) - \min_{1 \leq k \leq n} \sum_{j=1}^{j=k} (r_j - \bar{r}_n) \right], \tag{13}$$

where $\hat{\sigma}_n(q)$ is the usual sample variance:

$$\hat{\sigma}_n(q) = \frac{1}{n} \sum_{j=1}^{j=n} (r_j - \bar{r}_n) + \frac{2}{n} \sum_{j=1}^{j=q} \left(1 - \frac{j}{q+1}\right) \sum_{i=j+1}^{i=n} (r_i - \bar{r}_n)(r_{i-j} - \bar{r}_n).$$

The first and second terms in the bracket of Equation (13) are the maximum of the partial sums of the first k deviations of r_j from the sample mean $\bar{r}_n$ and the minimum of the same sequence of partial sums, respectively.

We show that the estimated Lo-modified R/S statistic increases with the lag q in the Panel B of Figure 3. Despite the sensitivity of the statistics to the selection of the number of lags, the overall results support the presence of long-range dependence in general. At the 10% significance level, with the confidence interval of $[0.861, 1.747]$, we reject the null hypothesis of no long-range dependence through 100 lags. At the 5% significance level with the confidence interval of $[0.809, 1.862]$, we find evidence of long-range dependence as long as $q \leqslant 16$.

3.5 *Leverage effect*

Leverage effect states that most measures of volatility of an asset are negatively correlated with the past return of that asset. It is also called volatility asymmetry, with the amplitude of price fluctuations or volatility having a tendency to increase when the price drops. Representing the volatility with subsequent squared returns, the leverage effect could be measured by $\text{corr}(|r_{t+q}|^2, r_t)$ Cont (2001). We graph $\text{corr}(|r_{t+q}|^2, r_t)$ as a function of the lag q in the Panel C of Figure 3. It turns out that the $\text{corr}(|r_{t+q}|^2, r_t)$ starts from a negative value which implies that negative returns lead to a rise in volatility. The simulated returns exhibit leverage effect as documented in many theoretical and empirical literature.[9]

4. Numerical analysis

After showing that the purely deterministic model are capable of generating a wide range of well-documented stylized facts, one shall extrapolate it to capture at least in part, if not all, fundamental factors of the complexity in financial market dynamics. At this point, we are more confident to take a step further to dig into such a model for the origins of return asymmetry, gradual bubbles and sudden crashes. In this section, we reproduce qualitative features and shade light on the origins of the phenomena of asymmetric returns as well as gradual bubbles and sudden crashes. Our analysis suggests that (i) returns are asymmetric because the most positive returns initiated by fundamentalist is weakened by chartists while the most negative return initiated by chartists is hardly affected by fundamentalists and (ii) price bubbles come up gradually but crashes happen suddenly, because when the price is above the fundamental, the upward price movements are counterbalanced while the downward movements are enhanced by fundamentalists.

4.1 *Asymmetric returns*

Returns are asymmetric in the sense that the largest upward return movement is not comparable with the absolute magnitude of the largest drawdown, that is, $\max(r_t, 0) < |\min(r_t, 0)|$. As shown in Table 1, the most positive return in our simulated sample is 27.8% while the most negative return is -31.1%, a match with the documented asymmetry in returns. As the statistical properties of returns have been studied in the previous section, we focus on the underlying mechanism of return asymmetry in this part. In line with Johansen and Sornette (2002) and Westerhoff (2003b), we support the idea that such asymmetry in returns are endogenous.

Figure 4 plots the absolute returns against the price level, with the hollow circle denoting the negative return and the solid circle denoting the absolute value of the negative return. It shows that extreme returns concentrate on low price levels.

What is the driving force behind the extreme returns? When price falls below its value, fundamentalists always buy in to shore up the asset price; chartists, however, either buy or sell, depending on their forecast of piece-wise short-term fundamental (see Equation (6)). At low price levels, extremely negative returns arise when the selling force of chartists outweighs the buying force of fundamentalists, which brings the price down sharply. Extremely positive returns could be generated if (i) chartists move in the same direction with fundamentalist to buy in the asset or (ii) the buying force of fundamentalists strongly exceeds the selling force of chartists. To have a clear picture of the internal mechanism, Figure 5 plots steps of price dynamics that generate returns below 10% percentile (the extremely negative returns) and above 90% percentile (the extremely positive returns). The dynamic steps associated with the extremely negative returns (top panel) all

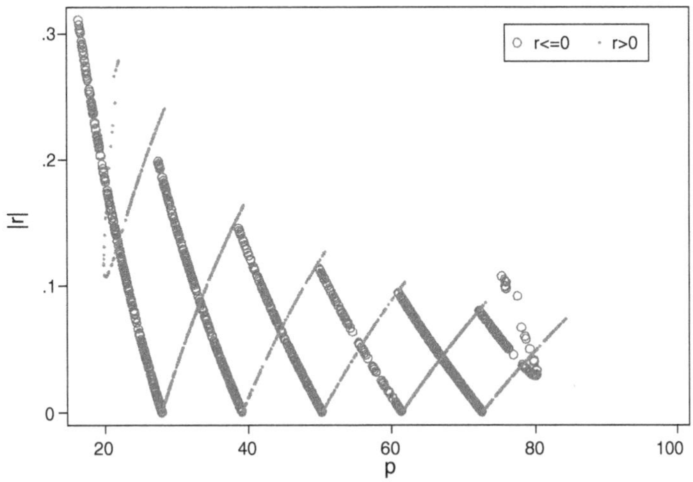

Figure 4. The distribution of absolute returns across different price levels. The positive returns are marked with hollow circles and the negative returns are marked with solid circles.

locate on the right-hand side of $p_{t-1} = 19.477$ (the dash vertical line), when the market fraction index m (dash dot line) is trivial.[10] It is equivalent to say that the collective selling of chartists gives rise to the extremely negative returns. The dynamic steps associated with the extremely positive returns (bottom panel) are associated with both trivial and non-trivial m. When m is not trivial that is $p_{t-1} < 19.477$, chartists generally find it optimal to sell,[11] extremely positive returns are generated because the buying force of the fundamentalists exceed that of the selling force of chartists. When m is not trivial, extremely positive returns arise because chartists who dominate the market buy in the asset in large volumes.

Why is the most negative return greater than the most positive return in terms of absolute magnitude? The most negative return (−31.1%) arises when the price falls from 22.435 to 16.445. When the price is 22.435, the market fraction of fundamentalists is trivial, the collective selling actions of chartists are hardly affected by fundamentalists. It is relative easy to move the price down for a large amplitude. The most positive return (27.8%) arises when the price jumps from 16.705 to 22.071. At the price level of 16.705, fundamentalists that are not trivial buy in the asset to increase the price. Their actions are, however, counterbalanced to some extent by the selling behaviour of chartists[12] that accounts for more than half of the market fraction (see the dash-dot line), which limits the upward movement of the subsequent return. In sum, returns are asymmetric because the most positive returns initiated by fundamentalist is weakened by the chartists while the most negative return initiated by chartists are hardly affected by fundamentalists.

4.2 *Gradual bubbles and sudden crashes*

Asset price moves up and down, accompanied by sporadic bubbles and crashes. The bull-run of equity price in 2006 and its collapse during credit crunch in 2007 are representative episodes of the bubble and the crash. Current heterogeneous agent models ascribe bubbles and crashes to the interaction among heterogeneous investors. Our simulation further supports this argument. Moreover, it captures the ubiquitous feature of gradual bubbles and sudden crashes that are rarely addressed in agent-based models. We argue that such characteristics could root in the facts

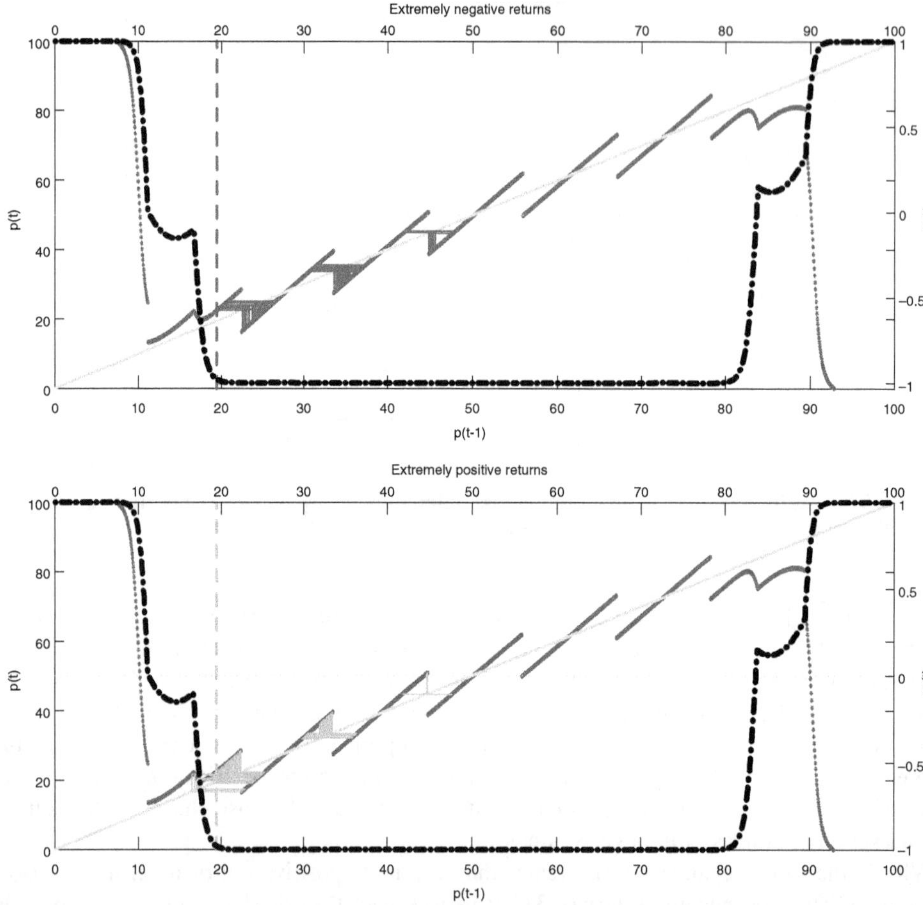

Figure 5. Steps of price dynamics for extreme returns. The dot line graphs the phase diagram of the price dynamics. The bold dash dot line is the market fraction index m. The solid lines plot the steps of price dynamics that generate the extremely negative returns (top) the extremely positive returns (bottom). The dash line represents $p_t = 19.477$, corresponding to the minimum price level associated with the extreme negative returns.

that upward price movements are counterbalanced while the downward movements are always enhanced by fundamentalists, when the price is above the fundamental.

We deviate first from the conventional concept of bubble[13] slightly, by focusing on a more general phenomenon – price booms characterized by an upward trend regardless of whether the price is above or below the fundamental. The upper left panel of Figure 6 shows that the simulated prices fluctuate randomly with booms and crashes. The typical episode of crash is reflected between period 174 and 306 (32 periods), when price falls from the peak, 84.184, to the bottom, 16.878 (declined by 67.306). The representative episode of price boom could be found from period 1346 to 1493 (47 periods), when the price bounces from the lowest point, 16.445, up to the regional peak, 83.394 (increased by 66.949). It seems to take longer for price to rise than to decline by a similar magnitude. In other words, the price crashes more quickly than its boom. In order to shade light on the phenomena of slow boom and sudden crash, the right panels of Figure 6

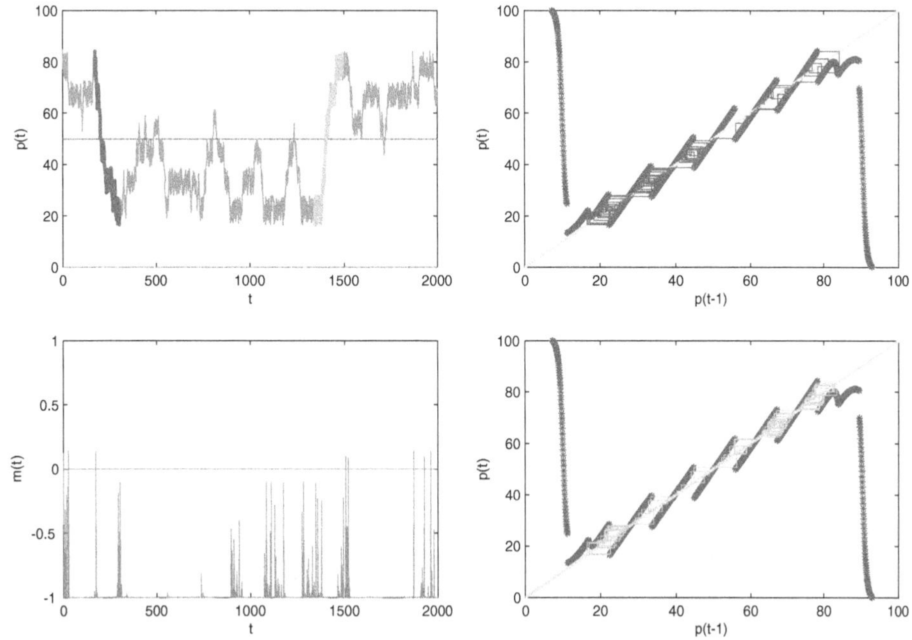

Figure 6. Price trajectory (upper left), market fraction index (bottom left), step-wise price dynamics of bubble (upper right) and crash (bottom right).

plot the step-wise price dynamics corresponding to these episodes of crash and boom. The crash starts when the price is very high above its value. At that high price level, fundamentalists sell asset to drag the price down towards its fundamental while chartists could either buy in or sell out, depending on their expected short-term fundamental. If the selling force of fundamentalists dominates the market, price goes down for sure. As the price declines, m decreases, which weakens the selling force of fundamentalists. The price stops falling if chartists find it optimal to buy in and their buying force is greater than the selling force of fundamentalists. As soon as the price is up, m increases, the collective selling force of fundamentalists is enhanced. The rising trend reverses when the selling force of fundamentalists exceeds the buying force of chartists. The battle between fundamentalists and chartists continues until the price is brought down to a level that chartists find it optimal to sell. That is the moment when the price starts to plunge. As the price move closer to the fundamental, chartists dominate the market (m is trivial) and continue to explore the trend of price, leading to a series of moderate and disturbing declines. Similarly, the boom starts with the battle between fundamentalists and chartists. When the price is up to a certain level, chartist dominate the market and continue to explore the trend, which eventually push the price far beyond its fundamental and forms a bubble.[14]

We now focus on the specific episode of the boom – the bubble, defined by the price span above the fundamental. Comparing the upper right and bottom panels of Figure 6, it is found from the density of the dynamic steps that price falls from the peak less disturbingly than it approaches the peak. Intuitively, when the price is above the fundamental, fundamentalists always buy in while chartists switch between buying and selling according to their latest update of the short-term fundamental. The upward price movements initiated by chartists are impaired, while the downward movements are enhanced by fundamentalists. Therefore, the price owes to drop

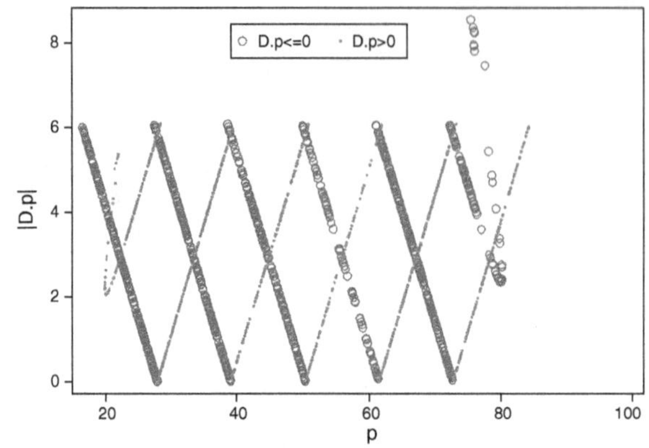

Figure 7. Asymmetric price movements. The solid circle denotes the upward movement and the hollow circle denotes absolute magnitude of the downward movement.

much easier than it climbs. Figure 7 illustrates such an asymmetry by plotting the absolute price movements against the price level. It shows that when the price is very high above the fundamental (e.g. $p > 70$), the downward price movements (denoted by hollow circles) are greater than the upward movements (denoted by solid circles) in terms of their absolute magnitudes. The former is, however, sparser than the latter. It implies that price drops in large scale with low frequency, while it increases in relatively small amplitude with high frequency.

For a technical explanation, we turn to the dynamics of the market fraction index, m. The bottom left panel of Figure 6 states that market index, m, fluctuates more disturbingly when the price falls from the peak than when the price approaches the peak. It suggests that the battle between fundamentalists and chartists lasts longer in forming bubbles than in generating crashes. When the price is at the peak, m is large. In this case, it is easy for fundamentalists to win the battle against chartists quickly and to drag the price down by a large scale. Whereas when the price is on the way towards the peak, as chartists push the price higher, m that is originally trivial increases gradually. The increased m fortifies the selling force of fundamentalists that counterbalances and even reverses chartists' effort to push the price up further. In sum, around the peak, it is easier for fundamentalists to win against chartists than vice versa. Therefore, price goes up easier than it falls. That is why bubbles tend to be gradual while crash tends to be sudden.

5. Conclusion

We show that it is possible for a deterministic heterogenous agent model, involving no random elements of any forms, to generate a wide range of stylized facts simultaneously. Specifically, the chaotic return series, simulated under the deterministic model in Huang, Zheng, and Chia (2010), exhibits characteristics of fat tails and volatility clustering, the two stylized facts receive the most intensive discussions in agent-based models. The tail index is around 3, in line with the cubic power low distribution of large returns. The volatility clustering decays with an exponent of 0.325, the value of which falls within the range of the empirical findings, suggesting a good match with the real data. Even without the inclusion of any normally distributed noise term or stochastic process, the simulated data reflect the properties of long-range dependence as well as leverage effect. The good performance of the chaotic model in reproducing stylized facts can be attributed to the endogenized non-linear dynamics, which is found to be important in capturing the salient feature in financial time series Kyrtsou and Terraza 2002; Kyrtsou and Vorlow 2009). Accounting for the chaotic behaviour through the non-linear deterministic dynamic is important in modelling the complexity in the financial market.

After verifying the solidity of the model by showing its capability to duplicate many stylized facts that are common across financial markets, we believe that the model has captured some, if not all, essential features of the complex market dynamics. So we take a step further to explore the phenomena of asymmetric returns as well as gradual bubbles and sudden crashes. Based on the same model and the same set of parameters, our numerical analysis suggests the followings: (i) returns are asymmetric because the most positive return initiated by fundamentalists are counterbalanced by chartists who trade in the opposite direction against fundamentalists, while the most negative returns initiated by chartists are hardly affected by fundamentalists. In other words, the net buying force of fundamentalists is not comparable with the collective selling forces of chartists, rendering the magnitude of the most positive return to be smaller than that of the most negative return, and (ii) bubbles form gradually while crashes happen suddenly because when the price is above its value, fundamentalists always sell assets to bring the price towards its fundamental, which strengthen the downward price movement but attenuate the upward movements driven by the collective buying force of chartists. Note again that the model is purely deterministic, our findings suggest that bubbles and crashes can arise even without external shocks. It indicates that regulations tend to be ineffective in preventing such phenomena from happening. However, policy-makers can still monitor the market to some extent by changing the market structure or by influencing behaviour of market participants. For example, they can step into the market and play the role of fundamentalists to boost the price up when the market is depressed and to stop the price from going too high. By doing so, they mitigate the size of bubbles and crashes.

Notes

1. See Johansen and Sornette (2002), Westerhoff (2003a) and Hong and Stein (2003) for models that can demonstrate asymmetric returns.
2. see, e.g. Day and Huang (1990), Frankel (2008), Gennotte and Leland (1990), Lux (1995) and He and Westerhoff (2005).
3. Kyrtsou and Terraza (2002) verify that interactions between heterogeneous investors contribute to the chaotic behaviour and excess volatility of financial time series.
4. The dynamic modelling of the normally distributed noise term could exhibit the features of fat tails even if the fundamental does change.
5. We thank the anonymous referee for pointing this out.
6. Studies that apply the piecewise set up in HAM include Westerhoff (2003a), Manzan and Westerhoff (2007), Tramontana, Westerhoff, and Gardini (2010). The findings in these papers suggest that accounting for such piecewise properties may improve the model performance in one way or another.
7. The non-stationarity in price series does not necessarily imply that price is unpredictable. The stationarity test is designed to evaluate whether shocks are permanent/temporary (Campbell, Lo, and MacKinlay 1997). Under the efficient market, shocks are expected to be permanent, which corresponds to a non-stationary process.
8. Any incompatibility between the data and the predicted behaviour of the R/S static under the null hypothesis of no long-range dependence may merely be a symptom of short-term memory, if conventional R/S is applied. That is, conventional R/S static is sensitive to short-range dependence. Lo-modified R/S static accounts for the effects of short-range dependence and is considerably more accurate.
9. See Bouchaud, Matacz, and Potters (2001) and the survey by Pagan (1996).
10. A trivial m ($m \to 0$) indicates a large proportion of chartists and almost no fundamentalists.
11. If there is no fundamentalists, one of the equilibria is that $p(t-1) = p(t) \approx 19$, below which chartists find it optimal to sell (see Equations (7) and (6)). As long as the price stays within the same trading window, the lower the price below the equilibrium price, the greater the selling force of chartists.
12. Note that at such price level, chartists' optimal strategy is to sell.

13. In the following context, we refer 'boom' to general upward trend and 'bubbles' to the upward trend when price is above the fundamental.
14. See Huang, Zheng, and Chia (2010) for a technical analysis.

References

Alfarano, S., T. Lux, and F. Wagner. 2008. Time variation of higher moments in a financial market with heterogeneous agents: An analytical approach. *Journal of Economic Dynamics and Control* 32, no. 1: 101–36.

Amilon, H. 2008. Estimation of an adaptive stock market model with heterogeneous agents. *Journal of Empirical Finance* 15, no. 2: 342–62.

Avramov, D. 2002. Stock return predictability and model uncertainty. *Journal of Financial Economics* 64, no. 3: 423–58. doi: 10.1016/s0304-405x(02)00131-9.

Bouchaud, J.-P., A. Matacz, and M. Potters. 2001. Leverage effect in financial markets: The retarded volatility model. *Physical Review Letters* 87, no. 22: 228701.

Brock, W.A., and C.H. Hommes. 1998. Heterogeneous beliefs and routes to chaos in a simple asset pricing model. *Journal of Economic Dynamics and Control* 22, nos. 8–9: 1235–74.

Campbell, J.Y., A.W. Lo, and C.A. MacKinlay. 1997. *The econometrics of financial markets*. Princeton: Princeton University Press.

Carhart, M.M. 1997. On persistence in mutual fund performance. *The Journal of Finance* 52, no. 1: 57–82.

Challet, D., M. Marsili, and Y.-C. Zhang. 2001. Stylized facts of financial markets and market crashes in Minority Games. *Physica A: Statistical Mechanics and its Applications* 294, nos. 3–4: 514–24.

Chen, S.-H., C.-L. Chang, and Y.-R. Du. 2009. Agent-based economic models and econometrics. *The Knowledge Engineering Review*: 1–46. doi: 10.1017/S0000000000000000.

Cont, R. 2001. Empirical properties of asset returns: Stylized facts and statistical issues. *Quantitative Finance* 1: 223–36.

Day, R.H., and W. Huang. 1990. Bulls, bears and market sheep. *Journal of Economic Behavior & Organization* 14, no. 3: 299–329.

Farmer, J.D., and S. Joshi. 2002. The price dynamics of common trading strategies. *Journal of Economic Behavior & Organization* 49, no. 2: 149–71.

Frankel, D.M. 2008. Adaptive expectations and stock market crashes. *International Economic Review* 49, no. 2: 595–619.

Gabaix, X., P. Gopikrishnan, V. Plerou, and H.E. Stanley. 2003. A theory of power-law distributions in financial market fluctuations. *Nature* 423, no. 6937: 267–70.

Gennotte, G., and H. Leland. 1990. Market liquidity, hedging, and crashes. *The American Economic Review* 80, no. 5: 999–1021.

He, X.-Z., and Y. Li. 2007. Power-law behaviour, heterogeneity, and trend chasing. *Journal of Economic Dynamics and Control* 31, no. 10: 3396–426.

He, X.-Z., and Y. Li. 2008. Heterogeneity, convergence, and autocorrelations. *Quantitative Finance* 8, no. 1: 5979.

He, X.-Z., and F.H. Westerhoff. 2005. Commodity markets, price limiters and speculative price dynamics. *Journal of Economic Dynamics and Control* 29, no. 9: 1577–96.

Hong, H., and J.C. Stein. 2003. Differences of opinion, short-sales constraints, and market crashes. *Review of Financial Studies* 16, no. 2: 487–525. doi: 10.1093/rfs/hhg006.

Huang, W., H. Zheng, and W.-M. Chia. 2010. Financial crises and interacting heterogeneous agents. *Journal of Economic Dynamics and Control* 34, no. 6: 1105–22.

Johansen, A., and D. Sornette. 2002. Large stock market price drawdowns are outliers. *Journal of Risk* 4, no. 2: 69–110.

Kirchler, M., and J. Huber. 2007. Fat tails and volatility clustering in experimental asset markets. *Journal of Economic Dynamics and Control* 31: 1844–74.

Kyrtsou, C., and M. Terraza. 2002. Stochastic chaos or ARCH effects in stock series? A comparative study. *International Review of Financial Analysis* 11, no. 4: 407–31. doi: 10.1016/s1057-5219(02)00067-4.

Kyrtsou, C., and C. Vorlow. 2009. Modelling non-linear comovements between time series. *Journal of Macroeconomics* 31, no. 1: 200–11. doi: 10.1016/j.jmacro.2008.02.001.

Lo, A.W. 1991. Long-term memory in stock market prices. *Econometrica* 59, no. 5: 1279–313.

Lux, T. 1995. Herd behaviour, bubbles and crashes. *The Economic Journal* 105, no. 431: 881–96.

Lux, T., and M. Marchesi. 1999. Scaling and criticality in a stochastic multi-agent model of a financial market. *Nature* 397, no. 6719: 498–500.

Lux, T., and M. Marchesi. 2000. Volatility clustering in financial markets: A microsimulation of interacting agents. *International Journal of Theoretical & Applied Finance* 3, no. 4: 675.

Mandelbrot, B.B. 1997. *Fractals and scaling in finance: Discontinuity, concentration, risk*. Berlin: Springer.

Manzan, S., and Westerhoff, F.H. 2007. Heterogeneous expectations, exchange rate dynamics and predictability. *Journal of Economic Behavior & Organization* 64, no. 1: 111–28.

Pagan, A. 1996. The econometrics of financial markets. *Journal of Empirical Finance* 3, no. 1: 15–102.

Shimokawa, T., K. Suzuki, and T. Misawa. 2007. An agent-based approach to financial stylized facts. *Physica A: Statistical Mechanics and its Applications* 379, no. 1: 207–25.

Sornette, D. 2004. *Critical phenomena in natural sciences : Chaos, fractals, selforganization, and disorder: Concepts and tools*. 2nd ed. Berlin and New York: Springer.

Tramontana, F., F. Westerhoff, and L. Gardini. 2010. On the complicated price dynamics of a simple one-dimensional discontinuous financial market model with heterogeneous interacting traders. *Journal of Economic Behavior & Organization* 74, no. 3: 187–205.

Veldkamp, L.L. 2005. Slow boom, sudden crash. *Journal of Economic Theory* 124, no. 2: 230–57.

Westerhoff, F.H. 2003a. Anchoring and psychological barriers in foreign exchange markets. *Journal of Behavioral Finance* 4, no. 2: 65–70.

Westerhoff, F. 2003b. Bubbles and crashes: Optimism, trend extrapolation and panic. *International Journal of Theoretical and Applied Finance* 6: 829–37.

Epidemics of rules, rational negligence and market crashes

Kartik Anand, Alan Kirman and Matteo Marsili

Structural changes in an economy or in financial markets can arise as a result of agents adopting rules that appear to be the norm around them. Such rules are adopted by implicit consensus as they turn out to be profitable for individuals. However, as rules develop and spread they may have consequences at the aggregate level which are not anticipated by individuals. To illustrate this, we develop a simple model, motivated by the 2007–2008 crisis in credit derivatives markets. This shows how coordination on simple and apparently profitable rules may weaken regulatory constraints, rendering the whole system more fragile. The rule, in the specific example, consists in deciding not to exercise due diligence in the evaluation of complex credit derivative products, free riding on information and operational costs. We show that such 'rational negligence', in the face of deteriorating macro-economic conditions, can bring a market to a sudden collapse.

1. Introduction

The standard vision of the economy, enshrined in modern macroeconomic models, remains the one characterized by a static equilibrium state or where the economy is in a steady state to which it returns when perturbed by an external shock. If the economy deviates suddenly and considerably from such a state this can only be, according to the paradigm, due to a major exogenous shock. This paper argues that such a framework is inappropriate, briefly examines the mechanics of the current crisis and proposes a simple model to demonstrate how the adoption of locally rational rules by the participants in a market can lead to a collapse at the aggregate level.

Before proceeding, it is worth restating some of the key problems with the standard equilibrium approach. A first problem with that view is that many models of the economy are characterized by multiple equibria (for a comprehensive survey, see Cooper 1999). Morris and Shin (2000) argued that radical changes or shifts between equilibria may result as a consequence of small modifications in the structure of the system. Such a change may not be simply reversible[1]. Such *phase transitions* cannot be corrected by remedial policies since there is no steady state or equilibrium path, but rather an evolution through a set of states.

A second issue concerns the origin of shifts in a models' parameters. We have become accustomed in the macroeconomic literature to the idea that periodically exogenous shocks temporarily knock the economy off course, but that it eventually returns to the steady-state path. This vision has led to the study of *impulse response functions*[2], which are supposed to measure the consequence of the external shocks.

However, none of this fits well with accounts of the evolution of the recent sub-prime crisis which we outline in the next section. In those accounts, words such as *trust*, *contagion* and *network* are commonly used. Each of these terms suggests that we have to consider the economy as an interactive system, which does not mean that markets cease to exist or be important, but that people's behavior in these markets is conditioned by the behavior of others around them. This is what Shiller (2008) refers to as *social contagion*. Furthermore, this evolution does not require a class of *dishonest* individuals who break the existing rules or norms because doing so is to their advantage and they have fewer scruples than their honest counterparts. In such a case one might just reflect on more effective regulatory systems to control and punish such behavior. What is, in fact at work, is the process by which what is acceptable changes, and it is this that underlies the collapse of such systems. In all of this there is no villain, no proximate cause, just a system evolving with a collective logic which does not correspond to that of the people who make it up.

In the next section, we draw from recent accounts on the crisis in credit derivatives which suggests that the diffusion of a certain type of behavioral rules among market participants has played a major role. In brief, two self-reinforcing concomitant factors were at play: On one side, the financial system was becoming less and less transparent. On the other, market participants had fewer and fewer incentives to gather correct information, given the increased costs of information and the apparent liquidity of the market. In the following section, we develop a simple model which reproduces this feedback mechanism, establishing *rational negligence* as a social norm. In the model, the participants in a market for securitized assets are led to buy without verifying the quality of the underlying assets, on the basis of their assessment of the likelihood that others will buy these assets. We show that, as this practice develops the whole system may finally break down. The final section discusses the results and offers some concluding remarks.

2. The sub-prime crisis

The outbreak of the sub-prime financial crisis, which can be dated to March 2007 with the revelation of losses by United States sub-prime investors Accredited Home Lenders Holding and New Century Financials, is similar to the bursting of previous asset bubbles. A number of in-depth studies have been produced since that time[3]. The following sketch highlights how particular rules for economic activity took root and addresses the deeper question, raised by Eichengreen (2008), which is 'how this belief in the efficacy of self-regulation was allowed to develop?'

Over the last 30 years there has been an explosion in the availability of credit for home-owner and entrepreneurs in the United States. This burst has been fueled by innovation in the financial sector and in particular by the advent of securitization. Following Fabozzi and Kothari (2007), we now briefly sketch the process. We identify as the *originator* a bank, or any financial intermediary, with a portfolio of assets on its balance sheet. These assets represent loans to home-owner and entrepreneurs who make regular installment payments (receivables) to the originator to clear their debts. A pool of these assets are selected and transferred to a *special purpose entity* (SPE), who pays for them by issuing securities. These securities are rated by credit agencies and bought by investors, who are paid back by the SPE from the stream of receivables. Investors are allowed to trade these asset-backed securities (ABS) with others.

Securitization gained popularity amongst banks as it allowed them to diversify their risks to a host of investors by the issuance of ABS via the SPE. As a result, banks were able to remove assets from their balance sheet. This, in turn, meant that their capital requirements – money that must be set aside to cover potential losses – were lower, thereby shoring up their liquidity and investment capabilities.

The growth of the ABS issuance has been nothing short of meteoric. As noted by Adrian and Shin (2009) in the second quarter of 2007, the total assets held by issuers of ABS in the United States – which the authors collectively refer to as the *shadow banking system* – were approximately 16 trillion dollars and substantially larger than those held by banks, which totaled approximately 12 trillion dollars. The growth rate of assets for ABS brokers, especially since the mid 1980s, has far exceeded those of commercial banks to the point that the vast majority of home-owner mortgages are held within the shadow banking system. As more and more prime-rated home-owner took on mortgages, the banks, being awash with liquidity, were more willing to underwrite mortgages for home-owners rated sub-prime. Paradoxically, as further discussed by Adrian and Shin (2009), many of the purchasers of the securities turned out to be the banks themselves.

We identify some of the factors that contributed to this exponential growth as follows:

- Investors adopted a decision rule whereby investments were made solely on the basis of publicly available signals and without performing independent credit analysis. Partly this was due to over-reliance on the information provided by rating agencies.[4,5,6]
- The market for ABS – and mortgage-based securities (MBS), in particular – was generally perceived to be liquid[7]. Hence buying MBS became acceptable, under the assumption that others considered MBS to be liquid (and hence tradable). This in turn reinforced the assumption that MBS were liquid. Therefore, as more and more investors adopted this rule i.e. trading in ABS without conducting independent credit analysis, it became profitable for others to follow suit and adopt the same rule in turn.
- A similar failure in information gathering also characterized the sub-prime mortgage market (see Rajan, Seru, and Vig 2010). The increased distance between risk origination (the sub-prime borrowers) and risk bearers (investors holding the ABS) induced intermediaries to grant sub-prime loans without appropriate due diligence concerning the reliability of borrowers. In other words, the network linking lenders and borrowers grew and evolved to increase opacity in the system. Despite the increased connectivity and density, information did not flow.

These conditions coupled with the spread of such seemingly rational rules amongst investors, led to a failure of markets to aggregate signals and reveal information on the fundamental value of assets. As a result, investors, seemingly blindly, bought into the ABS market and unwittingly assumed far greater risks.

Indeed, the dire consequences of these developments were made painfully apparent when the sub-prime mortgage bubble burst and a financial crisis developed. From 2004 to 2006, the Federal Reserve systematically raised interest rates to cool the markets. However, as indicated by the Case Shiller index, housing prices continued raising until the end of 2005 and then started to fall. The combined effect of higher interest rates and falling house prices culminated in the sharp rise in home owner defaults in 2006. In this situation, it became more difficult to re-sell the property to recoup the original value This, in turn meant that the price of all the securities diminished since it was not clear which were 'toxic'. As the prices of securities plummeted, investors started losing trust in the future profitability of the issuers of securities and chose instead to horde their liquidity. This resulted in a freeze of the credit and credit derivatives markets, thereby causing a large increase in ABS spreads.

This story of asymmetric information and herding of investors is endemic to all previous asset-pricing and credit bubbles, including the 1920s telecommunication, as recounted by Eichengreen and Mitchener (2003), and the 1990s dot-com boom and the subsequent burst. In the most recent crisis, it has become clear that the problem was exacerbated by the collective 'decision' not to gather information.

3. The model

Our goal is to model the general mechanism whereby investors, as a rule, trade securities without giving due diligence to fundamental information. The rationale motivating investors is simply that it is profitable to adopt this rule, because other investors have already adopted it.

The system consists of $i = 1, \ldots, N$ agents, who, in the case of the sub-prime crisis, we can think of as the banks who were both the issuers – via SPEs – and the investors in these ABS. Each agent i is characterized by a variable $z_i \in \{0, 1\}$ which specifies whether she follows ($z_i = 1$) or not ($z_i = 0$) the following behavior, or *rule* for short:

> purchase an ABS, relying on signals from the rating agencies, *without* independently evaluating the fundamental value of underlying assets,

$$z_i = \begin{cases} 1 & \texttt{if agent follows the rule,} \\ 0 & \texttt{if agent performs independent risk analysis.} \end{cases} \quad (1)$$

The rationale for adopting the rule, as we will see, is not based on the fundamental quality of the asset but rather on the fact that others also follow the rule. If, in fact, enough other participants do so, the agent becomes convinced, not irrationally that the ABS is highly liquid and hence easy to trade.

Let us assume that the ABS is *toxic* with probability p. By toxic we mean, for example, that the underlying asset was incorrectly graded and that the original borrower of loan has already defaulted or has a higher probability of defaulting. The cost of purchasing a security is $c < 1$ whereas the payoff from successfully re-selling the security is normalized to unity[8]. Denoting $\chi_i > 0$ to be the cost of due diligence and checking whether the underlying asset is toxic for agent i, we have the following payoff table.

	check and toxic	no check
$z_i = 1$	$-c$	$1 - c$
$z_i = 0$	$-\chi_i$	$1 - c - \chi_i$

(2)

Agents are linked together with trading partners in a financial network. Let N_i be the set of neighbors[9] of agent i and $k_i = |N_i|$ its cardinality. This captures the fact that the market for trading ABS and other credit derivatives is not centralized but instead takes place over-the-counter with traders in one firm directly calling up other traders to sell their securities (see Sabarwal 2006). The limit where N_i coincides with the set of all agents corresponds to the case of a centralized market.

When agent i receives an offer to buy new ABS, she considers whether or not to follow the rule. The line of reasoning she pursues is to first determine the probability that, if she adopts the rule and subsequently attempts to re-sell the security, the potential buyer, agent j in N_i will refuse to buy the security. This will be because agent j does not follow the rule and, as such, may verify that the underlying asset is toxic and, hence, not liquid. In this event, agent i will incur a loss of c

with probability $p(1-z_j)$. The expected payoff to i from following the rule, i.e. $z_i = 1$, is

$$\begin{aligned} u_i(z_i = 1) &= E[-p(1-z_j)c + [1 - p(1-z_j)](1-c)] \\ &= 1 - p(1-\bar{z}_i) - c, \end{aligned} \tag{3}$$

where $\bar{z}_i = \mathbb{E}[z_j]$ is the expected value of z_j for $j \in N_i$. We assume that the probability p that assets are toxic is known to agents[10]. When agent i buys the asset, she does not know *ex ante* to whom she will sell the security nor which neighbors follow the rule. In other words, agent i cannot observe the type z_j of her neighbors, but can instead estimate the probability $\bar{z}_i$ that a buyer in her neighborhood follows the rule. For simplicity, we take

$$\bar{z}_i = \frac{1}{k_i} \sum_{j \in N_i} z_j.$$

The expected payoff to agent i from not following the rule is $u_i(z_i = 0) = (1-p)(1-c) - \chi_i$. Here, $\chi_i > 0$ is the cost of gathering information. The rationale here is that, if agent i determines the asset to be toxic, she will only incur the cost of performing the risk analysis. If the asset turns out not to be toxic, with probability $1-p$, she will be able to easily re-sell the security and hence the payoff is $1 - c - \chi_i$.

In sum, the best response of agent i, when she gets the opportunity of buying a new ABS is[11]

$$\begin{aligned} z_i^* &= \Theta[u_i(1) - u_i(0)] \\ &= \Theta\left[p\left(\frac{1}{k_i}\sum_{j \in N_i} z_j - c\right) + \chi_i\right]. \end{aligned} \tag{4}$$

We model the dynamics, starting from any given set of initial conditions for z_i as follows. At each time t, we randomly select agents i and j whereby i receives an offer to buy an ABS from j. Agent i updates her value of z_i as the best response $z_i = z_i^*$. This dynamics goes on until the population reaches a fixed point.

In order to address the stochastic stability of fixed points, it is useful to generalize the dynamics introducing a probabilistic choice model. A standard way of introducing such stochastic trembles[12] consists in replacing Equation (4), in the dynamics, by a probabilistic choice of the logit type:

$$P\{z_i = 1\} = \frac{e^{Bu_i(z_i=1)}}{e^{Bu_i(z_i=0)} + e^{Bu_i(z_i=1)}}. \tag{5}$$

The parameter B modulates the randomness in the choice and is often referred to as intensity of choice. In the limit $B \to \infty$ the choice model Equation (5) reduces to Equation (4).

Numerical simulations based on the dynamics with both Equations (4) and (5), are presented in Figure 1. The state where everybody follows the rule ($z_i = 1,\ \forall i$) is a fixed point of the $B \to \infty$ dynamics for all values of p. Indeed, when everybody follows the rule, no trade is ever refused, independently of the quality of the assets, precisely because no-one checks. For large values of $p > p_c$, however, this fixed point coexists with one where most of the agents perform their independent credit analysis ($z_i = 0$).

Figure 1 also shows, however, that the rule-dominated equilibrium loses stability for high p, if the intensity of choice parameter B is not large. For intermediate values of B, as p increases, one has a sharp transition from the state where the vast majority follows the rule, to a situation where most of the agents do not follow it.

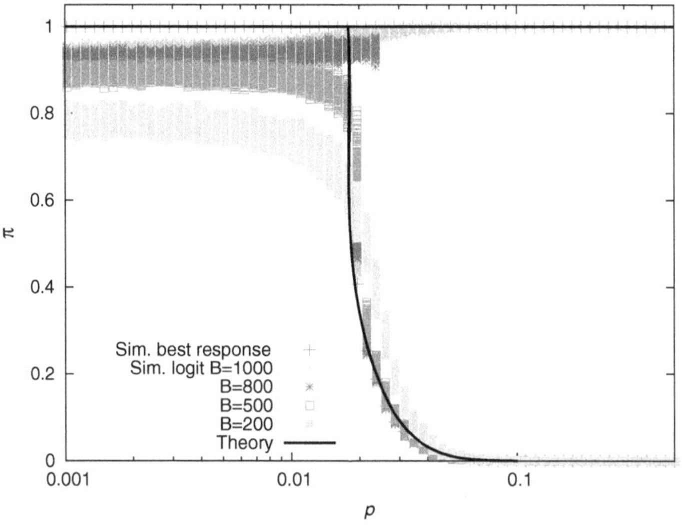

Figure 1. Prevalence $\bar{\pi} = E[z]$ of rule followers, as a function of p, for $c = 0.9$ and $k = 11$ and an exponential distribution for χ_i with mean $\lambda = 0.01$. The results of numerical simulations (best response) are compared with the theory (full line). Results for noisy best response $P\{z_i = 1\} = e^{Bu_i(1)}/(e^{Bu_i(1)} + e^{Bu_i(0)})$, with $B = 200, 500, 800$ and 1000 are also shown.

In order to see how this model leads to herding, imagine starting from a market in which there are only fundamentalists, i.e. no one follows the rule ($z_i = 0\ \forall i$). Those agents with cost $\chi_i > p_c$ will find it profitable to adopt the rule. A large cost may be understood as the securities being very complex, for example, after multiple repackaging. This, in turn, will make it appear to be profitable for some of their neighbors to also follow the rule and similarly for the neighbors of these neighbors. If the rule spreads to the extent that $\bar{z} > c$ all agents, even those for whom information is available for free, will follow the rule, then no one will look for information.

3.1 *Mean-field analysis*

We may shed further light on the results of numerical simulations using a mean-field analysis for the theory. We limit our analysis to the case where $B \to \infty$. Furthermore, we consider, for the sake of simplicity, a network with homogenous degrees, i.e. $k_i = |N_i| = k$. Defining $\pi(\chi) = P\{z_i = 1|\chi_i = \chi\}$ to be the probability that agent i follows the rule, given a cost for information equal to χ, we have that

$$\pi(\chi) = \sum_{\ell > (c-\chi/p)k} \binom{k}{\ell} \bar{\pi}^{\ell}(1-\bar{\pi})^{k-\ell}. \tag{6}$$

The probability that a randomly chosen neighbor of agent i follows the rule is given by $\bar{\pi} = E_\chi[\pi(\chi)]$. In deriving Equation (6), we assume that the probability that each of i's neighbors decide to follow the rule is independent of others[13] Considering Equation (4), the probability that i adopts the rule is simply the probability that at least $(c - \chi/p)k$ other neighbors follow the same rule.

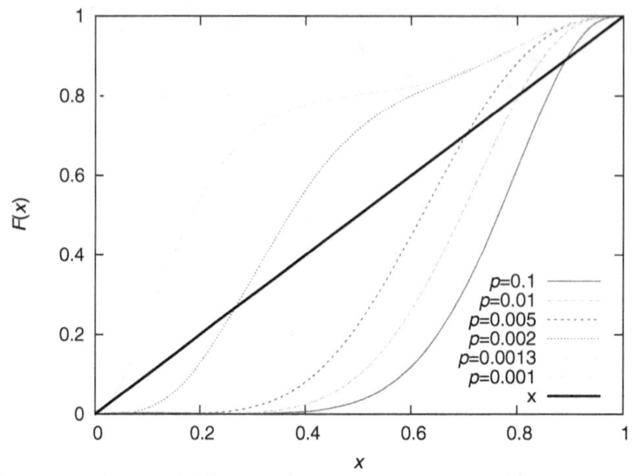

Figure 2. Function $F(\bar{\pi})$ on the right-hand side of Equation (7), as a function of $\bar{\pi}$, for different values of p (0.1, 0.01, 0.005, 0.002 and for 0.001). Here $\chi = \chi_0 = 0.01$ for 80% of the population, whereas the remaining minority has $\chi = 0$. $k = 11$ and $c = 0.8$. For this particular choice of the distribution of χ_i, the phase diagram is shown in Figure 3.

Taking the expectation of Equation (6) over costs χ one gets the following self-consistent equation for $\bar{\pi}$.

$$\bar{\pi} = F(\bar{\pi}) = \mathbb{E}_\chi \left[\underbrace{\sum_{\ell > (c-\chi/p)k} \binom{k}{\ell} \bar{\pi}^\ell (1-\bar{\pi})^{k-\ell}}_{p_\ell} \right]$$

$$= \sum_{\ell=0}^{k} \binom{k}{\ell} \bar{\pi}^\ell (1-\bar{\pi})^{k-\ell} P\left\{ \chi > p\left(\frac{c-\ell}{k}\right) \right\}. \tag{7}$$

The solution of these equations are shown in Figure 2 for different values of p, where for small p, the solution $\bar{\pi} = 1$ is the only fixed point. For $p > p_c$ the fixed point $\bar{\pi} = 0$ appears, with a basin of attraction (the interval in $\bar{\pi}$ where $F(\bar{\pi}) < \bar{\pi}$) that grows with p. However, noting that since $F(\bar{\pi} = 1) = 1$, the fixed point $\bar{\pi} = 1$ is, in fact, always a solution.

The mean-field solution accurately matches the results of numerical simulations, as shown in Figure 1, where the costs χ_i were drawn from an exponential distribution. For this choice of distribution, we may simplify our results further. In the limit $k \gg 1$, by the de Moivre–Laplace theorem, the binomial distribution in Equation (7) becomes sharply peaked around the mean, so that we can replace $\ell/k \simeq \bar{\pi}$ in it, which yields

$$\bar{\pi} \cong P\{\chi > p(c-\bar{\pi})\} = \min\{1, e^{\lambda p(c-\bar{\pi})}\}, \tag{8}$$

where the second equality holds for an exponential distribution of costs χ_i, with a mean value equal to $1/\lambda$. The solution with $\bar{\pi} < 1$ exists for large p and it ceases to exist when $F'(\bar{\pi}) = 1$. The latter equation, combined with $\bar{\pi} = F(\bar{\pi})$, implies that the boundary of the coexistence region is given by the equation

$$\lambda p = e^{\lambda pc-1} \tag{9}$$

and, more precisely, by the largest root (in p) of this equation. This is shown in Figure 3.

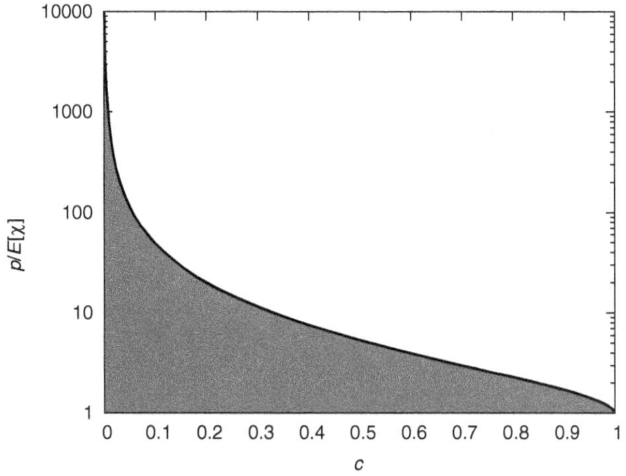

Figure 3. Phase diagram in the $(c, p/E[\chi])$ plane for a model with an exponential distribution for χ.

4. Discussion

It has been forcefully argued by Shiller (2008) and others that, by 2007 considerable evidence as to the bad credit quality of sub-prime-based ABS had been steadily accumulating. In addition, falling prices in the housing market, made it more difficult to recover the investment in defaulted loans. These two processes, in our stylized model, correspond to increasing the probability p that the underlying asset is toxic and increasing the cost c of the security, respectively. In both cases, one expects a sharp transition, for intermediate values of the intensity of choice B, from the state where the vast majority trades without gathering information on the underlying assets, to a situation where most of the agents actually perform independent credit analysis (see Figure 3).

It can be argued that default probabilities were grossly under-estimated by rating agencies. This was partly due to misaligned incentives arising from the fact that rating agencies were paid by the very issuers of the securities they were rating. This would suggest, within the naïve picture of the crisis provided by our model, that investors were basing their choice of whether to adopt the rule or not on the basis of a hypothetical value of p which was lower than the real one. Eventually, however, the disclosure of information on defaults of sub-primes and revelation of losses in financial institutions percolated through the market, which quickly realigned investors' beliefs (i.e. p). This suggests that during the crisis, the increase in the perceived probability p of toxicity was sharp rather than gradual.

A further element worth mentioning again, relates to the cost of information. With the introduction of more and more innovations in financial engineering of securitization, financial products became more and more complex. The cost of assessing the quality of credit derivatives has, in consequence, been increasing in the last decade. This made it even more profitable to follow the rule of trading without conducting credit analysis as opposed to undertaking the latter[14]. Lastly, this raises the possibility of the emergence of a third strategy, which is simply not to participate in the market at all, if the cost of finding information is high and the value of underlying assets whether toxic or not is falling, then traders may simply wish to become inactive. This would account for the 'freezing' of the market for these assets. Nevertheless, there is still hope for the prospects of remedial regulation with the introduction of appropriate Pigovian taxes, as outlined by Morris and Shin (2008).

Finally, the argument of this paper can be summarized as saying that the following of simple but not irrational rules by market participants can lead a market to a fragile state in which the very justification of the rules is undermined. Small changes in the macroeconomic environment coupled with the contagious spread of behavioral rules can gradually but almost imperceptibly undermine the system. Unfortunately, the result of these gradual changes can be catastrophic at the aggregate level.

Acknowledgements

In terms of financial support, I would like to acknowledge the support of the Deutsche Forschungsgemeinschaft through the Collaborative Research Center (Sonderforschungsbereich) SFB 649 on 'Economic Risks'.

Notes

1. Economists are familiar with the idea of a system which evolves along a surface and then may, as a result of a continuous change in variables, slide suddenly on to a different surface. The applications of catastrophe theory and later chaos theory to economics are illustrative of this (see Rosser 2000).
2. See, for example, Dridi, Guaya, and Renault (2007) and Hall et al. (2009).
3. See, for example, Ashcraft and Schuermann (2008), Dell'Ariccia, Igan, and Laeven (2008), Acharya and Richardson (2009), Adrian and Shin (2009), Hume and Sentance (2009) and Smaghi (2010).
4. The role of credit agencies in facilitating the smooth operation of financial markets may be summarized as correcting the problem of asymmetric information, first analyzed explicitly, in the context of a used-car market by Akerlof (1970). The issuer of an ABS typically has more information than the buyer on the value of the underlying asset, and hence its price. The buyer is quoted a certain price and must determine whether this reflects the true value. Rating agencies, as independent third-party entities should, in principles, circumvent the conflict of interest between buyers and sellers by providing an impartial assessment of the asset. In practice, however, rating agencies are not paid for their services by the investors but instead by the issuers of these securities. Thus, contrary to the original concept, there is a direct conflict of interest which leads to a friction whereby investors are unable to determine whether the rating agencies are being honest or not. Indeed, similar questions as to the moral hazards for rating agencies were raised (see Cheung and Tam 2009) in the aftermath of the East-Asian crisis of 1997. A detailed analysis of the various effects related to asymmetric information and moral hazard is provided by Ashcraft and Schuermann (2008).
5. The Financial Stability Forum (2008) observed that '[...] some institutional investors have relied too heavily on ratings in their investment guidelines and choices, in some cases fully substituting ratings for independent risk assessment and due diligence.' As a reaction to this document, some organizations (such as the European Fund and Asset Management Association) laid out guidelines to avoid the over-reliance on ratings agencies.
6. In September 2009, the U.S. Securities and Exchange Commission (2009), voted to regulate rating agencies better. Concerning the proposed measures, the chairman of the Commission, Mary Schapiro, said, 'These proposals are needed because investors often consider ratings when evaluating whether to purchase or sell a particular security. That reliance did not serve them well over the last several years.' See also Adrian and Shin (2009).
7. The Bond Market Association, an organization which does not exist any longer, issued an 'Investor's guide to mortgage-backed securities' in 2002, which explicitly declared that over-the-counter markets for MBS and credit-card-based securities were liquid markets. See also Sabarwal (2006).
8. A more detailed derivation of the payoffs is as follows. An agent buys a security at price p_0. If she re-packages and is able to sell it right away, i.e. the subsequent buyer follows the rule or she performs the risk analysis and verifies that the asset is not toxic, the security is sold for the price $p_1 > p_0$. In our set up, we do not allow for fire-sales or other events where the selling price of the security is less than the purchase price. Hence the payoff in this case is $1 - c = p_1 - p_0$. If, however, she does not sell, she will nevertheless receive future coupon payments from the issuer of the security. However, discounting for degradations in the assets' rating and also time, the effective price of the security held by the agent is $p_2 < p_0$ and hence the payoff is $-c = p_2 - p_0$. If one takes $p_1 = 1 + p_2$ and $p_0 = p_2 + c$ this is the model in the main text. This choice has the advantage of reducing the number of parameters by one.
9. The network may be directed as the set of traders agent i buys from need not be the same set to whom she sells securities.
10. The case where agents rely on over-optimistic estimates of default probabilities, such as those issued by rating agencies, can be dealt with easily. The final section comments briefly on this issue.

11. $\Theta(x) = 1$ for $x > 0$ and $\Theta(x) = 0$ otherwise.
12. This model has been also proposed in order to capture the trade-off between exploration of new rules and exploitation by Weisbuch et al. (1998).
13. This is appropriate if the network has a locally tree-like structure. This is the case, e.g. on random graphs with homogeneous degree, where loops are typically of length $\log N$. If statistical dependence decays with distance, different neighbors of the same agent can be considered as independent.
14. The particular case discussed in Equation (9) makes this point clear. Indeed, if the average cost $1/\lambda$ of information increases, the phase transition line moves upwards.

References

Acharya, V.V., and M.P. Richardson. 2009. Causes of the financial crisis. *Critical Review* 21, nos. 2–3: 195–210.

Adrian, T., and H.S. Shin. 2009. The shadow banking system: Implications for financial regulation. *Banque de France Financial Stability Review*, no. 13: 1–10.

Akerlof, G. 1970. The market for 'lemons'. *Quarterly Journal of Economics* 84, no. 3: 488–500.

Ashcraft, A.B., and T. Schuermann. 2008. Understanding the securitization of subprime mortgage credit. Federal Reserve Bank of New York Staff Report No. 318.

Cheung, L., and C.-S. Tam. 2009. Role of credit in equity market booms and bust. Hong Kong Monetary Authority working paper no. 04/2009.

Cooper, R.W. 1999. *Coordination games: complementarities and macroeconomics.* New York: Cambridge University Press.

Dell'Ariccia, G., D. Igan, and L. Laeven. 2008. The US subprime mortgage crisis: A credit boom gone bad? www.voxeu.org/index.php?q=node/905.

Dridi, R., A. Guaya, and E. Renault. 2007. Indirect inference and calibration of dynamic stochastic general equilibrium models. *Journal of Econometrics* 136, no. 2: 397–430.

Eichengreen, B. 2008. Origins and responses to the current crisis. *CESifo Forum* 2008, no. 4: 6–11.

Eichengreen, B. and K. Mitchener. 2003. The great depression as a credit boom gone wrong. Bank for International Settlements working paper no. 137.

Fabozzi, F.J., and V. Kothari. 2007. Securitization: The tool of financial transformation. Yale School of Management International Center for Finance working paper no. 07-07.

Hall, A., A. Inoue, J.M. Nason, and B. Rossi. 2009. Information criteria for impulse response function matching estimation of dsge models. Economic Research Initiatives at Duke, working paper no. 29.

Hume, M., and A. Sentance. 2009. The global credit boom: Challenges for macroeconomics and policy. *Journal of International Money and Finance* 28, no. 8: 1426–61.

Financial Stability Forum. 2008. *Report of the financial stability forum on enhancing market and institutional resilience.* Technical Report, Financial Stability Board.

U.S. Securities and Exchange Commission. 2009. Sec votes on measures to further strengthen oversight of credit rating agencies. http://www.sec.gov/news/press/2009/2009-200.html.

Morris, S., and H.S. Shin. 2000. Rethinking multiple equilibria in macroeconomic modeling. In *NBER Macroeconomics Annual*, ed. B.S. Bernanke and K. Rogoff, 139–82. Boston: MIT Press.

Morris, S., and H.S. Shin. 2008. *Financial regulation in a system context*, Brookings Papers on Economic Activity, 229–74. Washington, DC: Brookings Institute Press.

Rajan, U., A. Seru, and V. Vig. 2010. The failure of models that predict failure: Distance, incentives and defaults. Chicago GSB research paper no. 08-19.

Rosser, J.B. 2000. *From catastrophe to chaos: A general theory of economic discontinuities.* Dordrecht: Kluwer Academic Publishers.

Sabarwal, T. 2006. Common structures of asset-backed securities and their risks. *Corporate Ownership and Control* 4, no. 1: 258–65.

Shiller, R.J. 2008. *The subprime solution: How today's global financial crisis happened, and what to do about it.* Princeton, NJ: Princeton University Press.

Smaghi, L.B. 2010. From boom to bust: Towards a new equilibrium in bank credit. http://www.ecb.int/press/key/date/2010/html/sp100129.en.html.

Weisbuch, G., O. Chenevez, A. Kirman, and J.-P. Nadal. 1998. A formal approach to market organization: Choice functions, mean field approximation and maximum entropy principle. In *Advances in Self-Organization and Evolutionary Economics*, ed. J. Lesourne and A. Orlean, 149–59. London: Economica.

A note on institutional hierarchy and volatility in financial markets

S. Alfarano, M. Milaković and M. Raddant

From a statistical point of view, the prevalence of non-Gaussian distributions in financial returns and their volatilities shows that the Central Limit Theorem (CLT) often does not apply in financial markets. In this article, we take the position that the independence assumption of the CLT is violated by herding tendencies among market participants, and investigate whether a generic probabilistic herding model can reproduce non-Gaussian statistics in systems with a large number of agents. It is well known that the presence of a herding mechanism in the model is not sufficient for non-Gaussian properties, which crucially depend on the details of the communication network among agents. The main contribution of this article is to show that certain hierarchical networks, which portray the institutional structure of fund investment, warrant non-Gaussian properties for any system size and even lead to an increase in system-wide volatility. Viewed from this perspective, the mere existence of financial institutions with socially interacting managers contributes considerably to financial volatility.

1. Introduction

Financial time series exhibit ubiquitous non-Gaussian statistical regularities across different countries, assets, and time frequencies. The two most prominent features concern the fluctuations in the prices of financial assets, which exhibit heavy tails and clustered volatility (see e.g. Pagan 1996; Cont 2001). From a statistical point of view, the prevalence of non-Gaussian distributions in returns and their volatilities testifies to the importance of long-range correlations, which ultimately prevent the application of the Central Limit Theorem (CLT). Traditional finance has paid little, if any, attention to the origins of these statistical regularities and to the possibly most challenging question implied by the violation of the CLT: how does a complex system like the financial market actually allow for a large-scale coordination of the trading positions among millions of agents? The established literature on informational cascades (see Banerjee 1992; Bikhchandani, Hirshleifer and Welch 1992; Chamley 2004) does not address this question because it considers a static, sequential Bayesian updating approach with a constant 'true' state of the world and lacks any connection to the stylized facts of financial returns. The three major strands of the agent-based finance literature, on the other hand, argue in unison that it is precisely the perpetually alternating coordination of trading strategies over time that is responsible for the stylized facts of financial returns. Yet each of the approaches has to deal with its own set of problems.

Percolation models of herd behavior exploit the properties of well-known critical systems from the statistical physics literature (see e.g. Stauffer and Sornette 1999; Cont and Bouchaud 2000; Bornholdt 2001; Iori 2002) but rely on carefully adjusted model parameters near criticality to produce non-Gaussian statistics, entirely leaving open how or why a financial market composed of millions of agents could self-organize into (and remain in) such a critical state. The second strand of models follows the seminal work of Brock and Hommes (1997) where agents interact globally rather than locally, namely through the price system and public information about the performance of strategies that are subject to noise (e.g. Hommes 2006; Chang 2007). The drawback of this class of models is that they need a careful fine-tuning of their 'signal-to-noise ratio' around unity in order to resemble the stylized facts. Finally the third strand, and starting point of this article, is inspired by entomological experiments concerning the foraging behavior of ant that Kirman (1991, 1993) utilized to propose a stochastic herding model of opinion formation among financial investors. These models endogenously create swings and herding behavior in aggregate expectations through *social agent interaction*, while the stationary distribution of the stochastic process of opinion formation describes the *statistical equilibrium* of the model.

The 'ant model' has been reasonably successful in replicating the statistical features of financial returns, but Alfarano, Lux and Wagner (2008) have shown analytically that Kirman's original model suffers from the problem of *self-averaging* or *N-dependence*:[1] the model's ability to replicate the stylized facts vanishes for a given parametrization when the system size N increases, a quite common feature in agent-based models that has received relatively minor attention so far (see Egenter, Lux and Stauffer 1999; Lux and Schornstein 2005; Aoki 2008). Alfarano and Milaković (2009) establish a direct link between N-(in)dependence and the communication network among agents in a generalized version of Kirman's original model. They show that the model is immune to self-averaging if the relative communication range of agents remains unchanged under an enlargement of system size. Interestingly and rather counter-intuitively, other network features like the functional form of the degree distribution, the average clustering coefficient, the graph diameter, or the extent of assortative mixing have no impact on the N-dependence property. Put differently, the average number of neighbors per agent has to increase linearly with the total number of agents N in order to overcome the problem of self-averaging in the generic herding model. Among prototypical network structures such as regular lattices, small-world, or scale-free networks (see, e.g. Newman 2003), it is only the random graph with constant linking probability that exhibits this feature, yet random graphs are hardly ever a realistic representation of socio-economic communication networks.

After all, the results of Alfarano, Lux and Wagner (2008) and Alfarano and Milaković (2009) establish the model's behavior when the number of agents tends to infinity, at the same time illustrating that simple proto-typical network structures (with the exception of the empirically unsatisfactory random graph) cannot overcome the problem of N-dependence. This article builds on these insights and investigates whether a certain class of core-periphery networks might be capable of overcoming the self-averaging property of the original model. Here, we consider a central network with bi-directional links between *core agents* or *opinion leaders* on one hand, and a relatively large number of unidirectionally linked *followers* in the periphery on the other. We vary the number of followers per core agent by randomly drawing from various distributions, and study the aggregate behavior of system-wide opinion dynamics under an increasing dispersion in the number of followers. In essence, the hierarchical network corresponds to a weighted version of the original model. As we argue below, the weighted version is a reasonable first approximation of the institutional structure of financial fund investment. The central idea is that many investors effectively transfer control over investment decisions to fund managers who in turn are socially interacting, with the opinions of some fund managers carrying greater weight than others, for instance, because they manage larger funds or have performed more successfully in the past. It turns out that the analytical mean-field prediction used in Alfarano and Milaković (2009) now significantly underestimates the volatility in system-wide opinion dynamics. The key implication of this result is that behavioral heterogeneity among interacting agents is not, as previously thought, the exclusive source of endogenously arising volatility in agent-based herding models, but that the hierarchical structure of fund investment is an important auxiliary source of financial volatility.

We take the position that investing in the presence of (actively managed) financial funds basically corresponds to the hierarchical core-periphery networks we study here. Investors who are not wealthy enough to afford a broadly diversified portfolio of assets, those who participate in retirement plans, or those who simply feel that they lack the skills or time to make investment decisions often invest in some type or the other of managed fund. Effectively such agents, who correspond to followers in the periphery of the network, transfer their wealth to the fund managers in the core, and ultimately allow those to make decisions for them. If fund managers socially interact with their peers, and empirical evidence by Hong, Kubik and Stein (2005) and Wermers (1999) strongly suggests that this is indeed the case, we arrive at the core–periphery networks that we study in this paper.

Essentially, core-periphery networks will lead to an increase of system-wide volatility because fluctuations in a disproportionately small but central part of the network are amplified on a system-wide level. Therefore, it seems rather ironic that investors who want to 'play it safe' by investing in a variety of managed funds will actually end up increasing system-wide volatility if they delegate investment decisions to herding-prone fund managers.

2. Generic herding model

In a prototypical interaction-based herding model of the Kirman type, the agent population of size N is divided into two groups, say, X and Y of sizes n and $N-n$, respectively. The time evolution of the group sizes is modeled as a Markov chain, characterized by a pair of transition rates that are sometimes also referred to as birth and death rates. Depending on the particular financial market framework, the two groups are typically labeled as fundamentalists and chartists, or optimists and pessimists, or buyers and sellers. The basic idea is that agents change state for personal reasons or under the influence of the *neighbors* with whom they socially interact during a given time period. The transition rate for an agent i to switch from state X to state Y in the Markov chain is

$$\omega_i^- \equiv \rho_i(X \to Y) = a_i + \lambda_i \sum_{j \neq i} D_Y(i,j), \tag{1}$$

where a_i governs the possibility of self-conversion due to idiosyncratic factors, e.g. the arrival of new information, while λ_i governs the interaction strength between i and its neighbors. The function $D_Y(i,j)$ is an indicator function serving to count the number of i's neighbors that are in state Y,

$$D_Y(i,j) = \begin{cases} 1 & \text{if } j \text{ is a Y-neighbor of } i, \\ 0 & \text{otherwise,} \end{cases} \tag{2}$$

hence the sum captures the (equally weighted) influence of the neighbors on agent i. Symmetrically, the transition rates in the opposite direction are given by

$$\omega_i^+ \equiv \rho_i(Y \to X) = a_i + \lambda_i \sum_{j \neq i} D_X(i,j). \tag{3}$$

Let $a = \sum_i a_i/N$ and $\lambda = \sum_i \lambda_i/N$ denote the averages of the behavioral parameters over agents, and let D denote the average number of neighbors per agent. If all links are bi-directional, $\lambda_i > 0 \, \forall i \in \{1, \ldots, N\}$, a mean-field argument (see Alfarano and Milaković 2009) shows that the transition rates for a single switch on the aggregated system-wide level are

$$\omega^- = n\left(a + \frac{\lambda D}{N}(N-n)\right), \tag{4}$$

for a switch from X to Y, and symmetrically

$$\omega^+ = (N-n)\left(a + \frac{\lambda D}{N}n\right), \tag{5}$$

for the reverse switch. An important result of the mean-field approach is that the *relative communication range* D/N ultimately determines whether the Markov chain is self-averaging or not. In the jargon of Alfarano, Lux, and Wagner (2008), the non-self-averaging case corresponds to 'non-extensive' transition rates with a constant relative communication range, while the 'extensive' transition rates, as in Kirman's original model, lead to self-averaging and hence to counter-factual statistics of returns.[2] Note that non-extensive transition rates depend on the respective *occupation numbers* n and $N - n$, while extensive transition rates depend on the *concentrations* n/N and $(N - n)/N$ of agents in the opposite state, and therefore on the average communication range per time period in the network. This apparently minor modification has a crucial impact on the aggregate properties of the herding model, as illustrated in Figure 1. Hence, in contrast to Kirman's original model, the generalized transition rates (4) and (5) illustrate that network structure matters because the average number of neighbors explicitly enters the transition rates.

At any time, the *state of the system* refers to the concentration of agents in one of the two states, say, $z = n/N$, which can be treated as a continuous variable for large N. None of the possible states of $z \in [0, 1]$ is an equilibrium in itself nor are there multiple equilibria in the orthodox economic sense. Equilibrium rather refers to the stationary distribution of the birth and death processes (4) and (5). The distribution, that is the statistical equilibrium, describes the proportion of time the system spends in state z and is known to be a Beta distribution (see, e.g. Alfarano, Lux, and Wagner 2008; Alfarano and Milaković 2009, for a detailed derivation of the following results)

$$p_e(z) = \frac{1}{B(\epsilon,\epsilon)} z^{\epsilon-1}(1-z)^{\epsilon-1}, \tag{6}$$

where $B(\epsilon, \epsilon) = \Gamma(\epsilon)^2/\Gamma(2\epsilon)$ is Euler's Beta function. The qualitative behavior of the process is parsimoniously encoded in the adimensional shape parameter ϵ of the distribution

$$\epsilon = \frac{aN}{\lambda D}. \tag{7}$$

When $\epsilon < 1$, the distribution is bimodal with probability mass having maxima at $z = 0$ and $z = 1$. For $\epsilon > 1$, the distribution is unimodal, and in the 'knife-edge' scenario $\epsilon = 1$ the distribution is

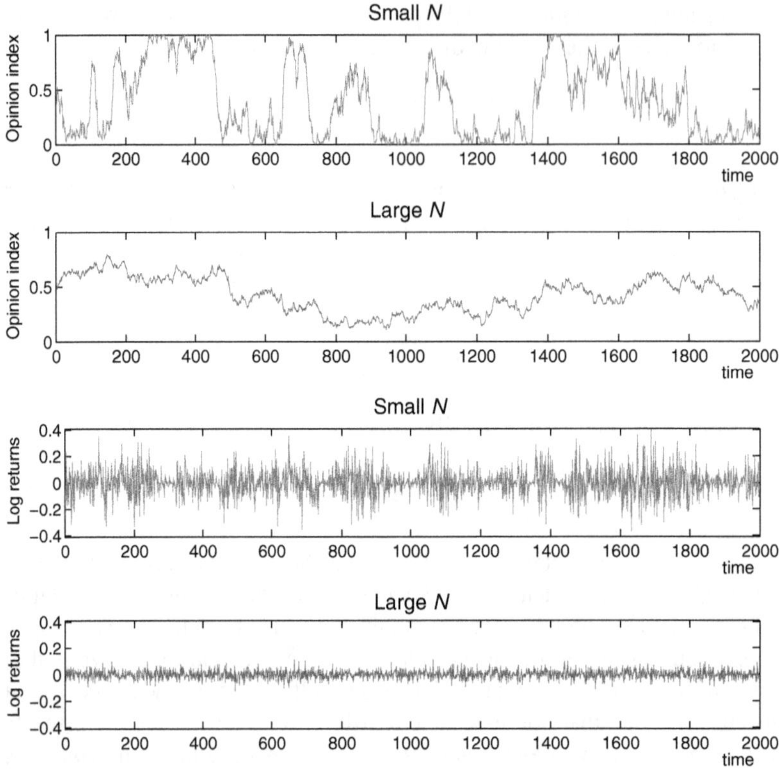

Figure 1. The two panels on the top illustrate the time evolution of aggregate opinion dynamics measured as the fraction of agents in one of the two states, say, $z = n/N$ (top panel $N = 500, a = 0.5, \lambda = 1, D = N$; second panel $N = 10,000, a = 0.5, \lambda = 1, D = 500$). The two panels on the bottom exhibit the corresponding time series of returns generated from a Walrasian pricing function, as for instance in Equation (13) of Section 3 (with $\kappa = 1$), where the level of excess demand depends on z. The bottom panel illustrates that an enlargement of system size under extensive transition rates will lead to counter-factual Gaussian returns and absence of volatility clustering.

uniform. The mean $E[z] = \frac{1}{2}$ is independent of ϵ, but the system exhibits very different characteristics depending on the modality of the distribution. In the bimodal case, the system spends the least of its time around the mean, instead mostly exhibiting very pronounced herding in either of the extreme states, as illustrated in the top panel of Figure 1. Finally, the variance of z,

$$\text{Var}(z) = E(z^2) - E(z)^2 = \frac{1}{4(2\epsilon + 1)} = \left[4\left(\frac{2aN}{\lambda D} + 1\right)\right]^{-1}, \tag{8}$$

is known to be a convenient summary measure of the model properties with respect to an enlargement of system size. If the variance of z remains constant (or even increases) when the system is enlarged, the leptokurtosis and volatility clustering of returns will be preserved in a standard Walrasian model of market clearing. A decreasing variance under enlargement of system size, on the other hand, is characteristic of self-averaging and thus leads to counter-factual Gaussian properties of returns, as shown in the bottom panel of Figure 1 and explained in more detail in the following section.

3. Financial market framework

For the sake of completeness, we briefly discuss how the Markov chain of the previous section would enter into a parsimonious model of an artificial financial market with interacting heterogeneous agents, where it is typically used as a metaphor of information diffusion among investors (see Kirman 1991, 1993; Alfarano, Lux and Wagner 2005; Alfarano and Lux 2007; Alfarano, Lux and Wagner 2008; Alfi et al. 2009; Irle et al. 2011, for more realistic or detailed implementations). Suppose that market participants are divided into two groups: the first group is populated by N_F *fundamentalists*, who buy (sell) assets when the price is below (above) its fundamental value P_F. Their excess demand for assets is given by $ED_F = N_F\gamma_F \log(P_F/P)$, where $\gamma_F > 0$ designates the sensitivity to deviations between the fundamental value and the market price P. Without loss of generality, the fundamental price is assumed to be constant over time. The second group is populated by N_{NT} *noise traders*, who are essentially driven by herd instincts in their investment strategies. Depending on their expectations of future price movements, noise traders can either be *optimists* (subscript O) or *pessimists* (subscript P). The excess demand of the noise trader group will be proportional to their aggregated state, $ED_{NT} = \gamma_{NT}(N_O - N_P)$, where N_O and N_P are the numbers of optimists and pessimists, respectively, with $N_{NT} = N_O + N_P$. The parameter $\gamma_{NT} > 0$ governs the impact of the noise traders' aggregate mood on the asset price. In line with the notation of the previous section, ED_{NT} can be parameterized as a function of $z = N_O/N_{NT}$ that is the fraction of optimists over the total number of noise traders

$$ED_{NT} = \gamma_{NT} \cdot N_{NT}(2z - 1). \tag{9}$$

While the share of fundamentalists and noise traders is constant over time (so there are no transitions between those two groups), switches from optimism to pessimism and vice versa do take place among the noise traders, and are governed by the Markov chain detailed in Section 2. Hence, noise traders change their opinions about the future prospects of an asset for idiosyncratic reasons or because of a tendency to follow the majority opinion of their peers.

Assuming sluggish price adjustments by a market maker in the presence of excess demand, one typically formalizes the price dynamics as

$$\frac{dP}{P \cdot dt} = \theta \cdot ED = \theta[ED_F + ED_{NT}], \tag{10}$$

where θ is the speed of price adjustment. As an approximation to the resulting disequilibrium dynamics, one may consider instantaneous market clearing ($\theta \to \infty$) or equivalently a Walrasian scenario ($ED = 0$) and solve Equation (10) for the equilibrium price

$$P = P_F \exp\left[\frac{N_{NT} \cdot \gamma_{NT}}{N_F \cdot \gamma_F}(2z - 1)\right] = P_F \exp[\kappa(2z - 1)], \tag{11}$$

where

$$\kappa = \frac{N_{NT} \cdot \gamma_{NT}}{N_F \cdot \gamma_F}. \tag{12}$$

Given a realization of the process z, we can see from Equation (11) that periods of undervaluation (compared with the fundamental price) will alternate with episodes of overvaluation. In the first case, the majority of noise traders are pessimists, while in the second case, most are optimists.

Finally, returns are typically defined as the log-increment of prices

$$r(t, \Delta t) = \log\left(\frac{P(t+\Delta t)}{P(t)}\right) = \kappa \Delta z, \tag{13}$$

and the third panel of Figure 1 shows the corresponding time series of log-returns for a 'small' number of traders ($N_{\mathrm{F}} = N_{\mathrm{NT}} = 500$), visually already indicating a leptokurtic return distribution and volatility clustering. In fact, Alfarano and Lux (2007) have shown that this very simple model quantitatively reproduces the stylized facts of financial returns with (i) a fat-tailed distribution of returns, (ii) an absence of auto-correlation in raw returns, and (iii) a slowly decaying positive auto-correlation in even functions of returns, i.e. volatility clustering. Increasing the number of agents, for instance, to $N_{\mathrm{F}} = N_{\mathrm{NT}} = 10,000$ (keeping $D = 500$) as shown in the bottom panel of Figure 1, turns the abrupt mood swings in z into much smoother paths and results in counter-factual Gaussian fluctuations of returns.

4. Network hierarchy and core weights

Essentially, we know that the relative communication range D/N in the transition rates (4) and (5) determines whether or not the model is self-averaging. Alfarano and Milaković consider prototypical networks with bi-directional links, in particular, regular lattices, random graphs, small-world networks of the Watts and Strogatz (1998) type, and the scale-free networks of Barabási and Albert (1999). Among these, it is only the random graph that exhibits a constant relative communication range since in that case $D = N\ell$, where ℓ designates the constant linking probability among agents in the random graph. On the other hand, D/N approaches zero for an increasing system size in the other network structures, unless one appropriately changes the respective parameters in the generating mechanisms of these networks.

From a socio-economic viewpoint, however, it is not at all clear how or why a complex system composed of many interacting agents could possibly coordinate an appropriate system-wide change in these parameters. The random graph is not a convincing mapping of socio-economic relationships either, because it implies that the average connectivity of agents increases linearly with system size.[3] Now suppose instead that N core agents are still bi-directionally linked among themselves, i.e. they still obey the Markov chain in Section 2. Additionally, each core agent has a constant number, W, of followers in the periphery, with unidirectional links emanating from the core to the periphery. Uni-directional linking implies that the state of peripheral followers corresponds to the state of the respective core agents. Then the total number of followers is $WN = F$, with a total of $F + N$ agents in the entire network. In this case, the system-wide concentration of agents in state X will be

$$z = \frac{Wn + n}{F + N} = \frac{n(W+1)}{N(W+1)} = \frac{n}{N}, \tag{14}$$

which just amounts to relabeling of variables. Put differently, in this special case, the system size $F + N$ can be expanded at will by simply adding followers F without encountering the self-averaging problem. Thus, we preserve system-wide fluctuations in a population of $F + N$ individuals, although only N socially interacting core agents are responsible for the fluctuations. At the same time, the hierarchical structure avoids the empirically unsatisfactory random graph structure in the entire population that would otherwise be necessary to preserve non-self-averaging fluctuations. The assumption of a constant number of followers per core agent, however, is quite artificial and unsatisfactory. Therefore, we want to investigate more general core-periphery structures by randomly drawing the number of followers per core agent from various distributions,

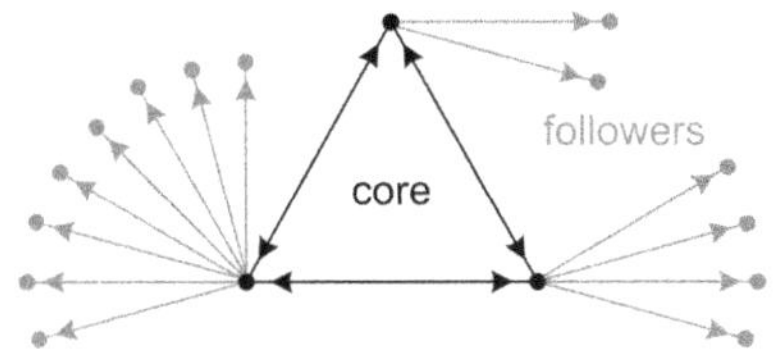

Figure 2. A stylized representation of a hierarchical core-periphery network, where core agents (black, bi-directional links) influence each other in their opinion formation, while peripheral followers (grey, unidirectional links) simply mimic their respective core agents. This basically corresponds to a weighted version of Kirman's original model.

keeping the total number of followers constant. We examine whether or how the dynamics of z change when the dispersion of followers increases. Note that the respective numbers of followers now act as *weights* in the opinion formation process of core agents, otherwise we recover the unweighted and already well-understood cases resulting in the large N limit of the generalized transition rates (4) and (5). Put differently, we would like to avoid the problem of self-averaging when enlarging the system, but without taking recourse to random graphs. Therefore, we turn to core–periphery networks as a stylized representation of the institutional structure of financial markets, and investigate whether these hierarchical networks overcome the problem of self-averaging when the core remains small relative to the periphery.

Figure 2 provides a stylized representation of the resulting core–periphery networks that reflect the organizational structure of managed fund investment. On one hand, peripheral agents who invest in managed funds effectively delegate all subsequent investment decisions to fund managers until they decide to withdraw their capital again. On the other hand, the fund managers in the core influence each other and are prone to herding effects, as in the empirical findings of Hong, Kubik and Stein (2005) or Wermers (1999). We can also interpret the number of followers per core agent as the size distribution of funds, thereby implicitly assuming that the influence of fund managers on each other's opinion is proportional to the size of the fund they are managing. While we are not aware of evidence that directly supports this assumption, the empirical size distribution of funds does in fact exhibit wide dispersion and leptokurtosis (see Gabaix et al. 2006; Schwarzkopf and Farmer 2008).

5. Simulation setup and results

It is important to recall that we can study the (non-)self-averaging property without actually increasing the number of agents in our subsequent simulations, because the addition of followers amounts to changing core agent *weights*. Note that adding core agents instead of followers would correspond to the scenario that Alfarano and Milaković (2009) already studied in detail, where the structure of the bi-directional (core) network determines whether the model is self-averaging or not in the large N limit. The introduction of weights, however, prevents a straightforward application of their mean-field technique: when the weights are widely dispersed, the average number of followers per core agent obviously no longer provides a good approximation. Therefore, we simulate the opinion dynamics in various core-periphery models, where we increase the dispersion of weights while drawing weights from different distributions, or altering the network structure in the core. We compare the resulting variance of z both to the mean-field prediction and to the variance in another limiting case that we have termed the *independent one-leader scenario* below.[4] After all, the variance of z is a useful summary measure of the different scenarios because we know that if it decreases relative to the mean-field benchmark, the weighted core-periphery networks will still suffer from the problem of self-averaging. If, on the other hand, the variance of z remains constant, the hierarchical model will be immune to self-averaging.

5.1 *Network-adapted transition rates*

To implement individual transition probabilities, in line with the transition rates (1) and (3), we first consider the (symmetric) adjacency matrix $E = e_{ij}$ for $i, j \in \{1, \ldots, N\}$ that keeps track of the links or *edges* between core agents, with $e_{ij} = 1$ if i and j are neighbors and $e_{ij} = 0$ otherwise.[5] The key element in the implementation of the transition rates is to determine for each agent i the number of neighbors that are in the opposite state, say n_i.

Let $\mathbf{e}(i)$ denote the ith column of the adjacency matrix E, which basically informs us of who is or is not an i-neighbor. While some of the neighbors will be in the same state as agent i, others will be in the opposite state, and these are the agents that we are interested in when implementing transition rates. To extract the i-neighbors that are in the opposite state, consider the projection matrix $S(i)$ of dimension $N \times N$ that keeps track of the i-neighbors that are in the opposite state: that is, for each i the off-diagonal elements of $S(i)$ are zero, $s_{ij} = 0$ if $i \neq j$, and obviously $s_{ii} = 0$ as well; on the diagonal of $S(i)$ we have $s_{jj} = 1$ if the state of neighbor j is opposite to that of agent i, and $s_{jj} = 0$ otherwise. Then the column vector $\mathbf{k}(i) = S(i)\mathbf{e}(i)$ expresses which i-neighbors are in the opposite state, and we finally have $n_i = \mathbf{k}^{\mathrm{T}}(i)\mathbf{k}(i)$.

Thus *in the absence of followers,* we would posit the transition probability $\tilde{\pi}_i = (a + \lambda n_i)\Delta t$ for switching states on the individual level. To ensure that $0 \leq \tilde{\pi}_i \leq 1\ \forall i$, we need $\Delta t \leq 1/(a + \lambda n_{\max})$, where $n_{\max}$ designates the number of neighbors of the node(s) with the highest degree in the network. Since an agent can be connected at most to all other agents, we utilize the transition probability

$$\tilde{\pi}_i = \frac{a + \lambda n_i}{a + \lambda N} \tag{15}$$

for individual switches, hence agent i's probability to remain in the current state is $0 \leq 1 - \tilde{\pi}_i \leq 1$.

In the presence of followers, we first need to make sure that our simulation results are comparable with the mean-field prediction arising from Equation (15), hence the individual transition probabilities need to be adapted to the core weights stemming from the hierarchical network setup. Let the column vector $\mathbf{w}$, with elements w_i, record the number of followers or weights for each core agent i, so $F = \sum_i w_i$ is the total number of followers in the network, and let $\langle f \rangle = F/N$ be the average number of followers per core agent. Now, we are interested in the weighted sum of core agents who are in the opposite state of an agent i, denoted f_i. Since $\mathbf{k}(i)$ describes the i-neighbors that are in the opposite state, the weighted sum of core agents in the opposite state is straightforwardly computed as $f_i = \mathbf{k}^{\mathrm{T}}(i)\mathbf{w} = \mathbf{e}^{\mathrm{T}}(i)S(i)\mathbf{w}$, and the probability Π_i to observe a change in the state of agent i in the weighted scenario is now given by

$$\pi_i = \frac{a + \lambda f_i/\langle f \rangle}{a + \lambda N}. \tag{16}$$

Note several points about the formulation of the herding term in the numerator of Equation (16). First, using the definition of $\langle f \rangle$, we can rewrite it as $f_i/\langle f \rangle = Nf_i/F$. Since $0 \leq f_i/F \leq 1$, we see that the denominator in Equation (16) ensures $0 \leq \pi_i \leq 1\ \forall i$. Put differently, since $0 \leq n_i \leq N$, the weighted formulation has the same boundaries as the unweighted one. Second, if all core agents have the same number of followers, we have that $\forall i f_i = n_i \langle f \rangle$, so we recover the unweighted original formulation (15). Third, the ratio $f_i / \langle f \rangle$ in the sum of Equation (16) is a direct measure of the dispersion of core weights, readily illustrating why we should not expect the mean-field approximation to be accurate when the dispersion becomes large.

5.2 *Simulation setup*

In our simulations, we fix the number of core agents at $N = 500$ and draw the number of followers from Gaussian, uniform, exponential and Pareto distributions with mean $\langle f \rangle = 1000$ such that each randomly drawn number is rounded to the nearest (absolute) integer value. Let N^+ and F^+, respectively, denote the number of core agents and followers that are in the optimistic state. The system-wide concentration of agents in the optimistic state is now $z = (N^+ + F^+)/M$, where $M = N + F$ is the total number of agents. In all scenarios, we set the parameters a and λ in such a way that $\epsilon = 1$, which yields a uniform distribution of z with $\mathrm{Var}(z) = \frac{1}{12} \approx 0.083$ when the mean-field approximation applies. One 'sweep' of the system corresponds to one round of sequential updating of all core agents in the system, thus requiring N steps per sweep, and each simulation run consists of half a million sweeps. Finally, we successively increase the standard deviation σ_f of the respective distribution while ensuring that the weights remain positive and record the variance of z for each sequence of increasing σ_f. Recall again that when $\mathrm{Var}(z)$ increases (decreases) above (below) the 'knife-edge' value of one twelfth, this implies that the distribution of z transforms from a uniform to a bimodal distribution with non-trivial averaging behavior (unimodal distribution with trivial self-averaging).

5.3 *Core structure and one-leader benchmark*

The simulation results for a fully connected core are magnified in the inset of Figure 3. When core weights are not overly dispersed, the mean-field prediction still performs well, but pronounced deviations ultimately do occur as the dispersion of weights increases. Intuitively, this happens because a few core agents become increasingly influential in the opinion formation dynamics of the system, thereby increasing the time during which the system is near one of the two extreme states. Hence, hierarchical networks are not only immune to self-averaging, but also actually *amplify* volatility in the system. It is noteworthy that the outcome does not depend on the functional form of the distribution from which the weights are drawn.

In order to determine the limit of the variance amplification, we consider an extreme case that we label as the *one-leader* scenario. In this case, we allocate an equal number of followers to all but one core agent (the leader), who is then assigned a weight such that the average number of followers corresponds again to $\langle f \rangle = 1000$. Let $1/N < p < 1$ denote the fraction of followers that are connected to the one-leader, such that the leader has pF followers, and assume that the remaining $(1 - p)F$ followers are allocated with equal weight among the $N - 1$ remaining core agents. When $p = 1/N$, all core agents have the same number of followers, F/N. Conversely when $p \to 1$, the system is almost entirely represented by the leader. In each new simulation run, we successively shift a larger number of followers to the leader by increasing p. The result is shown in Figure 3, with $\mathrm{Var}(z)$ intuitively approaching a value of one-fourth since the leading agent will represent almost the entire system by itself, and cannot be influenced by others anymore. Thus, its actions will consist of random switches between the two states, while the few remaining core

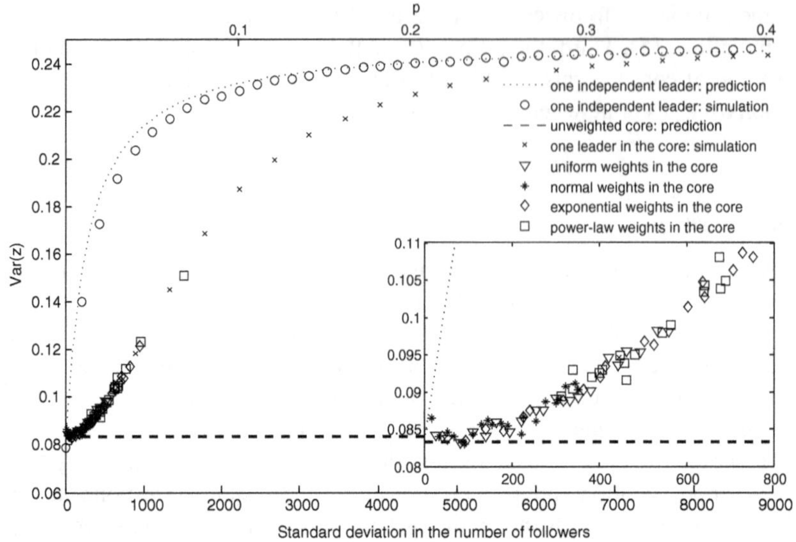

Figure 3. The impact of increasing heterogeneity in core weights on system-wide volatility. The simulations (with a fully connected core $D = N$ and behavioral parameters $a = \lambda = 1$, so $\epsilon = 1$) demonstrate that rising heterogeneity leads to increasing volatility, irrespective of the particular distribution from which the weights are drawn.

agents mimic the leader's behavior. Hence, the system spends half its time in one state and half in the other, resulting in a variance of one-fourth.

In addition, we present some analytical results for the related benchmark scenario of an *independent* leader who in a sense acts 'outside' the core network: in contrast to the preceding one-leader scenario, the independent leader now does not care about the state of other core agents. We explain the details of this benchmark setup and how we simulated it in Appendix 1. Figure 3 also illustrates the benchmark outcome of both the prediction and the simulation for the independent leader scenario. In summary, the figure establishes two central results. First, the mean-field approximation works reasonably well if the dispersion in the number of followers is relatively small, that is, when the core is fairly homogeneously weighted. Second, a heterogeneously weighted core actually leads to increasing system-wide volatility, asymptotically approaching the independent one-leader scenario, which constitutes the most extreme degree of heterogeneity. The heterogeneity of core agents thus represents an auxiliary source of fluctuations in the model. Basically, the simulations establish the model's behavior between the mean field and independent leader benchmarks, illustrating that the core-periphery setup quickly diverges from the mean-field approximation and asymptotically approaches the independent leader benchmark. The social interactions among core agents are crucial for overcoming N-dependence, because a vanishing herding propensity would lead to independently acting core agents, and thereby to a degenerate self-averaging distribution of their aggregate opinion with a sharply peaked mean of one-half. Moreover, if the core was enlarged (instead of the periphery), we would also confront the self-averaging problem, unless the core network was the empirically unsatisfactory random graph. It is, therefore, the contemporaneous presence of a hierarchical network with a relatively small core, and the social interactions in the core that ultimately overcomes the problem of N-dependence.

5.4 *Varying the core structure*

Our previous investigations show that a hierarchical network with a fully connected core not only overcomes the self-averaging problem, but also amplifies volatility. A remaining issue is whether these results are robust with respect to the network structure in the core itself. On that account, we perform another series of simulations with varying core network structures, and record how the different core networks respond to an increasing dispersion of weights.

For comparison with our previous findings, we keep the size of the core fixed at $N = 500$, and construct the following networks in the core: a circle with neighborhood 40, a random network with linking probability of 10%, and a scale-free network with an average of 5000 links. For the random and the scale-free graph, we construct 10 different realizations of the core network, and run the simulations again for half a million sweeps, subsequently averaging over the 10 respective core realizations. The details of the respective network parametrizations are not crucial, because in each scenario, we set $\lambda = 1$ in the transition rates (16), and adapt the behavioral parameter a in light of a particular parametrization of D such that the mean-field prediction would again yield a uniform distribution ($\epsilon = 1$). The simulation results in Figure 4 demonstrate that the core network structure has merely second-order effects on the macroscopic properties of the model. As before, an increasing dispersion of followers increases volatility, while the mean-field prediction holds true if the dispersion of weights is not too large.

We also simulated a very extreme scenario by considering a scale-free graph with deterministically assigned core weights that are proportional to the degree of a core agent. We can think of such a *proportional weights* structure as the asymptotic limit of *positive feedback* effects in the time evolution of the network, for instance, if highly central core agents increasingly attract the

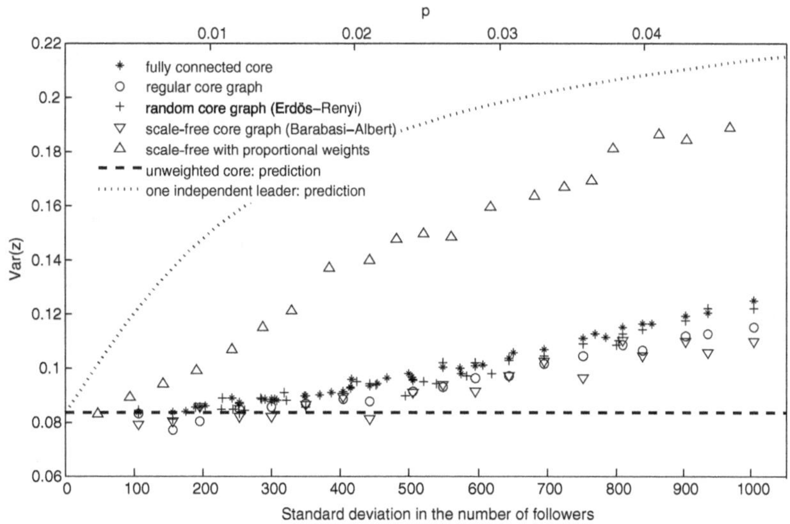

Figure 4. The impact of different core network structures on system-wide volatility has merely second-order effects, except for the 'proportional weights' scenario: if the core is a scale-free graph with core weights that are proportional to the degree of each agent in the core, the mean-field approximation immediately fails to produce accurate results and the variance of z rapidly increases, almost doubling compared to the other scenarios, where core weights are still randomly assigned when varying the network structure in the core. As before, the simulations were conducted for $N = 500$ agents with $\lambda = 1$, and a and D set in such a way that $\epsilon = 1$.

interest and wealth of investors, or if core agents with a large weight become increasingly connected among their peers in the core. Whatever the ultimate reason might be for observing such a double-weighted hierarchy, it is noteworthy that volatility increases considerably compared with the other scenarios shown in Figure 4, even for very small deviations in the number of followers.

6. Conclusion

Hierarchical core-periphery structures turn out to overcome the problem of N-dependence in probabilistic herding models of the Kirman type. On one hand, this is a good news from the viewpoint of the model's asymptotic properties, because one is able to replicate the stylized facts of financial returns with behaviorally heterogeneous agents for any system size, without having to tune any of the behavioral parameters. On the other hand, our findings have somewhat stark implications from the viewpoint of investment strategy, and they also raise pressing new questions about the origins of hierarchical network structures.

The introduction of hierarchical network structures represents an additional source of volatility on top of the behavioral heterogeneity that has previously been considered as the exclusive source of volatility in social interaction models. If one accepts our premise that hierarchical networks are a useful representation of fund investor relationships in financial markets, then popular and traditional investment advice to 'diversify one's portfolio' has to be judged with caution. Investors who are not wealthy enough to broadly diversify their portfolios, those who participate in funded retirement plans, or those who simply feel that they lack the skills or time to make appropriate investment decisions might very well delegate their investment decisions to institutional investors. But if these fund managers are socially interacting and influencing each other in their investment decisions, as the quoted empirical evidence suggests, this becomes a self-defeating strategy because we have argued that system-wide volatility increases under such circumstances. Put in more provocative terms, all the good intentions of investors to diversify risk can lead to the opposite effect if fund managers are prone to social interaction effects. Moreover, the presence of positive feedback effects in the time evolution of hierarchical networks seems to worsen the situation further, rather than improving it, since positive feedbacks would significantly increase the level of volatility in our simulations.

From the viewpoint of policy-making, our study indicates that a reduction of financial volatility would be facilitated by a shrinking degree of hierarchical organization in financial markets, corresponding to an increasing decentralization of investment decisions. While such advice sounds straightforward in principle, its implementation would most likely be more painful and complex: our results suggest that already very small values of p (or market share for that matter) lead to a sudden and pronounced increase in volatility. Keeping p very close to zero, on the other hand, would more or less imply getting rid of managed funds altogether, which hardly appears to be a feasible option.

Acknowledgements

We gratefully acknowledge the financial support by the Volkswagen Foundation through their grant on 'Complex Networks As Interdisciplinary Phenomena'. S.A. is thankful for financial support from the Spanish Ministry of Science and Innovation under research project ECO2008-00510 and the Universitat Jaume I-Bancaixa under the research project P11A2009-09. M.M. is thankful for financial support from the Research Promotion Plan 2010 of Universitat Jaume I, received during his visit to Castellón in that year. Comments by Albrecht Irle, Jonas Kauschke, Thomas Lux, and two anonymous referees are greatly appreciated.

Notes

1. Aoki utilizes the terms *(non-)self-averaging* in lieu of N-(in)dependence, and we will subsequently use both terms interchangeably.
2. The next section explains in more detail how the Markov chain typically enters Walrasian models of the financial market.
3. A simple example illustrates this implausibility. Suppose you live in Smallville, where you closely interact with, say, 30 people. Moving to Metropolis, with a population about 300 times the size of Smallville, a constant linking probability would imply that you now closely interact with a number of agents on the order of 10^5.
4. Appendix 1 contains an analytical treatment of this case.
5. By convention, $e_{ii} = 0$, so there are no 'self-loops' in the network.
6. The Polya distribution converges to the Beta distribution for large N. The results of this section, however, do not significantly depend on whether we use a continuous or discrete approach (material upon request).

References

Alfarano, S., and T. Lux. 2007. A noise trader model as a generator of apparent financial power laws and long memory. *Macroeconomic Dynamics* 11, no. S1: 80–101.

Alfarano, S., and M. Milaković. 2009. Network structure and N-dependence in agent-based herding models. *Journal of Economic Dynamics and Control* 33, no. 1: 78–92.

Alfarano, S., T. Lux, and F. Wagner. 2005. Estimation of agent-based models: The case of an asymmetric herding model. *Computational Economics* 26, no. 1: 19–49.

Alfarano, S., T. Lux, and F. Wagner. 2008. Time-variation of higher moments in a financial market with heterogeneous agents: An analytical approach. *Journal of Economic Dynamics and Control* 32, no. 1: 101–36.

Alfi, V., M. Cristelli, L. Pietronero, and A. Zaccaria. 2009. Minimal agent based model for financial markets I. *European Physical Journal B* 67, no. 3: 385–97.

Aoki, M. 2008. Thermodynamic limits of macroeconomic or financial models: One- and two-parameter Poisson–Dirichlet models. *Journal of Economic Dynamics and Control* 32, no. 1: 66–84.

Banerjee, A.V. 1992. A simple model of herd behavior. *Quarterly Journal of Economics* 107, no. 3: 797–817.

Barabási, A.-L., and R. Albert. 1999. Emergence of scaling in random networks. *Science* 286, no. 5439: 509–12.

Bikhchandani, S., D. Hirshleifer, and I. Welch. 1992. A theory of fads, fashion, custom, and cultural change as informational cascades. *Journal of Political Economy* 100, no. 5: 992–1026.

Bornholdt, S. 2001. Expectation bubbles in a spin model of markets: Intermittency from frustation across scales. *International Journal of Modern Physics C* 12, no. 5: 667–74.

Brock, W.A., and C.H. Hommes. 1997. A rational route to randomness. *Econometrica* 65, no. 5: 1059–95.

Chamley, C.P. 2004. *Rational herds*. New York: Cambridge University Press.

Chang, S.-K. 2007. A simple asset pricing model with social interactions and heterogeneous beliefs. *Journal of Economic Dynamics and Control* 31, no. 4: 1300–25.

Cont, R. 2001. Empirical properties of asset returns: Stylized facts and statistical issues. *Quantitative Finance* 1, no. 2: 223–36.

Cont, R., and J.P. Bouchaud. 2000. Herd behaviour and aggregate fluctuations in financial markets. *Macroeconomic Dynamics* 4, no. 2: 170–96.

Egenter, E., T. Lux, and D. Stauffer. 1999. Finite-size effects in Monte Carlo simulations of two stock market models. *Physica A* 268, nos. 1–2: 250–6.

Gabaix, X., P. Gopikrishnan, V. Plerou, and H.E. Stanley. 2006. A theory of power-law distributions in financial market fluctuations. *Quarterly Journal of Economics* 121, no. 2: 461–504.

Garibaldi, U., M.A. Penco, and P. Viarengo. 2003. An exact physical approach to market participation models. In *Heterogeneous agents, interactions and economic performances*, ed. R. Cowan and N. Jonard, Lecture Notes in Economics and Mathematical Systems, 91–103. Berlin: Springer.

Hommes, C.H. 2006. Heterogeneous agent models in economics and finance. In *Handbook of computational economics*, vol. 2, ed. L. Tesfatsion and K.L. Judd, 1109–1186, Amsterdam: North-Holland.

Hong, H., J.D. Kubik, and J.C. Stein. 2005. Thy neighbor's portfolio: Word-of-mouth effects in the holdings and trades of money managers. *Journal of Finance* 60, no. 6: 2801–24.

Iori, G. 2002. A micro-simulation of traders' activity in the stock market: the role of heterogeneity, agents' interactions and trade friction. *Journal of Economic Behavior and Organization* 49, no. 2: 269–85.

Irle, A., J. Kauschke, T. Lux, and M. Milaković. 2011. Switching rates and the asymptotic behavior of herding models. *Advances in Complex Systems* 14, no. 3: 359–76.
Kirman, A. 1991. Epidemics of opinion and speculative bubbles in financial markets. In *Money and financial markets*, ed. M.P. Taylor, 354–68. Cambridge: Blackwell.
Kirman, A. 1993. Ants, rationality, and recruitment. *Quarterly Journal of Economics* 108, no. 1: 137–56.
Lux, T., and S. Schornstein. 2005. Genetic learning as an explanation of stylized facts of foreign exchange markets. *Journal of Mathematical Economics* 41, nos. 1–2: 169–96.
Newman, M. 2003. The structure and function of complex networks. *SIAM Review* 45, no. 2: 167–256.
Pagan, A. 1996. The econometrics of financial markets. *Journal of Empirical Finance* 3, no. 1: 15–102.
Schwarzkopf, Y., and J.D. Farmer. 2008. Time evolution of the mutual fund size distribution. arXiv/0807.3800.
Stauffer, D., and D. Sornette. 1999. Self-organized percolation model for stock market fluctuation. *Physica A* 271, nos. 3–4: 496–506.
Watts, D.J., and S.H. Strogatz. 1998. Collective dynamics of 'small-world' networks. *Nature* 393, no. 6684: 440–2.
Wermers, R. 1999. Mutual fund herding and the impact on stock prices. *Journal of Finance* 54, no. 2: 581–622.

Appendix 1. Independent one-leader benchmark

Let us start by considering an arbitrary agent in the fully connected core who is always in a *fixed* state and does not change the opinion. As before, let $1/N < p < 1$ denote the fraction of followers that are connected to the fixed-opinion agent, or an *independent leader*, such that the agent has pF followers, and assume that the remaining $(1-p)F$ followers are allocated with equal weight among the remaining core agents, indexed by $i = 1, \dots, N-1$. When $p = 1/N$, all core agents have the same number of followers, F/N. Conversely, when $p \to 1$, the system is almost entirely represented by the leader. For ease of notation, let us write the transition probability as

$$\pi_i = \left(a + \frac{\lambda N F_i}{F}\right)\Delta t \quad \text{for } i = 1, \dots, N-1, \tag{A1}$$

where F_i denotes the *system-wide number of followers in the opposite state*, so the $N-1$ equally weighted core agents will obey the transition rate (A1). As before, we set $\Delta t = 1/(a+\lambda N)$. Furthermore, let β be an indicator function that takes on the value 0 or 1 depending on whether the state of agent i equals or is different from the state of the fixed-opinion agent. Then we can rewrite the herding term in Equation (A1), NF_i/F, taking into account the fixed opinion of the leader (say, being optimistic)

$$N\frac{F_i}{F} = \frac{N}{F}\left(Fp\beta + (n-1)\frac{F(1-p)}{N-1}\right), \tag{A2}$$

which yields the modified version of the transition probability (A1),

$$\begin{aligned}\pi_i &= \left(a + \lambda N p\beta + \lambda\frac{N}{N-1}(1-p)n\right)\Delta t \\ &\approx (a + \lambda N p\beta + \lambda(1-p)n)\Delta t\end{aligned} \tag{A3}$$

for large N. Depending on the value of the indicator function β, the transition probabilities of agent i are either

$$\pi_i = (\varepsilon + (1-p)n)\lambda\Delta t \quad \text{or} \tag{A4}$$

$$\pi_i = (\varepsilon + Np + (1-p)n)\lambda\Delta t, \tag{A5}$$

where we adapted ε to the definition (7) by noting that a fully connected core implies $D = N$.

Fixing the opinion of one agent is equivalent to creating an asymmetry in the autonomous component that stems from the additional term Np in the modified transition rates. Put simply, the system exhibits a tendency towards the fixed opinion that depends on p. A straightforward mean-field argument (see, e.g. Alfarano and Milaković 2009) results in the following system-wide transition probabilities, analogous to an extensive version of the transition rates (4) and (5),

$$\pi^- = \frac{n}{N}\frac{\varepsilon + (1-p)(N-n)}{\varepsilon + N}, \tag{A6}$$

$$\pi^+ = \frac{(N-n)}{N}\frac{\varepsilon + Np + (1-p)n}{\varepsilon + N}. \tag{A7}$$

The equilibrium distribution of such a unary Markov process is (see e.g. Garibaldi, Penco, and Viarengo 2003) the *Polya distribution* $R(\varepsilon_1, \varepsilon_2; z)$, with $z = n/N$ and shorthands[6]

$$\varepsilon_1 = \frac{\varepsilon + Np}{1-p}, \quad \varepsilon_2 = \frac{\varepsilon}{1-p}. \tag{A8}$$

Increasing the value of the control parameter p leads to an increasingly asymmetric distribution peaked around the opinion of the leader. Fixing the opinion of one agent, however, yields a very unsatisfactory approximation for the simulations in Section 5, where the leader is not in a fixed state but rather switches states as well. Therefore, we proceed by assuming that the 'independent' leader switches opinion randomly, without being influenced by other agents, which basically means that the autonomous term in the mean-field transitions (A6) and (A7) is now stochastic and time-dependent, hinging on the random realizations of the leader's state.

Such a situation is harder to tackle analytically because it leads to a stochastic differential equation with random coefficients. In order to approximate the full mathematical problem, we employ a so-called *adiabatic* approximation that neglects the adjustment of the system to the switching of the leader by assuming that the leader's switches are slow enough in order for the $N-1$ agents to reach statistical equilibrium. Then we can consider the system as being in statistical equilibrium most of the time and, consequently, the resulting equilibrium distribution G_e becomes the superposition of two independent equilibrium distributions, corresponding to the two possible configurations of the leader,

$$G_e = \tfrac{1}{2}R(\varepsilon_1, \varepsilon_2; z) + \tfrac{1}{2}R(\varepsilon_2, \varepsilon_1; z), \tag{A9}$$

which is an average of the previous asymmetric distributions among the two alternative configurations of the leader. The equilibrium distribution is now symmetric (note the interchange of the parameters ε_1 and ε_2) and U-shaped. From Equation (A9), the second moment of the equilibrium distribution $M_{2,e}$ is given by

$$M_{2,e} = \tfrac{1}{2}M_2(\varepsilon_1, \varepsilon_2) + \tfrac{1}{2}M_2(\varepsilon_2, \varepsilon_1), \tag{A10}$$

where $M_2(\cdot,\cdot)$ denotes the second moment of the respective asymmetric Polya distribution with parameters ε_1 and ε_2, and the variance of the equilibrium distribution for a given p is

$$\mathrm{Var}[z]_p = \tfrac{1}{2}\mathrm{Var}[\varepsilon_1, \varepsilon_2] + \tfrac{1}{2}\mathrm{Var}[\varepsilon_2, \varepsilon_1] + \tfrac{1}{2}\{M_1^2[\varepsilon_1, \varepsilon_2] + M_1^2[\varepsilon_2, \varepsilon_1]\} - (\tfrac{1}{2})^2, \tag{A11}$$

where M_1 designates the first moment of the respective asymmetric Polya distribution, and $\frac{1}{2}$ is obviously the mean of the equilibrium distribution G_e. The two variances are equal since they are the same under an exchange of the two parameters ε_1 and ε_2, hence the previous equation can be written as

$$\mathrm{Var}[z]_p = \mathrm{Var}[\varepsilon_1, \varepsilon_2] + \tfrac{1}{2}\{M_1^2[\varepsilon_1, \varepsilon_2] + M_1^2[\varepsilon_2, \varepsilon_1]\} - \tfrac{1}{4}. \tag{A12}$$

It is possible to show (see, e.g. Garibaldi, Penco, and Viarengo 2003) that

$$M_1[\varepsilon_1, \varepsilon_2] = \frac{\varepsilon_1}{\varepsilon_1 + \varepsilon_2}, \tag{A13}$$

$$\mathrm{Var}[\varepsilon_1, \varepsilon_2] = \frac{\varepsilon_1\varepsilon_2}{(\varepsilon_1 + \varepsilon_2)^2}\frac{\varepsilon_1\varepsilon_2 + N}{N(\varepsilon_1\varepsilon_2 + 1)}, \tag{A14}$$

and utilizing these in Equation (A12) yields

$$\mathrm{Var}[z] = \frac{1}{4} - \frac{\varepsilon_1\varepsilon_2}{(\varepsilon_1 + \varepsilon_2)(\varepsilon_1 + \varepsilon_2 + 1)}. \tag{A15}$$

Finally, recalling the shorthands in Equation (A8), we obtain the variance as a function of the control parameter p,

$$\mathrm{Var}[z]_p = \frac{1}{4} - \frac{1 + pN}{(2 + pN)(3 + pN - p)}, \tag{A16}$$

under the parameter choice $\varepsilon = 1$, i.e. $\lambda = 1$ and $a = 1$. For $N \gg 1$, we immediately see that Equation (A16) provides boundary values that are consistent with our previous findings: if $p = 1/N$, the variance tends to $\frac{1}{12}$, representing the correct value for the uniform distribution (recall the parameter choice $\varepsilon = 1$); if $p \to 1$, the variance tends to $\frac{1}{4}$, representing a distribution concentrated either in 0 or 1. We simulated the modified model with a randomly switching leader, successively increasing the control parameter p in a fully connected core of size $N = 500$ with a total of $F = 500{,}000$ followers. As before, we simulated each parametrization with half a million sweeps.

The results, along with the prediction (A16), are shown in Figure 3. For easier comparison with the simulation results in Figures 3 and 4, we calculate the standard deviation in the number of followers for each parametrization of p, which is

$$\sigma = \sqrt{\frac{1}{N}(pF)^2 + \frac{N-1}{N}\left(\frac{(1-p)F}{N-1}\right)^2 - \left(\frac{F}{N}\right)^2}, \tag{A17}$$

and invert the relation to obtain

$$p = \frac{\sigma\sqrt{N-1}}{F} + \frac{1}{N}. \tag{A18}$$

While the independent leader scenario exhibits a quicker convergence to the limiting variance of one-fourth than the one-leader model, both versions are qualitatively similar in the sense that there is a sudden and pronounced increase in volatility already for small values of p. The main difference between the independent versus one-leader scenarios is that the independent leader switches randomly (thus independently) between the two states, while the switches of the one-leader in Section 5.3 still depend on the interactions with the other core agents, which intuitively slows down the variance amplification relative to the independent leader case. As far as the creation of fluctuations and therefore risk is concerned, the important common feature of both models is that they exhibit a sudden and pronounced increase in system-wide volatility as soon as a relatively small number of core agents obtains a disproportionately large weight in the core network.

Identifying reference companies using the book-to-market ratio: a minimum spanning tree approach

David Brookfield, Halim Boussabaine and Chen Su

There is substantial evidence to suggest that the book-to-market (BM) ratio is an important factor in explaining stock market returns. Its role has proved difficult to isolate, however, due to statistical problems in its construction and to its observational equivalence to a number of risk and behavioural explanations. In addition, now widely recognised complex behaviour in financial markets has called into question modelling approaches that are limited in their ability to uncover relationships that are possibly masked during financial crises, for example. As one response, our research explores the value of a newly applied technique which examines the topological properties of minimum spanning trees as applied to both the BM ratio and market returns. Our intention is to identify and report investment signals as determined by the BM ratio and to assess the relationships of these signals to returns outcomes. The approach enables highly nonlinear behaviour to be addressed and the relationships we set out to capture to be reported in novel ways. We motivate and evidence a previously unreported role for BM as an investment signal which is effective over varying stock market conditions, including the financial crisis that began in 2008.

1. Introduction

The financial crisis that struck banking sectors in many countries beginning in 2008 has led to calls for significant reforms in risk governance and risk management methods. In particular, stress-testing financial risk models for 'fat-tail' events has become a priority to facilitiate effective price-finding mechanisms (Ackermann 2008). One difficulty in finding such mechanisms is reflected in the fairly widely held view that the time series of stock market prices, for example, exhibit nontrivial properties in addition to excess volatility of both short- and long-term memory effects, skewness, and a level of complexity such that price return distributions alter between normal and extreme periods (Bonanno, Lillo, and Mantegna 2001a; Ang and Chen 2002). Indeed, it may be profoundly difficult to stress-test fat tail events if the effects of market instability are the result of unidentified endogenous dynamic processes (Kyrtsou and Terraza 2002; Kyrtsou 2008).

A different modelling approach is, therefore, called-for that that recognises different levels of complexity in financial market behaviour as one response to modelling deficiencies exposed by the financial crisis, but for which adverse opinion and evidence has been emerging for some time (Malliaris and Stein 1999; Daníelsson 2002; Kyrtsou and Terraza 2003; Sornette 2003; Haldane

2009; Farmer and Foley 2009; Lux and Westerhoff 2009; but see Ball's 2009 counter-view). Our concern is with portfolio construction in stock markets and how portfolio choice may be modelled in a manner that exploits economic signals which might facilitate investment decision-making in a complex economic environment. Specifically, we look to assess how information extraction methods, such as spanning trees, can be economically motivated, modelled, applied and results reported that are capable of replication. Our method is theoretically grounded, *ex ante*, by which we mean it is able to offer predictions that are testable. Our predictions are motivated by an economic rationale that has two parts: first it looks at the book-to-market (BM) ratio as an investment signal of future stock returns and its role as a possible referencing device which can identify companies that are central to stock market behaviour and explains under what conditions the BM ratio can signal future stock market returns. Second, we economically motivate our modelling methodology using a segmented market analysis that positions a minimum spanning tree (MST) approach as an appropriate analytical method. This modelling approach recognises the inherent complexity of stock market behaviour by using a nonlinear clustering procedure that has had significant success in identifying industrial sectors. However, the research to date has lacked theoretical underpinning and our view is that only a theoretical motivation will lead to further significant steps in the research agenda. We believe our tentative proposals are a step forward in this direction.

That the BM ratio is of significance in explaining market returns has been known since the work of Fama and French (1992). Continuing research, however, into the exact role the BM ratio plays as an explanation of stock market returns is unresolved. For example, at a broad level, there is currently no resolution to opposing views as to whether there is a risk-based explanation for the role of BM (Fama and French 1993, 1996; Zhang 2005) or whether it arises as a result of mispricing, thus allowing a role for non-risk based (behaviourial) explanations (Lakonishok, Shleifer, and Vishny 1994; Haugen 1995; Asgharian and Hansson 2010). On top of that, as Daniel and Titman (2006) argue, BM is a 'catch-all' variable that is able to proxy for a variety of macroeconomic conditions and therefore its actual role may be undiscernable. This is not unexpected since both high BM figures ('value' stocks) and low BM figures ('growth' stocks) have been suggested as being economically meaningful: that is, if the BM ratio is meaningful over the complete range of values, there is no counterfactual to effectively dispute its role. So, for example, BM as associated with market returns over the business cycle will always have a relevance *but for different reasons* (see also Penman 1996). There is also evidence, reported as far back as Fama and French (1995) that the BM ratio is associated with persistent properties in earnings: high BM stocks exhibit less profitability than low BM stocks for at least a 5-year holding period after a ranking period determination. The relationship between BM and earnings is also observable in the relationship of BM to returns: 'the common factors in returns mirror common factors in earnings suggests that the market, size, and book-to-market factors in earnings are the source of the corresponding factors in returns.' (Fama and French 1995, 133). Thus, there is likely a persistence in over-performance in returns associated with low BM ratios. The nature of this persistance will be important for our own replicating portfolio work explained below.

Moreover, even the statistical significance of BM is routinely related to stock returns in a potentially spurious manner for two further reasons. First, there is a basic issue in the construction of the BM ratio which is rarely mentioned, but is not unknown (Pontiff and Schall 1998).[1] The basic issue is that book value changes infrequently while market value changes as often as is effectively sampled. At most, book value will alter four times a year for quarterly US accounting reporting cycles and, for Europe, twice yearly. The statistical problem arises because the value of 'B' in the BM ratio is persistent compared with the value of 'M'. The result is to produce a positive bias in parameter estimates of the persistent variables on future returns which becomes more pronounced over longer-run regressions (Kendall 1954). And second, Daniel and Titman (2006) argue that tests that rely on a categorisation by BM value (as done in Fama and French 1993) effectively 'wash out' any variation in factor loadings on returns that are independent of BM. The consequence is that 'even if the loadings on a proposed factor are only loosely correlated with the expected returns of the individual assets in the economy, the sorting procedure will result in a set of test portfolios where there is a close to perfect linear relation between loadings on the proposed factor and expected returns'. (Daniel and Titman 2006, 5).

Apart from statistical problems, it appears that the discovery of the role of BM may arise as a slow accumulation of evidence, possibly from a number of different perspectives. Our contribution is to offer a new perspective that takes, as its departure point, the view that BM is unavoidably a catch-all variable and then to try to discern the structural properties within the BM ratio that are associated with structural properties in returns in a manner that has not previously been addressed. This is different to estimations of factor loadings or calculations of mimicking portfolio returns. Specifically, the structural properties we seek to examine are the topological characteristics of an MST of both BM and stock market returns over the period 2005–2009. Using daily data for returns and six monthly data for BM, we examine listed UK companies during that period and evaluate successive six-monthly MSTs as one way of seeking to understand the role of BM as an investment tool used in portfolio construction. We deliberately choose a time to study BM in what was an exceptionally volatile period for the stock market. In so doing, we seek to make two key contributions. First, research has been reported concerning the potential economic significance of MSTs as a new technique that is able to mimic industry correlations and Markowitz portfolios (Mantegna 1999; Onnela et al. 2002). We extend and explain why MSTs can be significant perspectives in evaluating *investment styles* and hence become relevant in a style portfolio construction sense and also offer a novel view of the role of BM that is consistent with known economic explanations, but is not restricted to either risk-based or non-risk based views. Our second major contribution is to report our key finding: that the BM ratio is able to detect, six months ahead, which stocks act as central indicators of stock market performance. This result is irrespective of market conditions and volatility, thus suggesting the value of BM as a signalling device consistent with economic theory previously developed, but which may also be suggestive of a deeper, core role for BM in relation to returns for which we provide an economic motivation. Subsidiary findings are also reported. The next section outlines our theoretical structure and further explores the role of BM as an investment style. We also offer, we believe for the first time, an economic motivation for clustering methodologies – such as the MST – that places such approaches firmly within a theoretical context that then facilitates applications of the methodology into a broader research arena.[2] We next present our methodological approach and explain how MSTs provide a test of the role of BM as a predictor of stock market returns. The following section reports our data, presents the results and offers an analysis of what we find. Conclusions are then drawn.

2. The relationship between book to market and returns and the economic relevance of MSTs

Our task in this section is, first, to establish the economic role of the BM ratio and determine under what conditions it may act as a signalling device for future returns and, second, to consider the theoretical requirements for a clustering methodology to be appropriate, thereby motivating the MST as a relevant device to discover the role of BM as a referencing signal.

When making portfolio allocation decisions, investors generally first categorise assets into broad classes and then decide how to allocate their portfolios across these asset classes (Brown and

Goetzmann 1997; Barberis and Shleifer 2003). Mullainathan (2000) reports that investors pursue asset-class investing as a method of categorisation and as one means of simplifying problems related to choice. Equity fund managers then position funds to reflect investor appetite and thus opportunities for style investing are created (Bernstein 1995). A number of styles have become recognisable: value, growth, size, momentum, rising to 12 different styles as reported in Sharpe (1992). Value and growth strategies are ordinarily indexed by the BM ratio with high values reflecting *value* investing opportunities and low values reflecting *growth* opportunities (Fama and French 1998). Returns-based style analysis is a statistical technique that compares stock returns to returns achieved by a set of market indices. The multiple regression model $\tilde{R}_i = [b_{i1}\tilde{F}_1 + b_{i2}\tilde{F}_2 + \cdots + b_{in}\tilde{F}_n] + \tilde{e}_i$ is applied by Sharpe (1992) with stock return and asset class returns being used as dependent and independent variables, respectively. The coefficients are interpreted as the measure of historic exposure to asset class returns. The Fama and French (1993) three-factor model is a variant of Sharpe's general model and an extension of the basic CAPM. The additional risk factors relate to size and value and are reflective of two of the main style categorisations that have been extensively investigated.

The theoretical relationship between BM and returns is derived from Pontiff and Schall (1998) which is based on the ability of BM to forecast cash flows $E_t(\mathrm{CF}_{t+1})$ – that is, a forecast of cash flows for period $t+1$ based on information available and expectation formed in period t. Specifically, in a one period model, book value, B_t is assumed to reflect shareholder cash flow next period with error: $B_t = E_t(\mathrm{CF}_{t+1}) + \eta$, where η is a zero-mean white noise process. The realised cash flow next period and forecast cash flow differ only in terms of a zero mean white noise error such that $\mathrm{CF}_{t+1} = E_t(\mathrm{CF}_{t+1}) + \varepsilon$. The relationship between $E_t(\mathrm{CF}_{t+1})$ and current market price M_t is the usual discounted value: $M_t = E_t(\mathrm{CF}_{t+1})/\kappa$, where $\kappa = 1 + r$ and r is the discount rate. Realised returns to investors next period are $R_{t+1} = [\mathrm{CF}_{t+1}/M_t] - 1$. If the cash flows are dividends then the foregoing becomes the dividend valuation model. With BM_t used as a forecasting tool for returns, then we can redefine realised returns in terms of the BM ratio to reveal the relationship. The BM ratio is, therefore, defined as

$$\mathrm{BM}_t = \frac{B_t}{M_t} = \frac{E_t\mathrm{CF}_{t+1} + \eta}{M_t} = \kappa + \frac{\eta\kappa}{E_t\mathrm{CF}_{t+1}} \tag{1}$$

which we can use to express realised returns in terms of the BM ratio as

$$R_{t+1} = \kappa + \frac{\varepsilon(\mathrm{BM}_t - \kappa)}{\eta} - 1. \tag{2}$$

Thus, as BM rises in period t above the discount rate, realised returns next period increase *but only* as a zero mean, white noise phenomenon. Employing expected values, expected returns would simply be equal to the discount rate. We expand on this below and explain what is required for BM to have a substantive role.

The foregoing theoretical development leaves the question unanswered as to whether or not it is a rational, risk-based model since the method of determination of the discount rate, κ, is not part of its structure. The discount rate is, therefore, a choice variable which may or may not be determined in a rational manner and is reflective of the debate that has ensued concerning the role of BM over the years. Risk-based explanations of BM understandably position it as a source of undiversifiable risk, separate to that of the market. Thus, the search for this new source of risk has taken place. Among the studies relevant to this debate suggest that this risk might relate to distress (Fama and French 1995, 1996; Davis, Fama, and French 2000), to liquidity (Pastor and Stambaugh 2003) and to default risk (Vassalou and Xing 2004), for example. Non-risk based explanations relate to 'errors' of various types in investor behaviour such as misformation of expectations as in Daniel and Titman (1997, 2006). While there is some evidence that market factors cannot capture all systematic risk, it is also likely that the BM ratio is possibly motivated by a latent (hard-to-define) non-risk-based explanation (Asgharian and Hansson 2010).

We now comment on the conditions required to establish BM, or any other variable, to have a substantive role in predicting returns. In undertaking this, we look to assess how BM can act as a leading indicator and then to establish what is required to suggest clustering as an enduring phenomenon in which signals from a leading indicator can be used in portfolio selection in one period to anticipate returns in the next period. We expand on this notion and the following is adapted from Menzly and Ozbas (2010). There are two aspects to developing this: first, to identify the conditions under which returns predictability is feasible and, second, to identify under what conditions clusters of entities might emerge. Turning to returns, predictability is likely to emerge if any of the following is true:

(i) information regarding firm fundamentals is unequally available among investors, or
(ii) some investors only process a subset of publicly available information because of limited processing capabilities or search costs are too high, or
(iii) there are limits to arbitrage.

The first condition is due to Hayek (1945) and is worth exploring since it seeks to clarify what is meant by economic analysis which is more broadly pertinent. In attempting to establish a rational economic order (such as an efficient stock market), Hayek explains that certain assumptions are required: that is, if agents 'possess all the relevant information .... start from a given set of preferences [and] command complete knowledge of the available means [then] the problem which remains is purely one of logic' (p. 519). In other words, there remains no practical problem to solve. In reality, the 'assumptions of a rational order do not exist in concentrated or integrated form, but purely as dispersed bits of incomplete and frequently contradictory knowledge ...' (p. 519). The consequence is that, under (i)–(iii), information diffusion becomes slow or is only partially reflected into prices and hence price adjustment is not sufficiently complete to avoid returns predictability (Hong and Stein 1999).

In order to create clustering, given any of the conditions in (i)–(iii), returns need to be *cross-predictable* so that firm prices co-move. Porter (1998) offers a broad discussion of business clusters and what may motivate firms to co-locate and/or co-operate, and provides a range of interesting examples in an industrial context. He identifies some of the factors supporting the clustering of business which are unobservable from a stock market perspective. An early economic analysis and motivation of clustering appears in Elton and Gruber (1970). Our approach is high-level, akin to that of Elton and Gruber (1970) and looks to establish clustering of returns in the stock market, using indicators of unobservable latent activity. The outcome is a segmentation of the market based on BM ratios that predicts a segmentation of the market in terms of subsequent returns. There is already available some evidence for this phenomenon: Boyer (2007) reports evidence of co-movement of stocks with similar BM ratios. We assess the economic conditions to establish segmentation in a market and, in so doing, identify the economic relevance of clustering methodologies, such as MSTs, as analytical approaches that explain economic phenomena and produce testable hypotheses.

The first observation to emphasise is that clustering will take place in a *rational* framework if related *clustering* risk factors are identified. This is essentially the work that has been undertaken to date, using spanning trees in the stock market with the identification of industrial clusters. These are, in fact, a reflection of clusters that are modelled by a single factor market index, such as the CAPM. BM has long been argued as a risk factor separate to that of the market index, but its exact role has been the source of some dispute. Even so, what existing work has not done and which we evidence here, is to establish the relationship between the BM ratio as an indicator that is both a phenomenon that identifies an economically meaningful stock market cluster *and* which has returns predictability. If clustering is reflective of latent activity, it is possible that the underlying relationship may be nonlinear. Such nonlinearity is not necessarily at variance with a risk-based explanation. For example, Chauvet and Potter (2000) construct a financial stock market indicator based on a broad information set and which is very likely to be nonlinear in relation to market states and which has been confirmed as being consistent within an optimising framework (Backus and Gregory 1993). In essence, clustering by MSTs is a method that is capable of revealing the role of latent nonlinear relationships (Fortunato 2010; Gorban, Smirnova, and Tykina 2010). Clustering, as Menzly and Ozbas (2010) argue, requires:

(iv) a sub-set of firms that have correlated fundamentals, or
(v) information is segmentally analysed.

Correlated fundamentals would be a consistent explanation at a firm level for the circumstances described in Porter (1998). Hong, Torous, and Valanov (2007) evidence industry performance preceding that of stock markets and which is based on a correlation of fundamentals. Their work then leads onto explaining how cross-correlations of returns within an industry emerge and offers predictability for (1 and 2 monthly) excess stock returns due to slow diffusion of information. Jegadeesh and Titman (1993) agree that slow diffusion can give rise to returns momentum (that is, period by period predictability using a trading rule that takes a long position in rising stocks and a short position in falling stocks). Moskowitz and Grinblatt (1999) confirm industry-based returns exhibit momentum which supports this case. These reports are consistent with that outlined above in relation to Hayek's view of the nature of the economic problem to be solved in the light of partial information access and/or incomplete information processing. Moreover, a key aspect of the work of Hong, Torous, and Valanov (2007) is the focus of attention of investors to only limited parts of the universe of stocks. In such circumstances, 'asset classes' emerge and style investment becomes a recognisable phenomenon. This leads us to the key hypothesis of the paper: we argue that it is the investment by style class that leads to clustering and that BM is a major style factor from which associated clustering of returns may be predicted. It should be noted that Barberis and Shleifer (2003) have shown that cross-correlations within styles do not have to arise as a response to correlations to fundamentals (cash flows), but merely emerge because of common style attributes. That is, 'analysts' analyse on the basis of styles. In any case, we observe that BM is an important style that could potentially give rise to a 'segmentation' with the implication that returns co-predictability emerges: Chan, Chen, and Lakonishok (2002) report that both size and BM in the Fama and French (1993) three-factor model do a good job in summarising mutual fund managers' investment styles, for example. Strong and Xu (1997) examine the cross-section of expected returns for UK equities and also find average returns significantly positively related to BM.

3. Methodology

Our empirical examination reflects portfolio choice in the manner of the mimicking portfolio techniques widely employed by other researchers. This section details our approach. In summary, we employ BM ratios to select stocks in a ranking period to form portfolios. Portfolio membership is determined by positions in an MST. We then compare performance with a returns-based MST in a subsequent holding period and look for similarities in portfolio membership as one indicator of returns predicability. The detailed considerations are as follows.

3.1 *MSTs and distance measures*

An MST is a connected network of nodes in which the sum of the weights of the links (arcs) is minimised. The information requirements of the MST are much less than the non-minimised networks. The non-minimised networks are of size $N \times N$ with $N(N-1)/2$ separate edges. The number of edges of an MST are $N - 1$. The practical advantage of this is that it is reflective of portfolio construction, using a shrinkage routine which, in our case, is based on style investment using BM ratios. Mantegna (1999) first applied a (Euclidean) distance metric based on correlations of returns between stocks which enabled geometric properties of the stock market to be explored although the formal relationship between correlation coefficients and Euclidean distances has been well-known for some time (Cronbach and Gleser 1953; Rohlf and Sokal 1965; Coxon 1982; Fox 1982; Sneath and Sokal 1973). Subsequently, MSTs have been reported as being economically meaningful in terms of identifying economic sectors, based on returns, within the market as clusters that map to industry sectors (Mantegna and Stanley 2000; Bonanno, Lillo, and Mantegna 2001a, 2001b; Song, Zhi-Qiang, and Wei-Xing 2009) and which has been extended to commodities markets (Sieczka and Hoyst 2009), currency markets (Matesanz and Ortega 2005; McDonald et al. 2005; Naylor, Rose, and Brendan 2007; Brida, Gómez, and Wiston 2009), examination of market crises (Sornette 2000, 2002, 2005; Lillo and Mantegna 2002; Onnela et al. 2003; Sornette and Helmstetter 2003; Araújo and Louçã 2005); market contagions (Matesanz and Ortega 2008); and to exchanges across the world (Coelhoa et al. 2007).

The topological properties of the MSTs we estimate offer new statistical measures that show how investment evaluations of BM ratios may be usefully related to individual stock correlations and thereby potentially reflect investment decisions that account for portfolio selection techniques and which relate differences in BM values to return correlation structures. The linkage between the MST methodology and the theory-based approaches is that both are essentially factor models which can then be related to returns. Our approach enables prediction in a manner identical to existing factor regression approaches and, for that reason, is methodologically distinct from research to date employing MSTs. Indeed, this addresses Lux's (2008) criticism that 'the major weakness of available research in this area is that it has confined itself to illustrating the application of a particular methodology' (pp. 18–19) as opposed to explaining the causes of the effects observed. Our contribution, as we explain below, is a direct *a priori* (predictive) test of relevance of the MSTs we construct which is a departure from the *a posteriori* work undertaken to date.[3] Additionally, our approach is able to offer a perspective on the role of BM in relation to the market as a whole that is immune to the statistical inadequacies we mention and is able to account for relationships undiscernable in the usual linear models.

If MSTs are to have a substantive economic role, then their interpretation and usefulness as predictive devices is dependent on the calculation of the distance metric. There are two stages to the creation of an MST: first, the choice of the source data variable and, second, the distance translation. The source data variable for the correlation of returns MST is the log ratio of daily stock prices. $r = (\ln(S_t/S_{t-1})$, where S is the stock price) and the correlation between returns of companies i and j is defined as: $\rho_{ij} = \mathrm{Cov}(r_i r_j)/\sigma_i\sigma_j$. Thus, nodes are represented by the companies and the links are weighted by the correlations in returns between the companies. The return correlations are then converted to Euclidean distances, using the distance transformation $d_{ij} = \sqrt{2(1-\rho_{ij})}$. This satisfies the properties of a distance metric (Mantegna 1999) and also ensures that correlation and its distance transformation are structurally equivalent (see Wasserman and Faust 2006, 366) and, hence, no information is lost in the transformation as long as the correlations are first standardised as zero mean, unit variance variables. Because of the exact structural equivalence in the correlation and its associated distance metric, we do not consider other distance metrics in our empirical analysis. The source data for the BM ratio is the book value per share divided by the stock price per share. For the BM ratio, the nodes are the companies and the links are the differences in BM ratios. We form matrices of size $N \times N$ of Euclidean-transformed BM differences, using the following transformation:

$$d_{ij} = \sqrt{(\mathrm{BM}_i - \mathrm{BM}_j)^2}. \tag{3}$$

The MST from this distance measure is reflective of search procedures for portfolio construction that is fully sympathetic to well-recognised investor behaviour. In other words, in order to identify a style class, investment managers group companies on the basis of similar BM ratios (with differences minimised) and select an investment portfolio from a subset that satisfies an investment style class requirement. For example, to identify a style group defined on the basis of 'high growth', companies will be sorted and grouped according to low values of the BM ratio. Once the distance measures are calculated, the MST is then formed.

3.2 *Portfolio construction*

We adopt a portfolio mimicking strategy that directly reflects investor behaviour and is widely used in the academic literature to attest performance. We use daily stock return data for all companies listed on the UK stock exchange over the period 2005–2009. Specifically, we collect daily stock price data from the beginning of July 2005 to the end of June 2009. For each six-month period beginning 1 July 2005, we calculate daily log returns and convert them into correlations between all stocks to form an $N \times N$ stock return correlation matrix. These are converted to Euclidean distances as described above. In relation to BM ratios, we collect all available BM ratios twice yearly at the end of May and the end of November. Thus, there are 8 series of data available from May 2005 to November 2008. As part of a mimicking portfolio strategy, we construct (Euclidean) differences between all values of BM as one measure that investors might use to detect value and/or growth stocks. In this way, we mimic the process by which investors search for value and growth through comparison of BM ratios. The advantage of using BM differences is that it enables BM pair-wise relationships to be identified which will be crucial to the calculation of the MST. Thus, with BM differences calculated for all pairs of stocks, we produce an $N \times N$ BM difference matrix. BM values can then be ordered and compared on economic grounds because BM Euclidean differences retain their underlying transitivity properties (Hill 2001) and thus decisions may be made on the basis of preferences: that is, by grouping together differences that are small, we are undertaking the same exercise as if we were grouping BM ratios that are similar in style. The benchmark implicit in this is a rank ordering similar to that used in portfolio minimum variance selection through selection by the lowest correlation (that is, correlation closest to -1). There is then a natural partnering and economic interpretation between BM ratio *differences* and the return correlation matrix constructed. Our intention, therefore, is to use the MST for BM differences to detect relationships of economic substance in the return correlation MST. The measures of economic substance we will search-for relate to the distance and centrality statistics outlined below. In this way, if BM has value as a predictive device for stock return correlations, then it should be able to detect or indicate the topological (distance and centrality) measures of stock return correlations six months hence.

The next part of the portfolio mimicking strategy relates to the time periods used that demarcate our portfolio ranking periods from holding periods. This establishes the predictive capability of the MSTs we produce. In portfolio selection that uses a leading indicator, such as the BM ratio, there is typically a ranking period to determine values of BM on which stock selection decisions are based. Once stock selection is determined, stock portfolios are created and held over what is known as the holding period. Thus, our first ranking period begins with the calculation of BM ratios at 31 May 2005. This is then paired with a holding period in which return correlations are calculated from 1 July 2005 to 31 December 2006. There is a one month gap between ranking and holding periods which is usual in this type of portfolio mimicking. Subsequent pair-wise ranking and holding periods are defined similarly. Thus, we end up with eight pairs of MSTs to compare. Some further observations are relevant at this point. First, in using six monthly ranking and holding periods, we are able to reflect investment practice that is based on the latest information available in BM ratios.[4] With a 6 month gap between calculating BM ratios, we ensure that there is at least a new BM ratio at each MST calculation and avoid the persistence problem referred to earlier. Moreover, there is a potentially a significant problem in employing longer time periods when economic and market conditions are varying. As Ang and Chen (2002) note, correlations are asymmetric when conditioned on market states. That is, they find equity market correlations of the US are, on average, 11.6% higher during market contractions compared with a normal distribution. Given the volatility of the market during our own sample period, estimating correlations over extended periods runs the risk of masking important effects we seek to account-for. Second, our data sample is restricted by data availability. Prior to 2005, available data on BM ratios is poor and does not cover the universe of stocks and will consequently provide a poor comparison base. At the time of drafting (March 2010), accounting results are not available that would allow BMs to be calculated to produce a comparison with holding returns ending December 2009, hence our final holding period is June 2009. Third, as demonstrated in Figure 1, our sampling period extends into the financial crisis. On the basis of this evidence, we are confident that the MSTs we calculate cover a range of exceptionally different and difficult market conditions and should provide a good examination of test robustness.

We calculate eight pairs of MSTs for BM ratios and returns correlation based on the matching periods described above. Our core hypothesis is that, from a topological perspective, BM spanning trees reflect returns correlation MSTs 6 months hence. We specifically compare distance, centrality and positional measures in order to determine this and which are core structural concepts (Wasserman and Faust 2006). Since the results are not distribution based, we do not offer,

Figure 1. FTSE All share index 2005–2009.

in common with most other researchers, statistical tests.[5] However, Tumminello et al. (2007) report bootstrap tests of link reliability in MSTs. Interestingly, they observe that link reliability in a returns correlation network is not strictly associated with the size (strength) of the correlation coefficient and conclude 'that the strength of a link and its reliability in correlation-based networks are carrying partially different information'. (p. 2325). Their results confirm the reliability of the MST as a clustering device of economically meaningful groupings by demonstrating that intra-cluster links are more reliable than inter-cluster links. We also acknowledge that Garas and Argyrakis (2009) have usefully generalised the MST approach to a dynamic setting by the introduction and demonstration of the idea of an Overlapping Tree Network which, akin to our own hypothesis and results, has been revealing of the role of central nodes in stock market networks.

3.3 *Tackling the curse of dimensionality*

In Markowitz portfolio optimsations, if the number of stocks (N) is greater than the number of historical returns per stock (T), then estimating the sample covariance matrix is subject to significant error and is dominated by noise (Jagannathan and Ma 2003; Tola et al. 2008) and using a sample covariance in such cirumstances can lead to a portfolio with very poor performance (Pantaleo et al. 2010). The dimension ratio T/N must always exceed 1 in order to begin to mitigate this. However, a note of caution is pertinant, here, to make sure that this problem is not over-stated in practical settings when meeting the requirements of an investment decision. The reality is that an unconstrained covariance matrix covering the entire stock market – or even a large proportion of it – is almost never used. As Ledoit and Wolf (2003) note, the sample covariance matrix is seldom employed since it contains insufficient structure. What happens in practice is that some sort of shrinkage of the dimension of the covariance matrix is applied, as would happen if a 'structure' is superimposed. In fact, Jagannathan and Ma (2003) show that shrinkage is implicit when short sales are ruled-out, for example, as they often are in portfolio optimisation, because it is known that it is difficult to create short sale positions in many circumstances, for many stocks, and even for the most active markets (D'Avolio 2002). In practical terms, shrinkage is a common occurrence.

Nonetheless, the problem must be recognised to avoid reporting potentially spurious results. If we are to shrink the value of N, which is implied by imposing a structure on the portfolio weights, then a motivation for the structure should be based on an economic rationale to remain consistent with a key objective of this paper. A theoretical structure most frequently involves calculating expected returns according to a factor model (from CAPM (Sharpe 1964; Lintner 1965; Merton 1973), to APT (Ross 1976), to the three factor models of Fama and French (1993), and augmented to four factors using Carhart's (1997) momentum results. This is the approach we adopt and have already motivated a returns based model in terms of the BM ratio. That is, we employ a ranking/holding period structure that mimics portfolio management and which assists with the dimension problem. The statistical benefit of such an approach is that the problem of estimating expected returns and standard deviations is de-coupled from that of the estimation of the correlation matrix, a procedure outlined in Tola et al. (2008). We offer a different perspective on this problem, based in spirit on the results in Tola et al. (2008). As will be reported below, a key result from our empirical work is that BM MSTs are able to suggest a very restricted portfolio structure in an investment ranking period compared with a returns MST in the subsequent holding period. That is, a portfolio determined in a ranking period based on the idea of a central referencing company (or companies) is able to predict returns in a subsequent investment holding period that has very similar central referencing properties. The investment benefit of this is that we are able to predict returns behaviour of central referencing companies *and* reduce the transactions costs surrounding portfolio diversification for large N. The whole idea of central referencing companies and the methodology we employ is that we are able to reduce the size of N in our portfolio and reduce transactions costs.

An economic motivation, as expressed in a factor model, then provides a justification for dealing with a statistical problem that also can lead to improved statistical performance: 'combining historical data with "expert knowledge" (which is usually done in practice) or drawing up some guidelines which must be observed by the decision maker can lead to more reasonable and well-diversified portfolios rather than relying on pure statistical portfolio optimization methods' (Frahm 2008, 792). Spanning tree methods is one approach to imposing structure. If the spanning tree is minimised over a factor model that is consistent with economic theory then we have the means of theoretically reducing the value of N and thus 'cleaning' the sample covariance matrix of noise. Thus, our method indicates a strategy whereby investment choice may be simplified since the identification of reference companies enables investment managers to ignore or drop many companies from consideration in portfolio choice and thereby reduce noise in the sample covariance matrix. We report results for 6 month and 2 year holding periods and note that our key results, as predicted, are unchanged.[6]

4. Results and analysis

4.1 *Introductory analysis*

As an initial analysis we show representative and truncated single linkage dendrogams for the BM ratio and returns in Figures 2 and 3. These are illustrative of some common themes we wish to draw out and will act as preparatory work for detailed analysis to follow. Full dendrograms contain upwards over 400+ companies and are too large to meaningfully represent here and for that reason we have truncated them. Ordinarily, this process would contain less information but, as we explain, the truncated versions highlight economically meaningful differences that we explain. In any case, we report full dendrograms for all periods in this article's companion website.[7]

Our calculation of the dendrograms is a nearest-neighbour single linkage clustering and are optimised automatically within SPSS for returns. Schwarz's Bayesian criterion is employed to determine clustering for returns. but such tests are inappropriate for BM.[8] The single linkage clustering method is selected because its relationship to the associated MST is well known. Tumminello et al. (2007) demonstrate the formal relationship between a single linkage cluster algorithm and that used to produce a MST and explain the nature of the additional information contained in the MST as being the result of the fact that 'hierarchical clustering disregards the role of single elements in the cluster merging process while in spanning trees such a role is taken into account' (p. 2320), an observation which is fully sympathetic to our search for single reference companies. Thus our analysis draws out the *economic* differences between the single linkage dendrogram and associated MSTs in the knowledge that the technical differences are identifiable and explicable.

While we have truncated the dendrograms they are, in fact, representative of the whole as can be seen from the full dendrograms. An immediate observation is that the BM dendrogram is not revealing of any clustering, except those arising from outliers, whilst the returns clusters exhibit some limited clustering. The Bayesian Information Criterion statistics do not confirm more than two clusters for returns and, hence, the information produced by the single linkage method is not very revealing of distinctions in the data for either case. In essence, this validates

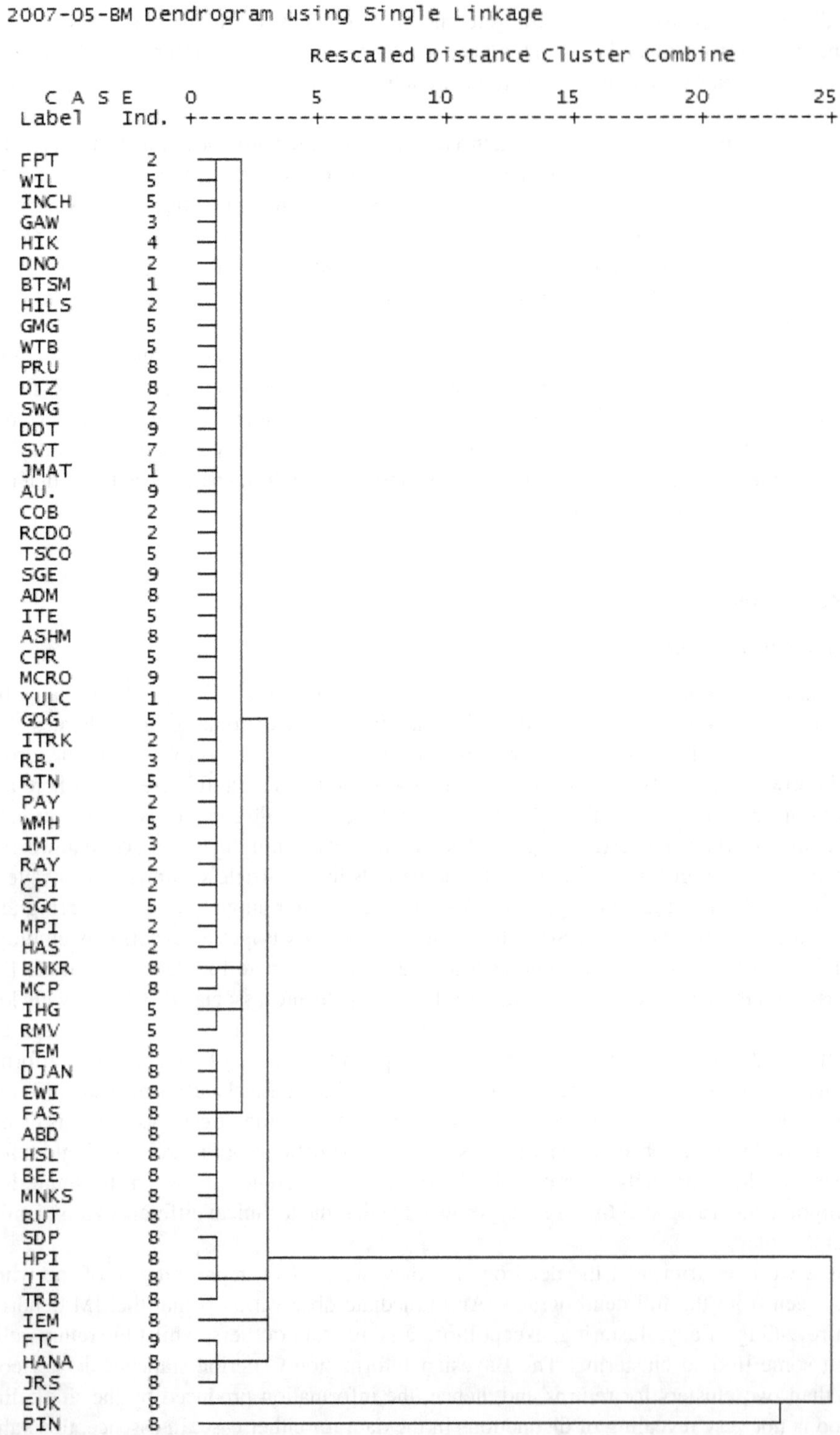

Figure 2. BM ratio truncated dendrogram.

Notes: First column is the firm acronym. The second column is the industry SIC membership of the firm and identified as: 0, oil and gas; 1, basic materials; 2, industrials; 3, consumer goods; 4, health care; 5, consumer services; 6, telecommunications; 7, utilities; 8, financials; 9, technology.

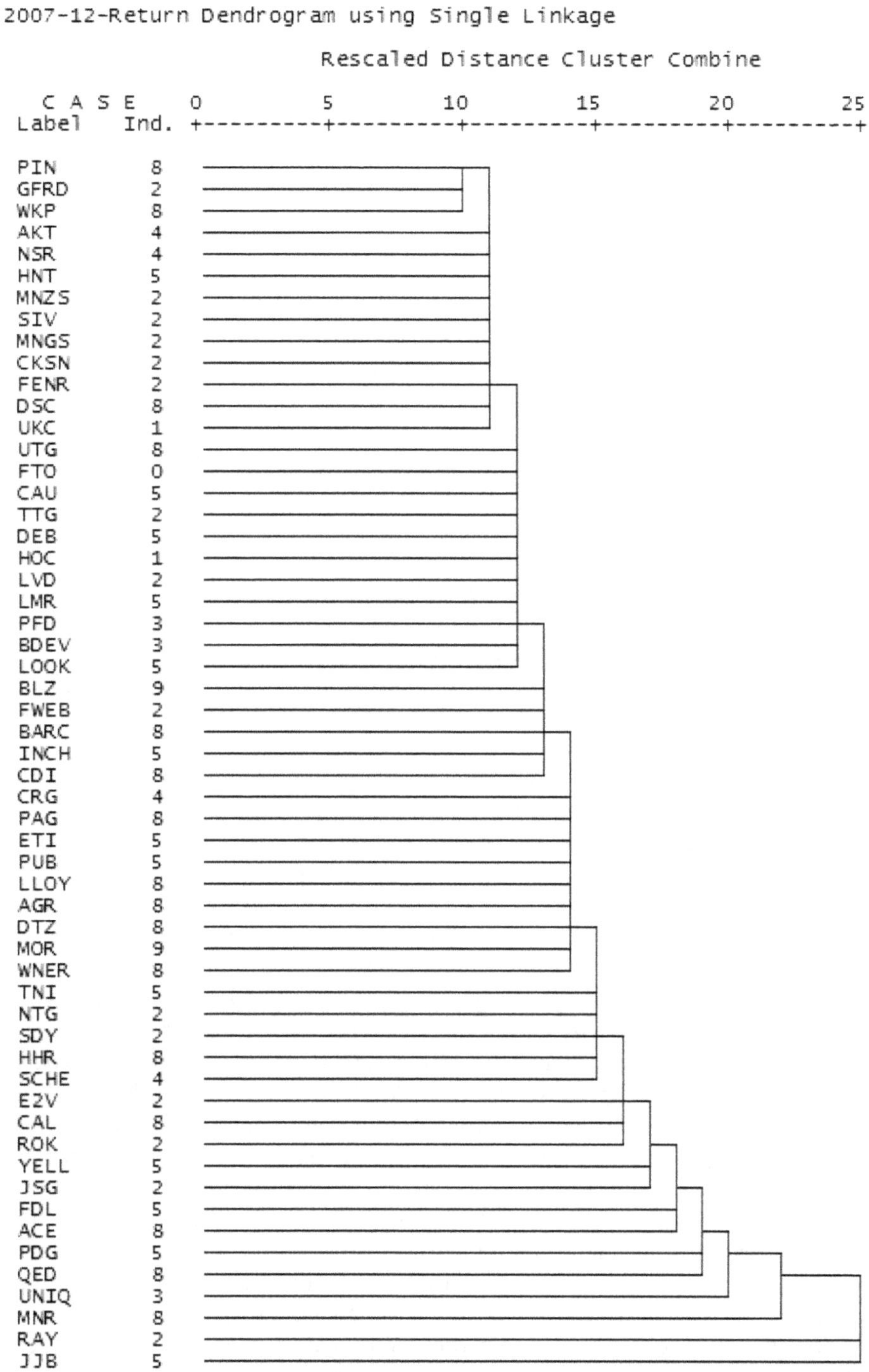

Figure 3. One year returns truncated dendrogram.
Notes: First column is the firm acronym. The second column is the industry SIC membership of the firm and identified as: 0, oil and gas; 1, basic materials; 2, industrials; 3, consumer goods; 4, health care; 5, consumer services; 6, telecommunications; 7, utilities; 8, financials; 9, technology.

the value of an information extraction method such as MST which we go on to demonstrate is able to draw-out economically meaningful groupings. Some economic sectors in returns are weakly discernable in terms of adjacency at the lowest 'leaf' level in the tree with Financial sector companies noticeable and also some evidence for 'Industrials'. Such a finding is consistent with other dendrogram methods employed to analyse the US stock market in Tumminello et al. (2010) and is also consistent with the economic groupings found for many works for correlated returns in MSTs (Mantegna 1999; Bonanno, Lillo, and Mantegna 2001b; Tumminello et al. 2007).

4.2 *Minimum spanning trees*

The eight pairs of MSTs are calculated and example trees for 2006 are shown in Appendix 1. Basic network statistics are reported in Table 1 and distance and centrality measures are reported in Table 2. The MST for returns reported in Appendix 1 look unsurprisingly similar to those reported elsewhere for other countries and with smaller samples of companies (for example, in Bonanno, Lillo, and Mantegna 2001b reporting on the USA) although there are some differences in appearance over the years (not shown). The temporal differences are best analysed via the statistics reported in Tables 1 and 2 since they are not influenced by presentation biases in the MST pictures.

The average degree of both returns and BM MSTs are very similar but are effectively a feature of the MST algorithm where, for a large number of nodes, there are at most two links and often only one. With n nodes and, for most nodes, two links then average degree will be somewhere between one and two, depending on the degree of clustering. As we subsequently demonstrate (Table 3), all MSTs are clustered around a few central nodes and average degree is persisently at approximately 1.9 across both types of tree and across all periods as reported in Table 1. Degree distributions for many real (non-MST) networks exhibit a power law relation with few nodes exhibiting many links and many nodes exhibiting few links. Power laws are of the form: $P(k) \sim k^{-\alpha}$. It is the value of α that is reported in Table 1 as the power law exponent. Dealing with returns correlations first: typical values for α are $\alpha > 2$, approximately (Onnela, Chakraborti, and Kaski 2003 report $\alpha = 2.1$ for the NYSE for 1980–1999; Vandewalle, Brisbois, and Tordoir 2001 report $\alpha = 2.2$ for 1999 on the NYSE, NASDAQ, and AMEX exchanges). Hence the values we report are low by comparison although, as Garas and Argyrakis (2007) observe, during financial crises returns correlations power law exponents fall: they report $\alpha = 1.9$ for the Greek stock exchange over the period 1987–2004 with a fall to $\alpha = 1.7$ for the crisis period of 1999–2001, a value consistent with that reported in Onnela, Chakraborti, and Kaski (2003) of $\alpha = 1.8$ for a value around Black Monday in 1987. Garas and Argyrakis (2007) note that this effect, at least for the Greek market, is associated with increased correlations (and reduced Euclidean distances). This finding is consistent with the evidence reported in Ang and Chen (2002) who report correlations for US equities on average 11.6% higher during US market contractions. More notable is the difference we report in the power law exponent compared with the BM network that typically reports α in excess of 4. The implication of this is that the BM MSTs exhibit average degrees that decline exponentially (much more sharply than the power law typical values). That is, the probability of finding a node with more links than the average becomes very small compared with an α close to 2 which is often referred to as having small world properties (Wang and Chen 2003). Thus, we expect to see in the BM MST fewer nodes with many connections than is the case with returns correlations. The implication of this, and for which we provide further evidence below, is that the BM MST is, in a sense, simplifying the structure of returns correlations if it is, as we hypothese, acting as a predictive tool for the returns correlations. This would make sense, intuitively, since we would

Table 1. Basic network statistics.

Panel A: BM	2005–2005	2005–2011	2006–2006	2006–2011	2007–2005	2007–2011	2008–2005	2008–2011
Average degree	1.97	1.97	1.98	1.94	1.94	1.95	1.96	1.96
Network centralisation %	0.29	0.26	0.25	0.37	0.72	0.24	0.25	0.55
Power law exponent	4.33	4.50	4.46	4.56	4.45	5.88	4.77	4.58
Panel B: Returns (6 months)	**2005–2012**	**2006–2006**	**2006–2012**	**2007–2006**	**2007–2012**	**2008–2006**	**2008–2012**	**2009–2006**
Average degree	1.99	1.99	1.99	1.99	1.99	1.99	1.99	1.99
Network centralisation %	27.44	16.63	13.27	17.61	18.35	19.68	18.3	16.34
Power law exponent	1.92	1.26	0.96	0.91	2.05	1.38	1.44	1.22
Panel C: Returns (2 years)	**2005–2012**	**2006–2006**	**2006–2012**	**2007–2006**	**2007–2012**	**2008–2006**	**2008–2012**	**2009–2006**
Average degree	1.99	1.99	1.99	1.99	1.99	1.99	1.99	N/A
Network centralisation %	26.27	14.89	15.30	28.35	18.16	16.26	18.3	N/A
Power law exponent	0.80	1.18	1.37	0.97	1.13	1.45	1.47	N/A

Notes: The average degree is the number of links attaching to a node divided by $n-1$. Network centralisation is the degree of variation in the degrees of nodes divided by the maximum degree variation. The power law exponent is the value of α in the power law relation $P(k) \sim k^{-\alpha}$. Two panels for returns are shown. Panel B reports results for returns based on correlations calculated over the 6 month period and Panel C reports results for returns based on correlations calculated over a 1 year period. Note that data unavailability means that there are no 2 year returns to present for the final period 2009–2006.

Table 2. Distance and centrality measures.

Panel A: BM	2005–2005	2005–2011	2006–2006	2006–2011	2007–2005	2007–2011	2008–2005	2008–2011
Average path length	6.58	6.88	6.61	6.93	6.68	6.83	6.98	6.25
Network diameter	16	18	16	15	15	17	16	14
Betweeness	1.56	1.48	1.41	1.35	0.43	1.29	1.32	1.15
Panel B: Returns (6 months)	**2005–2012**	**2006–2006**	**2006–2012**	**2007–2006**	**2007–2012**	**2008–2006**	**2008–2012**	**2009–2006**
Average path length	2.45	4.38	4.23	3.67	3.16	5.65	4.36	4.53
Network diameter	8	14	12	12	10	16	14	14
Betweeness	0.40	0.85	0.81	0.60	0.48	1.02	0.74	0.71
Panel C: Returns (2 years)	**2005–2012**	**2006–2006**	**2006–2012**	**2007–2006**	**2007–2012**	**2008–2006**	**2008–2012**	**2009–2006**
Average path length	2.77	4.78	3.408	3.38	3.45	3.56	4.40	N/A
Network diameter	9	13	8	11	10	9	11	N/A
Betweeness	0.556	0.904	0.680	0.575	0.494	0.591	0.800	N/A

Table 3. Identification of central nodes and degree values.

Panel A: BM															
2005–2005		2005–2011		2006–2005		2006–2011		2007–2005		2007–2011		2008–2005		2008–2011	
Company	Degree	Company	Degree	Company	Degree	Company	Degree	Company	Degree	Company	Degree	Company	Degree	Company	Degree
AV	23	RIO	15	ALL	18	RB	18	RB	23	HSD	20	HSD	20	AVV	27
BLND	10	AAL	14	SBRY	9	ROI	11	RIO	13	BAY	12	BAY	12	EMG	12
RBS	10	PMO	10	FEV	9	AZN	11	WTB	12	PSN	11	TATE	9	LII	11
GSK	9	BAY	10	RCP	9	ANTO	11	LMI	10	VED	10	AHI	9	SBRY	10
YELL	9	BDEV	10	PMO	9	CLDN	9	MAB	10	GFS	9	REX	8	CCL	10
VED	6	SBRY	10	EMG	9	SUS	9	LAD	10			BARC	8	WPP	10
Panel B: Returns (6 months)															
2006–2012		2006–2006		2006–2012		2007–2006		2007–2012		2008–2006		2008–2012		2009–2006	
Company	Degree	Company	Degree	Company	Degree	Company	Degree	Company	Degree	Company	Degree	Company	Degree	Company	Degree
AV	274	BB.	135	BB	149	RB	302	RB	321	HSD	205	HSD	232	AVV	172
ATST	68	AAL	128	ALL	128	AV	47	CLDN	50	JAM	59	RB	74	SBRY	109
		AV	41	AV	30	WTAN	28	RDSB	30	TATE	49	TATE	42	MKS	72
		WTAN	35	WTAN	25	TRG	27	AV	11	REX	35	REX	25	FRCL	44
		PNN	17	FWP	21	TEM	20	WTAN	11	ITRK	24	GEO	10	BYG	11
		BTEM	11	FEV	20					WTAN	21			JMG	10
Panel C: Returns (1 year)															
2006–2012		2006–2006		2006–2012		2007–2006		2007–2012		2008–2006		2008–2012		2009–2006	
Company	Degree	Company	Degree	Company	Degree	Company	Degree	Company	Degree	Company	Degree	Company	Degree	Company	Degree
AV	249	EMG	166	PNN	129	RB	328	RB	332	HSD	199	HSD	164	N/A	N/A
ATST	44	AZN	85	AAL	125	CLDN	29	CLDN	17	RB	83	RB	74		
		FRCL	45	BTEM	38	WTAN	17	WTAN	17	TATE	80	TATE	68		
		TMPL	28	PMO	34	HNE	10	RDSB	11	JAM	20	RDSA	33		
		AVV	23	FEV	12					ABF	13	VED	26		
		RIO	18									WTAN	21		
		WPP	18									REX	19		

Notes: We report clusters of more than five for BM and more than nine for returns. Two panels for returns are shown. Panel B reports results for returns based on correlations calculated over the 6-month period and Panel C reports results for returns based on correlations calculated over a 1-year period. Note that data unavailability means that there are no 2 year returns to present for the final period 2009–2006. Appendix 2 lists the companies referred to in acronym form.

expect the signalling device to be a more parsimonious representation of the reality we are trying to predict in order to help our understanding of more complex situations. Network centralisation is the degree of variation in the degrees of nodes divided by the maximum degree variation. It is a measure of node connectedness. A more centralised network will have more nodes that have more links (see Wasserman and Faust 2006). Thus, it is clear that the returns tree has more companies that are more connected than is reflected in the BM tree. This is consistent with our view, to be developed, that the BM tree is able to extract information in a relatively efficient (unclustered) manner from the returns information it is hypothesised to forecast.

Average path length is the average number of links between all connecting nodes. The network diameter is the maximum path length. The betweeness index is a measure of how nodes are vital for communication with other nodes: it is a 'go-between' concept and is an important indication of the flow of information in a network (Wasserman and Faust 2006). Two panels for returns are shown. Panel B reports results for returns based on correlations calculated over the 6-month period and Panel C reports results for returns based on correlations calculated over a 1-year period. Note that data unavailability means that there are no 2 year returns to present for the final period 2009–2006.

Table 2 reports tree diameters and maximum path lengths which are very similar for both BM and returns. In combination with the average degree, we observe that node connections and the distances between nodes in both networks are very similar and, from a distance point of view and in replicating the linkages involved between BM and returns, the two MSTs are topologically very similar. This is consistent with results reported consistently elsewhere and referred to above. However, as we report in Table 2, the betweeness centrality figures are very different. Betweeness is a reflection of how many companies are central to the communications channels within a network. It is analogous to a 'go-between' concept. Nodes, or companies, that act as go-between in this sense are extremely important to the information flows within a network. The more betweeness that a network exhibits the more there is likely to be a 'reference' node. In the evidence we report, betweeness is substantially higher in the BM tree than in returns (of the order of twice as large approximately). Betweeness is another measure of centralisation which indicates how the network is positioned around a few dominant companies, but it is different to the centralisation reported in Table 1. Thus the return networks are the most highly centralised on degree centralisation, but not on betweeness centralisation. This result indicates that returns are more clustered than BM, but that BM exhibits more influential companies. This would be intuitively reasonable for a predictive device that the BM ratio is meant to be: if BMs are used to select companies for portfolio inclusion then we should as a first step identify which are the most influential companies. These companies might otherwise be referred to as 'reference companies'. Such companies represent 'bell-weather' stocks that investors look to as indicators of more general performance and betweeness represents a parsimonious representation of a large amount of information. Thus, it may be possible that BM is able to extract central reference companies from very different clustering regimes between the two data sets. We now evidence this proposition.

Table 3 reports a ranking of the most connected companies for BM and returns for each of the periods under study. The data reflect the heavier clustering of returns with nodes exhibiting higher connectivity. What appears remarkable in Table 3 is the consistent choice in the ranking of most connected companies: in six out of eight periods for 6 month return holding periods, BM and returns choose the same company to connect. This is not an artefact of the calculation for a number of reasons, we would argue. First, the BM ranking appears 6 months prior to the returns ranking and so is a prediction of company positioning ahead of time. Second, companies only occupy the top spot for at most two periods so there is work for the prediction to do in accounting for changed circumstances and still retain its predictive ability. In fact, in all periods the BM ranking is able to identify one of the top two companies that the returns ranking presents. Third, the sample companies run into hundreds for each of the periods involved and hence the identification of central companies out of the morass of information available looks to be a significant feat. Fourth, the economic circumstances that featured quite dramatic change over our sample period indicate clearly, we would suggest, that the signal that BM is producing in terms of identifying reference companies is robust to quite volatile markets. Fifth, the dynamics of the BM centrality findings are consistent with known explanations of correlation dynamics over different economic circumstances. That is, over the period of study correlations have increased which is consistent with the view that distance has reduced and that the market behaves in a more self-consistent manner. This is reflected, too, in the centrality measures we report with the consequence that reference companies become *more dominant* or clustered during times when the market is experiencing closer correlation. For the period under observation, the behaviour of the market was characterised by a bull run during 2007–2008 followed by the financial crisis. Our results, in this sense, are completely consistent with those reported for correlation movements over the same period in, for example, Aste, Shaw, and Di Matteo (2010). The idea of a reference stock is not new (Moore, Boehm, and Banerji 1994; Chauvet and Potter 2000) but, to our knowledge, this is the first presentation of predictive ability in identifying a reference stock from another information source that is consistently used in the investment industry. Appendix 2 lists the companies referred to in acronym form in Table 3.

Previous work has been restricted to examining MSTs in relation to identifying economically meaningful taxonomies of various financial markets. We should mention that only Bonanno et al. (2003) have attempted a mapping of market factors to returns, but have restricted their work to the single factor CAPM and have not attempted any predictive, portfolio selection work as we have done. Their work was to look for topological similarities between actual returns and returns simulated from the CAPM. Their conclusion was that the CAPM model failed to describe the topological properties of the MST of a portfolio of stocks for the NYSE using daily data. In Bonanno, Lillo, and Mantegna (2001b), they demonstrate that the structure of the MST varies with the time horizon used to calculate returns. Our results are different since we construct time horizons with meaningful economic substance based on an investment horizon linked to the most frequent periodicity available for the investment signal (i.e. six monthly book values in the BM ratio). The MST so determined can then be interpreted in that context. The MST for US data over the period 1987–1998 provided in Bonanno, Lillo, and Mantegna (2001b) (their Figure 1) is again similar to the figures presented in the appendix of this paper. The single factor CAPM MST (their Figure 2) contains a large central cluster with satellite nodes and is different, as presented, to the MSTs for BM we report.[9] Bonanno et al. (2003) calculate returns from the CAPM and compare with the observed returns. This, naturally, brings with it all of the estimation problems concerned with CAPM, such as non-stationary betas. The CAPM MST cannot identify clusters in the Bonanno et al. (2003) paper. However, they do identify General Electric as one of their central nodes. Their power law exponent is 2.6 for actual returns. Their highest observed degree was General Electric with $k_{max} = 115$. They also find reference companies to be important (another example is Coca Cola) and also calculate the relevant statistics for a random MST, but they do not appear helpful in any way. For the CAPM MST, $k_{max} = 718$ and with a rapidly decaying distribution (they do not report the exponent value). In sum, they argue that the CAPM and actual returns MST are very different due, as they argue, to the noise present in real data that is washed-out in the calculated (simulated, as they put it) returns from the CAPM. But their approach is not a stock selection approach and is only a test of the one factor model against real data. It is interesting, they note, that the r-squared value of the CAPM is in excess of 80%, hence the CAPM is relevant in a 'usual' sense (that is, regression-based). But the MSTs display a disconnection that leads them to question the use of the CAPM as an explanatory device for stock returns. Their conclusion is quite revealing 'The MST of real market shows a more structured hierarchy of the importance of the stocks which is not captured by the considered models [*CAPM and the random MST*]. The topology of the stock return correlation-based MST shows large-scale correlation properties characteristic of complex networks in the native, as well as in an oriented form. Such properties cannot be reproduced at all, even as a first approximation, by simple models as a random model or the widespread one-factor model'. (p. 4). Our interpretation of this result is that the use of MSTs as comparators has to be carefully judged as they will not always be applicable. In agreeing with their conclusions regarding the lack of value of the CAPM in explaining the topological properties of actual returns correlations, our findings show that they are appropriate in portfolio selection and that, perhaps, BM is a more useful signal than is the market index inherent in CAPM. This should not be surprising given our acceptance of the assertion that BM is a catch-all factor. What we do show for the first time is the value of BM as a company referencing device. The findings presented here show that view to be supported.

5. Conclusions

Our aim is to look again at the value of the BM ratio in its role as a predictor of returns. We adopt a portfolio approach and place into a theoretical context why BM might be important as a predictor of future cash flows and thereby formalise the relationship between returns and BM. We do not, however, claim that this is a rational investor model since we do not identify the process by which the discount rate is determined. At this stage, we do not think this is important to our results since we have sought only to set-out the potential value in BM rather than contributing to the wider debate on whether BM is a valid risk factor or not.

For the first time to our knowledge, we have used an MST approach that links an investment decision to investment outcome. We have constructed BM trees as devices to predict certain topological properties of returns trees. The statistics we produce assert relationships between BM and returns not previously reported and are revealing of certain structural features of the respective networks that have not previously been identified. Key to our work was to construct the BM comparison tree as a portfolio manager might, so adding weight to the economic substance underlying our work.

Our results show some similarities and some key differences between the two sets of data and perhaps signal where additional work might be fruitful. In particular, the distance properties reveal that both BM and returns exhibit similar characteristics and that this is a consistent feature across different market conditions. The clear economic interpretation of this is that the length of communication patterns bewteen companies as described by the BM ratios and as described by their returns correlations are very similar indeed. This offers support to the theoretical relation outlined in the paper that BM is a predictive device for cash flows and subsequent returns. Clustering between the two trees was different, but this is to be expected: if BM is to act as a signal extraction device then it should be able to present information in a more parsimonious manner than is presented in the returns tree. What was of value, as we evidenced, was the difference in the role of betweeness centrality where it appeared that the BM trees consistently demonstrated a greater concentration of companies which acted as 'go-betweens'. The economic interpretation to this is that the BM tree was able to offer reference companies which were reflective of BM performance across the entire stock market and across our sample period. The final test then rested on whether the BM tree could select reference companies that would be meaningful in the returns tree six months ahead of time. Our evidence showed this to be clearly the case.

In sum, we have demonstrated how an MST technique could be usefully applied in a portfolio context and have interpreted in an economic sense the topological characteristics we observe. We have placed firmly our methodology into a theoretical and practical investment context and have shown and evidenced a new role for the BM ratio.

Acknowledgements

This paper has benefited substantially from editorial and anonymous referee reviews. Without implicating them in any errors and opinions, the authors wish to gratefully acknowledge this contribution.

Notes

1. As Pontiff and Schall detail in their own paper: 'We construct an aggregate book-to-market ratio by dividing the DJIA [Dow Jones Industrial Average] book value by the DJIA index's level. A monthly book-to-market ratio is constructed by dividing the most recent year's book value by the contemporaneous level of the DJIA. Thus, our book-to-market ratio in March 1988 is the book value from December 1987 divided by the level of the DJIA in March 1988; our measure in February 1988 is the book value from December 1986 divided by the level of the DJIA in February 1988. We expect this construction to produce a book-to-market variable that incorporates as much contemporaneous information as possible'. (p. 143). Thus, they are forced to use a 1986 book value as related to a February 1988 market value because the accounting results for the year-end 1987 are not available at the earliest until March 1988, at which time a new book value becomes 'contemporaneous'.
2. MSTs are one method of clustering data with, in this paper, cluster measures based on distance metrics (Schaeffer 2007).
3. Existing work relates only the fact that MSTs coincide with industry correlation structure and minimum variance Markowitz portfolios: they are not a direct test of any hypothesis.
4. Professional money managers are often assessed on their intra-year returns relative to a pre-specified benchmark (Lucas, van Dijk, and Kloek 2002).
5. Random networks are produced in some research but these are not direct tests of MSTs since any randomly determined network is unlikely to be a spanning tree.
6. A 2-year holding period will produce $T/N > 1$ with T (2 years) $\approx$490 and our maximum sample size $N = 432$.
7. We make available full dendrograms and some underlying date along with details of sofware employed in the article's companion website available at: http://www.liv.ac.uk/managementschool/DavidBrookfield/EJF-Brookfield/paper.htm
8. BM ratios are single valued variables at each portfolio ranking period and hence there is no variation in the BM individual data points on which to construct parametric tests.
9. It should be noted that the drawing of MSTs is arbitrary in the sense that there is no single picture which is always representative. This arises literally because of the two-dimensionality of the paper that the diagram is printed on and cannot be reflective of the higher dimensionality of the true network. The MST statistics are the only reliable and consistent basis of comparison between MSTS.

References

Ackermann, J. 2008. The subprime crisis and its consequences. *Journal of Financial Stability* 4, no. 4: 329–37.

Ang, A., and J. Chen. 2002. Asymmetric correlations of equity portfolios. *Journal of Financial Economics* 63, no. 1: 443–94.

Araújo, T., and F. Louçã. 2005. The geometry of crashes – a measure of the dynamics of stock market crises. Paper provided by Department of Economics at the School of Economics and Management (ISEG), Technical University of Lisbon in its series. Working Papers with number 2005/15. http://pascal.iseg.utl.pt/~depeco/wp/wp152005.pdf

Asgharian, H., and B. Hansson. 2010. Book-to-market and size effects: Compensations for risks or outcomes of market inefficiencies? *The European Journal of Finance* 16, no. 2: 119–36.

Aste, T., W. Shaw, and T. Di Matteo. 2010. Correlation structure and dynamics in volatile markets. *New Journal of Physics* 12: 1–21.

Backus, D.K., and A.W. Gregory. 1993. Theoretical relations between risk premiums and conditional variances. *Journal of Business and Economic Statistics* 11, no. 2: 177–85.

Ball, R. 2009. The global financial crisis and the efficient markets hypothesis: What have we learned? *Journal of Applied Corporate Finance* 21, no. 4: 8–16.

Barberis, N., and A. Shleifer. 2003. Style investing. *Journal of Financial Economics* 68, no. 2: 161–99.

Bernstein, R. 1995. *Style investing: Unique insight into equity management*. New York: John Wiley & Sons.

Bonanno, G., F. Lillo, and R.N. Mantegna. 2001a. Levels of complexity in financial markets. *Physica A* 299, nos. 1–2: 16–27.

Bonanno, G., F. Lillo, and R.N. Mantegna. 2001b. High-frequency cross-correlation in a set of stocks. *Quantitative Finance* 1, no. 1: 96–104.

Bonanno, G., G. Caldarelli, F. Lillo, and F.N. Mantegna. 2003. Topology of correlation-based minimal spanning trees in real and model markets. *Physical Review E* 68, no. 046130: 1–4.

Boyer, B.H. 2007. *Comovement among stocks with similar book-to-market ratios*. Utah: Brigham Young University. http://marriottschool.byu.edu/emp/boyer/Research/Feb14_2006.pdf

Brida, J.G., D.M. Gómez, and R.A. Wiston. 2009. Symbolic hierarchical analysis in currency markets: An application to contagion in currency crises. *Expert Systems with Applications* 36, no. 4: 7721–28.

Brown, S., and W. Goetzmann. 1997. Mutual fund styles. *Journal of Financial Economics* 43, no. 3: 373–99.

Carhart, M.M. 1997. On persistence in mutual fund performance. *Journal of Finance* 52, no. 1: 57–82.

Chan, K.C., H.L. Chen, and J. Lakonishok. 2002. On mutual fund investment styles. *Review of Financial Studies* 15, no. 5: 1407–37.

Chauvet, M., and S. Potter. 2000. Coincident and leading indicators of the stock market. *Journal of Empirical Finance* 7, no. 1: 87–111.

Coelhoa, R., C.G. Gilmore, B. Lucey, P. Richmond, and S. Hutzler. 2007. The evolution of interdependence in world equity markets. *Physica A* 376 (July): 455–66.

Coxon, A.P.M. 1982. *The user's guide to multi-dimensional scaling*. Exeter, NH: Heinemann.

Cronbach, L.J., and G.C. Gleser. 1953. Assessing similarity between profiles. *Psychological Bulletin* 50, no. 6: 456–73.

Daniel, K., and S. Titman. 1997. Evidence on the characteristics of cross sectional variation in stock returns. *Journal of Finance* 52, no. 1: 1035–58.

Daniel, K., and S. Titman. 2006. *Testing factor-model explanation of market anomalies*. Austin, TX: Kellog School of Management and University Texas.

Daníelsson, J. 2002. The emperor has no clothes: Limits to risk modeling. *Journal of Banking & Finance* 26, nos. 2–3: 1273–96.

Davis, J.L., E.F. Fama, and K.R. French. 2000. Characteristics, covariances, and average returns: 1929–1997. *Journal of Finance* 55, no. 1: 389–406.

D'Avolio, G. 2002. The market for borrowing stock. *Journal of Financial Economics* 66, nos. 2–3: 271–306.

Elton, E.J., and M.J. Gruber. 1970. Homogenous groups and the testing of economic hypotheses. *The Journal of Financial and Quantitative Analysis* 4, no. 4: 581–602.

Fama, E.F., and K.R. French. 1992. The cross-section of expected stock returns. *Journal of Finance* 47, no. 2: 427–65.

Fama, E.F., and K.R. French. 1993. Common risk factors in the returns on stocks and bonds. *Journal of Financial Economics* 33, no. 1: 3–56.

Fama, E.F., and K.R. French. 1995. Size and book-to-market factors in earnings and returns. *Journal of Finance* 50, no. 1: 131–55.

Fama, E.F., and K.R. French. 1996. Multifactor explanations of asset pricing anomalies. *Journal of Finance* 51, no. 1: 55–84.

Fama, E., and K. French. 1998. Value versus growth: The international evidence. *Journal of Finance* 53, no. 6: 1975–99.

Farmer, J.D., and D. Foley. 2009. The economy needs agent-based modelling. *Nature* 460 (August): 685–6.

Fortunato, S. 2010. Community detection in graphs. *Physics Reports* 486 (December): 75–174.

Fox, J. 1982. Selective aspects of measuring resemblance for taxonomy. In *Classifying social data*, ed. H.C. Hudson, 127–51. San Fransisco, CA: Jossey-Bass.

Frahm, G. 2008. Linear statistical inference for global and local minimum variance portfolios. *Statistical Papers* 51 (September): 789–812.

Garas, A., and P. Argyrakis. 2007. Correlation study of the Athens stock exchange. *Physica A* 380 (July): 399–410.

Garas, A., and P. Argyrakis. 2009. Filtering of complex systems using overlapping tree networks. *Europhysics Letters* 86, no. 28005: 1–6.

Gorban, A.N., E.V. Smirnova, and T.A. Tykina. 2010. Correlations, risk and crisis: From physiology to finance. *Physica A: Statistical Mechanics and its Applications* 389 (August): 3193–217.

Haldane, A.G. 2009. Rethinking the financial network. Speech delivered at the Financial Student Association, Amsterdam, April. http://www.finextra.com/Finextra-downloads/featuredocs/speech386.pdf

Haugen, R. 1995. *The new finance: The case against efficient markets*. Englewood Cliffs, NJ: Prentice Hall.

Hayek, F.A. 1945. The use of knowledge in society. *American Economic Review* 35, no. 4: 519–30.

Hill, R.J. 2001. Measuring inflation and growth using spanning trees. *International Economic Review* 42, no. 1: 167–85.

Hong, H., and J. Stein. 1999. A unified theory of underreaction, momentum trading, and overreaction in asset markets. *Journal of Finance* 54 (December): 2143–84.

Hong, H., W. Torous, and R. Valanov. 2007. Do industries lead stock markets? *Journal of Financial Economics* 83, no. 2: 367–96.

Jegadeesh, N., and S. Titman. 1993. Returns to buying winners and selling losers: Implications for stock market efficiency. *Journal of Finance* 48, no. 1: 65–91.

Jagannathan, R., and T. Ma. 2003. Risk reduction in large portfolios: Why imposing the wrong constraints helps. *Journal of Finance* 58, no. 4: 1651–83.

Kendall, M.G. 1954. Note on bias in the estimation of autocorrelation. *Biometrics* 41, no. 3: 403–4.

Kyrtsou, C. 2008. Re-examining the sources of heteroskedasticity: The paradigm of noisy chaotic models. *Physica A* 387 (December): 6785–89.

Kyrtsou, C., and M. Terraza. 2002. Stochastic chaos or ARCH effects in stock series? A comparative study. *International Review of Financial Analysis* 11, no. 4: 407–31.

Kyrtsou, C., and M. Terraza. 2003. Is it possible to study chaotic and ARCH behaviour jointly? Application of a Noisy Mackey–Glass equation with Heteroskedastic errors to the Paris Stock Exchange Returns series. *Computational Economics* 21, no. 3: 257–76.

Lakonishok, J., A. Shleifer, and R.W. Vishny. 1994. Contrarian investment, extrapolation, and risk. *Journal of Finance* 49, no. 5: 1541–78.

Ledoit, O., and M. Wolf. 2003. Improved estimation of the covariance matrix of stock returns with an application to portfolio selection. *Journal of Empirical Finance* 10, no. 5: 603–21.

Lillo, F., and R.N. Mantegna. 2002. Dynamics of financial market index after a crash. Manuscript, http://arXiv.org/abs/cond-mat/0209685

Lintner, J. 1965. The valuation of risk assets and the selection of risky investments in stock portfolios and capital budgets. *Review of Economics and Statistics* 47 (February): 13–37.

Lucas, A., R. van Dijk, and T. Kloek. 2002. Stock selection, style rotation, and risk. *Journal of Empirical Finance* 9, no. 1: 1–34.

Lux, T. 2008. Applications of statistical physics in finance and economics. Kiel Working Papers 1425. http://www.ifw-members.ifw-kiel.de/publications/applications-of-statistical-physics-in-finance-and-economics/KWP_1425_Applications%20of%20Statistical%20Physics.pdf

Lux, T., and F. Westerhoff. 2009. Economic crisis. *Nature Physics* 5, no. 1: 2–3.

Malliaris, A.G., and N.F. Stein. 1999. Methodological issues in asset pricing: Random walk or chaotic dynamics. *Journal of Banking and Finance* 23, no. 11: 1605–35.

Mantegna, R. 1999. Hierarchical structure in financial markets. *European Physical Journal B* 11, no. 1: 193–7.

Mantegna, R.N., and H.E. Stanley. 2000. *An introduction to econophysics: Correlations and complexity in finance.* Cambridge: Cambridge University Press.

Matesanz, D., and G.J. Ortega. 2005. Cross-country hierarchical structure and currency crisis. Department of Physics, Universidad de Buenos Aires and CONICET Ciudad Universitaria, Argentine.

Matesanz, D., and G.J. Ortega. 2008. Network analysis of exchange data: Interdependence drives crisis contagion. Universidad de Buenos Aires and CONICET Ciudad Universitaria, Argentine. http://mpra.ub.uni-muenchen.de/7720/1/MPRA_paper_7720.pdf

McDonald, M., O. Suleman, S. Williams, S. Howison, and N.F. Johnson. 2005. Detecting a currency's dominance or dependence using foreign exchange network trees. *Physical Review E* 72, no. 046106: 1–11.

Menzly, L., and O. Ozbas. 2010. Market segmentation and cross-predictability of returns. *Journal of Finance* 65, no. 4: 1555–80.

Merton, R.C. 1973. Theory of rational option pricing. *Bell Journal of Economics and Management Science* 4, no. 4: 141–83.

Mullainathan, S. 2000. Thinking through categories. Unpublished Working Paper, MIT.

Moore, G.H., E.A. Boehm, and A. Banerji. 1994. Using economic indicators to reduce risk in stock market investments. *International Journal of Forecasting* 10, no. 3: 405–17.

Moskowitz, T.J., and M. Grinblatt. 1999. Do industries explain momentum? *Journal of Finance* LIV, no. 4: 1249–90.

Naylor, M.J., L.C. Rose, and J. Brendan. 2007. Topology of foreign exchange markets using hierarchical structure methods. *Physica A* 382 (March): 199–208.

Onnela, J.-P., A. Chakraborti, and K. Kaski. 2003. Dynamics of market correlations: Taxonomy and portfolio analysis. *Physical Review E* 68, no. 056110: 1–12.

Onnela, J.-P., A. Chakrabortia, K. Kaskia, and J. Kertesza. 2002. Dynamic asset trees and portfolio analysis. *European Physical Journal* B 30 (August): 285–8.

Onnela, J.-P., A. Chakrabortia, K. Kaskia, and J. Kertesza. 2003. Dynamic asset trees and Black Monday. *Physica A* 324 (June): 247–52.

Pantaleo, E., M. Tumminello, F. Lillo, and R.N. Mantegna. 2010. When do improved covariance matrix estimators enhance portfolio optimization? An empirical comparative study of nine estimators. Available at SSRN: http://ssrn.com/abstract=1596865

Pastor, L., and R.F. Stambaugh. 2003. Liquidity risk and expect stock returns. *Journal of Political Economy* 111 (June): 642–85.

Penman, S.H. 1996. The articulation of price-earnings ratios and market to book ratios and the evaluation of growth. *Journal of Accounting Research* 34, no. 2: 235–59.

Pontiff, J., and L.D. Schall. 1998. Book-to-market ratios as predictors of market returns. *Journal of Financial Economics* 49, no. 2: 14–160.

Porter, M.E. 1998. Clusters and the new economics of competitions. *Harvard Business Review*, (November-December): 77–90.

Rohlf, F.J., and R.R. Sokal. 1965. Coefficients of correlation and distance in numerical taxonomy. *The University of Kansas Science Bulletin* 45 (October): 3–27.

Ross, S. 1976. The arbitrage theory of capital asset pricing. *Journal of Economic Theory* 13 (December): 341–60.

Schaeffer, S.E. 2007. Graph clustering. *Computer Science Review* 1, no. 1: 27–64.

Sieczka, P., and J.A. Hoyst. 2009. Correlations in commodity markets. *Physica A* 388 (April): 1621–30.

Sharpe, W.F. 1964. Capital asset prices – a theory of market equilibrium under conditions of risk. *Journal of Finance* 19, no. 3: 425–42.

Sharpe, W.F. 1992. Asset allocation: Management style and performance measurement. *Journal of Portfolio Management* 18 (Winter): 7–19.

Song, D.-M., J. Zhi-Qiang, and J. Wei-Xing. 2009. Statistical properties of world investment networks. *Physica A* 388 (July): 2450–60.

Sornette, D. 2000. The Nasdaq crash of April 2000: Yet another example of log periodicity in a speculative bubble ending in a crash. *European Physical Journal B* 17, no. 2: 319–28.

Sornette, D. 2002. *Why stock markets crash (critical events in complex financial systems).* Princeton, NJ: Princeton University Press.

Sornette, D. 2003. *Why stock markets crash: Critical events in complex financial systems.* Princeton, NJ: Princeton University Press.

Sornette, D. 2005. Endogenous versus exogenous origins of crises. In *monograph entitled "Extreme Events in Nature and Society", Series: The Frontiers Collection*, ed. S. Albeverio, V. Jentsch and H. Kantz, 95–119. Heidelberg: Springer. http://arxiv.org/abs/physics/0412026

Sornette, D., and A. Helmstetter. 2003. Endogenous versus exogenous shocks in systems with memory. *Physica A* 318 (June): 577–9.

Sneath, P.H.A., and R.R. Sokal. 1973. *Numerical taxonomy: The principles and practice of numerical classification*. San Francisco, CA: Freeman.

Strong, N., and X.G. Xu. 1997. Explaining the cross-section of UK expected stock returns. *British Accounting Review* 29, no. 1: 1–23.

Tola, V., F. Lillo, M. Gallegati, and R.N. Mantegna. 2008. Cluster analysis for portfolio optimization. *Journal of Economic Dynamics & Control* 32, no. 1: 235–58.

Tumminello, M., C. Coronnello, F. Lillo, S. Micciche, and R.N. Mantegna. 2007. Spanning trees and bootstrap reliability estimation in correlation-based networks. *International Journal of Bifurcation and Chaos* 17, no. 7: 2319–29.

Tumminelloa, M., F. Lillo, and R.N. Mantegna. 2010. Correlation, hierarchies, and networks in financial markets. *Journal of Economic Behavior & Organization* 75, no. 1: 40–58.

Vandewalle, N., F. Brisbois, and X. Tordoir. 2001. Non-random topology of stock markets. *Quantitative Finance* 1, no. 3: 372–4.

Vassalou, M., and Y. Xing. 2004. Default risk in equity returns. *Journal of Finance* 59, no. 2: 831–68.

Wang, X.F., and G. Chen. 2003. Complex networks: Small-world, scale-free and beyond. *IEEE Circuits and Systems Magazine* First quarter: 6–20.

Wasserman, S., and K. Faust. 2006. *Social network analysis: Methods and applications.* Cambridge: Cambridge University Press.

Zhang, L. 2005. The value premium. *Journal of Finance* 60, no. 1: 67–103.

Appendix 1. Example MSTs for BM differences and returns correlations

BM Minimum Spanning Tree May 2006

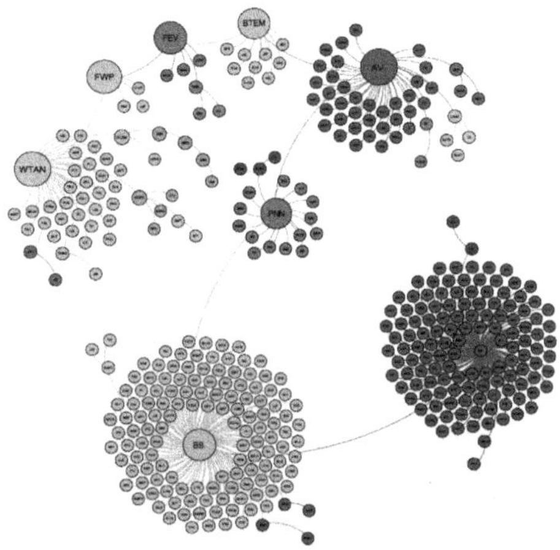

Returns Minimum Spanning Tree December 2006 (6 month)

Appendix 2. Reference company identification and industry sector

Code	Full name	Industry	Code	Full name	Industry
AAL	Anglo American	1	JMG	JPMorgan Emerging Mkts Inv Trust	8
ANTO	Antofagasta	1	LGEN	Legal & General Group	8
ATST	Alliance Trust (The)	8	LII	Liberty International	8
AV.	Aviva	8	LMI	Lonmin	1
AVV	Aveva Group	9	MAB	Mitchells & Butlers	5
AZN	AstraZeneca	4	MKS	Marks & Spencer Group	5
BARC	Barclays	8	PMO	Premier Oil	0
BAY	British Airways	5	PNN	Pennon Group	7
BB.	Bradford & Bingley	8	RB	Reckitt Benckiser Group	3
BDEV	Barratt Developments	3	RBS	Royal Bank Of Scotland Group	8
BLND	British Land Co	8	RCP	RIT Capital Partners	8
BTEM	British Empire Sec & General Tst	8	RDSB	Royal Dutch Shell B	0
BYG	Big Yellow Group	8	REX	Rexam	2
CCL	Carnival	5	RIO	Rio Tinto	1
CLDN	Caledonia Investments	8	SBRY	Sainsbury (J)	5
EMG	Man Group	8	TATE	Tate & Lyle	3
FEV	Fidelity European Values	8	TEM	Templeton Emerging Markets IT	8
FRCL	Foreign & Col Invest Trust	8	TRG	TR European Growth Trust	8
FWP	Finsbury Worldwide Pharmaceutical	8	ULE	Ultra Electronics Holdings	2
GEO	Gartmore European Inv Trust	8	VED	Vedanta Resources	1
GFS	G4S	2	WPP	WPP Group	5
GSK	GlaxoSmithKline	4	WTAN	Witan Inv Tst	8
ITRK	Intertek Group	2	WTB	Whitbread	5
JAM	JPMorgan American IT	8	YELL	Yell Group	5

Industry Classification Benchmark (ICB) issued by FTSE and Dow Jones as of March 2008. 0, oil and gas; 1, basic materials; 2, industrials; 3, consumer goods; 4, health care;5, consumer services; 6, telecommunications; 7, utilities; 8, financials; 9, technology.

Risk sharing in a financial market with endogenous option prices

Jan Wenzelburger

This article investigates a financial market in which investors may trade in risk-free bonds, stock and put options written on the stock. In each period, stock and option prices are simultaneously determined by market clearing. While the introduction of put options will decrease the systematic risk in the financial market, it will increase the price of risk. Investors with mean-variance preferences will generally hold portfolios containing the primary asset and the put option and may use the option to increase the risk in their wealth position in exchange for higher returns. Aggregate wealth is unaffected by an option market when there are no spillover effects on stock prices, and it is shown that short selling of options will increase the volatility of individual wealth positions. Investors with erroneous beliefs may on average be better off not trading in put options.

1. Introduction

The standard technique of pricing a derivative asset is to compute its arbitrage-free price. Resting on the foundations laid out by Black and Scholes (1973) and Merton (1973), the key element of this method is to construct a portfolio of assets which replicates the payoff of the derivative asset. The derivative asset, whose payoff depends on another traded asset, is thereby treated as a redundant asset. In the absence of arbitrage, the price of the derivative asset must therefore be equal to the price of the replicating portfolio. The key assumption for this method to work is that the introduction of a derivative asset will not alter the prices of the primary assets which constitute its replicating portfolio.

This assumption is in stark contrast to a result by Detemple and Selden (1991) who demonstrate that primary and derivative asset markets in a two-period general equilibrium model interact generically. For markets in which a stock and a call option written on the stock is traded, they show that investors will generally hold a portfolio mix consisting options and the underlying stock and that the stock price will depend on the exercise price. For a version of the classical capital asset pricing model (CAPM) of Mossin (1966), they demonstrate that the stock price increases when a call option contract is introduced.

Detemple and Selden's (1991) findings imply that the price of a primary asset cannot be taken as given if a derivative asset is newly introduced into the market. This result contradicts the standard assumption in pricing derivative assets which takes prices of primary assets as exogenously given. For this reason, this traditional paradigm provides no microeconomic foundation as to why investors hold portfolios which contain the primary and the derivative asset. With the arbitrage-free valuation as the price of a derivative asset, an investor is indifferent between holding the derivative asset and the portfolio that replicates its payoff. Therefore, standard trading strategies such as a *covered call*, in which a trader buys a call option and sells the underlying asset, or a *protective put*, in which a trader buys stock and put options written on the stock, have no foundation as an optimal portfolio of a decision problem. In addition to these findings, empirical evidence to date suggests that pricing tools such as the Black and Scholes formula may not be an accurate enough to price derivatives (see e.g. Franke, Stapleton, and Subrahmanyam 1999). These caveats motivate this article.

This article extends the approach of Detemple and Selden (1991) by incorporating option markets into a class of agent-based models which may be seen as a dynamic extension of the traditional CAPM. These models in which heterogeneous investors with one-period planning horizons interact have three main structural elements (see e.g. Wenzelburger 2009). First, a *temporary equilibrium map* which determines asset prices in each period, given the characteristics of investors such as preferences and subjective beliefs regarding the future evolution of markets. Second, *forecasting rules* which stipulate the way in which agents form and update these beliefs. Third, a model for exogenous perturbations which captures all influences which are not modeled explicitly such as dividend payments, random endowments or noise-traders' activities.

The first two components constitute a deterministic dynamical system in which investors' sentiments feed back into the actual evolution of asset prices and thus into their portfolio holdings. Together with the third component, one obtains a deterministic dynamical system in a random environment. The temporary equilibrium map may be understood in the sense of Grandmont (1982) and determines market-clearing prices from an aggregate excess demand function. This demand function may be derived from expected-utility maximizing investors as, for example, in Böhm, Deutscher, and Wenzelburger (2000) and Horst (2005) or from mean-variance preferences as in Brock and Hommes (1997, 1998), Chiarella and He (2002), Wenzelburger (2004) or Böhm and Chiarella (2005).

The behavioral element in these models is the use of forecasting rules which model the way in which agents form and update their beliefs. This behavioral approach is reconciled with the rational expectations paradigm in Wenzelburger (2004) by introducing *perfect forecasting rules* which generate rational expectations for a group of investors, while the beliefs of other market participants may be erroneous. It turns out that perfect forecasting rules are the key to extend fundamental concepts of the traditional CAPM to a dynamic setting with diverse beliefs.

In this article, investors are characterized by mean-variance preferences and are allowed to trade in three assets, a risk-free bond, a stock and a put-option written on the stock. Stock and option prices of each period are simultaneously determined by market clearing in the respective markets, where the put option contracts are in zero net supply. We investigate how these endogenously formed option prices impact on prices and allocations of the underlying primary asset. Investors with mean-variance preference will generally use put-option contracts to increase the risk in their wealth positions in exchange for higher returns and will hold portfolios which contain the stock and the option. The focus of the article is on two investors, one expert trader who is able to correctly predict the first two moments of future prices and option values, and a chartist who uses simple updating techniques to forecast the future evolution of the assets. The model shows that stock and option prices interact as soon as beliefs are heterogeneous and thus confirms the result of Detemple and Selden (1991) that these prices interact generically.

The main findings of the article are the following. The price of risk will generally increase with the introduction of an option market, although systematic risk decreases. Under homogeneous second-moment beliefs the introduction of an option market will not affect the aggregate wealth process of the financial market. Short selling of option contracts, however, will increase the risk of individual wealth positions as the volatility of individual wealth increases quadratically with the trading volume of the option contract. Investors with erroneous beliefs may therefore on average be better off not trading in put options. It is shown that that heterogeneous beliefs will cause market prices for options to deviate from their arbitrage-free valuations.

The results of the article may have interesting implication for pension funds which use financial derivatives as financial instruments to safeguard investments. In order not to obscure the effects from the market for option contracts, we do not allow investors to choose between different trading strategies as in Brock and Hommes (1997, 1998). The dynamic effects resulting from investors who switch between different strategies in option contracts may be an interesting avenue for further research. So is an extension to other derivative assets.

The article is organized as follows. In Section 2, a two-fund separation theorem for stock and option contracts is established. Section 3 develops the main features of the model. In Section 4, the joint evolution of a stock and an option market is analyzed. The main results are developed in Section 5 and conclusions are provided in Section 6. All proofs are relegated to an appendix.

2. Demand for stock and option contracts

Before we develop a dynamic model in Section 3, this section analyzes the demand behavior of an investor with mean-variance preferences who is allowed to trade in three assets, a risk-free bond, a stock and a put-option written on the stock.

2.1 *Prerequisites*

Consider the investment decision of an investor with a one-period planning horizon who needs to transfer wealth between two periods $t = 0, 1$. Her endowment consists of $w_0 > 0$ units of a non-storable consumption good in period 0 and none in period 1. The investment opportunities consist of one risk-free and two risky assets. The risk-free asset is a bond which pays a constant return $R_f = 1 + r_f > 0$ per unit and the bond price is normalized to unity. The risky assets consists of a stock and an *European put option* written on the stock. The stock is characterized by a stochastic gross return $\widetilde{q}_{s1} = \widetilde{p}_{s1} + \widetilde{d}_1$ which is composed of an *ex-dividend* price $\widetilde{p}_{s1}$ and a stochastic dividend $\widetilde{d}_1$. The dividend payment $\widetilde{d}_1$ is assumed to be randomly drawn from some subset of $\mathbb{R}_+$. The payoff of the put option contracts at date 1 depends on the ex-dividend price $\widetilde{p}_{s1}$ of period 1 and the strike price κ set in period 0 and takes the form

$$\widetilde{\tau}_1 = (\kappa - \widetilde{p}_{s1})^+.$$

The two risky assets are thus characterized by stochastic gross returns $\widetilde{q}_1 = (\widetilde{q}_{s1}, \widetilde{\tau}_1)$ per unit and take values in $\mathbb{R}^2_+$.

A portfolio is represented by a vector $(x, y) \in \mathbb{R}^2 \times \mathbb{R}$. The vector $x = (x_s, x_o)$ describes the portfolio of risky assets with x_s denoting the amount of stock and x_o denoting the amount of options in the portfolio. The scalar y describes the number of risk-free bonds in the portfolio (x, y). The total amount of risky assets is $(\bar{x}, 0) \in \mathbb{R}^2_+$ such that the option is in zero net supply.

Let $p = (p_s, p_o) \in \mathbb{R}^2$ denote the price vector of the risky asset and the option contract. Without short-sale constraints, the investor's budget constraint is

$$w_0 = y + \langle p, x\rangle = y + p_s x_s + p_o x_o,$$

where $\langle \cdot, \cdot \rangle$ denotes the scalar product on $\mathbb{R}^2$. Substituting for y, the investor's second-period wealth associated with the portfolio $x \in \mathbb{R}^2$ of risky assets becomes

$$W(w_0, p, \widetilde{q}_1, x) = R_f w_0 + \langle \widetilde{q}_1 - R_f p, x\rangle.$$

The uncertainty of second-period wealth rests with the random gross return $\widetilde{q}_1$ of risky assets, when the investor treats the asset price p of the first period as a parameter of her decision problem. The uncertainty is described by some subjective probability distribution ν of the future ex-dividend stock price $\widetilde{p}_{s1}$ and some probability distribution of the exogenous dividend $\widetilde{d}_1$. The expected future ex-dividend price of the stock with respect to her subjective probability distribution ν is

$$\mathbb{E}_\nu[\widetilde{p}_{s1}] = \int p_s \ \nu(\mathrm{d}p_s).$$

Since the option payoff $\widetilde{\tau}_1 = (\kappa - \widetilde{p}_{s1})^+$ is a function of the stock price $\widetilde{p}_{s1}$ and the strike price κ, the subjectively expected option value becomes

$$\mathbb{E}_\nu[\widetilde{\tau}_1] = \int (\kappa - p_s)^+ \ \nu(\mathrm{d}p_s).$$

In a CAPM framework an investor will base her evaluation of the uncertain return solely on the mean and the variance of second-period wealth rather than its full probability distribution. Based on ν, denote the expected stock return by $\mathbb{E}_\nu[\widetilde{q}_{s1}] = \mathbb{E}_\nu[\widetilde{p}_{s1}] + \mathbb{E}[\widetilde{d}_1]$ and the vector of the subjectively expected stock return and the expected option value by $\overline{q} := (\mathbb{E}_\nu[\widetilde{q}_{s1}], \mathbb{E}_\nu[\widetilde{\tau}_1]) \in \mathbb{R}^2_+$. Let

$$V(\kappa) := \begin{pmatrix} \mathbb{V}\mathrm{ar}_\nu[\widetilde{q}_{s1}] & \mathbb{C}\mathrm{ov}_\nu[\widetilde{q}_{s1}, \widetilde{\tau}_1] \\ \mathbb{C}\mathrm{ov}_\nu[\widetilde{q}_{s1}, \widetilde{\tau}_1] & \mathbb{V}\mathrm{ar}_\nu[\widetilde{\tau}_1] \end{pmatrix} \tag{1}$$

be the subjective covariance matrix of the stock return and the payoff of the option contract. The covariance matrix (1) is by definition symmetric and positive semi-definite but not necessarily positive definite. An investor with mean-variance preferences, however, will have a well-defined demand for put-option contracts only if the covariance matrix (1) is positive definite and hence invertible. This is guaranteed by the following assumption which, in effect, ensures that the option is not a redundant asset.

ASSUMPTION 1 *The probability distribution* ν *and the exercise price* κ *satisfy* $0 < \nu(\tilde{p}_{s1} < \kappa) < 1$. *If, in addition,* ν *is discrete, then the future stock price* $\tilde{p}_{s1}$ *takes on at least three distinct values with positive probability.*

Let $\pi := \overline{q} - R_f p$ be the vector of expected excess returns. Based on ν, the expected wealth and its standard deviation associated with a portfolio of risky assets $x \in \mathbb{R}^2$ become

$$\mu_w(w_0, p, x) := \mathbb{E}_\nu[W(w_0, p, \cdot, x)] = R_f w_0 + \langle \pi, x\rangle$$

and

$$\sigma_w(x) := \mathbb{V}\mathrm{ar}[W(w_0, p, \cdot, x)]^{1/2} = \langle x, V(\kappa)x\rangle^{1/2},$$

respectively. Assumption 1 ensures that $\sigma_w(x) > 0$ unless $x = 0$.

Risk preferences of an investor are characterized by an utility function $U(\mu, \sigma)$ which is a function of mean μ and standard deviation σ. $U(\mu, \sigma)$ is assumed to be continuously differentiable, strictly increasing in μ, strictly decreasing in σ and strictly quasiconcave. From Section 3 onwards we will restrict ourselves to the standard case in which U is linear, but considering the more general case in this section will provide an important insight into the risk-taking behavior of investors.

With the above assumptions on U and ν, the decision problem of an investor takes the form

$$\max_{x \in \mathbb{R}^2} U(\mu_w(w_0, p, x), \sigma_w(x)). \tag{2}$$

To ensure existence of a solution to Equation (2), we need the concept of a *limiting slope* of an indifference curve as adopted in Nielsen (1987). The limiting slope of the indifference curve starting in $(R_f w_0, 0)$ is defined by

$$\rho_U := \sup \left\{ -\frac{(\partial U/\partial \sigma)(\mu, \sigma)}{(\partial U/\partial \mu)(\mu, \sigma)} : (\mu, \sigma) \in \mathbb{R} \times \mathbb{R}_+ \text{ s.t. } U(\mu, \sigma) = U(R_f w_0, 0) \right\}. \tag{3}$$

From convex analysis it is well known that ρ_U is either positive and finite or plus infinity.[1]

2.2 *Two-fund separation*

With the prerequisites of the previous section it is straightforward to formulate a two-fund separation theorem for the case in which the risky assets consist of a stock and a put option. Following Wenzelburger (2010), we will first construct the efficient frontier, assuming that borrowing and lending at the safe rate R_f is allowed. Consider the optimization problem

$$\begin{aligned} \min_{x \in \mathbb{R}^2} \quad & \tfrac{1}{2}\sigma_w(x)^2 \\ \text{s.t.} \quad & \mu_w(w_0, p, x) \geq \mu, \end{aligned} \tag{4}$$

where $\mu \geq R_f w_0$, first considered by Markowitz (1952). The solution to problem (4) is a portfolio with the minimum variance for a given return, commonly referred to as an *efficient portfolio*, and given by

$$x_{\text{eff}}(\mu, \pi, V) := \frac{\mu - R_f w_0}{\langle \pi, V^{-1}\pi \rangle} V^{-1}\pi, \quad \mu \geq R_f w_0. \tag{5}$$

The standard deviation of any efficient portfolio (5) is

$$\sigma_{\text{eff}} = \frac{\mu - R_f w_0}{\sqrt{\langle \pi, V^{-1}\pi \rangle}}, \tag{6}$$

which implies that its risk-return characteristics $(\sigma_{\text{eff}}, \mu)$ satisfy the relation

$$\mu = R_f w_0 + \rho\sigma, \tag{7}$$

where $\rho := \sqrt{\langle \pi, V^{-1}\pi \rangle}$ is referred to as the *perceived price of risk*. Equation (7) is of course nothing but the *efficient frontier* expressed in terms of wealth rather than returns. Observe, however, that in this setting the slope ρ of the efficient frontier (7) depends on the investor's subjective beliefs, hence the term '*perceived* price of risk'.

The efficient frontier (7) is now used to formulate the *two-fund separation theorem* which dates back to Tobin (1958) and Lintner (1965).

PROPOSITION 1 *Let the above hypotheses be satisfied and $V = V(\kappa)$ be symmetric and positive definite. Then for any w_0 and any $\pi \in \mathbb{R}^2$ with $\langle \pi, V^{-1}\pi\rangle^{1/2} < \rho_U$, the optimization problem* (2) *has a unique maximizer $x_\star \in \mathbb{R}^2$. The corresponding asset demand function takes the form*

$$x_\star = \Phi(w_0, \pi, V) := \begin{cases} \dfrac{\phi(w_0, \langle \pi, V^{-1}\pi\rangle^{1/2})}{\langle \pi, V^{-1}\pi\rangle^{1/2}} V^{-1}\pi & \textit{if } \pi \neq 0, \\ 0 & \textit{otherwise}, \end{cases} \tag{8}$$

where for each $0 \leq \rho < \rho_U$,

$$\phi(w_0, \rho) := \underset{\sigma \geq 0}{\operatorname{argmax}}\, U(R_f w_0 + \rho\sigma, \sigma) \tag{9}$$

is finite.

A proof of Proposition 1 is found in Wenzelburger (2010). Proposition 1 shows that an investor with mean–variance preferences will treat the put-option just as another risky asset and demand a portfolio that consists of a mix of the put option and the underlying stock. The interpretation of the two-fund separation theorem is therefore standard. Given $\pi = (\pi_s, \pi_o)$ and $V = \left(\begin{smallmatrix} V_{11} & V_{12} \\ V_{12} & V_{22}\end{smallmatrix}\right)$, the optimal portfolio $x_\star$ is collinear to

$$V^{-1}\pi = \frac{1}{\det V}\begin{pmatrix} V_{22}\pi_s - V_{12}\pi_o \\ -V_{12}\pi_s + V_{11}\pi_o \end{pmatrix} \tag{10}$$

and hence an efficient portfolio.[2] Thus, investors with the same beliefs $(\overline{q}, V)$ will invest in the same two funds, the risk-free asset on the one hand and a 'mutual fund' with the same mix of risky assets. Since $\sigma_w(x_\star) = \phi(w_0, \rho)$, the function ϕ describes the investor's *willingness to take on risk*. This willingness and hence the amount of the endowment invested into risky assets will depend on the investor's preferences, while the portfolio mix is independent thereof.

With the help of the two-fund separation theorem we will show next that an investor with mean–variance preferences will demand put options because she expects to be rewarded with a higher price of risk, that is, a better trade-off between risk and return. To this end, consider an economy in which the stock is the only risky asset and assume that V_{11} is the subjective variance of the stock and π_s its excess return. Analogous to Equation (6), we find that the efficient portfolio is $\tilde{x}_{\text{eff}} = (\mu - R_f w_0)/\pi_s$. The standard deviation of $\tilde{x}_{\text{eff}}$ is $\tilde{\sigma}_{\text{eff}} = (\mu - R_f w_0)/\tilde{\rho}$, where $\tilde{\rho} = \pi_s/\sqrt{V_{11}}$ is the perceived price of risk. The well-known fact that the variance of an efficient portfolio will decrease with the introduction of an additional asset now takes the following form.

LEMMA 1 *Let $\pi = (\pi_s, \pi_o)$ and $V = \left(\begin{smallmatrix} V_{11} & V_{12} \\ V_{12} & V_{22}\end{smallmatrix}\right)$ be arbitrary. Then the following holds:*

(i) *The standard deviation of the efficient portfolio $x_{\text{eff}}(\mu, \pi, V)$ with a put option is less than the standard deviation of the efficient portfolio $\tilde{x}_{\text{eff}} = (\mu - R_f w_0)/\pi_s$ without a put option, that is, $\sigma_{\text{eff}} \leq \tilde{\sigma}_{\text{eff}}$.*
(ii) *The perceived price of risk of the economy with put options is higher than in the market without put options, i.e. $\rho \geq \tilde{\rho}$.*

Both inequalities are strict whenever $-V_{12}\pi_s + V_{11}\pi_o \neq 0$.

Equation (10) reveals that an efficient portfolio will contain put options whenever $-V_{12}\pi_s + V_{11}\pi_o \neq 0$. Lemma 1 therefore states that the variance of an efficient portfolio will *ceteris paribus* decrease unless it is not optimal to hold the option, i.e. unless $-V_{12}\pi_s + V_{11}\pi_o = 0$. The second statement of Lemma 1 is of course immediate from the first, as the efficient frontier (7) implies that

$$\rho = \frac{\mu - R_f w_0}{\sigma_{\text{eff}}} \geq \frac{\mu - R_f w_0}{\tilde{\sigma}_{\text{eff}}} = \tilde{\rho}.$$

Since the perceived price of risk will, in general, be higher if put options are tradeable, the two-fund separation theorem implies that an investor with mean–variance preferences will demand a mix of stock and put options, as such a portfolio will on average grant her a higher level of utility. More formally, we arrive at the following result:

THEOREM 1 *Let* $\pi = (\pi_s, \pi_o)$ *and* V *with* $-V_{12}\pi_s + V_{11}\pi_o \neq 0$ *be given. Then the following holds true*:

(i) *The optimal portfolio with put options is preferred to the portfolio without put options, i.e.* $U(\mu_w^*, \sigma_w^*) > U(\mu_{\tilde{w}}^*, \sigma_{\tilde{w}}^*)$;
(ii) *The risk of the portfolio with put options,* σ_w^**, is larger than the risk of the portfolio without put options,* $\sigma_{\tilde{w}}^*$*, if and only if* $\phi(w_0, \rho)$ *is increasing in* $\rho \in [S(R_f w_0, 0), \rho_U)$*, that is, if and only if*

$$\frac{\partial S}{\partial \mu}(R_f w_0 + \rho\phi(w_0, \rho), \phi(w_0, \rho))\phi(w_0, \rho) < 1.$$

While *ceteris paribus* a portfolio with put options will always be preferred, the second assertion of Theorem 1 states that, whether or not an investor will use options to decrease the risk of her future wealth will depend on her preferences. This observation is illustrated in Figure 1. If the willingness to take on risk is increasing with the perceived price of risk, then the introduction of an option market will lead to an increased demand for risk. Such an investor will use options to invest into a riskier portfolio. This situation occurs for the standard case with linear mean–variance preferences $U(\mu, \sigma) = \mu - (1/2a)\sigma^2$, where a denotes the risk tolerance of the investor. In this case, the willingness to take on risk is proportional to the perceived price of risk, i.e. $\phi(w_0, \rho) = a\rho$. In the $\mu - \sigma$ plane, the resulting 'price offer curve' is illustrated in Figure 1(a).

If, however, an investor's willingness to accept risk is decreasing with the perceived price of risk ρ, then options will be used to reduce the risk in future wealth. Such a situation is captured

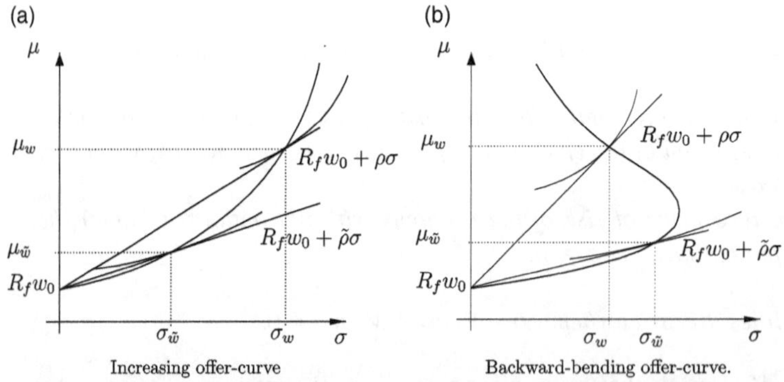

Figure 1. The willingness to take on risk. (a) Increasing offer-curve and (b) backward-bending offer-curve.

by a utility function of the form $U(\mu, \sigma) = -e^{-\mu} - \sigma$. The willingness to take risk is given by

$$\phi(w_0, \rho) = \max\left\{\frac{1}{\rho}(\ln \rho - R_f w_0), 0\right\}, \quad \rho \geq 0.$$

This case results in a backward bending price offer-curve as in Figure 1(b), showing that the investor will reduce the risk of her portfolio above a certain threshold for ρ.[3]

This discussion shows that whether or not an investor will use put options to reduce risk will depend on her preferences. For the remainder of this article, we restrict our analysis to the standard case with linear mean-variance preferences in which investors' willingness to take on risk is increasing with the perceived price of risk.

3. Model

Consider a financial market that is operated by two myopic investors $i = 1, 2$ with a one-period planning horizon who maximize expected future wealth given their beliefs. The investment opportunities consist of a risk-less asset, a risky stock and a put option written on the stock. Investor i's attitude towards risk is characterized by linear mean-variance utility function of the form

$$U^{(i)}(\mu, \sigma) = \mu - \frac{1}{2a^{(i)}}\sigma^2$$

with $a^{(i)}$ denoting the risk tolerance of investor i. Let $q_t^{(i)} \in \mathbb{R}_+^2$ denote the vector of investor i's subjective mean values of the cum-dividend stock price and the option value and $V_t^{(i)}$ be her subjective covariance matrix based on information available at date t. Given subjective beliefs $(q_t^{(i)}, V_t^{(i)})$ in period t, investor i's demand for risk assets is given by the demand function

$$\Phi^{(i)}(q_t^{(i)}, V_t^{(i)}, p) = a^{(i)} V_t^{(i)-1}(q_t^{(i)} - R_f p), \quad i = 1, 2. \tag{11}$$

Noise traders are restricted to the stock market. Their stock holdings after trading in period t are described by the random quantity ξ_t. With the option in zero net supply, the total amount of retradeable risky assets in the economy is $\bar{z} = (\bar{x}, 0) \in \mathbb{R}_+^2$.

3.1 *Asset prices*

Stock prices and put-option prices of each period are determined by simultaneous market clearing in the two markets. Market clearing in an arbitrary period t requires that the sum of demand functions (11) and stock holdings of noise-traders are equal to the total amount $\bar{z}$ of assets, such that

$$\Phi^{(1)}(q_t^{(1)}, V_t^{(1)}, p) + \Phi^{(2)}(q_t^{(2)}, V_t^{(2)}, p) + \begin{pmatrix}\xi_t \\ 0\end{pmatrix} \stackrel{!}{=} \bar{z}. \tag{12}$$

Solving the market clearing condition (12) for p, one obtains an explicit functional form for the asset price vector p_t at date t, which for arbitrary beliefs $(q_t^{(i)}, V_t^{(i)})$, $i = 1, 2$ is given by[4]

$$p_t = A_t^{(1)} q_t^{(1)} + A_t^{(2)} q_t^{(2)} - A_t \begin{pmatrix}\bar{x} - \xi_t \\ 0\end{pmatrix} \tag{13}$$

with

$$A_t := \frac{1}{R_f}(a^{(1)} V_t^{(1)-1} + a^{(2)} V_t^{(2)-1})^{-1} \tag{14}$$

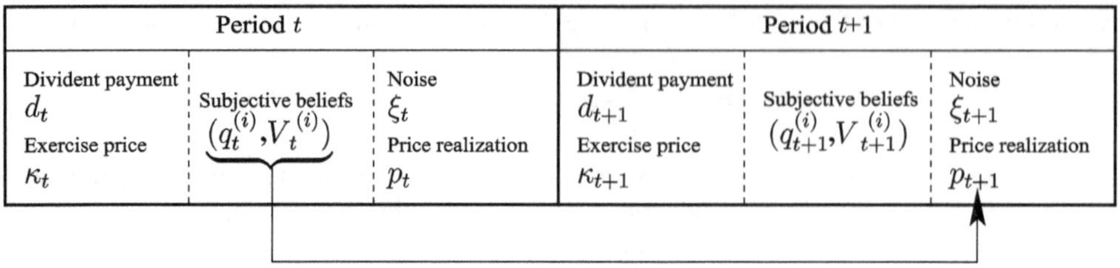

Figure 2. Timing of subjective expectations.

and

$$
\begin{aligned}
A_t^{(1)} &:= a^{(1)} A_t V_t^{(1)-1} = \frac{1}{R_f}\left(I + \frac{a^{(2)}}{a^{(1)}} V_t^{(1)} V_t^{(2)-1}\right)^{-1}, \\
A_t^{(2)} &:= a^{(2)} A_t V_t^{(2)-1} = \frac{1}{R_f}\left(I + \frac{a^{(1)}}{a^{(2)}} V_t^{(2)} V_t^{(1)-1}\right)^{-1}.
\end{aligned} \tag{15}
$$

The dating of expectations relative to prices implies that beliefs $q_t^{(i)} = (q_{st}^{(i)}, \tau_t^{(i)})$ and $V_t^{(i)}$ of date t are formed without knowledge of the prices $p_t = (p_{st}, p_{ot})$ which prevail in that period. This dating is referred to as an expectational lead in the price law (13) and is illustrated in Figure 2.

The entries of the matrices (15) and (14) are

$$
A_t^{(i)} = \begin{pmatrix} A_{t,11}^{(i)} & A_{t,12}^{(i)} \\ A_{t,21}^{(i)} & A_{t,22}^{(i)} \end{pmatrix} \quad \text{and} \quad A_t = \begin{pmatrix} A_{t,11} & A_{t,12} \\ A_{t,21} & A_{t,22} \end{pmatrix} \tag{16}
$$

and take a particular form which is reported in Appendix A.1. Since $A_t^{(1)} + A_t^{(2)} = (1/R_f)I$ and the put option is in zero net supply, the price law (13) takes the form

$$
\begin{aligned}
p_{st} &= A_{t,11}^{(1)} q_{st}^{(1)} + A_{t,11}^{(2)} q_{st}^{(2)} + A_{t,12}^{(2)} (\tau_t^{(2)} - \tau_t^{(1)}) - A_{t,11}(\bar{x} - \xi_t), \\
p_{ot} &= \frac{1}{R_f} \tau_t^{(1)} + A_{t,21}^{(2)} (q_{st}^{(2)} - q_{st}^{(1)}) + A_{t,22}^{(2)} (\tau_t^{(2)} - \tau_t^{(1)}) - A_{t,21}(\bar{x} - \xi_t).
\end{aligned} \tag{17}
$$

The key insight of the price law (17) is that simultaneous market clearing will link the stock price to the option price through subjective beliefs regarding future stock prices and option values. This confirms a result first noted by Detemple and Selden (1991) that stock and option prices interact generically.[5] Note in particular that apart from R_f and the coefficients of risk tolerance, the coefficients $A_{t,nm}^{(i)}$ are exclusively composed of heterogeneous second moment beliefs. This observation will be exploited later.

3.2 *Wealth, portfolio allocation and insurance*

Let $x_t^{(i)} = (x_{st}^{(i)}, x_{ot}^{(i)})$ denote the portfolio of investor i after trading in period t, where $x_{st}^{(i)}$ denotes her stock holding and $x_{ot}^{(i)}$ her holdings in options. If $w_t^{(i)}$ denotes initial wealth of investor i in period t, her wealth after trading is

$$
w_{t+1}^{(i)} = R_f w_t^{(i)} + (p_{st+1} + d_{t+1} - R_f p_{st}) x_{st}^{(i)} + (\tau_{t+1} - R_f p_{ot}) x_{ot}^{(i)} \tag{18}
$$

which becomes her initial wealth of the subsequent period $t+1$. Given beliefs $(q_t^{(i)}, V_t^{(i)})$ in period t, the portfolios held by investors after trading in period t at equilibrium prices p_t take the form

$$\begin{aligned} x_t^{(1)} &= \Phi^{(1)}(q_t^{(1)}, V_t^{(1)}, p_t) = B_t^{(1)} \begin{pmatrix} \bar{x} - \xi_t \\ 0 \end{pmatrix} - B_t(q_t^{(2)} - q_t^{(1)}), \\ x_t^{(2)} &= \Phi^{(2)}(q_t^{(2)}, V_t^{(2)}, p_t) = B_t^{(2)} \begin{pmatrix} \bar{x} - \xi_t \\ 0 \end{pmatrix} + B_t(q_t^{(2)} - q_t^{(1)}), \end{aligned} \tag{19}$$

where

$$B_t^{(1)} := \left(I + \frac{a^{(2)}}{a^{(1)}} V_t^{(2)-1} V_t^{(1)} \right)^{-1}, \quad B_t^{(2)} := \left(I + \frac{a^{(1)}}{a^{(2)}} V_t^{(1)-1} V_t^{(2)} \right)^{-1}, \tag{20}$$

and

$$B_t := \left(\frac{1}{a^{(1)}} V_t^{(1)} + \frac{1}{a^{(2)}} V_t^{(2)} \right)^{-1}. \tag{21}$$

The next lemma which is proved in Appendix A.2 establishes the relation between stock holdings and holdings in options of the two investors. It shows how the two investors adjust their portfolios if a put-option market is introduced.

LEMMA 2 *Under the above hypotheses, the following holds*:

(i) *Investor* 1 *holds a short and investor* 2 *a long position in the option*, $x_{ot}^{(2)} = -x_{ot}^{(1)} > 0$, *if and only if*

$$g_t(q_{st}^{(2)} - q_{st}^{(1)}) + (\tau_t^{(2)} - \tau_t^{(1)}) > \frac{V_{t,12}^{(1)} V_{t,11}^{(2)} - V_{t,11}^{(1)} V_{t,12}^{(2)}}{a^{(2)} V_{t,11}^{(1)} + a^{(1)} V_{t,11}^{(2)}} (\bar{x} - \xi_t),$$

where

$$0 < g_t := -\left(\frac{a^{(2)} V_{t,12}^{(1)} + a^{(1)} V_{t,12}^{(2)}}{a^{(2)} V_{t,11}^{(1)} + a^{(1)} V_{t,11}^{(2)}} \right) < 1.$$

(ii) *The stock holdings of the two traders are*

$$\begin{aligned} x_{st}^{(1)} &= \tilde{x}_{st}^{(1)} + g_t x_{ot}^{(1)}, \\ x_{st}^{(2)} &= \tilde{x}_{st}^{(2)} + g_t x_{ot}^{(2)}, \end{aligned}$$

where

$$\tilde{x}_{st}^{(1)} = \frac{a^{(1)} V_{t,11}^{(2)}}{a^{(2)} V_{t,11}^{(1)} + a^{(1)} V_{t,11}^{(2)}} (\bar{x} - \xi_t) - \frac{a^{(1)} a^{(2)}}{a^{(2)} V_{t,11}^{(1)} + a^{(1)} V_{t,11}^{(2)}} (q_{st}^{(2)} - q_{st}^{(1)}), \tag{22}$$

$$\tilde{x}_{st}^{(2)} = \frac{a^{(2)} V_{t,11}^{(1)}}{a^{(2)} V_{t,11}^{(1)} + a^{(1)} V_{t,11}^{(2)}} (\bar{x} - \xi_t) + \frac{a^{(1)} a^{(2)}}{a^{(2)} V_{t,11}^{(1)} + a^{(1)} V_{t,11}^{(2)}} (q_{st}^{(2)} - q_{st}^{(1)}). \tag{23}$$

Assertion (i) states that investor 2 will hold a long position in the options, $x_{ot}^{(2)} > 0$, and investor 1 a short position, $x_{ot}^{(1)} = -x_{ot}^{(2)} < 0$, if she believes that the future value of the stock and the option are sufficiently above the values investor 1 anticipates.

Assertion (ii) of Lemma 2 establishes how stock holdings of the two investors respond if options are traded. It is straightforward to see that Equations (22) and (23) are the respective portfolios the investors would hold if no option market existed.[6] In particular, if $x_{ot}^{(2)} > 0$, then investor 2 will, relative to a market without the possibility to trade in options, hold more stock $x_{st}^{(2)} > \tilde{x}_{st}^{(2)}$. Specifically, she will increase her position in stock by $g_t x_{ot}^{(2)} > 0$ units and insure this position by buying $x_{ot}^{(2)}$ option contracts from investor 1. Since $g_t < 1$, investor 2 '*over-insures*' this increased position.

If, on the contrary, investor 1 believes that the future value of the stock and the option are sufficiently *above* the values investor 2 anticipates, then relative to a market without put options, investor 2 will hold a reduced position in stock and a short position in options, thereby insuring investor 1's increased position in stock.

4. Dynamics with heterogeneous beliefs

To describe the evolution of asset prices and wealth, we need to specify how investors form their expectation regarding the future evolution of the economy and the nature of the exogenous noise in the markets. We begin with stipulating our assumptions regarding the two noise processes.

ASSUMPTION 2

(i) *Stock holdings of noise-traders* $\{\xi_t\}_{t\in\mathbb{N}}$ *are governed by an exogenous i.i.d. process with mean value* 0 *and variance* σ_ξ.
(ii) *Dividend payments* $\{d_t\}_{t\in\mathbb{N}}$ *are governed by an exogenous i.i.d. process with finite mean value and finite variance; the process is uncorrelated with the process defined in* (i) *and each dividend payment* d_t *is known to investors at time* $t-1$.

The assumption on the noise traders is made to rule out the possibility of perfect foresight on ex-dividend prices which would render the option useless. The assumption that dividend payments are known when deciding on portfolios is made to simplify the exposition of the model.

4.1 *Exercise prices*

In order to formulate a tractable dynamics, we assume for the remainder of this paper that the exercise price in period $t-1$ is stipulated as

$$\kappa_{t-1} = \mathbb{E}_{t-1}[p_{st}] - \beta\sqrt{\mathbb{V}\mathrm{ar}_{t-1}[p_{st}]}, \tag{24}$$

where $\mathbb{E}_{t-1}[p_{st}]$ is the mean stock price conditional on time $t-1$ information, $\sqrt{\mathbb{V}\mathrm{ar}_{t-1}[p_{st}]}$ is its standard deviation, and $\beta \leq 1$ some fixed constant. With this exercise price, the true first and second moments of stock and option prices (17) have a distinct form. Recall that all coefficients (16) depend exclusively on information available at date $t-1$. Taking expectations conditional on information at date $t-1$, we therefore obtain

$$\mathbb{E}_{t-1}[p_{st}] = A_{t,11}^{(1)} q_{st}^{(1)} + A_{t,11}^{(2)} q_{st}^{(2)} + A_{t,12}^{(2)}(\tau_t^{(2)} - \tau_t^{(1)}) - A_{t,11}\bar{x} \tag{25}$$

for the mean value of the stock price and

$$\sigma_{t-1} := \sqrt{\mathbb{V}\mathrm{ar}_{t-1}[p_{st}]} = A_{t,11}\sigma_\xi \tag{26}$$

for its standard deviation. With this notation, the first part in Equation (17) may be rewritten as

$$p_{st} = \mathbb{E}_{t-1}[p_{st}] + \sigma_{t-1}\frac{\xi_t}{\sigma_\xi}. \tag{27}$$

Define now an auxiliary random variable by setting

$$\zeta_t := -\left(\beta + \frac{\xi_t}{\sigma_\xi}\right). \tag{28}$$

Inserting Equation (24) into Equation (27), the expression for the option value then takes the form

$$\tau_t = (\kappa_{t-1} - p_{st})^+ = \sigma_{t-1}\zeta_t^+. \tag{29}$$

This implies that the option will be exercised whenever $\xi_t < \beta\sigma_\xi$. Its mean value then is

$$\mathbb{E}_{t-1}[\tau_t] = \sigma_{t-1}\mathbb{E}[\zeta_t^+] \tag{30}$$

and positive as $\beta < 1$. Since $\mathbb{V}\mathrm{ar}[\zeta_t] = 1$, the covariance structure of the two auxiliary variables ζ_t and ζ_t^+ is described by

$$b := \mathbb{C}\mathrm{ov}[\zeta_t, \zeta_t^+] \quad \text{and} \quad c := \mathbb{V}\mathrm{ar}[\zeta_t^+]. \tag{31}$$

With these preparations the covariance structure of ex-dividend prices (27) and option values (29) takes the particularly simple form

$$\Sigma_{t-1} = \begin{pmatrix} \mathbb{V}\mathrm{ar}_{t-1}[p_{st}] & \mathbb{C}\mathrm{ov}_{t-1}[p_{st}, \tau_t] \\ \mathbb{C}\mathrm{ov}_{t-1}[p_{st}, \tau_t] & \mathbb{V}\mathrm{ar}_{t-1}[\tau_t] \end{pmatrix} = \sigma_{t-1}^2 \begin{pmatrix} 1 & -b \\ -b & c \end{pmatrix}. \tag{32}$$

Since dividend payments d_t and noise-trader portfolios ξ_t are uncorrelated and d_t is known at date $t-1$, the covariance matrix (32) coincides with covariance matrix of *cum-dividend stock prices* and option values[7], implying

$$\Sigma_{t-1} = \begin{pmatrix} \mathbb{V}\mathrm{ar}_{t-1}[q_{st}] & \mathbb{C}\mathrm{ov}_{t-1}[q_{st}, \tau_t] \\ \mathbb{C}\mathrm{ov}_{t-1}[q_{st}, \tau_t] & \mathbb{V}\mathrm{ar}_{t-1}[\tau_t] \end{pmatrix}.$$

From Equation (26) we infer that this covariance structure is driven by investors' second moment beliefs via the coefficient $A_{t,11}$, the general form of which is given in Equation (A1) in Appendix A.1. Moreover, Equation (32) also shows that if b and c are known, an investor knows the whole covariance structure as soon as she knows the stock price volatility σ_{t-1}.

4.2 *Perfect forecasting rules*

The forecasting behavior of investors is described by adopting the concept of a *forecasting rule* in the sense of Grandmont (1982). *A priori*, there is a great degree of freedom in specifying forecasting rules. An abundant amount of literature (e.g. Hens and Schenk-Hoppé 2009), uses this flexibility in search for a better understanding of how financial investors behave in reality and for a better match of empirically observed price patterns.

While this would be an interesting avenue for future work, the focus of this article is on a benchmark case in which investor 2 knows the correct first two moments of the evolving price process while investor 1 applies a simple *technical trading rule* to estimate the trend of the asset prices. In the literature, investor 1 is also referred to as a *chartist* and investor 2 may be referred to as an *expert trader*. Since investors are endowed with mean-variance preferences, an expert trader will have rational expectations when the first two moments of her subjective probability distributions are correct. For brevity, we will therefore adopt the term *rational expectations* to describe the situation in which investor 2 is able to correctly predict the first two moments of the stock-price and option-value processes while investor 1 may have non-rational beliefs. Following Wenzelburger (2004), we will establish existence of a *perfect forecasting rule for first moments*, also referred to as an *unbiased forecasting rule*, and the existence of a *perfect forecasting rule for second moments* for future stock prices and option values.

To keep matters simple, we assume that investor 1 uses weighted averages to predict future stock prices and option values. Specifically, we assume that based on information available at date t, her predicted cum-dividend stock price for period $t+1$ is

$$q_{st}^{(1)} = \sum_{n=1}^{N} D_n p_{st-n} + d_t, \tag{33}$$

where $D_1, \ldots, D_N$ are some positive weights, and her predicted future option value is the moving average

$$\tau_t^{(1)} = \frac{1}{N}\sum_{n=1}^{N} \tau_{t-n} \tag{34}$$

of option values τ_{t-n}, $n = 1, \ldots, N$ observed in the past N periods.

We are now left to determine the perfect forecasting rules of investor 2. The condition for the forecast $q_{st-1}^{(2)}$ of period $t-1$ to be unbiased is

$$\mathbb{E}_{t-1}[q_{st}] = q_{st-1}^{(2)}. \tag{35}$$

Since by Assumption 2, d_t is known at date $t-1$, we have $\mathbb{E}_{t-1}[q_{st}] = \mathbb{E}_{t-1}[p_{st}] + d_t$. Inserting (25), condition (35) reads

$$A_{t,11}^{(1)} q_{st}^{(1)} + A_{t,11}^{(2)} q_{st}^{(2)} + A_{t,12}^{(2)} (\tau_t^{(2)} - \tau_t^{(1)}) - A_{t,11}\bar{x} = q_{s,t-1}^{(2)} - d_t. \tag{36}$$

Solving Equation (36) for $q_{st}^{(2)}$, one obtains

$$q_{st}^{(2)} = \frac{1}{A_{t,11}^{(2)}} [q_{st-1}^{(2)} - d_t - A_{t,11}^{(1)} q_{st}^{(1)} + A_{t,12}^{(2)} (\tau_t^{(1)} - \tau_t^{(2)}) + A_{t,11}\bar{x}]. \tag{37}$$

Following Wenzelburger (2004), the expression (37) is referred to as an unbiased forecasting rule for stock prices. Note that the right-hand side of Equation (37) is entirely based on information available at date t and thus describes a forecasting rule in the sense of Grandmont (1982). Hence, if investor 2 chooses $q_{st}^{(2)}$ according to the forecasting rule (37), then condition (36) is met, implying that the forecast $q_{st-1}^{(2)}$ formed at time $t-1$ is unbiased.

Inserting the forecasting rules (33), (34) and (37) into the first equation of (17), the core difference equations which drive the stock prices are given by

$$\begin{aligned} p_{st} &= q_{st-1}^{(2)} - d_t + A_{t,11}\xi_t, \\ q_{st}^{(2)} &= \frac{1}{A_{t,11}^{(2)}} (q_{st-1}^{(2)} - d_t) - \frac{A_{t,11}^{(1)}}{A_{t,11}^{(2)}} q_{st}^{(1)} + \frac{A_{t,12}^{(2)}}{A_{t,11}^{(2)}} (\tau_t^{(1)} - \tau_t^{(2)}) + \frac{A_{t,11}}{A_{t,11}^{(2)}} \bar{x}, \end{aligned} \tag{38}$$

$$q_{st}^{(1)} = \sum_{n=1}^{N} D_n p_{st-n} + d_t,$$

$$\tau_t^{(1)} = \frac{1}{N} \sum_{n=1}^{N} \tau_{t-n}.$$

In view of Equation (30), investor 2's ability to correctly forecast the option value τ_t rests on her ability to forecast the stock price volatility, whereby we assume that the characteristics of the exogenous noise (28) are known. To complete the description of the price dynamics, we therefore need to specify how second-moment beliefs are formed and how investor 1 forms expectations about future option values.

4.3 *Dynamics of stock and option prices*

To limit the amount of heterogeneity in second moment beliefs, we assume that both investors know the covariance structure of the exogenous noise (31) but disagree on the stock price variance by a small factor $\gamma > 0$.[8] In view of Equation (32), the subjective covariance matrices of the two investors are then multiples of each other so that

$$V_{t-1}^{(1)} = \frac{1}{\gamma} V_{t-1}^{(2)}. \tag{39}$$

In this case, the coefficient matrices (14) and (15) take the particularly simple form

$$A_t = \frac{1}{R_f(\gamma a^{(1)} + a^{(2)})} V_t^{(2)}, \quad A_t^{(1)} = \frac{\gamma a^{(1)}}{R_f(\gamma a^{(1)} + a^{(2)})} I, \quad A_t^{(2)} = \frac{a^{(2)}}{R_f(\gamma a^{(1)} + a^{(2)})} I, \tag{40}$$

such that the system of stochastic difference equations (38) which describes the evolution of stock prices takes the form

$$\begin{aligned} p_{st} &= q_{st-1}^{(2)} - d_t + \frac{1}{R_f(\gamma a^{(1)} + a^{(2)})} V_{t,11}^{(2)} \xi_t, \\ q_{st}^{(2)} &= R_f \left(1 + \frac{\gamma a^{(1)}}{a^{(2)}}\right) (q_{st-1}^{(2)} - d_t) - \frac{\gamma a^{(1)}}{a^{(2)}} q_{st}^{(1)} + \frac{1}{a^{(2)}} V_{t,11}^{(2)} \bar{x}, \\ q_{st}^{(1)} &= \sum_{n=1}^{N} D_n p_{st-n} + d_t. \end{aligned} \tag{41}$$

With $V_{t,11}^{(2)}$ denoting investor 2's subjective expectation for the variance of the stock price at time t, the difference equations (41) show that there is no spillover from the option market if second-moment beliefs obey the relation (39).

The perfect forecasting rule for second moments is now obtained by stipulating $V_{t,11}^{(2)}$ in such a way that the subjective covariance matrix $V_{t-1}^{(2)}$ coincides with the true covariance matrix Σ_{t-1}. This is carried out as follows. Using the fact that dividend payments are known, the first part in Equation (41) implies that the true standard deviation of the cum-dividend stock price

$q_{st} = p_{st} + d_t$ satisfies

$$\sqrt{\mathbb{V}\mathrm{ar}_{t-1}[q_{st}]} = \sqrt{\mathbb{V}\mathrm{ar}_{t-1}[p_{st}]} = \frac{\sigma_\xi}{R_f(\gamma a^{(1)} + a^{(2)})} V_{t,11}^{(2)}.$$

The condition for the subjective variance $V_{t-1,11}^{(2)}$ to be correct therefore is

$$\frac{\sigma_\xi}{R_f(\gamma a^{(1)} + a^{(2)})} V_{t,11}^{(2)} = \sqrt{V_{t-1,11}^{(2)}}.$$

Solving for $V_{t,11}^{(2)}$, one obtains

$$V_{t,11}^{(2)} = \frac{R_f}{\sigma_\xi}[\gamma a^{(1)} + a^{(2)}]\sqrt{V_{t-1,11}^{(2)}}. \tag{42}$$

The expression (42) determines the perfect forecasting rule for second moments of investor 2, as the correct second moment belief becomes

$$V_t^{(2)} = V_{t,11}^{(2)} \begin{pmatrix} 1 & -b \\ -b & c \end{pmatrix}. \tag{43}$$

Observe that Equation (42) is a deterministic one-dimensional difference equation with a fixed point

$$V_{\star,11}^{(2)} = \left(\frac{R_f}{\sigma_\xi}[\gamma a^{(1)} + a^{(2)}]\right)^2 \tag{44}$$

which is globally asymptotically stable such that the stock price volatility will converge to $V_{\star,11}^{(2)}$. This shows that the stock price dynamics is driven by Equations (41) and (42) which is a stable stationary process provided that the moduli of all eigenvalues of the coefficient matrix of (41) are less than unity. In fact, the dynamics is a linear variant of a system considered in Horst and Wenzelburger (2008) without option contracts.

The analysis so far shows that under the assumption that investors have homogeneous beliefs on second moments up to a constant γ, there are no spillover effects from the option market to the stock market. In particular, in the case under consideration, the introduction of a put-option market will have no effect on stock prices.

The evolution of option prices is as follows. As investor 2 correctly predicts second moments of the price process using the forecasting rule (43), she is also able to correctly predict the expected value of the put option, by setting

$$\tau_t^{(2)} = \sqrt{V_{t,11}^{(2)}}\, \mathbb{E}[\zeta_{t+1}^{+}]. \tag{45}$$

Since the forecast for the stock price variances is correct, $V_{t,11}^{(2)} = \sigma_t^2$, the forecast (45) for the option value (29) is correct as well such that

$$\tau_t^{(2)} = \mathbb{E}_t[\tau_{t+1}].$$

In view of Equation (17), the evolution of put-option prices is thus driven by

$$p_{ot} = \frac{1}{R_f}\left(\mathbb{E}_t[\tau_{t+1}] + \frac{\gamma a^{(1)}}{\gamma a^{(1)} + a^{(2)}}(\tau_t^{(1)} - \mathbb{E}_t[\tau_{t+1}]) - \frac{b}{\gamma a^{(1)} + a^{(2)}} V_{t,11}^{(2)}(\bar{x} - \xi_t)\right),$$

$$\mathbb{E}_t[\tau_{t+1}] = \sqrt{V_{t,11}^{(2)}}\ \mathbb{E}[\zeta_{t+1}^{+}], \tag{46}$$

$$\tau_t^{(1)} = \frac{1}{N}\sum_{n=1}^{N} \tau_{t-n}.$$

Note that investor 2 correctly anticipates the expected value of the put option while investor 1 will in general be wrong and therefore can, in principle, drive the option price p_{ot} arbitrarily far away from a traditional arbitrage-free valuation. Thus Equation (46) offers an explanation as to why options may be mispriced when using traditional arbitrage-free valuations.

The system of stochastic difference equations consisting of Equations (41), (42) and (46) describe the joint evolution of stock and option prices in which there are no spillovers from option prices to stock prices. This allows us to separate pure wealth effects from price effects. Pure wealth effects of holding put options will be studied in the next sections. The investigation of a more general price dynamics with perhaps more realistic forecasting rules is left for future research.

5. Allocation of risk and wealth distribution

In this section, we investigate the effects of an option market on the allocation of risk and the evolution of wealth of the two investors. The focus is on the situation in which stock prices receive no spillovers from the option market. As seen before, this case occurs if second-moment beliefs of investors are homogeneous up to a factor γ. Consider two economies, an economy with three assets, a risk-free bond with return R_f, a stock and a put option written on the stock as described before and the same economy without the possibility of trading in the put option. The respective beliefs of the two investors $i = 1, 2$ regarding future stock prices are the same in both economies. Under these conditions, it was shown in the previous section that the stock price processes of the two economies coincide and are governed by the same set of stochastic difference equations (41) and (42). The option price process for the economy with an option market is governed by the additional stochastic difference equations (46).

5.1 *Market price of risk*

We show first that the market prices of risk in the economy with a market for options are higher than the market prices of risk in the economy without the possibility to trade in options. As the market price for risk is a reward for taking on risk, this result will subsequently be used to establish that investors will take on more risk if they are allowed to trade in put options.

The market price of risk at time t is defined by the slope of the capital market line at time t. From Section 3.1, we know that the matrix of second moments of future payoffs, i.e. the covariance matrix (32) of stock prices and option values at date t is

$$\Sigma_t = \sigma_t^2 \begin{pmatrix} 1 & -b \\ -b & c \end{pmatrix},$$

The vector of excess returns $\pi_t = (\pi_{st}, \pi_{ot})$ is defined by

$$\pi_{st} = \mathbb{E}_t[q_{st+1}] - R_f p_{st} \quad \text{and} \quad \pi_{ot} = \mathbb{E}_t[\tau_{t+1}] - R_f p_{ot}.$$

Formally, the market price of risk of the economy with a market for options at time t is then defined as

$$\rho_t = \sqrt{\langle \pi_t, \Sigma_t^{-1} \pi_t \rangle}. \tag{47}$$

Analogously, the market price of risk of the economy without put options at time t is defined as

$$\tilde{\rho}_t = \frac{\pi_{st}}{\sigma_t}.$$

These definitions naturally extend the well-known concept of market price of risk to the situation in which investors' beliefs are heterogeneous. Note that the *perceived price of risk* of an investor which was defined earlier coincides with the correct market price of risk, if beliefs are rational. The first result is the following.

THEOREM 2

(i) *The market price of risk in the economy with a market for options is higher, that is,* $\rho_t \geq \tilde{\rho}_t$, *where the inequality is strict whenever*

$$b\pi_{st} + \pi_{ot} \neq 0. \tag{48}$$

(ii) *If, in addition, investor 2 has rational expectations and second-moment beliefs are homogeneous up to some factor* $\gamma > 0$, *then condition* (48) *is satisfied for*

$$b(\mathbb{E}_t[q_{st+1}] - q_{st}^{(1)}) \neq \tau_t^{(1)} - \mathbb{E}_t[\tau_{t+1}],$$

that is, whenever the option is traded.

COROLLARY 1 *The market price of risk* ρ_t *is strictly increasing with the magnitude of investor 1's forecast error on the future option value* $|\mathbb{E}_t[\tau_{t+1}] - \tau_t^{(1)}|$.

Theorem 2 establishes a key result of the paper which is that the reward for taking on risk is higher in an economy with a put option whenever the option is traded. As the proof of the theorem shows, this result holds for the general case with spillover effects from the put-option market. Corollary 1 demonstrates that this reward increases with the magnitude of the investor 1's forecast error on option values.

5.2 *Allocation of risk*

Let $\{w_t^{(i)}\}_{t\in\mathbb{N}}$, $i = 1, 2$ denote the wealth processes of the two investors in the economy with a market for put options. Using Equation (18), expected future wealths are

$$\mathbb{E}_t[w_{t+1}^{(i)}] = R_f w_t^{(i)} + \langle \pi_t, x_t^{(i)} \rangle,$$

whereas the respective conditional variances are

$$\mathbb{V}\mathrm{ar}_t[w_{t+1}^{(i)}] = \mathbb{V}\mathrm{ar}_t[p_{st+1}](x_{st}^{(i)})^2 + 2\mathbb{C}\mathrm{ov}_t[p_{st+1}, \tau_{t+1}]x_{st}^{(i)}x_{ot}^{(i)} + \mathbb{V}\mathrm{ar}_t[\tau_{t+1}](x_{ot}^{(i)})^2. \tag{49}$$

On the other hand, denote by $\{\tilde{w}_t^{(i)}\}_{t\in\mathbb{N}}$, $i = 1, 2$ the wealth processes of the respective investors in the economy in which put options cannot be traded. Expected future wealths of holding pure positions in stock $\tilde{x}_{st}^{(i)}$ are then

$$\mathbb{E}_t[\tilde{w}_{t+1}^{(i)}] = R_f\tilde{w}^{(i)} + \pi_{st}\tilde{x}_{st}^{(i)}$$

and the respective conditional variances compute as

$$\mathbb{V}\mathrm{ar}_t[\tilde{w}_{t+1}^{(i)}] = \mathbb{V}\mathrm{ar}_t[p_{st+1}](\tilde{x}_{st}^{(i)})^2. \tag{50}$$

In the economy with a market for put options, aggregate wealth in period t is $w_t = w_t^{(1)} + w_t^{(2)}$ and it follows from Equation (18) that

$$w_{t+1} = R_f w_t + (p_{st+1} + d_{t+1} - R_f p_{st})(\bar{x} - \xi_t).$$

Since there are no spillover effects on stock prices and the option is in zero net supply, this aggregate wealth process is the same as in the economy without options. In particular, if both economies start from the same initial distribution of wealth $w_0^{(i)} = \tilde{w}_0^{(i)}, i = 1, 2$ at time 0 and both are exposed to the same path of noise-trader portfolios $\{\xi_t\}_{t\in\mathbb{N}}$ and dividend payments $\{d_t\}_{t\in\mathbb{N}}$, then $w_{t+1} = \tilde{w}_{t+1}^{(1)} + \tilde{w}_{t+1}^{(2)}$ for all times t. This implies that the first two moments of the aggregate wealth process coincide for both economies. Contrary to this finding, however, the next proposition shows that individual risk in future wealth positions will increase for both investors, once the put option is traded.

PROPOSITION 2 *Suppose that under the above assumptions, put options are traded. Then the conditional variances of individual future wealth increase, that is,*

$$\mathbb{V}\mathrm{ar}_t[w_{t+1}^{(i)}] = \mathbb{V}\mathrm{ar}_t[\tilde{w}_{t+1}^{(i)}] + \frac{\det \Sigma_t}{\sigma_t^2}(x_{ot}^{(i)})^2$$

for both investors $i = 1, 2$ and all times t.

Proposition 2 shows that the volatility in both of the investors' future wealth increases quadratically with the trading volume of the option. This result has an interesting implication. If the stock price dynamics has no spillover effects from the option market, the correct forecast of investor 2, i.e. the expert trader, is independent of investor 1's forecast $\tau_t^{(1)}$. An over-estimation of the option value $\tau_t^{(1)} > \mathbb{E}_t[\tau_{t+1}]$ by investor 1 will increase the current option price p_{ot} as given in Equation (46) and, if sufficiently high, leave investor 1 in a long position of the option. Similarly, an under-estimation of the option value $\tau_t^{(1)} < \mathbb{E}_t[\tau_{t+1}]$ will decrease the current option price p_{ot} and, if sufficiently low, leave investor 1 in a short position of the option. Both over- and under-estimation enhances the volatility in the wealth process of both investors.

The next theorem now shows that only the expert trader with the correct beliefs will on average be rewarded for taking on extra risk.

THEOREM 3 *Under the previous assumptions, suppose $w_t^{(i)} = \tilde{w}_t^{(i)}, i = 1, 2$ in a period t. Then the following holds*:

(i)

$$\mathbb{E}_t[w_{t+1}^{(1)}] \leq \mathbb{E}_t[\tilde{w}_{t+1}^{(1)}] \quad and \quad \mathbb{V}\mathrm{ar}_t[w_{t+1}^{(1)}] \geq \mathbb{V}\mathrm{ar}_t[\tilde{w}_{t+1}^{(1)}]$$

(ii)

$$\mathbb{E}_t[w_{t+1}^{(2)}] \geq \mathbb{E}_t[\tilde{w}_{t+1}^{(2)}] \quad and \quad \mathbb{V}\mathrm{ar}_t[w_{t+1}^{(2)}] \geq \mathbb{V}\mathrm{ar}_t[\tilde{w}_{t+1}^{(2)}],$$

where all of the above inequalities are strict whenever

$$b(\mathbb{E}_t[q_{st+1}] - q_{st}^{(1)}) \neq \tau_t^{(1)} - \mathbb{E}_t[\tau_{t+1}],$$

that is, whenever the option is traded.

Theorem 3 establishes the wealth distributional effects of introducing an option market. The introduction of an option market will increase the risks of individual wealth positions, whereas aggregate wealth and aggregate risk in the two economies remain the same. On average, the informed expert trader will be rewarded by taking on extra risk, while the uninformed chartist will be penalized with a reduction in future wealth.

5.3 *Systematic and non-systematic risk*

The separation principle discussed in Section 2.2 states that a portfolio $x_t^{(i)}$ of investor i with mean-variance preferences is efficient with respect to her subjective beliefs $(q_t^{(i)}, V_t^{(i)})$. Another way of expressing this result is that an investor will choose a portfolio which she expects to earn the highest possible Sharpe ratio. This perceived Sharpe ratio is by construction equal to her perceived price of risk. With respect to the true moments of the actual price process, however, such a portfolio will *ex post* not earn the highest possible Sharpe ratio if beliefs turn out to be erroneous. This is so because investors with heterogeneous beliefs will most often not hold a portfolio that is collinear to the market portfolio. It is therefore not obvious which portfolios will attain the highest Sharpe ratio.

For financial markets without derivatives, this issue has been addressed in Wenzelburger (2004) who introduces a *modified market portfolio* which is *efficient* in the sense of Markowitz with respect to the true first two moments, and which attains the highest possible Sharpe ratio. The purpose of this section is to adapt this concept to a derivative market, to discuss the security market line for heterogeneous beliefs, and to extend the CAPM concepts of *systematic* and *non-systematic* risk to the model under consideration.

A modified market portfolio which accounts for the diversity in investors' beliefs can be introduced as follows. If π_t denotes the vector of expected excess returns in period t introduced in Section 5.1, a *modified market portfolio* of period t may be defined by setting

$$x_t^{\mathrm{ref}} := \Sigma_t^{-1}\pi_t. \tag{51}$$

The portfolio x_t^{ref} is a 'fictitious' portfolio as it is not necessarily held by an investor and will henceforth be referred to as *reference portfolio*.[9] Since the value of this reference portfolio at prices p_t is $\langle p_t, x_t^{\mathrm{ref}}\rangle$, its return is

$$R_{t+1}^{\mathrm{ref}} = \frac{\langle q_{t+1}, x_t^{\mathrm{ref}}\rangle}{\langle p_t, x_t^{\mathrm{ref}}\rangle} - 1. \tag{52}$$

The reference portfolio has two key properties. The first one is that its standard deviation is equal to the market price of risk, i.e. $\rho_t = \sqrt{\langle x_t^{\mathrm{ref}}, \Sigma_t x_t^{\mathrm{ref}}\rangle}$. The reference portfolio may therefore be seen as an indicator for aggregate risk. The second property[10] of the reference portfolio is the fact that its Sharpe ratio is equal to the market price of risk, that is,

$$\frac{\mathbb{E}_t[R^{\mathrm{ref}}_{t+1}] - r_f}{\sqrt{\mathbb{V}\mathrm{ar}_t[R^{\mathrm{ref}}_{t+1}]}} = \rho_t, \tag{53}$$

where $r_f = R_f - 1$ is the safe rate. The main results of this section can now be formulated as follows. Let $x^{(i)}_t$ denote the portfolio of risky assets held by investor i in period t after investing $w^{(i)}_t$. Then the return of i's portfolio realized in period $t+1$ is

$$R^{(i)}_{t+1} = r_f + \frac{1}{w^{(i)}_t}\langle q_{t+1} - R_f p_t, x^{(i)}_t\rangle. \tag{54}$$

In relating the return (54) to the return of the reference portfolio (52), the next proposition establishes a generalized security market line result first developed in Wenzelburger (2004).

PROPOSITION 3 *Let i be an arbitrary investor and assume asset markets clear in each period $t \in \mathbb{N}$ at prices p_{st}. Then for each $t \in \mathbb{N}$,*

$$\mathbb{E}_t[R^{(i)}_{t+1}] - r_f = \beta^{(i)}_t(\mathbb{E}_t[R^{\mathrm{ref}}_{t+1}] - r_f) \quad \textit{where } \beta^{(i)}_t := \frac{\mathbb{C}\mathrm{ov}_t[R^{(i)}_{t+1}, R^{\mathrm{ref}}_{t+1}]}{\mathbb{V}\mathrm{ar}_t[R^{\mathrm{ref}}_{t+1}]}. \tag{55}$$

Proposition 3 is a generalization of the *security market line* (see Luenberger 1998 or LeRoy and Werner 2001) to asset markets with heterogeneous beliefs. It states that the expected rate of return of a portfolio increases linearly as its covariance with the reference portfolio or, equivalently, as its $\beta^{(i)}_t$ increases.[11] An immediate implication of Proposition 3 is that the risk premium of a portfolio $x^{(i)}_t$ can only be higher than the risk premium of the reference portfolio x^{ref}_t at the expense of higher risk, i.e. $\mathbb{V}\mathrm{ar}_t[R^{(i)}_{t+1}] \geq \mathbb{V}\mathrm{ar}_t[R^{\mathrm{ref}}_{t+1}]$.

A slightly more convenient formulation of the security market line (55) follows from the following consideration. The *Sharpe ratio* of a portfolio $x^{(i)}_t$ conditional on information at date t is

$$\frac{\mathbb{E}_t[R^{(i)}_{t+1}] - r_f}{\sqrt{\mathbb{V}\mathrm{ar}_t[R^{(i)}_{t+1}]}}.$$

Dividing Equation (55) by the standard deviation $\sqrt{\mathbb{V}\mathrm{ar}_t[R^{(i)}_{t+1}]}$, we see that the Sharpe ratio of the portfolio $x^{(i)}_t$ satisfies

$$\frac{\mathbb{E}_t[R^{(i)}_{t+1}] - r_f}{\sqrt{\mathbb{V}\mathrm{ar}_t[R^{(i)}_{t+1}]}} = \mathbb{C}\mathrm{or}_t[R^{(i)}_{t+1}, R^{\mathrm{ref}}_{t+1}]\left(\frac{\mathbb{E}_t[R^{\mathrm{ref}}_{t+1}] - r_f}{\sqrt{\mathbb{V}\mathrm{ar}_t[R^{\mathrm{ref}}_{t+1}]}}\right), \tag{56}$$

where $-1 \leq \mathbb{C}\mathrm{or}_t(R^{(i)}_{t+1}, R^{\mathrm{ref}}_{t+1}] \leq 1$ denotes the correlation coefficient between $R^{(i)}_{t+1}$ and R^{ref}_{t+1}. This shows that the Sharpe ratio of a portfolio is bounded from above by the Sharpe ratio of the reference portfolio. Since any portfolio of risky assets $\tilde{x}_t = \lambda x_t$ with $\lambda > 0$ will have the same Sharpe ratio as $x_t \in \mathbb{R}^2$, only the mix of a portfolio has an influence on its Sharpe ratio. It follows that the expert trader will hold portfolios which are efficient in the original sense of Markowitz and thus attain the highest possible Sharpe ratios. Using Equation (53), we see that upper bounds for the Sharpe ratios (56) are the respective market prices of risk ρ_t which are generated by the endogenous price process.

We show next that the modified beta, $\beta_t^{(i)}$, as given in Proposition 3 is an appropriate measure of risk if investors' beliefs are heterogeneous. Choose a random variable $\varepsilon_{t+1}^{(i)}$ such that the random return of $x_t^{(i)}$ may be written as

$$R_{t+1}^{(i)} = r_f + \beta_t^{(i)}(R_{t+1}^{\text{ref}} - r_f) + \varepsilon_{t+1}^{(i)}. \tag{57}$$

Taking expectations, Proposition 3 implies $\mathbb{E}_t[\varepsilon_{t+1}^{(i)}] = 0$. Taking the conditional covariance between R_{t+1}^{ref} and Equation (57) and using the definition of the modified beta, we see that $\mathbb{C}\text{ov}_t[\varepsilon_{t+1}^{(i)}, R_{t+1}^{\text{ref}}] = 0$. Thus, the variance of $R_{t+1}^{(i)}$ becomes the sum of two parts:

$$\mathbb{V}\text{ar}_t[R_{t+1}^{(i)}] = (\beta_t^{(i)})^2\mathbb{V}\text{ar}_t[R_{t+1}^{\text{ref}}] + \mathbb{V}\text{ar}_t[\varepsilon_{t+1}^{(i)}]. \tag{58}$$

The first term in Equation (58) may be termed *systematic risk* and takes the form

$$sr_t^{(i)} = (\beta_t^{(i)})^2\mathbb{V}\text{ar}_t[R_{t+1}^{\text{ref}}] = \mathbb{C}\text{or}_t[R_{t+1}^{(i)}, R_{t+1}^{\text{ref}}]^2\mathbb{V}\text{ar}_t[R_{t+1}^{(i)}]. \tag{59}$$

This risk is associated with the market in period t as a whole. If $x_t^{(i)}$ consisted of a single asset, then this risk could not be diversified away because every asset with a nonzero beta contains this risk. The second term in Equation (58) may be termed *non-systematic* or *idiosyncratic risk* and takes the form

$$\mathbb{V}\text{ar}_t[\varepsilon_{t+1}^{(i)}] = (1 - \mathbb{C}\text{or}_t[R_{t+1}^{(i)}, R_{t+1}^{\text{ref}}]^2)\mathbb{V}\text{ar}_t[R_{t+1}^{(i)}]. \tag{60}$$

This risk is uncorrelated with the market and could be reduced by diversification, namely by choosing a combination of the risk-free asset and the reference portfolio.

The last theorem now shows that systematic risk in the above sense decreases with the introduction of a put-option market while the non-systematic risk increases.

THEOREM 4 *Let the general hypothesis of this section be satisfied. Consider a portfolio* $x_t^{(i)} = (x_{st}^{(i)}, 0)$ *that consists of stock only. Then the following holds*:

(i) *The portfolio's systematic risk* $\text{sr}_t^{(i)}$ *in an economy with a put-option market is lower than its systematic risk* $\widetilde{\text{sr}}_t^{(i)}$ *in an economy without a put-option market.*
(ii) *The portfolio's non-systematic risk in an economy with a put-option market is higher than its non-systematic risk in an economy without a put-option market.*

Theorem 4 provides a rationale for boundedly rational investors. Since the introduction of a put-option market increases the non-systematic risk of the economy, it is *ex ante* rational to participate in the put-option market in order to reduce the non-systematic risk of a portfolio. However, in a market with two investors, only one investor will on average be rewarded with attaining higher Sharpe ratios and thus a higher level of expected utility for trading in options.

6. Conclusion

This article investigated a financial market in which investors are allowed to simultaneously trade in stock and input options written on the stock. In each period, put-option prices were determined by market clearing in the put-option market. The focus was on a special case in which put option prices have no spillovers on stock prices. It was shown that while the introduction of a put-option market will decrease systematic risk in the financial market, it will increase the price of risk. The higher price of risk will be used by investors with linear $\mu - \sigma$ preferences to increase the risk of individual portfolio holdings. While aggregate risk in the market remains unaltered, individual risk of individual portfolio holdings increases. An investor with erroneous beliefs will on average not be rewarded for the additional risk of holding put options. She therefore may be better off not trading in put options. The model provided some insight as to why endogenous option prices may deviate from their traditional arbitrage-free valuations. The findings of the article may have interesting implication for pension funds which use financial derivatives to safeguard investments. Future research will look into spillover effects from option prices and into more realistic forecasting behavior of investors.

Acknowledgements

I would like to thank Matthias Schleef for his contributions to an early draft of this article and Jürgen Eichberger for valuable discussions. An earlier version of the paper was entitled *Risk Sharing in a Dynamic CAPM with Endogenous Option Prices*.

Notes

1. It is also well known that the indifference curves of concave utility functions U all have the same limiting slope (see Rockafellar 1970).
2. All entries of $V^{-1} = (1/\det V)\begin{pmatrix} V_{22} & -V_{12} \\ -V_{12} & V_{11} \end{pmatrix}$ are strictly positive, where $\det V = V_{11}V_{22} - V_{12}^2 > 0$.
3. In this case $\phi(w_0, \rho)$ is unimodal with respect to ρ. It is increasing for ρ below the threshold value $\rho_\star = e^{(1+R_f w_0)}$ and decreasing for ρ above $\rho_\star$. See Wenzelburger (2010) for details.
4. In view of Assumption 1, we assume that the exercise price κ_t is such that both subjective covariance matrices are non-degenerate. Conditions that ensure this will be given below.
5. The result here is more general regarding the degree of heterogeneity in beliefs and less general regarding risk preferences.
6. See also Appendix A.2.
7. It is straightforward to see that $0 < c < b < 1$ and $\det\begin{pmatrix} 1 & -b \\ -b & c \end{pmatrix} = c - b^2 > 0$, so that all covariance matrices are non-degenerate and thus invertible.
8. The results of the article will carry through for γ subject to small random noise. For simplicity, we assume that γ is constant.
9. It is not hard to see that x_t^{ref} is collinear to the market portfolio $(\bar{x}, 0)$ if beliefs are homogeneous and noise traders are absent. This justifies the name *modified market portfolio* as it indeed accounts for the diversity in investors' beliefs. Note that x_t^{ref} is well defined since according to Section 3.1, all covariance matrices are Σ_t, $t \in \mathbb{N}$ are invertible. Thus, x_t^{ref} can be associated with any price process with non-degenerate second moments.
10. This follows from the efficient frontier (7) in a straightforward manner. See the first part of the proof of Proposition 3 below for details.
11. An important observation is that the proof of Proposition 3 requires no assumption on the preferences of investors and, apart from a non-degenerate covariance structure, no assumption on the nature of the price process.

References

Black, F., and Scholes, M.J. 1973. The pricing of options and corporate liabilities. *Journal of Political Economy* 81, no. 3: 637–54.

Böhm, V., and Chiarella, C. 2005. Mean variance preferences, expectations formations, and the dynamics of random asset prices. *Mathematical Finance* 15, no. 1: 61–97.

Böhm, V., Deutscher, N., and Wenzelburger, J. 2000. Endogenous random asset prices in overlapping generations economies. *Mathematical Finance* 10, no. 1: 23–38.

Brock, W.A., and Hommes, C.H. 1997. Models of complexity in economics and finance. In *Systems dynamics in economic and finance models*, ed. B. Hanzon, C. Heij, J. Schumacher, and C. Praagman, chap. 1, 3–44. New York: Wiley.

Chiarella, C., and He, X.-Z. 2002. Heterogenous beliefs, risk and learning in a simple asset pricing model. *Computational Economics* 19: 95–132.

Detemple, J., and Selden, L. 1991. A general equilibrium analysis of option and stock market interactions. *International Economic Review* 32, no. 2: 279–303.

Franke, G., Stapleton, R.C., and Subrahmanyam, M.G. 1999. When are options overpriced? The Black–Scholes model and alternative characterisations of the pricing kernel. *European Finance Review* 3: 79–102.

Grandmont, J.-M. 1982. Temporary general equilibrium theory. In *Handbook of mathematical economics*, ed. K. Arrow and M. Intrilligator. Amsterdam: North-Holland.

Hens, T., and Schenk-Hoppé, K.R. 2009. *Handbook of financial markets – dynamics and evolution, Handbooks in Finance*. Amsterdam: Elsevier.

Hommes, C.H. 1998. On the consistency of backward looking expectations: the case of the Cobweb. *Journal of Economic Behavior & Organisation* 33: 333–62.

Horst, U. 2005 Financial price fluctuations in a stock market model with many interacting agents. *Economic Theory* 25, no. 4: 917–32.

Horst, U., and Wenzelburger, J. 2008. On non-ergodic asset prices. *Economic Theory* 34, no. 2: 207–34.

Krasa, S. 1989 Existence of competitive equilibria for option markets. *Journal of Economic Theory* 47: 413–21.

LeRoy, S., and Werner, J. 2001. *Principles of financial economics*. Cambridge: Cambridge University Press.

Lintner, J. 1965. The valuation of risky assets and selection of risky investment in stock portfolios and capital budgets. *Review of Economics and Statistics* 47: 13–37.

Luenberger, D.G. 1998. *Investment science*. Oxford: Oxford University Press.

Markowitz, H. 1952. Portfolio selection. *Journal of Finance* 7: 77–91.

Merton, R.C. 1973. An intertemporal capital asset pricing model. *Econometrica* 41, no. 5: 867–88.

Mossin, J. 1966 Equilibrium in a capital asset market. *Econometrica* 34: 268–90.

Nielsen, L.T. 1987. Portfolio selection in the mean–variance model: a note. *Journal of Finance* 42, no. 5: 1371–6.

Rockafellar, T.R. 1970. *Convex analysis*. Princeton, NJ: Princeton University Press.

Tobin, J. 1958. Liquidity preference as behavior towards risk. *Review of Economic Studies* 25: 65–86.

Wenzelburger, J. 2004. Learning to predict rationally when beliefs are heterogeneous. *Journal of Economic Dynamics and Control* 28, no. 10: 2075–104.

Wenzelburger, J. 2009 Perfect forecasting, behavioral heterogeneities, and asset prices. In *Handbook of financial markets – dynamics and evolution*, ed. T. Hens and K.R. Schenk-Hoppé, *Handbooks in Finance*, chap. 6, 345–401. Amsterdam: Elsevier.

Wenzelburger, J. 2010. The two-fund separation theorem revisited. *Annals of Finance* 6, no. 2: 221–39.

A. Mathematical appendix

A.1 *Matrix coefficients*

It is straightforward to see that the entries of the matrix coefficients (16) in the price law (17) take the following form:

$$A_{t,11}^{(1)} = \frac{(a^{(1)}/a^{(2)})(V_{t,22}^{(1)}V_{t,11}^{(2)} - V_{t,12}^{(1)}V_{t,12}^{(2)}) + (a^{(1)}/a^{(2)})^2 \det V_t^{(2)}}{R_f \det(V_t^{(1)} + (a^{(1)}/a^{(2)})V_t^{(2)})},$$

$$A_{t,12}^{(1)} = \frac{(a^{(1)}/a^{(2)})(V_{t,11}^{(1)}V_{t,12}^{(2)} - V_{t,12}^{(1)}V_{t,11}^{(2)})}{R_f \det(V_t^{(1)} + (a^{(1)}/a^{(2)})V_t^{(2)})}, \quad A_{t,21}^{(1)} = \frac{(a^{(1)}/a^{(2)})(V_{t,22}^{(1)}V_{t,12}^{(2)} - V_{t,12}^{(1)}V_{t,22}^{(2)})}{R_f \det(V_t^{(1)} + a^{(1)}/a^{(2)}V_t^{(2)})},$$

$$A_{t,22}^{(1)} = \frac{(a^{(1)}/a^{(2)})(V_{t,11}^{(1)}V_{t,22}^{(2)} - V_{t,12}^{(1)}V_{t,12}^{(2)}) + (a^{(1)}/a^{(2)})^2 \det V_t^{(2)}}{R_f \det(V_t^{(1)} + (a^{(1)}/a^{(2)})V_t^{(2)})}$$

and

$$A_{t,11}^{(2)} = \frac{1}{R_f} - A_{t,11}^{(1)}, \quad A_{t,12}^{(2)} = -A_{t,12}^{(1)}, \quad A_{t,21}^{(2)} = -A_{t,21}^{(1)}, \quad A_{t,22}^{(2)} = \frac{1}{R_f} - A_{t,22}^{(1)},$$

as well as

$$A_{t,11} = \frac{V_{t,11}^{(2)} \det V_t^{(1)} + (a^{(1)}/a^{(2)}) V_{t,11}^{(1)} \det V_t^{(2)}}{a^{(2)} R_f \det(V_t^{(1)} + (a^{(1)}/a^{(2)}) V_t^{(2)})} > 0, \tag{A1}$$

$$A_{t,21} = \frac{V_{t,12}^{(2)} \det V_t^{(1)} + (a^{(1)}/a^{(2)}) V_{t,12}^{(1)} \det V_t^{(2)}}{a^{(2)} R_f \det(V_t^{(1)} + (a^{(1)}/a^{(2)}) V_t^{(2)})} < 0. \tag{A2}$$

A.2 *Portfolio holdings*

This section determines allocations of stock and option contracts for given subjective beliefs of the two investors. Consider the coefficient matrices in Equation (19) and write

$$B_t = \begin{pmatrix} B_{t,11} & B_{t,12} \\ B_{t,12} & B_{t,22} \end{pmatrix}, \quad B_t^{(1)} = \begin{pmatrix} B_{t,11}^{(1)} & B_{t,12}^{(1)} \\ B_{t,21}^{(1)} & B_{t,22}^{(1)} \end{pmatrix} \quad \text{and} \quad B_t^{(2)} = \begin{pmatrix} B_{t,11}^{(2)} & B_{t,12}^{(2)} \\ B_{t,21}^{(2)} & B_{t,22}^{(2)} \end{pmatrix}.$$

Using the definitions (20) and (21), the relevant components of these matrices take the form:

$$B_{t,11} = \frac{a^{(1)} a^{(2)}}{\det(a^{(2)} V_t^{(1)} + a^{(1)} V_t^{(2)})} (a^{(2)} V_{t,22}^{(1)} + a^{(1)} V_{t,22}^{(2)}),$$

$$B_{t,12} = \frac{-a^{(1)} a^{(2)}}{\det(a^{(2)} V_t^{(1)} + a^{(1)} V_t^{(2)})} (a^{(2)} V_{t,12}^{(1)} + a^{(1)} V_{t,12}^{(2)}),$$

$$B_{t,22} = \frac{a^{(1)} a^{(2)}}{\det(a^{(2)} V_t^{(1)} + a^{(1)} V_t^{(2)})} (a^{(2)} V_{t,22}^{(1)} + a^{(1)} V_{t,22}^{(2)}),$$

as well as

$$B_{t,11}^{(2)} = \frac{a^{(1)} a^{(2)}}{\det(a^{(2)} V_t^{(1)} + a^{(1)} V_t^{(2)})} \left(\left(\frac{a^{(2)}}{a^{(1)}} \right) \det V_t^{(1)} + V_{t,11}^{(1)} V_{t,22}^{(2)} - V_{t,12}^{(1)} V_{t,12}^{(2)} \right),$$

$$B_{t,21}^{(2)} = \frac{a^{(1)} a^{(2)}}{\det(a^{(2)} V_t^{(1)} + a^{(1)} V_t^{(2)})} (V_{t,12}^{(1)} V_{t,11}^{(2)} - V_{t,11}^{(1)} V_{t,12}^{(2)}),$$

and, using $B_t^{(1)} + B_t^{(2)} = I$,

$$B_{t,11}^{(1)} = 1 - B_{t,11}^{(2)}, \quad B_{t,21}^{(1)} = -B_{t,21}^{(2)}.$$

With these coefficients the effective stock holdings in Equation (19) are

$$x_{st}^{(1)} = B_{t,11}^{(1)} (\bar{x} - \xi_t) - (B_{t,11} (q_{st}^{(2)} - q_{st}^{(1)}) + B_{12} (\tau_t^{(2)} - \tau_t^{(1)})), \tag{A3}$$

$$x_{st}^{(2)} = B_{t,11}^{(2)} (\bar{x} - \xi_t) + (B_{t,11} (q_{st}^{(2)} - q_{st}^{(1)}) + B_{12} (\tau_t^{(2)} - \tau_t^{(1)})), \tag{A4}$$

while the effective holdings in options become

$$x_{ot}^{(1)} = B_{t,21}^{(1)} (\bar{x} - \xi_t) - (B_{t,12} (q_{st}^{(2)} - q_{st}^{(1)}) + B_{22} (\tau_t^{(2)} - \tau_t^{(1)})), \tag{A5}$$

$$x_{ot}^{(2)} = B_{t,21}^{(2)} (\bar{x} - \xi_t) + (B_{t,12} (q_{st}^{(2)} - q_{st}^{(1)}) + B_{22} (\tau_t^{(2)} - \tau_t^{(1)})). \tag{A6}$$

For homogeneous beliefs $q_t^{(1)} = q_t^{(2)}$ and $V_t^{(1)} = V_t^{(2)}$, we obtain $x_{ot}^{(1)} = x_{ot}^{(2)} = 0$ and thus recover the fundamental result of the traditional *Capital Asset Pricing Model* which states that investors hold a portion of the market portfolio. As a consequence, options contracts which are in zero net-supply will not be traded under homogeneous beliefs in first and second moments.

A.3 *Proofs of theorems*

Proof of Lemma 1 By construction of the respective decision problems, $\sigma_{\text{eff}} \leq \tilde{\sigma}_{\text{eff}}$. This inequality is an equality if and only if the respective efficient portfolios $x_{\text{eff}} \in \mathbb{R}^2$ and $\tilde{x}_{\text{eff}} \in \mathbb{R}$ satisfy $x_{\text{eff}} = (\tilde{x}_{\text{eff}}, 0)$. Otherwise, the inequality is strict. In view of Equation (10), this is equivalent to

$$\frac{1}{\det V}\begin{pmatrix} V_{22}\pi_s - V_{12}\pi_o \\ -V_{12}\pi_s + V_{11}\pi_o \end{pmatrix} = \begin{pmatrix} \frac{\pi_s}{V_{11}} \\ 0 \end{pmatrix}. \tag{A7}$$

It is now straightforward to verify that Equation (A7) is satisfied if and only if $-V_{12}\pi_s + V_{11}\pi_o = 0$. This yields the first assertion. The second assertion follows from the first and Equation (5), noting that $\rho \geq \tilde{\rho}$ if and only if $\sigma_{\text{eff}} \leq \tilde{\sigma}_{\text{eff}}$.

Proof of Theorem 1 The assertions follow from Wenzelburger (2010, Proposition 2).

Proof of Lemma 2 The first part follows straightforwardly from Equation (A6). The second part follows directly from subtracting $\tilde{x}_t^{(i)}$ from the respective stock holdings in Equation (A4) which were computed in Appendix A.2.

Proof of Theorem 2 (i) Let $x_t^{\text{ref}} = \begin{pmatrix} x_{st}^{\text{ref}} \\ x_{ot}^{\text{ref}} \end{pmatrix}$ be the reference portfolio as defined by Equation (51), which takes the form

$$\begin{pmatrix} x_{st}^{\text{ref}} \\ x_{ot}^{\text{ref}} \end{pmatrix} = \frac{\sigma_t^2}{\det \Sigma_t}\begin{pmatrix} c\pi_{st} + b\pi_{ot} \\ b\pi_{st} + \pi_{ot} \end{pmatrix}, \tag{A8}$$

and $\tilde{x}_t^{\text{ref}} = \pi_{st}/\sigma_t^2$ be the reference portfolio of the economy without a put option market. It is not difficult to see that x_t^{ref} decomposes into

$$x_t^{\text{ref}} = \begin{pmatrix} x_{st}^{\text{ref}} \\ x_{ot}^{\text{ref}} \end{pmatrix} = \begin{pmatrix} \tilde{x}_t^{\text{ref}} \\ 0 \end{pmatrix} + x_{ot}^{\text{ref}}\begin{pmatrix} b \\ 1 \end{pmatrix}. \tag{A9}$$

Using Equation (A9) and the fact that

$$\Sigma_t\begin{pmatrix} b \\ 1 \end{pmatrix} = \begin{pmatrix} 0 \\ \frac{\det \Sigma_t}{\sigma_t^2} \end{pmatrix},$$

the market price of risk takes the form

$$\rho_t^2 = \langle x_t^{\text{ref}}, \Sigma_t x_t^{\text{ref}} \rangle = \sigma_t^2(\tilde{x}_t^{\text{ref}})^2 + \frac{\det \Sigma_t}{\sigma_t^2}(x_{ot}^{\text{ref}})^2 = \tilde{\rho}_t^2 + \frac{\det \Sigma_t}{\sigma_t^2}(x_{ot}^{\text{ref}})^2. \tag{A10}$$

This implies that $\rho_t \geq \tilde{\rho}_t$, where the inequality is strict if and only if $x_{ot}^{\text{ref}} \neq 0$. It follows from (A8) that $\rho_t > \tilde{\rho}_t$ if and only if

$$b\pi_{st} + \pi_{ot} \neq 0. \tag{A11}$$

(ii) The assumptions on the beliefs now imply that Equations (14) and (14) take the form (40), i.e.

$$A_t = \frac{1}{R_f(\gamma a^{(1)} + a^{(2)})}\Sigma_t, \quad A_t^{(1)} = \frac{\gamma a^{(1)}}{R_f(\gamma a^{(1)} + a^{(2)})}I, \quad A_t^{(2)} = \frac{a^{(2)}}{R_f(\gamma a^{(1)} + a^{(2)})}I.$$

With these coefficients, it follows from the price law (17) that

$$\begin{aligned} \pi_{st} &= \frac{\gamma a^{(1)}}{\gamma a^{(1)} + a^{(2)}}(\mathbb{E}_t[q_{st+1}] - q_{st}^{(1)}) + \frac{\sigma_t^2\bar{x}}{R_f(\gamma a^{(1)} + a^{(2)})}, \\ \pi_{ot} &= \frac{\gamma a^{(1)}}{\gamma a^{(1)} + a^{(2)}}(\mathbb{E}_t[\tau_{t+1}] - \tau_t^{(1)}) - \frac{(\sigma_t^2 b)\bar{x}}{R_f(\gamma a^{(1)} + a^{(2)})}. \end{aligned} \tag{A12}$$

Inserting Equation (A12) into Equation (A11) then yields the assertion because

$$b\pi_{st} + \pi_{ot} = \frac{\gamma a^{(1)}}{\gamma a^{(1)} + a^{(2)}}(b(\mathbb{E}_t[q_{st+1}] - q_{st}^{(1)}) + \mathbb{E}_t[\tau_{t+1}] - \tau_t^{(1)}). \tag{A13}$$

Proof of Corollary 1 Inserting Equation (A13) into Equation (A10), one obtains

$$\rho_t^2 = \tilde{\rho}_t^2 + \left(\frac{\gamma a^{(1)}}{\gamma a^{(1)} + a^{(2)}}\right)^2 \frac{\sigma_t^2}{\det \Sigma_t}(b(\mathbb{E}_t[q_{st+1}] - q_{st}^{(1)}) + \mathbb{E}_t[\tau_{t+1}] - \tau_t^{(1)})^2.$$

Thus ρ_t^2 is a quadratic function of the forecast error $(\mathbb{E}_t[\tau_{t+1}] - \tau_t^{(1)})$. Moreover, ρ_t^2 achieves its minimum $\tilde{\rho}_t^2$ for $\mathbb{E}_t[\tau_{t+1}] - \tau_t^{(1)} = b(q_{st}^{(1)} - \mathbb{E}_t[q_{st+1}])$.

Proof of Proposition 2 Subtracting the respective variances (49) and (50) implies

$$\mathbb{V}\text{ar}_t[w_{t+1}^{(i)}] - \mathbb{V}\text{ar}_t[\tilde{w}_{t+1}^{(i)}] = \sigma_t^2(c(x_{ot}^{(i)})^2 - 2bx_{st}^{(i)}x_{ot}^{(i)} + (x_{st}^{(i)} - \tilde{x}_{st}^{(i)})(x_{st}^{(i)} + \tilde{x}_{st}^{(i)})). \tag{A14}$$

By Lemma 2, $x_{st}^{(i)} - \tilde{x}_{st}^{(i)} = bx_{ot}^{(i)}$. Since investor 2 has correct second moments, the assertion now follows from inserting this into (A14) and rearranging.

Proof of Theorem 3 The assertions regarding the variances follow from Proposition 2. Consider investor 2 first and compare the risk-return characteristics of her future wealth in the two economies. By Proposition 1, the risk-return characteristics of the future wealth $w_{t+1}^{(2)}$ in an economy with an option market satisfy

$$\mathbb{E}_t[w_{t+1}^{(2)}] = R_f w_t^{(2)} + \rho_t \mathbb{V}\text{ar}_t[w_{t+1}^{(2)}]^{1/2},$$

where ρ_t is the price of risk in the economy with an option market. In an economy without an option market, the risk return characteristics of the future wealth $\tilde{w}_{t+1}^{(2)}$ satisfy

$$\mathbb{E}_t[\tilde{w}_{t+1}^{(2)}] = R_f w_t^{(2)} + \tilde{\rho}_t \mathbb{V}\text{ar}_t[\tilde{w}_{t+1}^{(2)}]^{1/2},$$

where $\tilde{\rho}_t$ is the price of risk in the economy with an option market. By Theorem 2, $\rho_t \geq \tilde{\rho}_t$ and by Proposition 2

$$\mathbb{V}\text{ar}_t[w_{t+1}^{(i)}] \geq \mathbb{V}\text{ar}_t[\tilde{w}_{t+1}^{(i)}], \quad i = 1, 2.$$

This implies (ii). Since aggregate wealth satisfies

$$w_{t+1} = w_{t+1}^{(1)} + w_{t+1}^{(2)} = \tilde{w}_{t+1}^{(1)} + \tilde{w}_{t+1}^{(2)},$$

one has

$$\mathbb{E}_t[w_{t+1}^{(1)}] = \mathbb{E}_t[w_{t+1}] - \mathbb{E}_t[w_{t+1}^{(2)}] \leq \mathbb{E}_t[w_{t+1}] - \mathbb{E}_t[\tilde{w}_{t+1}^{(2)}] = \mathbb{E}_t[\tilde{w}_{t+1}^{(1)}].$$

Since all inequalities are strict whenever $b(\mathbb{E}_t[q_{st+1}] - q_{st}^{(1)}) \neq \tau_t^{(1)} - \mathbb{E}_t[\tau_{t+1}]$, this yields the theorem.

Proof of Proposition 3 (see Wenzelburger 2009) Since the value of this reference portfolio at prices p_t is $\langle p_t, x_t^{\text{ref}}\rangle$, its return is

$$R_{t+1}^{\text{ref}} = \frac{\langle q_{t+1}, x_t^{\text{ref}}\rangle}{\langle p_t, x_t^{\text{ref}}\rangle} - 1.$$

Its conditional variance computes as

$$\mathbb{V}\text{ar}_t[R_{t+1}^{\text{ref}}] = \frac{\langle x_t^{\text{ref}}, \Sigma_t x_t^{\text{ref}}\rangle}{\langle p_t, \Sigma_t^{-1}\pi_t\rangle^2} = \frac{\langle \pi_t, \Sigma_t^{-1}\pi_t\rangle}{\langle p_t, \Sigma_t^{-1}\pi_t\rangle^2} \tag{A15}$$

and hence is proportional to the squared market price of risk $\langle \pi_t, \Sigma_t^{-1}\pi_t\rangle$. This implies that the *risk premium* of the reference portfolio satisfies

$$\mathbb{E}_t[R_{t+1}^{\text{ref}}] - r_f = \langle \pi_t, \Sigma_t^{-1}\pi_t\rangle^{1/2}\mathbb{V}\text{ar}_t[R_{t+1}^{\text{ref}}]^{1/2}, \tag{A16}$$

so that its risk-return characteristics lie on the capital-market line of period t.

Let $x_t^{(i)}$ denote the portfolio of risky assets held by investor i in period t after investing $w_t^{(i)}$. Then the expected return on i's portfolio in period $t+1$ is

$$\mathbb{E}_t[R_{t+1}^{(i)}] = r_f + \frac{1}{w_t^{(i)}}\langle \pi_t, x_t^{(i)} \rangle.$$

The conditional covariance $\mathbb{C}\mathrm{ov}_t[R_{t+1}^{(i)}, R_{t+1}^{\mathrm{ref}}]$ between $R_{t+1}^{(i)}$ and the return of the reference portfolio x_t^{ref} is

$$\mathbb{C}\mathrm{ov}_t[R_{t+1}^{(i)}, R_{t+1}^{\mathrm{ref}}] = \frac{1}{w_t^{(i)}\langle p_t, x_t^{\mathrm{ref}} \rangle}\langle x_t^{(i)}, \Sigma_t x_t^{\mathrm{ref}} \rangle. \tag{A17}$$

Inserting Equation (51) into Equation (A17), we see that the risk premium associated with the portfolio $x_t^{(i)}$ becomes

$$\mathbb{E}_t[R_{t+1}^{(i)}] - r_f = \langle p_t, \Sigma_t^{-1}\pi_t \rangle \mathbb{C}\mathrm{ov}_t[R_{t+1}^{(i)}, R_{t+1}^{\mathrm{ref}}]. \tag{A18}$$

Thus the risk premium of investor i's portfolio is proportional to the covariance between its return and the return of the reference portfolio. Combining Equation (A18) with Equation (A15) and (A16) yields the theorem.

Proof of Theorem 4 By Theorem 2, $\rho_t \geq \tilde{\rho}_t$, where the inequality is strict whenever

$$b(\mathbb{E}_t[q_{st+1}] - q_{st}^{(1)}) \neq \tau_t^{(1)} - \mathbb{E}_t[\tau_{t+1}]. \tag{A19}$$

As there are no spillover effects on the stock market, the Sharpe ratio of $x_t^{(i)} = (x_{st}^{(i)}, 0)$ will not change with the introduction of an option market. Using Equation (56) one has

$$\frac{\mathbb{E}_t[R_{t+1}^{(i)}] - r_f}{\sqrt{\mathbb{V}\mathrm{ar}_t[R_{t+1}^{(i)}]}} = \mathbb{C}\mathrm{or}_t[R_{t+1}^{(i)}, R_{t+1}^{\mathrm{ref}}]\rho_t = \mathbb{C}\mathrm{or}_t[R_{t+1}^{(i)}, \tilde{R}_{t+1}^{\mathrm{ref}}]\tilde{\rho}_t.$$

Thus, $\rho_t \geq \tilde{\rho}_t$ implies $\mathbb{C}\mathrm{or}_t[R_{t+1}^{(i)}, R_{t+1}^{\mathrm{ref}}] \leq \mathbb{C}\mathrm{or}_t[R_{t+1}^{(i)}, \tilde{R}_{t+1}^{\mathrm{ref}}]$ and hence $sr_t^{(i)} \leq \tilde{sr}_t^{(i)}$, where the inequalities are strict, whenever Equation (A19) holds.

Performance analysis of a collateralized fund obligation (CFO) equity tranche

Shady Aboul-Enein, Georges Dionne and Nicolas Papageorgiou

This article examines the performance of the junior tranche of a collateralized fund obligation (CFO), i.e. the residual claim (equity) on a securitized portfolio of hedge funds. We use a polynomial goal programming model to create optimal portfolios of hedge funds, conditional to investor preferences and diversification constraints (maximum allocation per strategy). For each portfolio, we build CFO structures that have different levels of leverage, and analyze both the stand-alone performance as well as potential diversification benefits (low systematic risk exposures) of investing in the equity tranche of these structures. We find that the unconstrained mean-variance portfolio yields a high performance, but greater exposure to systematic risk. We observe the exact opposite picture in the case of unconstrained optimization, where a skewness bias is added, thus proving the existence of a trade-off between stand-alone performance and low exposure to systematic risk factors. We provide evidence that leveraged exposure to these hedge fund portfolios through the structuring of CFOs creates value for the equity tranche investor, even during the recent financial crisis.

1. Introduction

In 2002, structured finance and hedge funds merged together for the first time. This union gave birth to *collateralized fund obligations* (CFO) which consists in the securitization of hedge fund portfolios. This new category of assets seems to offer the best of both worlds. On the one hand, it provides investors with a new vehicle through which to obtain exposure to hedge fund returns, and on the other hand offers to the financial engineers a new and quite unique pool of assets to securitize. The variety of strategies and low correlations with traditional assets makes hedge funds an ideal candidate as a collateral for securitization transactions. Although the theoretical justification of CFOs has been firmly established in financial literature (Cheng 2002; Mahadevan and Schwartz 2002; Stone and Zissu 2004; Missinhoun and Chacowry 2005), there are still many misgivings as to their practical pertinence.

Thus, despite the rapid growth of the CDO market over the past two decades, there were no more than 20 CFO transactions prior to 2008. A lack of interest by investors in the equity tranche of these structures seems to be the source of the slow proliferation. The perception of low added-value and high inherent leverage, made it difficult to solicitate interest in the junior tranche of CFOs. That said, given the novelty and the complexity of these products, which belong to a vast family of derivatives, it is logical to suppose that the distinctive fundamental characteristics and benefits of the exposure to a CFO equity tranche have yet to be carefully scrutinized. This article provides a thorough analysis of the factors that might influence the performance of various hypothetical CFO equity tranches. Using data on historical hedge fund returns, the goal is to structure various CFOs based on a variety of underlying portfolios and investigate the returns of the equity tranche both in terms of stand alone performance and in terms of potential diversification benefits.

More specifically, the first objective, from the viewpoint of a CFO equity owner, is to define the optimal capital structure(s) as well as the general attributes for the diversification of the optimal portfolio of hedge funds for the securitization transaction. The analysis is, therefore, far more thorough than that observed in existing literature on the subject of CFOs. In order to investigate the impact of strategy selection and diversification in the underlying hedge fund portfolio, we implement an optimization model that allows us to specify preferences for higher moments. This polynomial goal-programming (PGP) approach generates optimal allocations conditional to specific investor preferences. For each 'optimal' portfolio, several debt-structured finance programs are then considered so as to account for a far broader range of scenarios. This is done in order to identify, on the basis of a number of performance indicators, the optimal composition of the collateral and the appropriate leverage to which the exposure should be subjected.

The second objective is to study the exposure of the CFO equity tranche to systematic risk factors, such as market, credit and liquidity. In this sense, the study will determine the degree to which returns are defined by the returns of readily available risk premia, and therefore provide a better idea of their risk exposures. This is achieved using a multivariate linear regression model.

The results indicate that CFOs create value from the equity holder's perspective. Nonetheless, there is a trade-off that must be made between the stand-alone performance of a CFO equity tranche and its' systematic risk exposure. We find that the unconstrained mean-variance portfolio yields a high performance, but exhibits greater exposure to systematic risk factors. We observe the exact opposite in the case of unconstrained optimization, where a preference for skewness is incorporated, thus proving the existence of a trade-off between performance and low-correlation with the financial markets. According to our results, an interesting compromise could be obtained by securitizing a well-diversified underlying portfolio of funds.

The article is structured as follows. Section 2 presents the three stage methodology. Section 3 describes and analyzes the data and Section 4 focuses on the empirical results. We also analyze the impact of the recent financial crisis on the results. Conclusions are presented in Section 5.

2. Methodology

The methodology consists of three steps. The first step concerns the allocation of hedge funds across the different strategies, the second relates to the structuring and evaluation of the CFO, and the final stage consists in the analysis of the systematic risk exposures of the resulting equity tranche of the CFO.

2.1 *Allocation across hedge fund strategies*

To decide on the asset allocation between the different investment strategies, we use a PGP optimization model. This approach was introduced by Tayi and Leonard (1988), and has been employed by Chunhachinda et al. (1997) and Sun and Yan (2003) to incorporate the effect of skewness on portfolio allocation decisions. Davies, Kat, and Lu (2009) use this approach to incorporate investor preferences for higher moments into the construction of funds of funds. They extend the original model in order to account not only for skewness but also for the kurtosis that is prevalent in hedge fund return distributions. This approach incorporates multiple, and often conflicting, objectives and considers the impact of a change in investor preferences on asset allocation.

2.1.1 *The PGP model*

Consider an environment with m risky assets, each with random return $\tilde{R}_i$, and x_i being the percentage of wealth invested in the ith asset. The risk-free rate r is constant and no short selling of the risky assets is permitted ($x_i \geq 0$ for all i). The percentage invested in the risk-free asset is determined by $x_{m+1} = 1 - \boldsymbol{I}^{\mathrm{T}}\boldsymbol{X}$, where $\boldsymbol{I}$ is an identity vector of dimension $m \times 1$ and $X = (x_1, x_2, \ldots, x_n)$. V is variance–covariance matrix for $\tilde{R} = (\tilde{R}_1, \tilde{R}_2, \ldots, \tilde{R}_m)$. The matrix V is positive definite and of dimension $m \times m$. The variance of the portfolios $\boldsymbol{X}^{\mathrm{T}}\boldsymbol{V}\boldsymbol{X}$ is set at one. Since the analysis concerns the relative performance invested in each asset, this restriction on the variance does not affect the results. Thus, the problem of portfolio selection can be defined using the PGP model:

$$\text{MIN} \quad Z = (1 + d_1)^{\alpha} + (1 + d_3)^{\beta} + (1 + d_4)^{\gamma} \tag{1}$$

$$\text{Subject to} \quad E[X^{\mathrm{T}}\tilde{R}] + x_{m+1}r + d_1 = Z_1^*, \tag{2}$$

$$E[X^{\mathrm{T}}(\tilde{R} - E[\tilde{R}])]^3 + d_3 = Z_3^*, \tag{3}$$

$$-E[X^{\mathrm{T}}(\tilde{R} - E[\tilde{R}])]^4 + d_4 = -Z_4^*, \tag{4}$$

$$d_1, d_3, d_4 \geq 0, \tag{5}$$

$$\boldsymbol{X}^{\mathrm{T}}\boldsymbol{V}\boldsymbol{X} = 1; x_i \geq 0; x_{m+1} = 1 - \boldsymbol{I}^{\mathrm{T}}\boldsymbol{X}, \tag{6}$$

where $Z_1^* = \text{Max}\{Z_1 \mid \boldsymbol{X}^{\mathrm{T}}\boldsymbol{V}\boldsymbol{X} = 1\}$ is the average return of the optimal mean-variance portfolio with a unit variance, $Z_3^* = \text{Max}\{Z_3 \mid \boldsymbol{X}^{\mathrm{T}}\boldsymbol{V}\boldsymbol{X} = 1\}$ is the skewness of the optimal skewness-variance portfolio with a unit variance, and $Z_4^* = \text{Max}\{Z_4 \mid \boldsymbol{X}^{\mathrm{T}}\boldsymbol{V}\boldsymbol{X} = 1\}$ is the kurtosis of the optimal kurtosis-variance portfolio with a unit variance; and where

$$Z_1 = E[X^{\mathrm{T}}\tilde{R}] + x_{m+1}r;$$

$$Z_3 = E[X^{\mathrm{T}}(\tilde{R} - E[\tilde{R}])]^3;$$

$$Z_4 = E[X^{\mathrm{T}}(\tilde{R} - E[\tilde{R}])]^4.$$

The optimal values Z_1^*, Z_3^*, and Z_4^* solve each particular objective without considering the other objectives. The solution of the PGP model considers all objectives simultaneously. α, β, and γ are non-negative parameters specific to the investor's subjective degree of preference with regard to the goal variables (average return (d_1), the skewness (d_2) and the kurtosis (d_4)) which account for the investor deviations from Z_1^*, Z_3^*, and Z_4^*, respectively. The form of the objective function ensures its monotone growth in d_1, d_3, and d_4 for all possible values.

Even though the technique does not require an investor-specific utility function, it can still be inferred that the investors' utility functions are of higher order than quadratic. Importantly, the model's parameters α, β, and γ have an explicit economic interpretation; they are directly linked to the concept of the marginal rate of substitution, which measures the desirability of the foregoing objective for achieving another. In short, the problem of a multi-objective PGP is solved in two stages. First, the optimal values for Z_1^*, Z_3^*, and Z_4^* are each obtained within a two-dimensional unit variance framework. Subsequently, these values are substituted in conditions (2)–(4) and the minimum value of Equation (1) is found for a given set of investor preferences $\{\alpha, \beta, \gamma\}$ within a four-moment framework.

All resulting portfolios are composed of risky assets (hedge fund strategies) and a risk-free asset so as to ensure the unicity of each optimal portfolio. We redistribute the risk-free rate allocation into the hedge fund strategies on a pro-rata basis such that the total investment in the risky assets equals 1. Thus $y_i = x_i/(x_1 + x_2 + \cdots + x_m)$ will be the percentage invested in the ith asset (hedge fund strategy) for the optimal portfolio.

Five sets of preference parameters $\{\alpha, \beta, \gamma\}$ are used for the optimization procedure. These are: $E_1 = \{\alpha = 1, \beta = 0, \gamma = 0\}$, $E_2 = \{\alpha = 1, \beta = 1, \gamma = 0\}$, $E_3 = \{\alpha = 1, \beta = 1, \gamma = 0.75\}$, $E_4 = \{\alpha = 2, \beta = 1, \gamma = 0.75\}$ and $E_5 = \{\alpha = 3, \beta = 1, \gamma = 0.25\}$. The goal is not to build portfolios with fully representative parameters, but to determine the relative importance that must be attributed to each of the higher-order moments of the distribution. Simultaneously, one of the main objectives is to characterize an optimal underlying from the viewpoint of a CFO equity owner and it is therefore reasonable to suppose that the five sets of preferences should easily suffice. Note that the preference set E_1 represents a traditional mean-variance optimization. We also perform constrained optimizations for each set of preferences, with maximum allocation to each strategy limited to 10%, 15%, 20%, 25%, and 50%. Finally, given the recent empirical evidence supporting the equally weighted (EW) portfolio (DeMiguel, Garlappi, and Uppal 2009) we also consider the $(1/m)$ portfolio allocation. In all, 31 portfolios will be analyzed. The notation that will be employed to refer to a given preference set and diversification constraint is E_{hk}, where h refers to the preference set and k to the maximum allocation per strategy.

2.2 *CFO structures*

In constructing the CFO structures, we follow the approach of Mahadevan and Schwartz (2002). Overall, 20 structures are analyzed, with each CFO_j $(j = 1, 2, \ldots, n)$ being distinguished by its debt-to-equity ratio. CFO_1 represents the zero-debt case, which is simply a direct, unleveraged exposure to the hedge fund portfolio.[1] The amount of debt within the structure is then increased in increments of 5% for each of the ensuing CFO structures, up to CFO_{20} in which the equity tranche represents only 5% of the structure. Table 1 presents the 20 structures.

Each CFO has a par value of \$400M and a maturity of 7 years.[2] As the proportion of debt increases so does the number of tranches. To this end, a number of assumptions are made so as to comply with the same economic logic across all structures. We, therefore, assume that the first 200 million in debt (50% of the structure) are senior rated (AA), which explains why no junior debt tranche appears prior to CFO_{12}. This new tranche (BBB) is capped at 20% of the structure (\$80M), so that when more than \$280M in debt accrues, the BB tranche of debt is added. This new tranche is capped at 15%. The final tranche (BB-) only appears in the two most leveraged structures. The cost of financing for the AAA tranche is 150 basis points over the 1-month LIBOR. This spread is 200 basis points for the AA tranche, 300 basis points for the BBB tranche and 450 basis points for the BB- tranche. This convex increase in costs (150–200, 200–300, 300–450 bps) allows us to emphasize the risk associated with the junior debt tranches.

The common costs underlying our CFO structures differ slightly from those of Mahadevan and Schwartz (2002). Specifically, the periodic cost of debt is directly calculated by adding the variation in basis points for each level to the one-month LIBOR rate. Consequently, it is assumed that the structures are perfectly hedged in terms of interest rate risk, which reduces the number of variables handled without, however, undermining the robustness of the analysis. The senior

Table 1. Structural assumptions for the 20 CFOs considered.

	CFO 1	CFO 2	CFO 3	CFO 4	CFO 5	CFO 6	CFO 7	CFO 8	CFO 9	CFO 10
Senior notes										
Rating		AA	AA	AA	AA	AA	AA	AA	AA	AA
Par value		$20M	$40M	$60M	$80M	$100M	$120M	$140M	$160M	$180M
% of structure		5%	10%	15%	20%	25%	30%	35%	40%	45%
Advance rate		60%	60%	60%	60%	60%	60%	60%	60%	60%
Class II notes										
Rating										
Par value										
% of structure										
Advance rate										
Class III notes										
Rating										
Par value										
% of structure										
Advance rate										
Class IV notes										
Rating										
Par value										
% of structure										
Advance rate										
Total Debt	–$	$20M	$40M	$60M	$80M	$100M	$120M	$140M	$160M	$180M
Equity tranche										
Par value	$400M	$380M	$360M	$340M	$320M	$300M	$280M	$260M	$240M	$220M
% of structure	100%	95%	90%	85%	80%	75%	70%	65%	60%	55%
% of MV gains distributed on a current basis	0%	0%	0%	0%	0%	0%	0%	0%	0%	0%
Total par value of CFO	$400M	$400M	$400M	$400M	$400M	$400M	$400M	$400M	$400M	$400M
D/E ratio	–	0.053	0.111	0.176	0.25	0.333	0.429	0.538	0.667	0.818

Costs and fees										
All in funding cost (spread in bps)	–	150	150	150	150	150	150	150	150	150
Senior management fee	N/A	50 bps	50 bps	50 bps	50 bps	50 bps	50 bps	50 bps	50 bps	50 bps
Up-front fees	N/A	3%	3%	3%	3%	3%	3%	3%	3%	3%
Benchmark	N/A	1M LIBOR	1M LIBOR	1M LIBOR	1M LIBOR	1M LIBOR	1M LIBOR	1M LIBOR	1M LIBOR	1M LIBOR
7-year swap rate @ $t = 0$	N/A	5.85%	5.85%	5.85%	5.85%	5.85%	5.85%	5.85%	5.85%	5.85%
Stated maturity (all securities)	7 Years	7 Years	7 Years	7 Years	7 Years	7 Years	7 Years	7 Years	7 Years	7 Years
	CFO 11	CFO 12	CFO 13	CFO 14	CFO 15	CFO 16	CFO 17	CFO 18	CFO 19	CFO 20
Senior notes										
Rating	AA	AA	AA	AA	AA	AA	AA	AA	AA	AA
Par value		$200M	$200M	$200M	$200M	$200M	$200M	$200M	$200M	$200M
% of structure		50%	50%	50%	50%	50%	50%	50%	50%	50%
Advance rate		60%	60%	60%	60%	60%	60%	60%	60%	60%
Class II notes										
Rating		BBB	BBB	BBB	BBB	BBB	BBB	BBB	BBB	BBB
Par value		$20M	$40M	$60M	$80M	$80M	$80M	$80M	$80M	$80M
% of structure		5%	10%	15%	20%	20%	20%	20%	20%	20%
Advance rate		75%	75%	75%	75%	75%	75%	75%	75%	75%
Class III notes										
Rating						BB	BB	BB	BB	BB
Par value						$20M	$40M	$60M	$60M	$60M
% of structure						5%	10%	15%	15%	15%
Advance rate						82%	82%	82%	82%	82%
Class IV notes										
Rating									BB-	BB-
Par value									$20M	$40M
% of structure									5%	10%
Advance rate									90%	90%
Total debt	$200M	$220M	$240M	$260M	$280M	$300M	$320M	$340M	$360M	$380M

(Continued)

Table 1. Continued

	CFO 1	CFO 2	CFO 3	CFO 4	CFO 5	CFO 6	CFO 7	CFO 8	CFO 9	CFO 10
Equity tranche										
Par value	\$200M	\$180M	\$160M	\$140M	\$120M	\$100M	\$80M	\$60M	\$40M	\$20M
% of structure	50%	45%	40%	35%	30%	25%	20%	15%	10%	5%
% of MV gains distributed on a current basis	0%	0%	0%	0%	0%	0%	0%	0%	0%	0%
Total par value of CFO	\$400M	\$400M	\$400M	\$400M	\$400M	\$400M	\$400M	\$400M	\$400M	\$400M
D/E ratio	1.00	1.222	1.50	1.857	2.333	3.00	4.00	5.667	9.00	19.00
Costs and fees										
All in funding cost (spread in bps)	150	200	200	200	200	300	300	300	450	450
Senior management fee	50 bps	50 bps	50 bps	50 bps	50 bps	50 bps	50 bps	50 bps	50 bps	50 bps
Up-front fees	3%	3%	3%	3%	3%	3%	3%	3%	3%	3%
Benchmark	1M LIBOR	1M LIBOR	1M LIBOR	1M LIBOR	1M LIBOR	1M LIBOR	1M LIBOR	1M LIBOR	1M LIBOR	1M LIBOR
7-year swap rate @ $t = 0$	5.85%	5.85%	5.85%	5.85%	5.85%	5.85%	5.85%	5.85%	5.85%	5.85%
Stated maturity (all securities)	7 Years	7 Years	7 Years	7 Years	7 Years	7 Years	7 Years	7 Years	7 Years	7 Years

Notes: This table presents the 20 capital structures considered. The characteristics of each structure appear on the vertical axis, while the 20 CFO structures are presented horizontally. The upper portion of the table shows the features of the five possible tranches and the lower one relates to cost assumptions. Blanks designate the absence of a certain tranche for a specific structure.

management fees of 0.5% per annum and the up-front fees of 3% add to the financial burden of the structure's liabilities. To prevent the up-front fees from disproportinately impacting the first month's results, the latter are financed by the structure via a gradually amortized loan at the 7-year Swap rate in effect at the time the vehicle is issued (5.85%).[3]

Thus, from the above information and a series of returns on a collateralized portfolio, it is possible to derive a periodic return on the equity tranche of any structure for any underlying portfolio. To calculate the monthly return of the equity tranche of $\mathrm{CFO}_{j,hk}$ at time $t(r_{j,hk,t})$ using the return on E_{hk}, the following formulas are used:

$$\mathrm{Equity}_{j,hk,t} = \left\{\left[\mathrm{NAV}_{t-1}(1 + r_{hk,t}) - D_j\left(\frac{\mathrm{LIBOR}_t + \mathrm{AFC}_j}{12}\right) - \left(\mathrm{NAV}_{t-1} * \frac{0.5\%}{12}\right) - \mathrm{PMT}\right] - D_j\right\} \tag{7}$$

$$r_{j,hk,t} = \frac{\mathrm{Equity}_{j,hk,t} - \mathrm{Equity}_{j,hk,t-1}}{\mathrm{Equity}_{j,hk,t-1}}, \tag{8}$$

where $\mathrm{Equity}_{j,hk,t}$ is the value of the equity of the structure j,hk at the end of month t; NAV_{t-1} is the structure's total value at the start of the month t; $r_{hk,t}$ is the return of the unlevered portfolio hk for month t; D_j is the value of the debt of CFO_j; LIBOR_t is the value of the 1-month LIBOR at the end of month t; AFC_j is the aggregated financing cost of CFO_j; $0.5\%/12$ corresponds to the senior management fees reported monthly; PMT corresponds to the monthly payment in the amount of \$174,441 concerning the amortization of up-front fees.

A monthly frequency is favored herein; all costs are, therefore, reported on a monthly basis and the income generated by the model is represented by a series of returns, each with 84 observations (7 years × 12 months). It is also important to mention that contrary to Mahadevan and Schwartz (2002), no distribution of market value gains will be performed during the seven years of the vehicles' existence. Implicitly, we assume a seven-year lock-up period for the equity tranche owners.

2.2.1 *Evaluating the equity tranche*

Given the 31 hedge fund portfolios and 20 possible CFO structures, we obtain 620 series of returns (31 × 20 CFO structures) containing 84 observations each.

An initial analysis of the results is performed using a number of performance measures. In addition to calculating the usual descriptive statistics and normality tests for return distributions,[4] several performance measures are calculated to evaluate the risk-adjusted performance of the different CFO structures. We employ two conventional measures, specifically, the Sharpe and Treynor ratios. We also calculate three more comprehensive measures, namely the Sortino ratio (Sortino and Price 1994), the modified Sharpe ratio (Gregoriou and Gueyi 2003; Lee 2007) and the Omega measure (Keating and Shadwick 2002; De Souza and Gokcan 2004). A brief description of the performance measures is presented in Table 2.

In sum, after having determined the CFO structures and optimal portfolios from the equity owner's viewpoint using the performance measures stated above, the attributes of the capital structure (D/E ratio) and the impact of the diversification constraints on the underlying strategies are analyzed. These results allow us to draw a first round of conclusions.

Table 2. Description of performance measures.

Performance measures	Formula	Description
Sharpe ratio	$\frac{E[r_p - r_f]}{\sigma_p}$	The ratio of excess return above the risk-free rate over total portfolio volatility
Treynor ratio	$\frac{E[r_p - r_f]}{\beta_p}$	The ratio of excess return over the systematic portfolio risk
Sortino ratio	$\frac{E[r_p - \text{MAR}]}{\text{DD}_p}$	The ratio of excess return above a minimum acceptable return (MAR) over the downside deviation below the MAR
Modified Sharpe ratio	$\frac{E[r_p - r_f]}{\text{VaR}}$	The ratio of excess return above the risk-free rate over the 95% value-at-risk measure
Omega	$\frac{\int_{\text{MAR}}^{\infty}(1 - F(r))\text{d}r}{\int_{-\infty}^{\text{MAR}} F(r)\text{d}r}$	The probability weighted ratio of gains over losses with respect to an MAR

Note: This table presents the description of the five performance measures used in the analysis.

2.3 *Analysis of the systematic risk exposure*

In order to verify whether the equity tranche of each CFO is exposed to systematic risk factors (market, credit, and liquidity), we estimate a multivariate linear regression. If the resulting regression coefficients are not significant, this would imply that returns on CFO equity tranches are not determined by systematic risk factors and hence could offer significant diversification benefits to traditional portfolios. The same analysis is performed on the returns of the underlying hedge fund portfolios so as to compare the diversification benefits resulting from a direct exposure to the hedge fund portfolios versus that of a CFO. The variables for the regression are presented in Section 4.3.

3. Data

The hedge fund data were provided by Desjardins Global Asset Management and includes HFR and TASS databases. As of January 2008, 7533 hedge funds were included in the database. The initial sample consists of monthly returns of hedge funds over a 17-year period, from February 1991 to January 2008. The database includes specific information about each fund, including the self-reported investment style.

Of the original 7533 hedge funds, many had to be eliminated from the study. First, 2523 funds of hedge funds were withdrawn because they are not strategy-specific funds. Similarly, 126 HFRI and HFRX indexes were deleted. Next, we eliminated 73 funds that did not report their after-fee returns. Also, to ensure the reliability of data used and avoid dealing with self-selection bias, 632 funds were withdrawn from the sample as they registered either less than 12 consecutive months of performance or the disclosure of their results had been interrupted at some point. Finally, 33 'Regulation D' funds were discarded since the latter category only appears as of the late 1990s. After these deletions, the returns of 4146 hedge funds make up the sample over a period of 204 months (17 years $\times$ 12 months).

We observe that across the 29 initial strategies, certain strategies have more than 300 funds while others have less than 30. To address this relative imbalance, we opt to aggregate similar strategies. Table 3 presents the distribution of hedge funds across strategies before and after aggregation.

We observe that the process results in three new aggregated strategies: *Emerging Markets* (*Asia, E. Europe/CIS, Global and Latin America*), *Fixed Income* (*arbitrage, convertible bonds, diversified, high yield and mortgage backed*) and *Sectorial* (*energy, financial, health care/biotechnology, miscellaneous, real estate and technology*). The number of strategies, therefore, decreases from 29 to 16 and the hedge funds are relatively well dispersed across the strategies.

In order to circumvent the issue of relative size of the strategies, avoid working with 4146 assets and counter the issue of survivorship bias, an EW index is constructed for each strategy. In other words, an average return per strategy is calculated for each date of the sample. This allows us to perform the portfolio optimization with 16 assets and obtain easily interpretable results in relation to the number, attributed weight and type of the different strategies so as to create the greatest possible value for the owners of a CFO equity tranche. In essence, this approach assumes that there is no value created by the CFO manager through active fund selection and ensures that we obtain the average return of all the available funds within a category.

Furthermore, in order to meet the objectives of the proposed empirical approach, the sample is split into two periods. The first 10 years of the sample are used for the optimization of hedge fund portfolios *ex ante*, and the final seven years provide out-of-sample data to which the CFO structures will be applied. Table 4 presents the statistics of each strategy index over the first 10 years and over the final seven years.

If we first make a general comparison between the data of the two periods, we note that hedge fund returns over period 1 are higher, more volatile and generally demonstrate a greater level of skewness and kurtosis. This result can mainly be explained by the fact that period 1 witnessed a very bullish market, while period 2 was more unpredictable and generated less value on the financial markets.[5] In this regard, it should be noted that the data only cover the beginning of the 2008 financial crisis. Nonetheless, despite the obvious disparities between the two periods, the strategies demonstrate similar behavior. We observe that the tests of Jarque-Bera, Lilliefors, and Genest and Remillard reject normality in the respective proportions of 81% (13/16), 56% (9/16) and 63% (10/16) for period 1 and 38% (6/16), 38% (6/16) and 56% (9/16) for period 2. This must be considered when testing the normality of returns of the constructed portfolios and CFOs.

As for the comparison between the strategies themselves, we first observe that the *Emerging Markets* and *Sectorial* strategies demonstrate the best average monthly returns while the *Short Selling* strategy is at the bottom of the ladder. In terms of volatility, the above three strategies are, quite logically, at the top of the list, alongside with the *Equity Non-Hedge* and *Managed Futures* strategies while the majority of market-neutral strategies demonstrate the least volatile returns. Secondly, *Foreign Exchange* strategy stands out with its positive skewness while the *Merger Arbitrage* and *Event Driven* strategies are distinguished by higher kurtosis.

Several other financial time series covering the period over which the CFO structures are distributed (2001–2008) are required to perform all the necessary calculations. These series, all expressed on a monthly basis, are obtained from *Bloomberg*. Table 5 summarizes the descriptive statistics for these secondary variables. The 1-month LIBOR and *T-bill* series both have the same average, but the returns on the latter are far more volatile. The 10-year *on-* and *off-the-run* government securities demonstrate almost identical statistical behavior, while 20-year *on-the-run* securities offer better average returns and are less volatile. Finally, we note that these three assets exhibit positive skewness (with the exception of the Russell 3000).

Table 3. Distribution of hedge fund strategies within sample.

	Strategy	Frequency	Relative frequency
Panel A: Sample before strategy aggregation			
1	Convertible arbitrage	100	2.39%
2	Distressed securities	112	2.68%
3	Emerging markets: Asia	88	2.11%
4	Emerging markets: E. Europe/CIS	71	1.70%
5	Emerging markets: Global	109	2.61%
6	Emerging markets: Latin America	26	0.62%
7	Equity hedge	1359	32.52%
8	Equity market neutral	263	6.29%
9	Equity non-hedge	135	3.23%
10	Event-driven	248	5.93%
11	Fixed income: arbitrage	75	1.79%
12	Fixed income: convertible bonds	25	0.60%
13	Fixed income: diversified	86	2.06%
14	Fixed income: high yield	67	1.60%
15	Fixed income: mortgage backed	56	1.34%
16	Foreign exchange	75	1.79%
17	Macro	293	7.01%
18	Managed futures	299	7.15%
19	Market timing	20	0.48%
20	Merger arbitrage	37	0.89%
21	Regulation D	33	0.79%
22	Relative value arbitrage	288	6.89%
23	Sector: energy	81	1.94%
24	Sector: financial	33	0.79%
25	Sector: health care/biotechnology	47	1.12%
26	Sector: miscellaneous	35	0.84%
27	Sector: real estate	41	0.98%
28	Sector: technology	58	1.39%
29	Short selling	19	0.45%
	Total	4179	100%
Panel B: Sample after strategy aggregation			
1	Convertible arbitrage	100	2.41%
2	Distressed securities	112	2.70%
3	Equity hedge	1359	32.78%
4	Equity market neutral	263	6.34%
5	Equity non-hedge	135	3.26%
6	Event-driven	248	5.98%
7	Foreign exchange	75	1.81%
8	Macro	293	7.07%
9	Managed futures	299	7.21%
10	Market timing	20	0.48%
11	Merger arbitrage	37	0.89%
12	Relative value arbitrage	288	6.95%
13	Short selling	19	0.46%
14	Emerging markets	294	7.09%
15	Fixed income	309	7.45%
16	Sectorial	295	7.12%
	Total	4146	100%

Notes: The table shows the absolute and relative frequencies of each of the hedge fund strategies in our sample. Panel A describes the sample before the aggregation of certain strategies while Panel B presents the sample after aggregation.

Table 4. Statistics of hedge fund strategy indexes.

	Convert. arbit.	Dist. securities	Equity hedge	E. mkt neutral	Equity n-hedge	Event-driven	FX	Macro	Mnged fut.	Market timing	Merger arbit.	Relat. val arbit.	Short selling	Emerg. mkts	Fixed inc.	Sectorial
	Period 1: 120 months (February 1991 to January 2001)															
Mean	0.0119	0.0151	0.0180	0.0101	0.0165	0.0165	0.0161	0.0138	0.0146	0.0152	0.0118	0.0145	−0.0039	0.0244	0.0109	0.0200
Standard deviation	0.0116	0.0216	0.0273	0.0111	0.0355	0.0225	0.0206	0.0213	0.0456	0.0257	0.0118	0.0114	0.0828	0.0659	0.0114	0.0410
Skewness	−0.1963	0.9182	0.0413	−0.2320	−0.6419	−0.5284	1.5295	0.2341	0.9591	0.7721	−2.5619	−0.7081	0.1929	−0.1586	−0.6013	−0.5642
Kurtosis	5.3599	7.4489	4.1026	2.5946	5.8056	8.8399	7.6032	3.9269	5.9506	4.9391	19.3466	4.501	4.8889	3.2656	6.2689	6.7705
Min	−0.0321	−0.0647	−0.0809	−0.0195	−0.1473	−0.0948	−0.0204	−0.0561	−0.0924	−0.0464	−0.0684	−0.0230	−0.3036	−0.1946	−0.0377	−0.1733
Max	0.0510	0.1086	0.1025	0.0338	0.1116	0.1094	0.1178	0.0826	0.2281	0.1154	0.0393	0.0402	0.2783	0.1874	0.0450	0.1399
JB test (df = 2)	28.62	115.82	6.11	1.90	47.60	176.11	152.74	5.39	61.93	30.72	1467.32	21.30	18.58	0.86	60.66	77.45
$\alpha = 5\%; x \leq 5.99$	1	1	1	0	1	1	1	0	1	1	1	1	1	0	1	1
Lilliefors test	0.007	0.001	0.50	0.02	0.50	0.16	0.001	0.17	0.04	0.16	0.008	0.003	0.008	0.50	0.10	0.01
$\alpha = 5\%; p \geq 5\%$	1	1	0	1	0	0	1	0	1	0	1	1	1	0	0	1
G & R test	0.00	0.00	0.89	0.09	0.59	0.01	0.00	0.19	0.01	0.06	0.00	0.00	0.00	0.95	0.04	0.02
$\alpha = 5\%; p \geq 5\%$	1	1	0	0	0	1	1	0	1	0	1	1	1	0	1	1
	Period 2: 84 months (February 2001 to January 2008)															
Mean	0.0064	0.0114	0.0086	0.0056	0.0103	0.0089	0.0069	0.0094	0.0105	0.0064	0.0052	0.0085	0.0049	0.0167	0.0067	0.0113
Standard deviation	0.0111	0.0134	0.0180	0.0064	0.0345	0.016	0.0099	0.0136	0.0279	0.0243	0.0086	0.0065	0.0470	0.0295	0.0083	0.0214
Skewness	−0.4950	−0.1774	−0.6148	−1.2205	−0.4870	−0.7719	1.4167	−0.0101	−0.0549	−0.0420	−0.1752	−0.6253	0.1632	−0.9236	−0.6435	−0.3815
Kurtosis	3.5464	3.2546	2.9455	5.7064	2.7287	3.6133	5.9688	2.7894	2.7363	2.5760	3.9317	3.6192	2.8247	3.3725	3.4356	2.5501
Min	−0.0284	−0.0240	−0.0414	−0.0196	−0.0774	−0.0342	−0.0067	−0.0224	−0.0570	−0.0514	−0.0210	−0.0127	−0.1013	−0.0679	−0.0176	−0.0395
Max	0.0339	0.0459	0.0444	0.0164	0.0774	0.0387	0.0444	0.0433	0.0719	0.0596	0.0260	0.0206	0.1281	0.0649	0.0236	0.0570
JB test (df = 2)	4.48	0.67	5.30	46.49	3.58	9.66	58.95	0.16	0.29	0.65	3.47	6.82	0.48	12.43	6.46	2.75
$\alpha = 5\%; x \leq 5.99$	0	0	0	1	0	1	1	0	0	0	0	1	0	1	1	0
Lilliefors test	0.12	0.18	0.05	0.02	0.07	0.003	0.006	0.50	0.50	0.38	0.02	0.13	0.39	0.001	0.09	0.15
$\alpha = 5\%; p \geq 5\%$	0	0	1	1	0	1	1	0	0	0	1	0	0	1	0	0
G & R test	0.03	0.44	0.01	0.01	0.09	0.00	0.00	0.92	0.99	0.78	0.04	0.09	0.35	0.00	0.02	0.03
$\alpha = 5\%; p \geq 5\%$	1	0	1	1	0	1	1	0	0	0	1	0	0	1	1	1

Notes: This table presents the descriptive statistics and the results of the Jarque-Bera, Lilliefors, and Genest-Remillard normality tests for every hedge fund strategy in the sample. Period 1 runs from February 1991 to January 2001, while period 2 covers the seven following years to January 2008. For both panels, the nature of the statistics appears on the left-hand side and the strategies feature horizontally. The descriptive statistics are monthly and include the first four moments of the distributions, as well as the minimum and maximum returns. With regard to the tests for normality, the value of the test statistic and a dummy variable indicating whether or not the value is significant at a confidence level of 95% are presented*. The dummy variable equals 1 when the null hypothesis of normality is rejected.

**p*-values are available upon request.

Table 5. Descriptive statistics of secondary data.

	Period 2: 84 months (February 2001 to January 2008)							
	LIBOR 1M	T-Bill 1M	Russel 3000	CDX.NA.IG_5Y[a,b]	LUCI_OAS[a]	USA_10Y (on-t-r)	USA_10Y (off-t-r)	USA_20Y
Mean	0.0026	0.0026	0.0015	4.4948	12.0387	0.0037	0.0037	0.0042
Variance	1.87E−06	5.10E−07	0.0016	1.5875	14.6199	1.50E−07	1.60E−07	1.10E−07
Skewness	0.1906	0.3597	−0.4743	0.9061	0.7873	−0.0265	−0.0301	0.3986
Excess kurtosis	−1.6071	−1.2216	0.3473	1.485	−0.5299	−0.4791	−0.5402	−0.5446
Max	0.0048	0.0042	0.0803	9.0417	21.7833	0.0045	0.0045	0.0049
Min	0.0009	0.0016	−0.1064	2.5419	7.5167	0.0028	0.0028	0.0036

Notes: The table presents the first four moments of the distribution as well as the maximum and minimum. The statistics appear on the vertical axis, while the time-series feature horizontally. They are all presented on a monthly return basis. 1M LIBOR and 1M T-Bill are relative to the money market while the Russell 3000 is relative to the stock market. CDX.NA.IG_5Y and LUCI_OAS relate to the corporate credit market while the three whose title starts with USA are related to the US government securities, 10- and 20-year maturities. For the 10-year maturity, on-the-run (on-t-r) and off-the-run (off-t-r) rates are presented.

[a]Data are shown in terms of spread in basis points.

[b]The statistics relative to this series are calculated from 58 months of available data.

4. Empirical results

4.1 *Optimal hedge fund allocations*

Table 6 presents, for three of the sets of preferences $E_h = \{\alpha, \beta, \gamma\}$, the composition of the optimized hedge fund portfolios.[6] We observe, conditional on the diversification constraint imposed, the weight y_i assigned to each strategy.

In analyzing the various distributions, we notice first of all that in the case of the mean-variance optimization ($\alpha = 1; \beta = 0; \gamma = 0$), with no weight constraint, one-third of the capital is allocated to *Relative Value Arbitrage* and *Foreign Exchange* strategies, respectively. This is logical since these two strategies have the highest reward-risk ratios for period 1, i.e. the time window allotted for the optimization process. As the diversification constraint on the optimized portfolio is increased, the *Equity Hedge* and *Distressed Securities* strategies obtain the largest possible allocations. It should be noted here that the two least constrained portfolios are identical. This means that even if we allow weights in excess of 50% of the portfolio, no portfolio will be positioned above this threshold for this set of preferences.

With regard to the set of preferences $E_2 = \{\alpha = 1; \beta = 1; \gamma = 0\}$, there is equal preference between returns and skewness; with no importance placed on the level of kurtosis. When the weights y_i are unconstrained, almost 45% of the capital is allocated to *Foreign Exchange* strategy, i.e. the one with the greatest level of positive skewness. However, it may be surprising to see that the *Equity Market Neutral* and *Convertible Arbitrage* strategies, which are both negatively skewned, are ranked second and third, respectively. This clearly demonstrates the trade-off between skewness and returns for this preference set. It is also interesting to note that as the maximum weight constraint becomes more significant, thereby forceably reducing the allocation in the *Foreign Exchange* strategy, the allocation to *Equity Market Neutral* and *Convertible Arbitrage* strategies practically disappear. It is at this point that the *Equity Hedge*, *Distressed Securities*, *Market Timing*, *Short Selling* and *Managed Futures* strategies start to emerge. All these strategies exhibit positive skewness and lower skewness-return ratios.

As for $E_3 = \{\alpha = 1; \beta = 1; \gamma = 0.75\}$, the relative significance of the kurtosis is evident for the first time. In this case, we note a more harmonious balance of funds across strategies from the very outset. Despite this, the *Foreign Exchange* strategy is still predominant (20% in the least-constrained case) along with *Distressed Securities* (13%) and *Market Timing* (16%). No other strategy obtains more than 10% of the capital. This allocation certainly takes root in the weak kurtosis observed in relation to the significance of the skewness levels of the three main strategies. For this set of preferences, the diversification constraints have little impact on the allocation of capital. In this regard, it will be interesting to compare the performance of these portfolios, where there is optimal allocation through all strategies, to that of EW funds that allocate the same proportion of capital to each strategy.

4.1.1 Performance analysis

Table 7 presents the descriptive statistics, the tests of normality and the performance measures attributable to the returns of the portfolios examined in period 2. These results are presented for the same sets of preferences as presented earlier, and for the EW portfolio.

In analyzing Table 7 with regard to the descriptive statistics for each series of returns, we first see that they are in line with those of their main components, i.e. the strategy indexes. For example, the funds of the set E_2 demonstrate the greatest level of skewness and the non-weight-constrained mean-variance portfolio dominates in terms of the return-variance ratio. These characteristics

Table 6. Composition of optimal portfolios for sets of preferences E_1, E_2, and E_3.

	$E_1 : \{\alpha = 1; \beta = 0; \gamma = 0\}$						$E_2 : \{\alpha = 1; \beta = 1; \gamma = 0\}$					
HF strategy	$y \leq 100\%$	$y \leq 50\%$	$y \leq 25\%$	$y \leq 20\%$	$y \leq 15\%$	$y \leq 10\%$	$y \leq 100\%$	$y \leq 50\%$	$y \leq 25\%$	$y \leq 20\%$	$y \leq 15\%$	$y \leq 10\%$
Convertible arbitrage				0.0267	0.0124	0.0828	0.1364	0.1372		0.0150	0.0799	0.0775
Distressed securities	0.0941	0.0941	0.0988	0.1154	0.1500	0.1000			0.2500	0.2000	0.1500	0.1000
Equity hedge	0.1195	0.1195	0.2023	0.1579	0.1500	0.1000			0.1288	0.2000	0.1500	0.1000
Equity market neutral						0.0522	0.1780	0.1774			0.0579	0.0659
Equity non-hedge												0.0270
Event-driven	0.0175	0.0175		0.0537	0.0484	0.0889				0.0003		0.0436
Foreign exchange	0.2986	0.2986	0.2500	0.2000	0.1500	0.1000	0.4418	0.4418	0.2500	0.2000	0.1500	0.1000
Macro						0.0077						0.0454
Managed futures				0.0013	0.0106	0.0241					0.1115	0.1000
Market timing	0.0482	0.0482	0.0582	0.0829	0.1046	0.0926	0.0419	0.0421	0.2500	0.2000	0.1500	0.1000
Merger arbitrage	0.0524	0.0524	0.0645	0.0777	0.1074	0.0949	0.0931	0.0935	0.0050		0.0226	0.0238
Relative value arbitrage	0.3154	0.3154	0.2500	0.2000	0.1500	0.1000	0.0147	0.0157	0.0248	0.0271	0.0412	0.0531
Short selling	0.0344	0.0344	0.0475	0.0486	0.0629	0.0587	0.0307	0.0307	0.0914	0.1103	0.0850	0.0923
Emerging markets	0.0198	0.0198	0.0211	0.0128	0.0273	0.0271				0.0209	0.0009	0.0153
Fixed income						0.0204	0.0635	0.0616			0.0011	0.0295
Sectorial			0.0077	0.023	0.0265	0.0505				0.0265		0.0266

Convertible arbitrage	0.0501	0.0501	0.0531	0.0510	0.0569	0.0659
Distressed securities	0.1326	0.1326	0.1347	0.1315	0.1340	0.1000
Equity hedge	0.0688	0.0688	0.0690	0.0678	0.0700	0.0792
Equity market neutral	0.0488	0.0488	0.0566	0.0503	0.0574	0.0714
Equity non-hedge	0.0154	0.0154	0.0133	0.0148	0.0197	0.0316
Event-driven	0.0360	0.0360	0.0247	0.0353	0.0367	0.0430
Foreign exchange	0.2055	0.2055	0.2018	0.2000	0.1500	0.1000
Macro			0.0335			0.0569
Managed futures	0.0538	0.0538	0.0606	0.0602	0.0926	0.0870
Market timing	0.1616	0.1616	0.1642	0.1633	0.1500	0.1000
Merger arbitrage	0.0226	0.0226	0.0253	0.0237	0.0248	0.0312
Relative value arbitrage	0.0480	0.0480	0.0460	0.0488	0.0513	0.0572
Short selling	0.0739	0.0739	0.0681	0.0735	0.0782	0.0828
Emerging markets	0.0268	0.0268	0.0159	0.0257	0.0199	0.0209
Fixed income	0.0279	0.0279	0.0198	0.0278	0.0337	0.0417
Sectorial	0.0283	0.0283	0.0133	0.0263	0.0248	0.0311

Notes: This table shows the composition of optimal portfolios for the first three sets of preferences. All hedge fund strategies appear on the vertical axis and the different portfolios (set of preference and diversification constraint) are presented horizontally. The sum of each column equals to 1, as the weights y are listed as a proportion of the total value and are between 0 and 1 (no-short constraint). Blanks refer to null allocations.

Table 7. Performance of optimal portfolios for sets of preferences E_1, E_2, E_3, and E_6.

	$E_1 : \{\alpha = 1; \beta = 0; \gamma = 0\}$					
	$y \leq 100\%$	$y \leq 50\%$	$y \leq 25\%$	$y \leq 20\%$	$y \leq 15\%$	$y \leq 10\%$
Mean	0.008077	0.008077	0.008095	0.008058	0.008215	0.008003
Variance	4.78E−05	4.78E−05	5.60E−05	6.35E−05	6.94E−05	7.10E−05
Skewness	−0.3793	−0.3793	−0.4507	−0.4436	−0.4165	−0.4582
Excess kurtosis	0.2581	0.2581	0.3661	0.3442	0.2639	0.2604
Max	0.0224	0.0224	0.0239	0.0249	0.0268	0.0265
Min	−0.0113	−0.0113	−0.0133	−0.0137	−0.0139	−0.0138
JB test (df = 2)	2.25	2.25	3.31	3.17	2.67	3.18
$\alpha = 5\%; x \leq 5.99$	0	0	0	0	0	0
Lilliefors test	0.50	0.50	0.09	0.03	0.08	0.15
$\alpha = 5\%; p \leq 5\%$	0	0	0	1	0	0
Genest and Rémillard test	0.40	0.45	0.11	0.06	0.03	0.02
$\alpha = 5\%; p \leq 5\%$	0	0	0	0	1	1
Sharpe	0.7972	0.7972	0.7393	0.6898	0.6785	0.6457
Treynor	0.0702	0.0702	0.0568	0.0481	0.0474	0.0461
Sortino MAR = 0	4.1199	4.1199	3.4138	3.0041	2.9266	2.6633
Sortino MAR = Rf	2.0198	2.0198	1.7276	1.5519	1.5263	1.3883
Sortino MAR = 0.004	1.2536	1.2536	1.0929	0.9896	0.9847	0.8910
Sortino MAR = 0.008	0.0151	0.0151	0.0171	0.0098	0.0350	0.0005
Sortino MAR = 0.012	−0.5255	−0.5255	−0.4957	−0.4775	−0.4495	−0.4623
Sortino MAR = 0.016	−0.7610	−0.7610	−0.7360	−0.7178	−0.6970	−0.7016
Modified Sharpe 95% ($\alpha = 5\%$)	1.3294	1.3294	1.0387	0.8847	0.8526	0.7606
Ω(MAR = 0)	16.3885	16.3885	12.6570	10.8673	10.2516	9.0137
Ω(MAR = Rf)	6.9654	6.9654	5.8272	5.2087	4.9906	4.6330
Ω(MAR = 0.004)	4.2247	4.2247	3.7307	3.4195	3.3414	3.1304
Ω(MAR = 0.008)	1.0288	1.0288	1.0337	1.0190	1.0682	1.0010
Ω(MAR = 0.012)	0.2149	0.2149	0.2368	0.2548	0.2856	0.2639
Ω(MAR = 0.016)	0.0443	0.0443	0.0525	0.0600	0.0683	0.0638
	$E_2 : \{\alpha = 1; \beta = 1; \gamma = 0\}$					
	$y \leq 100\%$	$y \leq 50\%$	$y \leq 25\%$	$y \leq 20\%$	$y \leq 15\%$	$y \leq 10\%$
Mean	0.006376	0.006378	0.007971	0.008180	0.007902	0.008110
Variance	3.81E−05	3.82E−05	7.04E−05	7.03E−05	6.86E−05	6.88E−05
Skewness	0.2493	0.2492	−0.0005	−0.1584	−0.1268	−0.2366
Excess kurtosis	−0.1148	−0.1160	0.1839	0.1600	−0.1919	−0.2506
Max	0.0228	0.0228	0.0300	0.0298	0.0277	0.0270
Min	−0.0068	−0.0068	−0.0149	−0.0136	−0.0110	−0.0115
JB test (df = 2)	0.92	0.92	0.12	0.44	0.35	1.00
$\alpha = 5\%; x \leq 5.99$	0	0	0	0	0	0
Lilliefors test	0.50	0.50	0.50	0.24	0.05	0.10
$\alpha = 5\%; p \leq 5\%$	0	0	0	0	1	0
Genest and Rémillard test	0.60	0.61	0.69	0.20	0.21	0.04

(*Continued*).

Table 7. Continued

	$E_2 : \{\alpha = 1; \beta = 1; \gamma = 0\}$					
	$y \le 100\%$	$y \le 50\%$	$y \le 25\%$	$y \le 20\%$	$y \le 15\%$	$y \le 10\%$
$\alpha = 5\%; p \le 5\%$	0	0	0	0	0	1
Sharpe	0.6174	0.6174	0.6446	0.6702	0.6447	0.6689
Treynor	0.7915	0.7981	0.0522	0.0553	0.1018	0.0916
Sortino MAR = 0	4.8478	4.8465	3.2773	3.2394	3.2702	3.3239
Sortino MAR = Rf	1.6841	1.6842	1.6107	1.6178	1.5771	1.6238
Sortino MAR = 0.004	0.8132	0.8136	1.0037	1.0289	0.9707	1.0153
Sortino MAR = 0.008	−0.3131	−0.3128	−0.0049	0.0301	−0.0161	0.0182
Sortino MAR = 0.012	−0.6963	−0.6961	−0.4793	−0.4573	−0.4834	−0.4620
Sortino MAR = 0.016	−0.8462	−0.8461	−0.7101	−0.6996	−0.7142	−0.7033
Modified Sharpe 95% ($\alpha = 5\%$)	1.1171	1.1169	0.9324	0.9382	0.8796	0.8952
Ω(MAR = 0)	16.8982	16.8859	11.0174	10.5652	10.6381	10.7006
Ω(MAR = Rf)	4.9259	4.9265	5.0842	5.1061	4.7611	4.8767
Ω(MAR = 0.004)	2.6800	2.6812	3.2992	3.3972	3.1035	3.2112
Ω(MAR = 0.008)	0.5219	0.5224	0.9912	1.0568	0.9711	1.0335
Ω(MAR = 0.012)	0.1044	0.1046	0.2932	0.3002	0.2666	0.2812
Ω(MAR = 0.016)	0.0208	0.0208	0.0808	0.0772	0.0705	0.0702

	$E_3 : \{\alpha = 1; \beta = 1; \gamma = 0.75\}$						E_6 : EW
	$y \le 100\%$	$y \le 50\%$	$y \le 25\%$	$y \le 20\%$	$y \le 15\%$	$y \le 10\%$	$y \le 6.25\%$
Mean	0.008031	0.008031	0.007940	0.008021	0.008091	0.008156	0.008597
Variance	6.90E−05	6.90E−05	6.92E−05	6.95E−05	7.18E−05	7.08E−05	9.88E−05
Skewness	−0.1314	−0.1314	−0.0869	−0.1205	−0.1384	−0.2457	−0.4270
Excess kurtosis	0.0175	0.0175	−0.0213	0.0046	−0.1070	−0.1832	−0.0592
Max	0.0278	0.0278	0.0279	0.0279	0.0280	0.0271	0.0291
Min	−0.0126	−0.0126	−0.0124	−0.0125	−0.0118	−0.0116	−0.0150
JB test (df = 2)	0.24	0.24	0.11	0.20	0.31	0.96	2.57
$\alpha = 5\%; x \le 5.99$	0	0	0	0	0	0	0
Lilliefors test	0.38	0.38	0.50	0.38	0.49	0.12	0.04
$\alpha = 5\%; p \le 5\%$	0	0	0	0	0	0	1
Genest and Rémillard test	0.33	0.47	0.58	0.33	0.24	0.03	0.00
$\alpha = 5\%; p \le 5\%$	0	0	0	0	0	1	1
Sharpe	0.6583	0.6583	0.6466	0.6549	0.6525	0.6649	0.6070
Treynor	0.0586	0.0586	0.0621	0.0597	0.0684	0.0731	0.0418
Sortino MAR = 0	3.2284	3.2284	3.2339	3.2186	3.2002	3.2059	2.3109
Sortino MAR = Rf	1.5932	1.5932	1.5808	1.5872	1.5851	1.5893	1.2827
Sortino MAR = 0.004	0.9993	0.9993	0.9812	0.9944	0.9968	1.0040	0.8658
Sortino MAR = 0.008	0.0052	0.0052	−0.0100	0.0035	0.0150	0.0254	0.0829
Sortino MAR = 0.012	−0.4733	−0.4733	−0.4814	−0.4733	−0.4610	−0.4539	−0.3614
Sortino MAR = 0.016	−0.7090	−0.7090	−0.7129	−0.7084	−0.6995	−0.6971	−0.6174

(*Continued*).

Table 7. Continued

	$E_3 : \{\alpha = 1; \beta = 1; \gamma = 0.75\}$						E_6 : EW
	$y \leq 100\%$	$y \leq 50\%$	$y \leq 25\%$	$y \leq 20\%$	$y \leq 15\%$	$y \leq 10\%$	$y \leq 6.25\%$
Modified Sharpe 95% ($\alpha = 5\%$)	0.9174	0.9174	0.9025	0.9110	0.8887	0.8778	0.6542
Ω(MAR = 0)	10.5186	10.5186	10.7024	10.4917	10.3898	10.1550	7.4065
Ω(MAR = Rf)	4.9892	4.9892	4.8924	4.9530	4.8828	4.8584	4.1459
Ω(MAR = 0.004)	3.2872	3.2872	3.2009	3.2638	3.2174	3.2272	2.9930
Ω(MAR = 0.008)	1.0097	1.0097	0.9817	1.0065	1.0276	1.0471	1.1620
Ω(MAR = 0.012)	0.2822	0.2822	0.2760	0.2829	0.2954	0.2918	0.3955
Ω(MAR = 0.016)	0.0766	0.0766	0.0764	0.0775	0.0802	0.0738	0.1117

Notes: The table presents the descriptive statistics, the results of the tests for normality and the performance measures of the optimal portfolios for sets 1, 2, and 3 of preference for the moments of distributions; the EW portfolio is also presented. Each of the indicators appears on the vertical axis and the different portfolios (set of preference and diversification constraint) are presented horizontally. The descriptive statistics are monthly and include the first four moments of the distributions, as well as the maximum and minimum returns. With regard to the tests for normality, the value of the test statistic and a dummy variable indicating whether or not the value is significant at a confidence level of 95% are presented*. The dummy variable equals 1 when the null hypothesisof normality is rejected. The performance measures (Sharpe, Treynor, Sortino, Modified Sharpe, and Omega) are also presented on a monthly basis. MAR levels of 0.8% and 1.2% monthly are used for the calculations of the Sortino ratio and the Omega measure. The Modified Sharpe is computed based on a value-at-risk calculation with a 95% confidence level. The weights y are the proportion of the total value and are between 0 and 1 (no-short constraint).
*p-Values are available upon request.

become diluted as diversification broadens, while the presence of other strategies gradually normalizes the allocations. It is also interesting to note that the EW portfolio demonstrates the best average returns and the most variance. In this sense, it is not surprising to see average returns decrease with the diversification of the set of preferences E_1 while variance also shows a sharp decrease. However, this same phenomenon does not apply to the other optimized portfolios for which allocation considers both skewness and kurtosis. In short, the mean of all average returns is 0.79 and there is mostly negative skewness and positive excess kurtosis.

With regard to the normality of returns, we first notice that normality is not rejected in all cases according to the Jarque-Bera test. With respect to the other two tests, the returns of five portfolios out of 31 (16.1%) reject the assumption of normality under the Lilliefors test, while six out of 31 (19.4%) do the same when the Genest and Remillard procedure is used. This is an interesting result. Although most hedge fund strategy indexes reject normality on an individual level, it would appear that when these strategies are combined together, the distributions of the portfolios are considerably more Gaussian. Let us also recall that the strategy indexes exhibit greater normality in period 2, which may be another plausible explanation. In sum, without completely casting aside rejection of the null hypothesis, the decrease in the proportion of rejections is undisputable. These results may seem small for a hedge fund environment, but they are still significant and confirm the relevance of using comprehensive performance measures, or at least those measures that account for all information contained in the tails of the distributions. It is also interesting to emphasize that normality is only rejected in the case of highly diversified portfolios; the normality of returns of the EW portfolio is rejected by the Lilliefors, and Genest and Remillard tests.

With regard to traditional performance measures, it is the unconstrained portfolio of set E_1 that has the highest Sharpe ratio at 0.80 while the EW portfolio comes in last at 0.61. For the other portfolios, the value of the Sharpe ratio varies between 0.62 and 0.67. Consequently, it appears that no distinction can be made between the portfolios using this performance measure. On the other hand, the unconstrained portfolios of sets E_2 and E_5 which differ in terms of the best Treynor ratio, presents a value of around 0.80 and 0.20. Their good performance in terms of Treynor ratio is largely due to the low-beta coefficient, i.e. the covariance of returns with those of the market. It should once again be noted that the EW portfolio has the lowest ratio at 0.04 and the highest beta coefficient at 0.14. Given the overall weakness of the beta coefficient values, we can put forth that the 31 hedge fund portfolios have very low correlation with the market. In sum, if we base the analysis on the Sharpe and Treynor ratios, we would conclude that incorporating preferences for higher moments does not generate value. Equal weighting is systematically an underperforming strategy and diversification generally undermines the performance of a hedge fund portfolio.

If we focus on the more comprehensive performance measures, it is possible to better evaluate and discern the advantages of accounting for higher moments. It should be noted here that for the Sortino ratio and the Omega measure, the monthly MAR used for the calculations are 0.8% and 1.2%. Table 8 summarizes the performance for all portfolios with regard to the comprehensive performance measure. In addition, a classification of each measure is included.

For the Sortino ratio and the Omega measure, the EW portfolio dominates, which is the exact opposite of the observation made using the two simple performance measures. Also, we deduce that equal weighting may be better than the highly diversified optimizations found using the PGP model. This is similar to the conclusions of DeMiguel, Garlappi, and Uppal (2009). Nevertheless, certain funds originating from the optimization procedure are always among the best performers. As for the lowest values, the unconstrained portfolios for the set of preferences E_2 and E_5 are ranked near the bottom, which directly contradicts the results of the Treynor ratio presented earlier. The mean-variance optimal portfolio (preference set E_1) no longer outperforms.

The modified Sharpe ratio offers a similar classification as the conventional Sharpe ratio. Unlike the Omega measure, the modified Sharpe ratio simply incorporates estimates of the skewness and kurtosis coefficients. It does not incorporate all information regarding the actual empirical distribution. Nonetheless, given the non-normality of the returns distributions of certain portfolios, this version of the ratio allows us to establish a more precise classification of the different portfolios of funds.

In short, there are eight portfolios that stand out from our performance analysis. These are: $E_{1;100\%}$, $E_{1;15\%}$, $E_{2;100\%}$, $E_{2;20\%}$, $E_{4;10\%}$, $E_{5;50\%}$, $E_{5;15\%}$ and $E_{6;6.25\%}$. It is clear that the underlying interests appear at two extremes of diversification. Indeed, they are either very little or highly diversified, which means that no unilateral deduction can be made unless it accounts for investor preference. In the following section, we shall determine whether these findings still apply from the viewpoint of a CFO equity owner.

4.2 *Performance of the CFOs′ equity tranche*

Table 9 presents the results of the equity of CFO structures 11, 15, and 18. These structures are those deemed optimal from the viewpoint of junior tranche owners. That said, the following remarks arise from the study of all of the structures. As in the previous section, the descriptive statistics, the results of tests of normality and the performance measures are included.

In analyzing the descriptive statistics, we observe that regardless of the securitized underlying portfolio, the linear increase of leverage within a CFO structure results in a relatively linear increase, at least at the outset, of the first four centered moments of the distribution of equity returns. This finding seems logical *a priori*. However, for a given aggregate cost of financing, where the maximum debt level has been reached, average returns seem to experience a local peak.

Table 8. Performance and rank of portfolios according to the comprehensive measures.

E_h	k	Sortino MAR = 0.008	Rank	Sortino MAR = 0.012	Rank	Modified Sharpe 95%	Rank	Ω (MAR = 0.008)	Rank	Ω (MAR = 0.012)	Rank
$E_1 : \{\alpha = 1;$	$y \leq 100\%$	0.0151	12	−0.5255	26	1.3294	1	1.0288	12	0.2149	26
$\beta = 0;$	$y \leq 50\%$	0.0151	12	−0.5255	26	1.3294	1	1.0288	12	0.2149	26
$\gamma = 0\}$	$y \leq 25\%$	0.0171	11	−0.4957	25	1.0387	7	1.0337	10	0.2368	25
	$y \leq 20\%$	0.0098	15	−0.4775	21	0.8847	22	1.0190	15	0.2548	24
	$y \leq 15\%$	0.0350	2	−0.4495	4	0.8526	29	1.0682	2	0.2856	12
	$y \leq 10\%$	0.0005	24	−0.4623	12	0.7606	30	1.0010	24	0.2639	23
$E_2 : \{\alpha = 1;$	$y \leq 100\%$	−0.3131	31	−0.6963	31	1.1171	5	0.5219	31	0.1044	31
$\beta = 1;$	$y \leq 50\%$	−0.3128	30	−0.6961	30	1.1169	6	0.5224	30	0.1046	30
$\gamma = 0\}$	$y \leq 25\%$	−0.0049	25	−0.4793	22	0.9324	10	0.9912	25	0.2932	9
	$y \leq 20\%$	0.0301	5	−0.4573	9	0.9382	9	1.0568	5	0.3002	6
	$y \leq 15\%$	−0.0161	27	−0.4834	24	0.8796	24	0.9711	27	0.2666	22
	$y \leq 10\%$	0.0182	10	−0.4620	11	0.8952	17	1.0335	11	0.2812	17
$E_3 : \{\alpha = 1;$	$y \leq 100\%$	0.0052	21	−0.4733	19	0.9174	11	1.0097	21	0.2822	15
$\beta = 1;$	$y \leq 50\%$	0.0052	21	−0.4733	19	0.9174	11	1.0097	21	0.2822	15
$\gamma = 0.75\}$	$y \leq 25\%$	−0.0100	26	−0.4814	23	0.9025	15	0.9817	26	0.2760	21
	$y \leq 20\%$	0.0035	23	−0.4733	18	0.9110	13	1.0065	23	0.2829	14
	$y \leq 15\%$	0.0150	14	−0.4610	10	0.8887	21	1.0276	14	0.2954	8
	$y \leq 10\%$	0.0254	8	−0.4539	7	0.8778	26	1.0471	8	0.2918	10
$E_4 : \{\alpha = 2;$	$y \leq 100\%$	0.0067	19	−0.4711	15	0.8944	18	1.0126	19	0.2811	18
$\beta = 1;$	$y \leq 50\%$	0.0067	19	−0.4711	15	0.8944	18	1.0126	19	0.2811	18
$\gamma = 0.75\}$	$y \leq 25\%$	0.0070	18	−0.4722	17	0.9029	14	1.0133	18	0.2794	20
	$y \leq 20\%$	0.0082	17	−0.4691	13	0.8907	20	1.0153	17	0.2832	13
	$y \leq 15\%$	0.0278	7	−0.4514	5	0.8797	23	1.0520	7	0.3019	5
	$y \leq 10\%$	0.0337	3	−0.4449	2	0.8531	28	1.0632	3	0.2977	7
$E_5 : \{\alpha = 3;$	$y \leq 100\%$	−0.2761	29	−0.6781	29	1.1416	4	0.5693	29	0.1170	29
$\beta = 1;$	$y \leq 50\%$	−0.2754	28	−0.6779	28	1.1439	3	0.5702	28	0.1172	28
$\gamma = 0.25\}$	$y \leq 25\%$	0.0087	16	−0.4700	14	0.9402	8	1.0156	16	0.3046	3
	$y \leq 20\%$	0.0293	6	−0.4515	6	0.8965	16	1.0553	6	0.3097	2
	$y \leq 15\%$	0.0318	4	−0.4476	3	0.8680	27	1.0603	4	0.3038	4
	$y \leq 10\%$	0.0236	9	−0.4572	8	0.8780	25	1.0439	9	0.2864	11
E_6 : EW (1/m)	$y = 6.25\%$	0.0829	1	−0.3614	1	0.6542	31	1.1620	1	0.3955	1

Notes: The table shows the results, on a monthly basis, of the Sortino ratio, the Modified Sharpe ratio and the Omega measure for all 30 optimal portfolios as well as the EW fund. The 31 portfolios and their characteristics (sets of preference and diversification constraint) appear on the vertical axis and the performance measures are presented horizontally. MAR levels of 0.8% and 1.2% monthly are used for the calculations of the Sortino ratio and the Omega measure. The Modified Sharpe was computed based on a value-at-risk calculation with a 95% confidence level. To the right of each measure is the rank of the portfolio for a given indicator; 1 indicates the best performing portfolio and 31, the worst performing one.

With regard to tests of normality, we see that the Jarque-Bera, Lilliefors, and Genest and Remillard tests reject normality in the respective proportions of 5% (28/589), 17% (102/589), and 21% (125/589). In all three cases, this represents an increase compared with the case of unlevered portfolio of hedge funds, which reinforces the interest of using more comprehensive performance measures. Generally speaking, it is possible to conclude that the securitization of hedge funds reduces the normality of the return distribution of the equity tranche. A closer look at the distribution of 'non-normality' across structures, we see a more frequent rejection of the

Table 9. Performance of CFOs 11, 15, and 18.

E_h	k	Mean	Variance	Skewness	Excess kurtosis	JB $\alpha = 5\%$	Lilliefors $\alpha = 5\%$	G&R $\alpha = 5\%$	Sharpe	Treynor	Sortino MAR = 0.008	Sortino MAR = 0.012	Modified Sharpe $\alpha = 5\%$	Ω MAR = 0.008	Ω MAR = 0.012
Panel A: CFO 11 (Debt = \$200M ; All−in funding cost = 150 bps over LIBOR 1 month)															
$E_1 : \{\alpha = 1;$	$y \leq 100\%$	0.0098	1.255E−04	−0.2858	−0.0136	0	0	0	0.6472	0.0602	0.9963	0.769	0.7509	1.5024	0.6018
$\beta = 0;$	$y \leq 50\%$	0.0098	1.255E−04	−0.2858	−0.0136	0	0	0	0.6472	0.0602	0.9963	0.769	0.7509	1.5024	0.6018
$\gamma = 0\}$	$y \leq 25\%$	0.0098	1.460E−04	−0.4064	0.0752	0	0	0	0.6017	0.0473	0.8977	0.713	0.6216	1.4668	0.6245
	$y \leq 20\%$	0.0098	1.667E−04	−0.4104	0.0762	0	0	0	0.5586	0.0391	0.8231	0.6628	0.5444	1.4090	0.6377
	$y \leq 15\%$	0.0100	1.817E−04	−0.4135	−0.0191	0	0	1	0.5524	0.0388	0.8173	0.6635	0.5292	1.4435	0.6826
	$y \leq 10\%$	0.0097	1.861E−04	−0.4443	−0.0123	0	1	1	0.5225	0.0377	0.7553	0.6162	0.4802	1.3567	0.6439
$E_2 : \{\alpha = 1;$	$y \leq 100\%$	0.0071	1.157E−04	0.4734	0.2580	0	0	0	0.4201	−0.5235	0.5943	0.4390	0.4786	0.8059	0.3329
$\beta = 1;$	$y \leq 50\%$	0.0071	1.158E−04	0.4729	0.2559	0	0	0	0.4202	−0.5181	0.5946	0.4393	0.4788	0.8064	0.3333
$\gamma = 0\}$	$y \leq 25\%$	0.0096	1.858E−04	0.0043	−0.2065	0	0	0	0.5179	0.0428	0.8107	0.6420	0.5497	1.3531	0.6461
	$y \leq 20\%$	0.0100	1.817E−04	−0.1852	−0.2746	0	0	0	0.5482	0.0467	0.8407	0.6739	0.5654	1.4338	0.6780
	$y \leq 15\%$	0.0095	1.808E−04	−0.1361	−0.4612	0	1	0	0.5194	0.1051	0.7842	0.6247	0.5270	1.3207	0.6303
	$y \leq 10\%$	0.0099	1.794E−04	−0.2355	−0.5394	0	0	1	0.5460	0.0909	0.8255	0.6596	0.5498	1.3960	0.6706
$E_3 : \{\alpha = 1;$	$y \leq 100\%$	0.0097	1.790E−04	−0.1204	−0.2906	0	0	0	0.5359	0.0497	0.8216	0.6545	0.5585	1.3785	0.6504
$\beta = 1;$	$y \leq 50\%$	0.0097	1.790E−04	−0.1204	−0.2906	0	0	0	0.5359	0.0497	0.8216	0.6545	0.5585	1.3785	0.6504
$\gamma = 0.75\}$	$y \leq 25\%$	0.0096	1.803E−04	−0.0757	−0.3115	0	0	0	0.5236	0.0531	0.8019	0.6374	0.5459	1.3396	0.6350
	$y \leq 20\%$	0.0097	1.803E−04	−0.1110	−0.3004	0	0	0	0.5329	0.0508	0.8170	0.6509	0.5547	1.3718	0.6497
	$y \leq 15\%$	0.0098	1.864E−04	−0.1286	−0.3860	0	0	0	0.5326	0.0609	0.8170	0.6528	0.5483	1.3868	0.6698
	$y \leq 10\%$	0.0099	1.835E−04	−0.2351	−0.4667	0	1	1	0.5448	0.0668	0.8258	0.6615	0.5476	1.4111	0.6826
$E_4 : \{\alpha = 2;$	$y \leq 100\%$	0.0097	1.791E−04	−0.1920	−0.1883	0	0	0	0.5366	0.0422	0.8139	0.6516	0.5473	1.3829	0.6489
$\beta = 1;$	$y \leq 50\%$	0.0097	1.791E−04	−0.1920	−0.1883	0	0	0	0.5366	0.0422	0.8139	0.6516	0.5473	1.3829	0.6489
$\gamma = 0.75\}$	$y \leq 25\%$	0.0097	1.775E−04	−0.1939	−0.1886	0	0	0	0.5393	0.0429	0.8185	0.6546	0.5517	1.3858	0.6481
	$y \leq 20\%$	0.0098	1.803E−04	−0.1847	−0.2076	0	0	0	0.5360	0.0431	0.8145	0.6519	0.5473	1.3840	0.6521
	$y \leq 15\%$	0.0100	1.870E−04	−0.1854	−0.3037	0	0	0	0.5406	0.0491	0.8283	0.6635	0.5513	1.4187	0.6849
	$y \leq 10\%$	0.0100	1.864E−04	−0.2818	−0.3614	0	1	1	0.5463	0.0531	0.8258	0.6639	0.5412	1.4294	0.6959

(Continued)

Table 9. Continued

E_h	k	Mean	Variance	Skewness	Excess kurtosis	JB $\alpha = 5\%$	Lilliefors $\alpha = 5\%$	G&R $\alpha = 5\%$	Sharpe	Treynor	Sortino MAR = 0.008	Sortino MAR = 0.012	Modified Sharpe $\alpha = 5\%$	Ω MAR = 0.008	Ω MAR = 0.012
$E_5 : \{\alpha = 3;$	$y \leq 100\%$	0.0074	1.159E−04	0.3280	−0.0388	0	0	0	0.4488	0.2628	0.6398	0.4747	0.5098	0.8689	0.3538
$\beta = 1;$	$y \leq 50\%$	0.0074	1.159E−04	0.3277	−0.0381	0	0	0	0.4496	0.2637	0.6412	0.4757	0.5111	0.8704	0.3543
$\gamma = 0.25\}$	$y \leq 25\%$	0.0097	1.890E−04	0.0167	−0.1873	0	0	0	0.5225	0.0403	0.8251	0.6536	0.5587	1.3806	0.6639
	$y \leq 20\%$	0.0100	1.899E−04	−0.1505	−0.2202	0	0	0	0.5364	0.0404	0.8271	0.6637	0.5512	1.4256	0.6860
	$y \leq 15\%$	0.0100	1.872E−04	−0.2307	−0.2506	0	0	0	0.5430	0.0456	0.8271	0.6650	0.5470	1.4285	0.6887
	$y \leq 10\%$	0.0099	1.795E−04	−0.2604	−0.3925	0	1	1	0.5497	0.0705	0.8313	0.6654	0.5522	1.4137	0.6768
E_6 : EW (1/m)	$y = 6.25\%$	0.0106	2.565E−04	−0.3987	−0.1921	0	1	1	0.5033	0.0345	0.7522	0.6283	0.4491	1.4854	0.8058
Panel B: CFO 15 (Debt = \$280M ; All-in funding cost = 200 bps over LIBOR 1 month)															
$E_1 : \{\alpha = 1;$	$y \leq 100\%$	0.0120	2.540E−04	−0.1768	−0.0826	0	0	0	0.5936	0.0568	0.9984	0.8212	0.6269	1.8739	1.0037
$\beta = 0;$	$y \leq 50\%$	0.0120	2.540E−04	−0.1768	−0.0826	0	0	0	0.5936	0.0568	0.9984	0.8212	0.6269	1.8739	1.0037
$\gamma = 0\}$	$y \leq 25\%$	0.0120	2.953E−04	−0.3433	0.0178	0	0	0	0.5520	0.0435	0.8855	0.7464	0.5221	1.7975	1.0072
	$y \leq 20\%$	0.0120	3.400E−04	−0.3646	0.0435	0	0	0	0.5104	0.0354	0.8034	0.6847	0.4571	1.6978	0.9963
	$y \leq 15\%$	0.0123	3.710E−04	−0.3883	−0.0460	0	1	1	0.5047	0.0351	0.7930	0.6801	0.4430	1.7162	1.0374
	$y \leq 10\%$	0.0119	3.789E−04	−0.4098	−0.0714	0	1	1	0.4779	0.0342	0.7347	0.6319	0.4063	1.6207	0.9830
$E_2 : \{\alpha = 1;$	$y \leq 100\%$	0.0082	2.646E−04	0.6583	0.6494	1	0	0	0.3473	−0.2364	0.5518	0.4412	0.3476	1.0343	0.5617
$\beta = 1;$	$y \leq 50\%$	0.0082	2.647E−04	0.6577	0.6468	1	0	1	0.3475	−0.2350	0.5522	0.4416	0.3478	1.0349	0.5621
$\gamma = 0\}$	$y \leq 25\%$	0.0118	3.824E−04	0.0606	−0.3049	0	0	0	0.4703	0.0390	0.7901	0.6657	0.4552	1.6278	0.9696
	$y \leq 20\%$	0.0122	3.666E−04	−0.1560	−0.4277	0	0	0	0.5035	0.0431	0.8248	0.6991	0.4732	1.7107	1.0270
	$y \leq 15\%$	0.0117	3.664E−04	−0.0863	−0.5361	0	1	1	0.4762	0.1154	0.7742	0.6517	0.4446	1.5821	0.9598
	$y \leq 10\%$	0.0121	3.595E−04	−0.1839	−0.6645	0	1	1	0.5042	0.0957	0.8214	0.6914	0.4686	1.6662	1.0157
$E_3 : \{\alpha = 1;$	$y \leq 100\%$	0.0119	3.594E−04	−0.0623	−0.4081	0	0	0	0.4935	0.0466	0.8147	0.6855	0.4733	1.6559	0.9894
$\beta = 1;$	$y \leq 50\%$	0.0119	3.594E−04	−0.0623	−0.4081	0	0	0	0.4935	0.0466	0.8147	0.6855	0.4733	1.6559	0.9894
$\gamma = 0.75\}$	$y \leq 25\%$	0.0117	3.626E−04	−0.0169	−0.4277	0	0	0	0.4814	0.0503	0.7952	0.6676	0.4617	1.6103	0.9655
	$y \leq 20\%$	0.0119	3.620E−04	−0.0530	−0.4179	0	0	0	0.4907	0.0479	0.8103	0.6816	0.4702	1.6481	0.9868
	$y \leq 15\%$	0.0121	3.736E−04	−0.0663	−0.4851	0	0	0	0.4914	0.0593	0.8123	0.6841	0.4679	1.6557	1.0078
	$y \leq 10\%$	0.0122	3.663E−04	−0.1794	−0.5968	0	1	1	0.5041	0.0660	0.8225	0.6942	0.4691	1.6829	1.0269

$E_4 : \{\alpha = 2;$	$y \le 100\%$	0.0119	3.607E−04	−0.1434	−0.3167	0	0	0	0.4932	0.0387	0.8023	0.6786	0.4623	1.6623	0.9907
$\beta = 1;$	$y \le 50\%$	0.0119	3.607E−04	−0.1434	−0.3167	0	0	0	0.4932	0.0387	0.8023	0.6786	0.4623	1.6623	0.9907
$\gamma = 0.75\}$	$y \le 25\%$	0.0119	3.570E−04	−0.1445	−0.3204	0	0	0	0.4959	0.0394	0.8078	0.6825	0.4662	1.6675	0.9913
	$y \le 20\%$	0.0120	3.624E−04	−0.1323	−0.3354	0	0	0	0.4932	0.0396	0.8045	0.6799	0.4636	1.6622	0.9938
	$y \le 15\%$	0.0122	3.729E−04	−0.1244	−0.4274	0	0	0	0.5001	0.0462	0.8244	0.6962	0.4725	1.6962	1.0282
	$y \le 10\%$	0.0123	3.709E−04	−0.2267	−0.4916	0	1	1	0.5063	0.0506	0.8229	0.6968	0.4658	1.7089	1.0403
$E_5 : \{\alpha = 3;$	$y \le 100\%$	0.0087	2.595E−04	0.4900	0.2461	0	0	0	0.3784	0.3634	0.6023	0.4826	0.3799	1.1096	0.5994
$\beta = 1;$	$y \le 50\%$	0.0087	2.594E−04	0.4902	0.2475	0	0	0	0.3792	0.3658	0.6039	0.4838	0.3810	1.1115	0.6002
$\gamma = 0.25\}$	$y \le 25\%$	0.0119	3.888E−04	0.0769	−0.2680	0	0	0	0.4750	0.0365	0.8048	0.6781	0.4637	1.6552	0.9910
	$y \le 20\%$	0.0122	3.844E−04	−0.1036	−0.3333	0	0	0	0.4922	0.0369	0.8116	0.6889	0.4644	1.7013	1.0274
	$y \le 15\%$	0.0123	3.732E−04	−0.1756	−0.3896	0	0	0	0.5025	0.0425	0.8217	0.6959	0.4688	1.7050	1.0348
	$y \le 10\%$	0.0122	3.569E−04	−0.1913	−0.5283	0	1	1	0.5097	0.0705	0.8319	0.7010	0.4765	1.6917	1.0250
E_6 : EW (1/m)	$y = 6.25\%$	0.0131	5.175E−04	−0.3569	−0.1135	0	1	1	0.4648	0.0315	0.7350	0.6429	0.3909	1.7174	1.1298
Panel C: CFO 18 (Debt = \$340M ; All-in funding cost = 300 bps over LIBOR 1 month)															
$E_1 : \{\alpha = 1;$	$y \le 100\%$	0.0149	6.779E−04	−0.0187	0.0959	0	0	0	0.4749	0.0474	0.8314	0.7326	0.4418	1.9585	1.3345
$\beta = 0;$	$y \le 50\%$	0.0149	6.779E−04	−0.0187	0.0959	0	0	0	0.4749	0.0474	0.8314	0.7326	0.4418	1.9585	1.3345
$\gamma = 0\}$	$y \le 25\%$	0.015	7.978E−04	−0.2632	0.2770	0	0	0	0.4394	0.0348	0.7237	0.6497	0.3682	1.8608	1.3082
	$y \le 20\%$	0.0149	9.408E−04	−0.3193	0.3499	0	0	0	0.4018	0.0276	0.6445	0.5839	0.3196	1.7455	1.2680
	$y \le 15\%$	0.0154	1.038E−03	−0.3688	0.3002	0	0	0	0.3974	0.0275	0.6325	0.5759	0.3092	1.7514	1.2960
	$y \le 10\%$	0.0147	1.047E−03	−0.3740	0.1657	0	1	0	0.3764	0.0267	0.5891	0.5366	0.2870	1.6642	1.2325
$E_2 : \{\alpha = 1;$	$y \le 100\%$	0.0087	8.573E−04	0.8688	1.2782	1	1	1	0.2080	−0.0990	0.3433	0.3004	0.1762	1.0600	0.7474
$\beta = 1;$	$y \le 50\%$	0.0087	8.573E−04	0.8682	1.2748	1	1	1	0.2082	−0.0986	0.3438	0.3008	0.1764	1.0607	0.7479
$\gamma = 0\}$	$y \le 25\%$	0.0146	1.092E−03	0.1824	−0.0811	0	0	0	0.3632	0.0306	0.6259	0.5633	0.3135	1.6629	1.2187
	$y \le 20\%$	0.0152	1.004E−03	−0.0837	−0.3054	0	0	0	0.3996	0.0347	0.6682	0.6024	0.3343	1.7538	1.2895
	$y \le 15\%$	0.0145	9.800E−04	0.0330	−0.4012	0	0	0	0.3799	0.1286	0.6379	0.5707	0.3214	1.6425	1.2108
	$y \le 10\%$	0.0151	9.415E−04	−0.0809	−0.6626	0	1	1	0.4096	0.0978	0.6893	0.6157	0.3444	1.7311	1.2769

(Continued)

Table 9. Continued

E_h	k	Mean	Variance	Skewness	Excess kurtosis	JB $\alpha = 5\%$	Lilliefors $\alpha = 5\%$	G&R $\alpha = 5\%$	Sharpe	Treynor	Sortino MAR = 0.008	Sortino MAR = 0.012	Modified Sharpe $\alpha = 5\%$	Ω MAR = 0.008	Ω MAR = 0.012
$E_3 : \{\alpha = 1;$	$y \leq 100\%$	0.0148	9.627E−04	0.0564	−0.3723	0	0	0	0.3943	0.0385	0.6726	0.6013	0.3400	1.7103	1.2484
$\beta = 1;$	$y \leq 50\%$	0.0148	9.627E−04	0.0564	−0.3723	0	0	0	0.3943	0.0385	0.6726	0.6013	0.3400	1.7103	1.2484
$\gamma = 0.75\}$	$y \leq 25\%$	0.0145	9.726E−04	0.1058	−0.4254	0	0	0	0.3832	0.0421	0.6553	0.5846	0.3304	1.6637	1.2176
	$y \leq 20\%$	0.0148	9.691E−04	0.0682	−0.3887	0	0	0	0.3921	0.0397	0.6693	0.5981	0.3381	1.7027	1.2436
	$y \leq 15\%$	0.0150	9.911E−04	0.0678	−0.4240	0	0	1	0.3960	0.0523	0.6781	0.6059	0.3421	1.7125	1.2634
	$y \leq 10\%$	0.0153	9.583E−04	−0.0742	−0.6260	0	0	0	0.4101	0.0600	0.6915	0.6187	0.3456	1.7465	1.2889
$E_4 : \{\alpha = 2;$	$y \leq 100\%$	0.0148	9.786E−04	−0.0544	−0.2381	0	0	0	0.3916	0.0307	0.6538	0.5876	0.3285	1.7100	1.2484
$\beta = 1;$	$y \leq 50\%$	0.0148	9.786E−04	−0.0544	−0.2381	0	0	0	0.3916	0.0307	0.6538	0.5876	0.3285	1.7100	1.2484
$\gamma = 0.75\}$	$y \leq 25\%$	0.0148	9.663E−04	−0.0537	−0.2516	0	0	0	0.3943	0.0313	0.6595	0.5922	0.3316	1.7162	1.2506
	$y \leq 20\%$	0.0149	9.791E−04	−0.0351	−0.2727	0	0	0	0.3927	0.0316	0.6586	0.5912	0.3311	1.7112	1.2508
	$y \leq 15\%$	0.0153	9.873E−04	−0.0033	−0.3939	0	1	0	0.4042	0.0385	0.6891	0.6171	0.3461	1.7537	1.2874
	$y \leq 10\%$	0.0154	9.708E−04	−0.1297	−0.5004	0	0	0	0.4125	0.0432	0.6923	0.6210	0.3439	1.7710	1.3017
$E_5 : \{\alpha = 3;$	$y \leq 100\%$	0.0094	8.231E−04	0.7112	0.8357	1	0	0	0.2395	0.7232	0.3967	0.3468	0.2053	1.1371	0.7980
$\beta = 1;$	$y \leq 50\%$	0.0095	8.222E−04	0.7120	0.8381	1	0	0	0.2403	0.7433	0.3984	0.3482	0.2061	1.1393	0.7993
$\gamma = 0.25\}$	$y \leq 25\%$	0.0148	1.111E−03	0.1996	−0.0070	0	0	0	0.3680	0.0284	0.6386	0.5749	0.3203	1.6894	1.2410
	$y \leq 20\%$	0.0153	1.059E−03	−0.0150	−0.1675	0	0	0	0.3901	0.0292	0.6576	0.5935	0.3295	1.7425	1.2836
	$y \leq 15\%$	0.0153	9.901E−04	−0.0701	−0.3556	0	0	0	0.4061	0.0349	0.6845	0.6145	0.3426	1.7594	1.2945
	$y \leq 10\%$	0.0152	9.250E−04	−0.0578	−0.5521	0	0	1	0.4165	0.0654	0.7057	0.6298	0.3553	1.7602	1.2916
E_6 : EW (1/m)	$y = 6.25\%$	0.0167	1.412E−03	−0.3207	0.3804	0	0	0	0.3771	0.0255	0.6070	0.5588	0.2906	1.7599	1.3623

Notes: This table presents the descriptive statistics, the results of the tests for normality and the performance measures of CFO structures 11 (panel A), 15 (Panel B), and 18 (Panel C) constructed from the 31 hedge fund portfolios. For each of the three CFO structures, the nature of the underlying fund (set of preference and diversification constraint) appears on the vertical axis and their statistics within the particular CFO structure are presented horizontally. As a reference, the value of the debt portion of the CFO's $400M and the all-in funding cost, in basis points over the 1M LIBOR, appear at the top of each panel. The descriptive statistics are monthly and include the first four moments of the distributions, as well as the minimum and maximum returns. With regard to the tests for normality, the value of the test statistic and a dummy variable indicating whether or not the value is significant at a confidence level of 95% are presented*. The dummy variable equals 1 when the null hypothesis of normality is rejected. The performance measures (Sharpe, Treynor, Sortino, Modified Sharpe, and Omega) are also presented on a monthly basis. For the Sortino ratio and the Omega measure, the calculations are made for MAR levels of 0.8% and 1.2% monthly. The Modified Sharpe is computed based on a value-at-risk calculation with a 95% confidence level.

**p*-Values are available upon request.

null hypothesis as the structure's leverage increases. Indeed, we note for example that using the method of Genest and Remillard, four out of 31 funds rejected the normality of equity returns in the case of CFO 2; the result is ten out of 31 for CFO 14.

As for the performance indicators, we will focus on the more sophisticated measures. First of all, the Sortino ratio increases as leverage increases, reaching a maximum for CFO 15, for both levels of MARs considered. In the case of the unconstrained mean-variance portfolio, the measure is close to 1 for a monthly MAR of 0.8%, and 0.82 for a monthly MAR of 1.2%. The ratio decreases beyond CFO 15. According to this measure however, there seems to be an optimal debt level for the equity owner, beyond which it is no longer beneficial to add leverage. With regard to the measure's overall behavior as leverage increases, we once again observe the phenomenon of local peaks for CFOs 11 and 18.

The Omega measure behaves in a similar manner to the Sortino ratio except for the fact that it decreases beyond a certain threshold when we consider a monthly MAR = 0.8%. More specifically, when the MAR is at this level, the maximum occurs at CFO 18 for a value of almost 1.96, and CFOs 11 and 15 are also distinguished by their local optimality. With monthly MAR = 1.2%, CFO 20 shows the highest values at levels above 1.40. However, if we compare this structure to that of CFO 18, we see that the highest values are very close and that the lowest values of CFO 20 are substantially lower than those of CFO 18. Thus, the benefits of leverage decrease for CFOs 19 and 20. Also, it is interesting to note that at this level of MARs, it is the EW portfolio that results in maximum 'intra-CFO' values rather than the portfolios resulting from the unconstrained optimization.

Finally, the modified Sharpe ratio behaves much the same way as the conventional Sharpe ratio. It systematically decreases between CFO 2 and CFO 20, and the rate at which the decrease occurs for CFOs 12, 16, and 19 is far more pronounced. The estimates of the higher moments used in the calculation of the modified Sharpe ratio are however subject to significant estimation error as the size of the sample is relatively small. Ultimately, we will rely exclusively on the Sortino and Omega measures given that they account more accurately for the actual empirical distribution of the returns.

In short, the performance analysis indicates that CFOs 11, 15, and 18, which maximize the debt levels for a given aggregate cost CFO structures, are clearly distinguished from the others. The optimal debt-to-equity ratios are therefore 1, 7/3, and 17/3. For every dollar of equity, there must therefore be at least one dollar of debt. In this sense, this supports the existence of an optimal debt level from the equity owner's viewpoint, the merit of CFOs and thus, the added-value of the latter for the investor. These results also show the outperformance of the CFO equity tranche, regardless of the structure, when compared with a direct exposure to the portfolio of hedge funds. Indeed, if we compare the results of the Sortino ratio and the Omega measure from one portfolio of hedge funds to another versus the CFO, the latter always outperform the former. It is important to emphasize that if we rely solely on simple performance measures, we would not come to these conclusions.

With regard to the relationship between the underlying portfolio and the performance of the CFO equity tranche, the results show more or less the same pattern as in the previous section. More specifically, the funds all behave in a similar manner from the equity owner's viewpoint, regardless of the amount of leverage. This means that the same eight portfolios are of interest to the CFO equity tranche owner and that once again, on the sole basis of risk-adjusted performance, no general conclusion can be drawn as to the diversification requirements for an equity owner. There appears to be independence between decisions concerning the underlying portfolio and the debt structure. This is indeed very interesting as CFOs are flexible instruments, meaning that it is possible to choose the types of underlying portfolio according to one's need for diversification and the extent of leverage based on one's appetite for risk.

4.3 *Systematic risk exposure of the equity tranche*

The following multivariate linear regression was estimated to test the diversification benefits of the equity tranches of 28 CFO structures identified in the previous section.

$$\begin{aligned}\mathrm{CFO}_{j,hk,t} &= \alpha_{j,hk} + \beta_{1j,hk}\mathrm{STOCK}_t + \beta_{2j,hk}\mathrm{DEF}_t + \beta_{3j,hk}\mathrm{LIQ}_t \\ &\quad + \beta_{4j,hk}\mathrm{TERM}_t + \beta_{5j,hk}\mathrm{TREND}_t + \varepsilon_{j,hk,t}, \qquad (9)\end{aligned}$$

where $\mathrm{CFO}_{j,hk,t}$ is the monthly return of CFO_j, constructed using the hedge fund portfolio subjected to the set of preference E_h and the diversification constraint k, at time t.

STOCK_t is the monthly return of the Russel 3000 stock index at time t. It is used as an indicator of financial market performance and is included so as to determine whether systematic exposure to equity returns has an explicative power with regard to the performance of a securitized hedge fund portfolio.

DEF_t, is the spread in basis points of the LUCI Total OAS[7] index at time t and is used as an indicator of the systematic default risk of credit markets. It is included in the model so as to ascertain whether the systematic default risk in the credit markets influences CFO returns. To this end, several variables are used in the literature to capture this notion of default. However, as stipulated in Longstaff, Mithal, and Neis (2005), among others, since the advent of the credit default swaps (CDS) market, it has become common practice to use the spreads on these instruments to identify the default risk embedded in the credit risk.[8]

LIQ_t is the spread in basis points between 10-year on-the-run and off-the-run government securities at time t. The variable is used as an indicator of the systematic liquidity risk of bond markets. This indicator is further explained in Longstaff, Mithal, and Neis (2005).

TERM_t is the spread in basis points between long-term (20-year) and short-term (1-month t-bills) government securities at time t. It is used as an indicator of systematic interest rate risk. This indicator is the same as that used in Fama and French (1993).

TREND_t is the typical time trend that is used when the variables are distributed over time. The idea is to eliminate any time trend effect that may result in autocorrelation in the data series.

Table 10 presents the value of the estimated coefficients and their respective *p-value*. We recall that the ideal scenario is that of completely uncorrelated returns, i.e. statistically null coefficients. In the case of the constant α, its statistical significance implies the presence of a fixed effect not captured by the model's variables.

We first note that the constant α and the coefficient β_5, which is attributed to the TREND variable, are always significant. This means, on the one hand, that returns are specific to each of the instruments. In addition, we see that the values taken by α are always positive and increase as leverage increases, thus reflecting greater added-value. On the other hand, the significance of β_5 confirms that there is indeed a trend in terms of CFO returns. It is also interesting to note that this coefficient is always negative, implying that returns decrease over the period studied (2001–2008).

When we consider the estimated coefficients of the variables of interest, β_1–β_4, it is important to emphasize at the very outset that the statistical significance of the coefficients follows a rather consistent pattern across the different CFO structures tested. Indeed, the same pattern in terms of the statistical significance of the regression coefficients is exhibited in the case of direct exposure

Table 10. Results of multivariate linear regressions for CFOs 1, 11, 15, and 18.

	Panel A: CFO 1 (Direct exposure to portfolio of HF)						
	Coefficients						
	$\{\alpha = 1; \beta = 0; \gamma = 0\}$ $y \leq 100\%$	$\{\alpha = 1; \beta = 1; \gamma = 0\}$ $y \leq 100\%$	$\{\alpha = 1; \beta = 1; \gamma = 0\}$ $y \leq 20\%$	$\{\alpha = 2; \beta = 1; \gamma = 0.75\}$ $y \leq 10\%$	$\{\alpha = 3; \beta = 1; \gamma = 0.25\}$ $y \leq 50\%$	$\{\alpha = 3; \beta = 1; \gamma = 0.25\}$ $y \leq 15\%$	1/m $y = 6.25\%$
α	0.025818	0.021177	0.024543	0.025677	0.020373	0.026133	0.026712
STOCK	0.061247	−0.008493	0.082277	0.077032	0.006984	0.087423	0.129787
DEF	−0.000675	−0.000480	−0.000671	−0.000603	−0.000451	−0.000659	−0.000639
LIQU	−21.324371	−20.243579	−11.967612	−21.047440	−20.423683	−17.897796	−16.064178
TERM	−2.305055	−2.320236	−2.013981	−2.712104	−2.214730	−2.580198	−2.646475
TREND	−0.000144	−0.000127	−0.000122	−0.000143	−0.000116	−0.000142	−0.000151
	p-Values						
	$\{\alpha = 1; \beta = 0; \gamma = 0\}$ $y \leq 100\%$	$\{\alpha = 1; \beta = 1; \gamma = 0\}$ $y \leq 100\%$	$\{\alpha = 1; \beta = 1; \gamma = 0\}$ $y \leq 20\%$	$\{\alpha = 2; \beta = 1; \gamma = 0.75\}$ $y \leq 10\%$	$\{\alpha = 3; \beta = 1; \gamma = 0.25\}$ $y \leq 50\%$	$\{\alpha = 3; \beta = 1; \gamma = 0.25\}$ $y \leq 15\%$	1/m $y = 6.25\%$
α	0.0000	0.0002	0.0005	0.0004	0.0005	0.0002	0.0005
STOCK	0.0016	0.6536	0.0006	0.0018	0.7177	0.0003	0.0000
DEF	0.0097	0.0649	0.0353	0.0671	0.0889	0.0398	0.0677
LIQU	0.3550	0.3830	0.6723	0.4734	0.3886	0.5297	0.6060
TERM	0.0511	0.0512	0.1633	0.0713	0.0678	0.0770	0.0969
TREND	0.0014	0.0049	0.0249	0.0119	0.0112	0.0098	0.0123

(*Continued*)

Table 10. Continued

	Panel B: CFO 11						
	Coefficients						
	$\{\alpha = 1; \beta = 0; \gamma = 0\}$ $y \leq 100\%$	$\{\alpha = 1; \beta = 1; \gamma = 0\}$ $y \leq 100\%$	$\{\alpha = 1; \beta = 1; \gamma = 0\}$ $y \leq 20\%$	$\{\alpha = 2; \beta = 1; \gamma = 0.75\}$ $y \leq 10\%$	$\{\alpha = 3; \beta = 1; \gamma = 0.25\}$ $y \leq 50\%$	$\{\alpha = 3; \beta = 1; \gamma = 0.25\}$ $y \leq 15\%$	1/m $y = 6.25\%$
α	0.037932	0.031745	0.035875	0.037632	0.030135	0.038319	0.038088
STOCK	0.098863	−0.022917	0.134674	0.122659	0.004186	0.142237	0.217518
DEF	−0.001056	−0.000803	−0.001073	−0.000942	−0.000749	−0.001033	−0.000944
LIQU	−49.959631	−46.930344	−35.537299	−49.574431	−48.093856	−45.137863	−41.680773
TERM	−3.254628	−3.444272	−2.654086	−3.858305	−3.212852	−3.641032	−3.606458
TREND	−0.000253	−0.000230	−0.000217	−0.000250	−0.000211	−0.000249	−0.000257
	p-Values						
	$\{\alpha = 1; \beta = 0; \gamma = 0\}$ $y \leq 100\%$	$\{\alpha = 1; \beta = 1; \gamma = 0\}$ $y \leq 100\%$	$\{\alpha = 1; \beta = 1; \gamma = 0\}$ $y \leq 20\%$	$\{\alpha = 2; \beta = 1; \gamma = 0.75\}$ $y \leq 10\%$	$\{\alpha = 3; \beta = 1; \gamma = 0.25\}$ $y \leq 50\%$	$\{\alpha = 3; \beta = 1; \gamma = 0.25\}$ $y \leq 15\%$	1/m $y = 6.25\%$
α	0.0000	0.0013	0.0013	0.0011	0.0024	0.0006	0.0017
STOCK	0.0015	0.4848	0.0005	0.0019	0.8991	0.0002	0.0000
DEF	0.0119	0.0744	0.0353	0.0738	0.0986	0.0429	0.0884
LIQU	0.1794	0.2437	0.4326	0.2925	0.2362	0.3205	0.3996
TERM	0.0861	0.0935	0.2495	0.1082	0.1203	0.1162	0.1529
TREND	0.0005	0.0032	0.0131	0.0061	0.0073	0.0047	0.0073

(Continued)

Table 10. Continued

Panel C: CFO 15							
	Coefficients						
	$\{\alpha = 1; \beta = 0; \gamma = 0\}$ $y \leq 100\%$	$\{\alpha = 1; \beta = 1; \gamma = 0\}$ $y \leq 100\%$	$\{\alpha = 1; \beta = 1; \gamma = 0\}$ $y \leq 20\%$	$\{\alpha = 2; \beta = 1; \gamma = 0.75\}$ $y \leq 10\%$	$\{\alpha = 3; \beta = 1; \gamma = 0.25\}$ $y \leq 50\%$	$\{\alpha = 3; \beta = 1; \gamma = 0.25\}$ $y \leq 15\%$	1/m $y = 6.25\%$
α	0.050856	0.044229	0.048016	0.050308	0.041476	0.051277	0.049340
STOCK	0.138615	−0.044203	0.191964	0.169802	−0.003430	0.201255	0.316547
DEF	−0.001428	−0.001170	−0.001481	−0.001271	−0.001080	−0.001401	−0.001199
LIQU	−81.254411	−76.995044	−62.397691	−80.775945	−79.772810	−75.565411	−69.526505
TERM	−4.251777	−4.744886	−3.253458	−5.024286	−4.336980	−4.723197	−4.471656
TREND	−0.000370	−0.000350	−0.000320	−0.000366	−0.000318	−0.000364	−0.000368
	p-Values						
	$\{\alpha = 1; \beta = 0; \gamma = 0\}$ $y \leq 100\%$	$\{\alpha = 1; \beta = 1; \gamma = 0\}$ $y \leq 100\%$	$\{\alpha = 1; \beta = 1; \gamma = 0\}$ $y \leq 20\%$	$\{\alpha = 2; \beta = 1; \gamma = 0.75\}$ $y \leq 10\%$	$\{\alpha = 3; \beta = 1; \gamma = 0.25\}$ $y \leq 50\%$	$\{\alpha = 3; \beta = 1; \gamma = 0.25\}$ $y \leq 15\%$	1/m $y = 6.25\%$
α	0.0001	0.0028	0.0022	0.0019	0.0048	0.0011	0.0037
STOCK	0.0017	0.3712	0.0004	0.0023	0.9445	0.0002	0.0000
DEF	0.0163	0.0841	0.0401	0.0868	0.1102	0.0507	0.1235
LIQU	0.1245	0.2043	0.3311	0.2243	0.1885	0.2378	0.3185
TERM	0.1135	0.1243	0.3183	0.1375	0.1594	0.1470	0.2073
TREND	0.0004	0.0029	0.0099	0.0045	0.0066	0.0034	0.0064

(Continued)

Table 10. Continued

	Panel D: CFO 18						
	Coefficients						
	$\{\alpha = 1; \beta = 0; \gamma = 0\}$ $y \leq 100\%$	$\{\alpha = 1; \beta = 1; \gamma = 0\}$ $y \leq 100\%$	$\{\alpha = 1; \beta = 1; \gamma = 0\}$ $y \leq 20\%$	$\{\alpha = 2; \beta = 1; \gamma = 0.75\}$ $y \leq 10\%$	$\{\alpha = 3; \beta = 1; \gamma = 0.25\}$ $y \leq 50\%$	$\{\alpha = 3; \beta = 1; \gamma = 0.25\}$ $y \leq 15\%$	1/m $y = 6.25\%$
α	0.074028	0.070676	0.069972	0.072836	0.064612	0.074630	0.066990
STOCK	0.218948	−0.099010	0.313963	0.262845	−0.027730	0.324006	0.534591
DEF	−0.002167	−0.002082	−0.002329	−0.001924	−0.001884	−0.002143	−0.001600
LIQU	−146.250322	−145.031986	−121.184595	−145.829989	−152.364230	−140.468397	−126.841879
TERM	−6.021820	−7.488111	−4.120773	−7.066956	−6.627699	−6.635288	−5.641108
TREND	−0.000590	−0.000613	−0.000512	−0.000579	−0.000546	−0.000579	−0.000563
	p-Values						
	$\{\alpha = 1; \beta = 0; \gamma = 0\}$ $y \leq 100\%$	$\{\alpha = 1; \beta = 1; \gamma = 0\}$ $y \leq 100\%$	$\{\alpha = 1; \beta = 1; \gamma = 0\}$ $y \leq 20\%$	$\{\alpha = 2; \beta = 1; \gamma = 0.75\}$ $y \leq 10\%$	$\{\alpha = 3; \beta = 1; \gamma = 0.25\}$ $y \leq 50\%$	$\{\alpha = 3; \beta = 1; \gamma = 0.25\}$ $y \leq 15\%$	1/m $y = 6.25\%$
α	0.0005	0.0075	0.0068	0.0056	0.0133	0.0034	0.0158
STOCK	0.0026	0.2660	0.0005	0.0037	0.7524	0.0003	0.0000
DEF	0.0264	0.0873	0.0514	0.1113	0.1178	0.0671	0.2110
LIQU	0.0934	0.1838	0.2559	0.1786	0.1592	0.1801	0.2700
TERM	0.1723	0.1766	0.4457	0.1990	0.2269	0.2119	0.3334
TREND	0.0005	0.0037	0.0127	0.0057	0.0088	0.0043	0.0112

Notes: The table shows the results of the multivariate linear regression model applied to the returns of CFO structures 1, 11, 15 and 18. For every structure, the value of the coefficients respective to each independent variable and their corresponding p-value are presented. The coefficient α is the model's constant. Within each panel (A to D), the independent variables appear on the vertical axis and the underlying funds (set of preference and diversification constraint) are presented horizontally. The weights y are the proportion of the total value and are between 0 and 1 (no-short constraint).

to the portfolio of hedge fund and CFO 11, whereas CFOs 15 and 18 present fewer significant coefficients. It can therefore be inferred that leverage has very little effect on the systematic diversification. The benefits of diversification are therefore not an argument in favor of CFOs.

Regardless of the choice of the underlying portfolio and of the selected capital structure, the coefficient estimates indicate that the liquidity (LIQ) and the slope of the term structure (TERM) variables do not significantly impact CFO returns. With respect to the STOCK variable, which relates to systematic equity market risk, we note that the estimated coefficient is almost always significant. The estimated coefficient for the default risk variable is less stable across the different CFO structures. In the case of exposure to CFO 1 and CFO 11, we see that the DEF variable has a significant, negative impact in the case of underlying portfolios $E_{1;100\%}$, $E_{2;20\%}$, and $E_{5;15\%}$. For CFOs 15 and 18, there is a gradual loss of significance of the estimated coefficient for the last two underlying portfolios ($E_{2;20\%}$ and $E_{5;15\%}$).

Thus, it is the unconstrained mean-variance portfolio that fairs the most poorly in terms of systematic risk exposures, while the unconstrained version of preference set E_2 is the big winner. However, we recall that this underlying portfolio underperforms in terms of most performance measures. It therefore appears necessary to reach a compromise between performance and decorrelation with the capital market as the best of both worlds cannot be achieved simultaneously. Two interesting alternatives appear to be that of $E_{4;10\%}$ and the EW portfolio that both exhibit a slight positive correlation with equity markets. Although not an optimal solution, these results provide strong evidence that it is possible to construct CFOs that generate value in terms of both performance and low systematic risk exposure.

On the basis of the results above, when the objective pursued by the investor in terms of CFO equity is either performance, or decorrelation, an unconstrained portfolio in which *Foreign Exchange* strategy is predominant is essential. Where one wishes to combine the two objectives, there must be substantial diversification of the underlying portfolio. With regard to the debt-to-equity ratio of the capital structure selected, there is almost no impact, notwithstanding exceptions. This therefore implies that CFOs represent added-value compared with a direct exposure to the portfolio of hedge funds, only in terms of performance however, not with regard to diversification in capital markets.

4.4 *Impact of the financial crisis*

In this section, we look at the impact that the financial crisis would have had on the performance of the three CFO structures that were identified as being the most attractive for equity tranche investors, namely CFO 11, CFO 15, and CFO 18. We also include the analysis for CFO 20, the most highly levered structure. For these four structures we extend the maturity of the analysis until the end of March 2009, the month during which the equity markets finally bottomed. In Table 11, we present the descriptive statistics for the 16 strategies over the January 2008 to March 2009 period. Although this was clearly a very difficult period for many strategies, particularly convertible arbitrage, emerging markets and equity non-hedge, it is interesting to note that certain strategies, notably short sellers and managed futures generated positive returns during this 15-month market correction.

In Table 12, we report the performance of the equity tranche for the extended sample for CFO 11, CFO 15, CFO 18, and CFO 20. The most significant result is that the holding period returns for the equity tranche remain positive for the three CFO structures that were identified earlier as being the most attractive to investors. The holding period returns are, not surprisingly, greatly reduced when we extend the sample to include the financial crisis. However, sufficient excess return had

Table 11. Statistics of hedge fund strategy indexes during financial crisis.

Strategy	Mean monthly return	Standard deviation	Minimum monthly return	Maximum monthly return	Maximum drawdown
Convertible arbitrage	−0.019	0.0565	−0.166	0.0553	−0.397
Distressed securities	−0.0195	0.0288	−0.090	0.0139	−0.293
Equity hedge	−0.0163	0.0329	−0.080	0.0262	−0.269
Equity market neutral	−0.0015	0.0133	−0.034	0.0169	−0.0621
Equity non-hedge	−0.0315	0.0614	−0.177	0.0575	−0.530
Event-driven	−0.0141	0.0289	−0.076	0.0212	−0.211
Foreign exchange	0.0032	0.0071	−0.007	0.0181	−0.0101
Macro	−0.0053	0.0174	−0.036	0.0319	−0.108
Managed futures	0.0085	0.0268	−0.038	0.0766	−0.049
Market timing	−0.0177	0.0361	−0.099	0.0360	−0.281
Merger arbitrage	−0.0024	0.0130	−0.026	0.0213	−0.040
Rel. value arbitrage	−0.0092	0.0281	−0.076	0.0216	−0.138
Short selling	0.0218	0.0411	−0.053	0.0974	−0.053
Emerging markets	−0.0332	0.0547	−0.163	0.0406	−0.540
Fixed income	−0.0137	0.0331	−0.105	0.0256	−0.233

Notes: This table presents the descriptive statistics for every hedge fund strategy for the period January 2008 to March 2009.

been generated over the previous seven years to absorb the losses. Only when we consider the most levered structure, CFO 20, does the equity tranche generate negative returns. In fact, with the exception of the EW portfolio, the equity tranche holding period returns are negative for all the CFO 20 portfolios, and in certain cases ($E_{2,100\%}$), the equity tranche is completely wiped out.

5. Conclusion

In response to suggestions that CFO equity tranches do not offer value to investors, we decided to undertake a thorough examination of the performance of this type of investment. The objective was to assess the performance of the equity tranche of CFOs both in terms of risk-adjusted return as well as systematic risk exposures. For this purpose, 30 optimal portfolios (each conditional to a set of preferences and weight constraints) and an EW portfolio were constructed using the 16-hedge fund strategy indexes. All of these underlying portfolios were then securitized using 19 capital structures, which allowed us to analyze the series of returns of the 620 CFO equity tranches.

Interestingly, we observe that if we consider the overall distribution of returns of a CFO equity tranche in analyzing the performance, securitizing and tranching the underlying portfolio of hedge funds add value to the end investor. Our analysis also finds that there was no direct relationship between the optimal portfolio to securitize and the capital structure decisions. With regard to the debt-to-equity ratio, we conclude that leverage is beneficial to the CFO equity holder when the level of debt is maximized for a given funding cost. In addition, our analysis shows that a trade-off takes place between performance and systematic diversification; if one considers a combination of the two objectives, we conclude that the underlying portfolio must be broadly diversified across the various hedge fund strategies. Thus, these conclusions suggest that market participants might have been too hasty in dismissing CFOs, and not taking greater advantage of the benefits offered by these investment vehicles.

Table 12. Performance of CFOs 11, 15, 18, and 20 during financial crisis.

Structure	Preferences	Weighting	Mean return	Standard deviation	HPR	HPR excl. crisis	% Reduction in HPR
CFO 11	$E_1 : \{\alpha = 1; \beta = 0; \gamma = 0\}$	$y \leq 100\%$	0.00673	0.0157	90.7%	125.9%	28.0%
		$y \leq 20\%$	0.0097	0.0129	83.3%	124.8%	33.3%
	$E_2 : \{\alpha = 1; \beta = 1; \gamma = 0\}$	$y \leq 100\%$	0.00701	0.0107	63.5%	80.3%	20.9%
		$y \leq 20\%$	0.00995	0.0135	82.6%	123.0%	32.8%
	$E_3 : \{\alpha = 1; \beta = 1; \gamma = 0.75\}$	$y \leq 100\%$	0.0097	0.0134	83.7%	123.9%	32.4%
		$y \leq 20\%$	0.0097	0.0134	82.9%	124.4%	33.4%
	EW	$y \leq 6.25\%$	0.0067	0.0211	89.6%	140.4%	36.2%
CFO 15	$E_1 : \{\alpha = 1; \beta = 0; \gamma = 0\}$	$y \leq 100\%$	0.00784	0.0216	110.1%	170.1%	35.3%
		$y \leq 20\%$	0.0118	0.0184	98.52%	168.0%	41.4%
	$E_2 : \{\alpha = 1; \beta = 1; \gamma = 0\}$	$y \leq 100\%$	0.0082	0.0162	65.53%	96.65%	32.2%
		$y \leq 20\%$	0.0122	0.0191	97.51%	172.9%	43.6%
	$E_3 : \{\alpha = 1; \beta = 1; \gamma = 0.75\}$	$y \leq 100\%$	0.0119	0.0189	99.1%	166.6%	40.5%
		$y \leq 20\%$	0.0119	0.0189	99.3%	166.1%	40.2%
	EW	$y \leq 6.25\%$	0.0080	0.0295	109.9%	193.0%	43.1%
CFO 18	$E_1 : \{\alpha = 1; \beta = 0; \gamma = 0\}$	$y \leq 100\%$	0.0084	0.0342	114.9%	237.8%	51.7%
		$y \leq 20\%$	0.0075	0.0404	93.8%	233.04%	59.7%
	$E_2 : \{\alpha = 1; \beta = 1; \gamma = 0\}$	$y \leq 100\%$	0.0086	0.0292	27.9%	99.2%	71.9%
		$y \leq 20\%$	0.0074	0.0402	91.6%	241.7%	62.1%
	$E_3 : \{\alpha = 1; \beta = 1; \gamma = 0.75\}$	$y \leq 100\%$	0.0075	0.0392	94.3%	230.4%	59.1%
		$y \leq 20\%$	0.0075	0.0392	94.6%	229.4%	58.8%
	EW	$y \leq 6.25\%$	0.0089	0.0465	114.9%	280.6%	59.1%
CFO 20	$E_1 : \{\alpha = 1; \beta = 0; \gamma = 0\}$	$y \leq 100\%$	−0.0025	0.097	−55.4%	323.7%	...
		$y \leq 20\%$	−0.044%	0.116	−70.8%	306.8%	...
	$E_2 : \{\alpha = 1; \beta = 1; \gamma = 0\}$	$y \leq 100\%$	−0.0182	0.502	−100%	−59.8%	...
		$y \leq 20\%$	−0.0005	0.109	−50.4%	328.7%	...
	$E_3 : \{\alpha = 1; \beta = 1; \gamma = 0.75\}$	$y \leq 100\%$	−0.0065	0.118	−77.4%	299.6%	...
		$y \leq 20\%$	−0.0073	0.120	−79.6%	297.2%	...
	EW	$y \leq 6.25\%$	0.0012	0.107	50.6%	439.92%	88.5%

Notes: This table presents the performance of the equity tranche of CFO structures 11, 15, 18, and 20 when the sample period is extended to March 2009. For each of the four CFO structures, we present results for three sets of preferences and two diversification constraints, as well as for the EW portfolio. The mean return, standard deviation, Holding period return (HPR), Holding period return excluding 2008 and 2009 (HPR excl. crisis), as well as the percent reduction in the HPR due to the crisis are presented (% reduction of HPR is one minus the ratio of HPR over HPR excluding crisis). The weights y are the proportion of the total value and are all comprised between 0 and 1 (no-short constraint).

Interestingly, when we look at the performance of the different hedge fund strategies during the 2008 crisis, the ones that historically had a positive skewness suffered the smallest drawdown, with certain strategies such as macro, managed futures and foreign exchange actually generating positive returns. This further underlines the importance of accounting for higher moments in the portfolio optimization, and shows that accounting for skewness is important in building a robust portfolio of hedge funds. Furthermore, it is interesting to note that very few of the debt tranches, with the exception of the most levered structures, suffer losses when the analysis is extended to include the financial crisis. This demonstrates that the value of CFOs reaches beyond the equity tranche and extends to the debt holders.

If the reputation of securitization had not already been undermined by its involvement in the current financial crisis, the impact of this two-dimensional analysis could have been rather different. However, given the present stigma attached to structured products, we should not expect to witness new CFO transactions anytime soon. This is unfortunate considering that the nature of the problem is one of inaccurate valuation rather than one of overexuberant financial engineering, as explained in Longstaff and Myers (2009). Global financial markets are currently seeking to rebuild a sound financial system and it will be interesting to see whether CFOs will be favored among the range of investments available to institutional investors. For this to transpire, securitization and financing practices must be rehabilitated in conjunction with proper governance rules that promote greater transparency.

Notes

1. Costs related to the structure's management and debt do not obviously apply in the case of this instrument.
2. These are representative of the size and maturity of a typical CFO transaction.
3. For the $12M originally due (3% × $400M), the monthly installment amounts to $174,441.
4. For a complete description of the tests of normality used, refer to Jarque and Bera (1980), Lilliefors (1967) and Genest and Rémillard (2004).
5. The Dow Jones Industrial Average Index recorded an increase of approximately 300% (14.9% on an annual basis) between February 1991 and January 2001, and less than 20% (2.5% on an annual basis) between February 2001 and January 2008.
6. For the purpose of brevity, only the results for preference sets E_1, E_2, and E_3 are presented in Tables 6 and 7.
7. LUCI is the acronym for Liquid US Corporate Indices, a series of bond indexes developed by Crédit Suisse. The Total OAS (Option Adjusted Spread) version captures the entire market, eliminating the specific nature of securities such as embedded options.
8. The original intention was to use the CDX.NA.IG index spread. However, a thorough study of the series shows that there is a lack of liquidity prior to 2004, which could bias the results. We are aware that there is a liquidity component in the CDS spreads.

References

Cheng, C. 2002. Securitization & hedge funds: Creating a more efficient market. Working paper, Intangis, Renaissance Capital Group, New York.

Chunhachinda, P., K. Dandapani, S. Hamid, and A. Prakash. 1997. Portfolio selection and skewness: Evidence from international stock markets. *Journal of Banking and Finance* 21, no. 2: 143–67.

Davies, R.J., H.M. Kat, and S. Lu. 2009. Fund of hedge funds portfolio selection: A multiple-objective approach. *Journal of Derivatives and Hedge Funds* 15, August: 91–115.

DeMiguel, A-V., L. Garlappi, and R. Uppal. 2009. Optimal versus naïve diversification: How inefficient is the 1/N portfolio strategy? *Review of Financial Studies* 22, no. 5: 1915–53.

De Souza, C., and S. Gokcan. 2004. Allocation methodologies and customizing hedge-fund multi-manager multi-strategy products. *Journal of Alternative Investments* 6, Spring: 7–21.

Fama, E., and K. French. 1993. Common risk factors in the returns on stocks and bonds. *Journal of Financial Economics* 33, no. 1: 3–56.

Genest, C., and B. Rémillard. 2004. Tests of independence and randomness based on the empirical copula process. *Test* 13, no. 2: 335–69.

Gregoriou, G.N., and J.-P. Gueyie. 2003. Risk-adjusted performance of funds of hedge funds using a modified Sharpe ratio. *Journal of Wealth Management* 6, no. 3: 77–83.

Jarque, C.M., and A.K. Bera. 1980. Efficient tests for normality, homoscedasticity and serial independence of regression residuals. *Economic Letters* 6, no. 3: 255–9.

Keating, C., and W.F. Shadwick. 2002. A universal performance measure. Working paper, The Finance Development Centre, London.

Lilliefors, H.W. 1967. On the Kolmogorov–Smirnov test for normality with mean and variance unknown. *Journal of the American Statistical Association* 62, June: 399–402.

Lee, S.L. 2007. Modified VAR and the allocation to real estate in the mixed-asset portfolio. International Real Estate Business School, University of Regensburg, Regensburg.

Longstaff, F.A., S. Mithal, and E. Neis. 2005. Corporate yield spreads: Default risk or liquidity? New evidence from the credit-default swap market. *Journal of Finance* 60, no. 5: 2214–54.

Longstaff, F.A., and B. Myers. 2009. Valuing toxic assets: An analysis of CDO equity. Working paper, NBER.

Mahadevan, S., and D. Schwartz. 2002. Hedge fund collateralized fund obligations. *Journal of Alternative Investments* 5, no. 2: 45–62.

Missinhoun, J., and L. Chacowry. 2005. Collateralized fund obligations: The value of investing in the equity tranche. *Journal of Structured Finance* 10, no. 4: 32–7.

Sortino, F.A., and L.N. Price. 1994. Performance measurement in a downside risk framework. *Journal of Investing* 3, Fall: 59–65.

Stone, C.A., and A. Zissu. 2004. Fund of fund securitizations. *Journal of Derivatives* 11, Summer: 62–9.

Sun, Q., and Y. Yan. 2003. Skewness persistence with optimal portfolio selection. *Journal of Banking and Finance* 27, no. 6: 1111–21.

Tayi, G., and P. Leonard. 1988. Bank balance sheet management: An alternative multiobjective model. *Journal of Operational Research Society* 39, no. 4: 401–10.

Optimal liquidation strategies regularize portfolio selection

Fabio Caccioli, Susanne Still, Matteo Marsili and Imre Kondor

We consider the problem of portfolio optimization in the presence of market impact, and derive optimal liquidation strategies. We discuss in detail the problem of finding the optimal portfolio under expected shortfall (ES) in the case of linear market impact. We show that, once market impact is taken into account, a regularized version of the usual optimization problem naturally emerges. We characterize the typical behavior of the optimal liquidation strategies, in the limit of large portfolio sizes, and show how the market impact removes the instability of ES in this context.

1. Introduction

The optimization of large portfolios is known to be highly unstable, due to large sample to sample fluctuations. This instability arises from the fact that risk measures need to be estimated from empirical observations in the market and for large portfolios we can never have enough data: by the very nature of portfolio selection, the sampling frequency cannot be high, and the look-back period cannot be too long. Therefore, the length T of the available time series cannot be sufficiently large compared to the number N of the different items in the portfolio: for large portfolios T may be, at best, of the same order of magnitude as N. Clearly, classical statistical methods cannot be expected to work in this regime.

This difficulty has been well known in portfolio theory, and a host of methods have been put forward to handle it (Jobson, Korkie, and Ratti 1979; Frost and Savarino 1986; Jorion 1986; Elton and Gruber 1995; Laloux et al. 1999, 2000; Macrae and Watkins 1999; Plerou et al. 1999, 2002; Jagannathan and Ma 2003; Ledoit and Wolf 2003, 2004a, 2004b; Burda et al. 2004; Potters and Bouchaud 2005; DeMiguel, Garlappi, and Uppal 2007; Garlappi, Uppal, and Wang 2007; Golosnoy and Okhrin 2007; Kan and Zhou 2007; DeMiguel et al. 2009; Frahm and Memmel 2009), but the problem was put in a particularly sharp light when it was recognized that for a critical value of the ratio N/T the estimation error actually diverges (Pafka and Kondor 2003; Kondor, Pafka, and Nagy 2007).

A similar statistical problem arises in many other areas, and methods known as regularization can be used as a remedy, see Still and Kondor (2009) and references therein. In the context of portfolio selection, regularization penalizes large excursions of the portfolio weight vector by imposing a constraint on the length, as measured in terms of a suitably chosen norm (Still and Kondor 2009). Regularized portfolio optimization, in general, then has two choices to make (Still and Kondor 2009): (i) which risk function to use, and (ii) which Lp-norm to use as a regularizer.

Regularized portfolio optimization was studied in Still and Kondor (2009) with the increasingly popular risk measure expected shortfall (ES) and the L2-norm. This scheme was shown in Still and Kondor (2009) to be related to support vector regression (Cortes and Vapnik 1995; Schölkopf et al. 2000), and Still and Kondor (2009) introduced the necessary modifications to the support vector machine algorithm which are required by the asymmetry of the ES risk measure and by the extra constraint imposed by the fixed budget. A number of other filtering techniques that use the variance as a risk measure also implement regularization (Macrae and Watkins 1999; Brodie et al. 2009), even when the link to statistical learning theory is not made explicit.[1]

The choice of the risk measure is a subject of ongoing debate (Szegö 2004). In this paper, we focus on the optimization of portfolios under the ES. ES is the mean loss above a high quantile.[2] The reason for our choice is that ES provides a more accurate estimate of risk when returns have fat-tailed distributions (Mandelbrot 1963; Fama 1965; Muller et al. 1990; Hols and Vries 1991; Mantegna and Stanley 1995) and it gives a more faithful representation of large losses than value at risk (VaR) (JP Morgan and Reuters 1996; Jorion 2000) that can be identified by the quantile itself. In addition, ES can be computed by fast linear programming algorithms (Rockafellar and Uryasev 2000) and, most significantly, it was shown (Acerbi 2002, 2004; Acerbi and Tasche 2002) to belong to the set of coherent risk measures (Artzner et al. 1999). These properties make it an attractive alternative to VaR which has been criticized for its lack of convexity (Artzner et al. 1999; Embrechts 2000; Acerbi, Nordio, and Sirtori 2001).

As for the choice of the regularizer, one has to realize that various regularizers act differently. The L2 norm has a tendency to favor equal weights, and thus acts as a diversification pressure (Bouchaud and Potters 2000; Still and Kondor 2009). The L1 norm can lead to more sparse solutions, see e.g., Tibshirani (1996) and Chen, Donoho, and Saunders (2001). In portfolio optimization, it corresponds to an exclusion of short positions (Brodie et al. 2009; DeMiguel et al. 2009). We refer the interested reader to Brodie et al. (2009), where its use with the variance as a risk measure is explored.[3] It is evident that the proper choice of the regularizer is merely not a matter of mathematical convenience: one has to motivate it on the basis of the nature of the problem in hand. In a Bayesian context, the choice of the regularizer expresses prior information, as it reflects what we know, or believe to know, about the possible structure in the data.

In this paper, we suggest that regularization inherently arises from considering the market impact of portfolio liquidation strategies, and we show how a linear assumption for the market impact leads to the L2 norm as a regularizer.

The fact that liquidity considerations effectively regularize portfolio selection is quite natural, in view of the origin of the instability and of the no-arbitrage hypothesis. In brief, it was shown (Kondor and Varga-Haszonits 2008; Varga-Haszonits and Kondor 2008) that the instability of risk measures arises because, when portfolio returns are estimated on a data set of finite length, then an *accidental arbitrage* may appear, corresponding to a zero cost portfolio which happens to have a positive return on that particular data set. When this occurs, the minimization of risk measures that have no lower bound (such as ES, for example) dictates to take an infinitely long position on these portfolios. However, in real markets, we expect that realized prices will react to the liquidation of a portfolio by adjusting prices in such a way as to eliminate accidental arbitrages. Therefore, taking the market impact of the liquidation into account as part of the portfolio optimization problem should intuitively regularize portfolio optimization.

The paper is organized as follows. In Section 2, we define the ES risk measure, set up the problem of its optimization, discuss its instability, and recall how to overcome this difficulty by regularization, as suggested in Still and Kondor (2009).

We show in Section 3 that regularization can be derived from estimating the risk of portfolio liquidation, within a linear assumption of market impact. This provides a clear financial motivation for choosing the L2-norm as a regularizer in the given problem. Note that this derivation does not depend on the choice of the risk function and that it therefore justifies and motivates the use of an L2-regularizer also in methods that use the variance as a risk measure. This market impact consideration is related to a recent proposal suggesting that portfolio optimization should be defined in terms of liquidation strategies (Acerbi and Scandolo 2007).

Section 4 provides a concrete illustration of how the regularizer works in typical cases. Following Ciliberti, Kondor, and Mezard (2007), we derive analytic results for typical instances of large portfolios, generated from a simple distribution. This shows that regularization, as suggested in Still and Kondor (2009), indeed removes the instability observed in Ciliberti, Kondor, and Mezard (2007), but it also shows the non-trivial role played by the confidence level: the more the risk measure is concentrated in the tail of the distribution, the weaker is the regularization induced by liquidity considerations.

The final section concludes with a short summary. Details of the derivation of the results presented in Section 4 are relegated to an appendix.

2. Expected shortfall, instability and regularization

We consider a portfolio $\{w_1 \dots w_N\}$ of N assets with returns $\{x_i\}$, with w_i the position of asset i. We impose a global budget constraint $\sum_{i=1}^N w_i = wN$ and we allow the weights $\{w_i\}$ to take any real value. The problem we address is that of finding the optimal weights $\{w_i\}$ that minimize the ES defined as follows. Given the loss $l(\{w_i\}|\{x_i\}) = -\sum_i w_i x_i$, the probability for such loss to be smaller than a threshold α is

$$P_<(\{w_i\},\alpha) = \int \prod_i \mathrm{d}x_i p(\{x_i\})\theta(\alpha - l(\{w_i\}|\{x_i\})), \tag{1}$$

with $\theta(x) = 1$ if $x > 0$ and $\theta(x) = 0$ otherwise. The associated β VaR is defined as

$$\beta\,\mathrm{VaR}(\{w_i\}) = \min\{\alpha : P_<(\{w_i\},\alpha) \geq \beta\}, \tag{2}$$

while the $\mathrm{ES}(\{w_i\})$ is given by

$$\mathrm{ES}(\{w_i\}) = \frac{1}{1-\beta}\int \prod_i \mathrm{d}x_i p(\{x_i\}) l(\{w_i\}|\{x_i\})\theta(l(\{w_i\}|\{x_i\}) - \beta\,\mathrm{VaR}(\{w_i\})). \tag{3}$$

The calculation of the ES (Rockafellar and Uryasev 2000) can be obtained through the minimization of the function

$$F_\beta(\{w_i\},v) = v + \frac{1}{1-\beta}\int \prod_i \mathrm{d}x_i p(\{x_i\})[l(\{w_i\}|\{x_i\}) - v]^+ \tag{4}$$

with respect to the auxiliary parameter v, where $[x]^+ = (x + |x|)/2$, i.e.

$$\mathrm{ES}(\{w_i\}) = \min_v F_\beta(\{w_i\},v). \tag{5}$$

Approximating the integral in Equation (4) by sampling the probability distributions of returns, the problem can be reduced to the calculation of the minimum of the cost function

$$E[v, \{u_\tau\}] = (1 - \beta)Tv + \sum_{\tau=1}^{T} u_\tau$$

under the constraints

$$u_\tau \geq 0 \quad \forall\tau,$$

$$u_\tau + v + \sum_{i=1}^{N} x_{i,\tau} w_i \geq 0 \quad \forall\tau$$

and

$$\sum_i w_i = wN,$$

where we have introduced a new set of variables defined as

$$u_\tau = \frac{(-v - \sum_{i=1}^{N} w_i x_{i,\tau}) + |(-v - \sum_{i=1}^{N} w_i x_{i,\tau})|}{2}.$$

Portfolio optimization often assumes that weights should satisfy a further constraint that fixes the expected return to some target value. However, it has been remarked (Merton 1980; Jagannathan and Ma 2003) that estimation error in sample expected returns is so large that nothing much is lost in ignoring this constraint altogether, with no appreciable effect on out-of-sample performance (Jorion 1986). Also, in applications such as index tracking, where the objective is to mimic a benchmark portfolio as closely as possible, this constraint is not needed. Finally, the issues we address below (Varga-Haszonits and Kondor 2008), the main argument and the results are not affected by the presence of a constraint on expected returns. So, for the sake simplicity, we omit this constraint in what follows.

2.1 *Instability of expected shortfall*

Being a conditional average, ES is not bounded from below: if a portfolio produces a large gain, rather than a loss, then ES takes a large negative value. Now, on a finite sample it may happen that one of the items, or a combination of items, *dominates* the others, i.e., produces a larger return at each time point than the rest. When such an apparent arbitrage occurs, the optimization of ES suggests to go as long as possible in the dominating asset and correspondingly short in the dominated ones. In particular, if there are no other constraints except for the fixed budget, then this leads to a runaway solution and to a seemingly infinite return. Therefore, for finite N and T the optimization of ES will have a finite solution with a probability always less than one. This probability quickly approaches one as N/T goes to zero, and quickly approaches zero as N/T goes to infinity. The transition between the two limits becomes sharper and sharper as N and T go to infinity such that their ratio is fixed, which is the realistic limit to consider for large institutional portfolios. In this limit there will be a critical value of the ratio N/T where a sharp transition occurs between the region where the optimization of ES leads to a finite solution and the one where it does not. This instability of ES was pointed out in Kondor, Pafka, and Nagy (2007), where the critical N/T as function of the cutoff beyond which the conditional average is calculated (i.e., the phase diagram) was determined numerically, while Ciliberti, Kondor, and Mezard (2007) derived an analytic expression for it by the help of tools borrowed from the statistical physics of random systems.

Although the ES is a specific case of the several possible risk measures, it was explicitly demonstrated (Kondor and Varga-Haszonits 2008) for all the coherent risk measures (Artzner et al. 1999) that the presence of apparent arbitrages constitutes a sufficient condition for the portfolio optimization problem to be unfeasible. Moreover, the same instability was shown to characterize also portfolio optimization problems under downside risk measures (Varga-Haszonits and Kondor 2008), including parametric VaR, one of the standard tools in banking. In the following, we will then focus on the specific case of ES with the idea that the results derived can be generalized to such wider classes of risk measures.

2.2 *Regularized portfolio optimization*

The essence of the problem discussed above, namely that the dimension (here N) is too high compared with the size of the statistical sample (T), is common to all fields where complex modelling or optimization problems arise. The field of statistical learning theory/machine learning (see, e.g., Vapnik and Chervonenkis 1971; Vapnik 1995, 1998) has developed powerful and systematic methods to deal with the difficulty of insufficient data. The insights gained in that area can be directly applied to portfolio optimization, as pointed out in Still and Kondor (2009).

The main observation is that the instability is caused by over-fitting, which in turn is caused by the fact that the empirical risk is minimized in a regime in which there is not enough data to guarantee small actual risk. The weights $\{w_i\}$ constitute a linear model of the observed returns, and the model capacity has to be constrained in order to avoid over-fitting. The capacity of the linear model is monotonic in the length of the weight vector, so that minimizing that length results in better generalization performance.

In the context of portfolio selection this means that the resulting portfolio better reflects the actual variations in the data by avoiding fluctuations due to small sample size effects. This line of reasoning leads to an optimization problem in which a modified version of ES is minimized (Still and Kondor 2009). The change that this introduces is known under the name of regularization, and if one chooses the L2-norm as a regularizer, then the resulting method is closely related (Still and Kondor 2009) to support vector regression (Cortes and Vapnik 1995; Schölkopf et al. 2000) and robust statistics (Huber 1981).

3. Regularization from market illiquidity

To generate cash, an investor has to liquidate (part of) his portfolio. The set up of the portfolio optimization problem above ignored the fact that this liquidation may have an impact on asset prices. Let us consider a situation in which an investor holds a portfolio of N assets and, at time t, liquidates a fraction of such portfolio $\vec{w}_t = (w_{1,t}, \dots, w_{N,t})$, with $w_{i,t}$ representing the position of asset i liquidated at time t. In the following, we assume that the liquidation of the portfolio $\vec{w}_t$ affects prices in a linear way

$$\vec{p}_{t+1} = \vec{p}_t + \vec{x}_t - \eta \vec{w}_t. \tag{6}$$

Here $\vec{x}_t$ is the vector of returns and η is an impact parameter. Note that investment is taken to move prices in the direction opposite to trading: selling ($w_{i,t} > 0$) will cause prices to fall and buying

($w_{i,t} < 0$) will push prices up. The cash flow generated on day t is then given by

$$c_t = \vec{w}_t \cdot \vec{p}_{t+1} = \vec{w}_t \cdot \vec{p}_t + \vec{w}_t \cdot (\vec{x}_t - \eta \vec{w}_t). \tag{7}$$

The first part $\vec{w}_t \cdot \vec{p}_t$ is known at time t, so risk only enters in the second part, $\vec{w} \cdot \vec{x} - \eta \|\vec{w}\|^2$, where we have dropped the subscript t to simplify the notation. Similarly to what is done in classical portfolio theory (Markowitz 1952), we consider the problem of finding the portfolio of minimal risk, for a given present value $\sum_i w_i p_{i,t} = wN$ of the realized cash flow. The parameter w plays the role of a normalization, and is customarily set to one, because risk is usually linear in the size of the portfolio. Here, however, the size of the portfolio matters as the impact of liquidation strategies on prices depends on the size. We therefore keep w as an independent parameter. In order to further simplify the notation, we consider $p_i = 1, \ \forall i$, so that we have the constraint

$$\sum_i w_i = wN. \tag{8}$$

As before, we take the ES as a risk measure. The loss is now given by $l(\{w_i\}|\{x_i\}) = -\vec{w} \cdot \vec{x} + \eta \|\vec{w}\|^2$, and we then have to find the minimum of the cost function

$$E_\eta[v, \{u_\tau\}] = (1-\beta)Tv + \sum_{\tau=1}^{T} u_\tau \tag{9}$$

under the constraints

$$u_\tau \geq 0 \quad \forall \tau, \tag{10}$$

$$u_\tau + v + \sum_{i=1}^{N} w_i x_{i,\tau} - \eta \|\vec{w}\|^2 \geq 0 \quad \forall \tau, \tag{11}$$

$$\sum_i w_i = wN. \tag{12}$$

All of the T inequality constraints contain a term that is independent of τ ($\tau = 1, \ldots, T$), given by

$$\epsilon = v - \eta \|\vec{w}\|^2. \tag{13}$$

Substitution of $\epsilon + \eta \|\vec{w}\|^2$ for v in the cost function, Equation (9), and multiplication by $1/2(1-\beta)T\eta$ leads us to the regularized ES problem proposed recently (see Still and Kondor 2009); Equation (7)–(10)):

$$\min_{\vec{w},\vec{u},\epsilon} \left[\frac{1}{2}\|\vec{w}\|^2 + C\left(\frac{1}{T}\sum_{\tau=1}^{T} u_\tau + (1-\beta)\epsilon \right) \right] \tag{14}$$

$$\text{s.t.} \quad \vec{w} \cdot \vec{x}_\tau + \epsilon + u_\tau \geq 0; \ u_\tau \geq 0 \quad \forall \tau, \tag{15}$$

$$\sum_i w_i = wN. \tag{16}$$

with

$$C = \frac{1}{2(1-\beta)\eta}. \tag{17}$$

We recognize that the term proportional to η in Equation (7) acts as a regularizer.

To develop a simple intuitive argument, imagine that there are two portfolios $\vec{w}^+$ and $\vec{w}^-$, each properly normalized (i.e., $\sum_i w_i^{\pm} = wN$), with $\vec{w}^+\vec{x}_\tau \geq \vec{w}^-\vec{x}_\tau$ for all $\tau = 1, \ldots, t$ and $\vec{w}^+\vec{x}_\tau > \vec{w}^-\vec{x}_\tau$ for at least one τ. Then, when $\eta = 0$, minimal ES would be realized by selling K units of $\vec{w}^-$ and buying $K + 1$ units of $\vec{w}^+$, with $K \to \infty$. This, as shown in Kondor and Varga-Haszonits (2008), is the origin of the instability in coherent risk measures. Such infinite returns cannot be realized, however, by liquidating a real portfolio because prices will adjust. In the linear approximation discussed here, when $\eta > 0$, the investment behavior discussed above is going to modify future returns, because $x_{i,t+1} \to x_{i,t+1} - \eta w_i$, thereby eliminating the apparent arbitrage. This effect reflects precisely the logic behind the no-arbitrage hypothesis.

4. Behavior of large random minimal risk portfolios under regularized expected shortfall

We have argued that the observed instability can be alleviated by regularization (Still and Kondor 2009). In particular, regularized portfolio selection under ES is related to support vector regression (Still and Kondor 2009). This opens up the way to apply the existing support vector algorithms, duly modified, to portfolio selection.

We will show here that, if we make an assumption on the distribution of the underlying data, then we can make progress by analytical means as well. We follow the calculation in Ciliberti, Kondor, and Mezard (2007) to see how the regularizer takes care of the instability. In the course of the calculation we make use of the powerful techniques of the statistical physics of random systems. Some details of the derivation are reported in the appendix, but these details are not necessary for the understanding of the result which is a very plausible extension of that in Ciliberti, Kondor, and Mezard (2007). Therefore, here we just quote the result and discuss its consequences, namely the removal of the singularity of the risk measure. We also refer the interested reader to the related literature within statistical learning theory, such as Opper (1995), Opper and Haussler (1995), Dietrich, Opper, and Sompolinsky (1999), Malzahn and Opper (2005) and references therein.

In the previous sections, both statistical and financial considerations led us to a cost function of the form

$$E[\epsilon, \{u_\tau\}] = (1-\beta)T\epsilon + \sum_{\tau=1}^{T} u_\tau + \tilde{\eta}\|w\|^2,$$

where $\tilde{\eta}$ can be expressed in terms of C or η. Starting from this expression, and averaging over the returns $\{x_{i,\tau}\}$ drawn from a Gaussian distribution[4] via the method described in the appendix, one arrives at a generalized cost function given in terms of three variational parameters Δ, $q_0 = \tilde{q}_0\Delta^2 = \sum w_i^2/N$, and $\epsilon = \tilde{\epsilon}\Delta$, as in Ciliberti, Kondor, and Mezard (2007)

$$E(\tilde{\epsilon}, \tilde{q}_0, \Delta) = \frac{w^2}{2\Delta} + \Delta\left[t(1-\beta)\tilde{\epsilon} - \frac{\tilde{q}_0}{2} + \frac{t}{2\sqrt{\pi}}\int_{-\infty}^{\infty} \mathrm{d}s e^{-s^2} g(\tilde{\epsilon} + s\sqrt{2\tilde{q}_0})\right] + \tilde{\eta}\tilde{q}_0\Delta^2, \quad (18)$$

where

$$g(x) = \begin{cases} 0, & x \geq 0, \\ x^2, & -1 \leq x \leq 0, \\ -2x - 1, & x < -1. \end{cases} \quad (19)$$

The difference with respect to Ciliberti, Kondor, and Mezard (2007) is that now we have an additional term proportional to q_0. Indeed, if one considers the definition of $\tilde{q}_0$, then the extra term $\tilde{\eta}\tilde{q}_0\Delta^2$ precisely maps into the term $\tilde{\eta}\|w\|^2$ added to the objective function.

Let us now discuss how the term proportional to $\|w\|^2$ in the cost function prevents the instability in the portfolio optimization problem. The first-order conditions on (18) with respect to the three variational parameters read

$$-1+\frac{t}{\sqrt{2\pi\tilde{q}_0}}\int \mathrm{d}s e^{-s^2} s g'(\tilde{\epsilon}+s\sqrt{2\tilde{q}_0})+2\tilde{\eta}\Delta=0, \tag{20}$$

$$1-\beta+\frac{1}{2\sqrt{\pi}}\int \mathrm{d}s e^{-s^2} g'(\tilde{\epsilon}+s\sqrt{2\tilde{q}_0})=0, \tag{21}$$

$$-\frac{w^2}{2\Delta^2}+t(1-\beta)\tilde{\epsilon}-\frac{\tilde{q}_0}{2}+\frac{t}{2\sqrt{\pi}}\int \mathrm{d}s e^{-s^2} g(\tilde{\epsilon}+s\sqrt{2\tilde{q}_0})+2\tilde{\eta}\Delta\tilde{q}_0=0. \tag{22}$$

In the original, non-regularized problem in Ciliberti, Kondor, and Mezard (2007) the instability of ES was indicated by the divergence of the parameter Δ which we will, therefore, call the susceptibility here. The divergence of this susceptibility is thus the signature of the instability, which made it expedient to rescale the variables as $\tilde{\epsilon}=\epsilon/\Delta$ and $\tilde{q}_0=q_0/\Delta^2$ in the first-order conditions. Note that the variables $\tilde{\epsilon}$ and $\tilde{q}_0$ are already finite.[5] This should be sufficient to conclude that all integrals over the variable s are finite. In order to see whether a solution with divergent susceptibility can exist, we now let $\Delta\to\infty$ in the first-order conditions. We first note that, in order for (22) to be satisfied, $\tilde{q}_0\Delta$ has to remain finite as $\Delta\to\infty$, i.e., $\tilde{q}_0=\alpha/\Delta$ with α finite. However, this is in contrast with a similar constraint we can deduce from Equation (20), where we find that a solution exists only if $\Delta\sqrt{\tilde{q}_0}$ is finite. Indeed, if we multiply all terms of (20) for $\sqrt{\tilde{q}_0}$ and impose $\tilde{q}_0=\alpha/\Delta$ we see that all the terms are bounded except the last one which diverges as $\sqrt{\Delta}$. We thus conclude that no solution with divergent susceptibility can be found as long as $\tilde{\eta}>0$.

The numerical solution of the first-order conditions confirms this prediction. In Figures 1 and 2, we show the behavior of $q_0=(1/N)\sum_i w_i^2$ and of Δ. We can clearly observe that the divergence, which is present for $\tilde{\eta}=0$, disappears as soon as $\tilde{\eta}>0$. This is further confirmed by Figure 3, where we show that, in the unfeasible region of the original problem, Δ diverges at $\tilde{\eta}=0$.

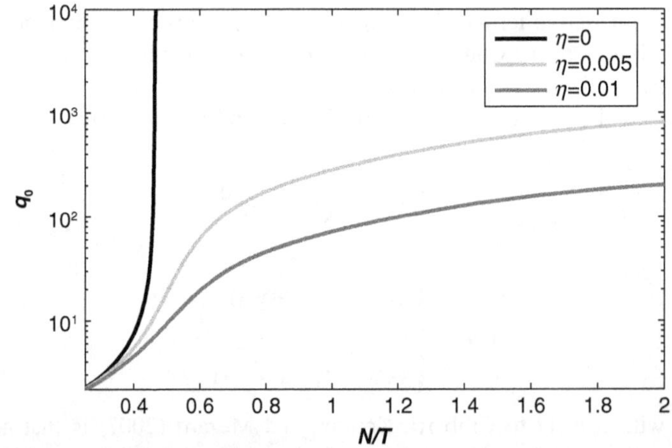

Figure 1. q_0 as a function of N/T for different values of $\tilde{\eta}$ and $\beta=0.7$.

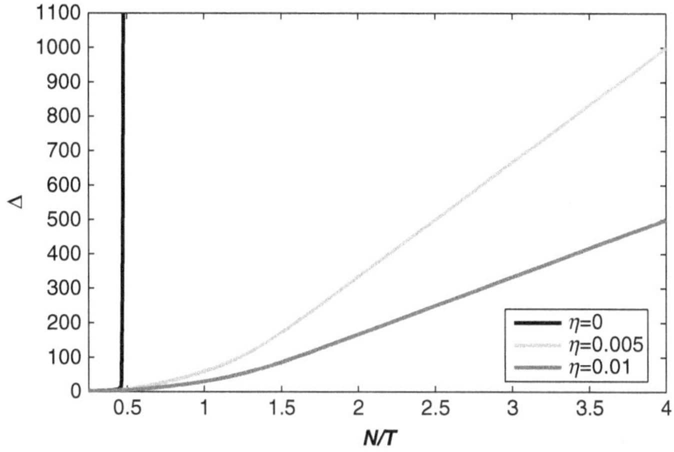

Figure 2. The susceptibility as a function of N/T for different values of $\tilde{\eta}$ and $\beta = 0.7$.

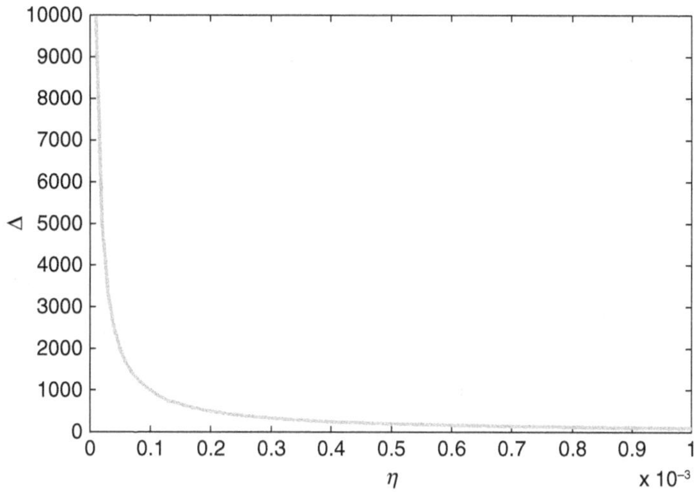

Figure 3. The susceptibility as a function of $\tilde{\eta}$ for the case $t = 1.5$ and $\beta = 0.7$.

5. Discussion

Let us now comment on the generality of the result. Concerning the linear assumption in Equation (6), which is standard in the econometric literature (Hasbrouck 1991), we observe that the estimate of market impact functions is a matter of active current research. Most of the empirical evidence suggests a convex shape (Eisler, Bouchaud, and Kockelkoren 2009), with the price impact growing slower than w. In double auction markets, if one restricts attention to the instantaneous impact of market orders, then the effect on the price depends on the shape of the order book. In order to discuss this case in some more detail, let $\rho_i(p,t)$ be the density of limit orders for asset i at time t, and consider the situation where a market order for a quantity w_i arrives at time t. If $p_{i,t-1}$ is the current price and $p_{i,t-1} + x_{i,t}$ is the price (of the transaction which occurred) just before the order arrives, then the price $p_{i,t}$ at which the transaction will take place is given by

$$w_i = \int_{p_{i,t-1}+x_{i,t}}^{p_{i,t}} \mathrm{d}p\rho_i(p,t). \tag{23}$$

A linear impact, as the one assumed in Equation (6), then corresponds to an order book with a constant density of limit orders. Hence, a measure of η is given by the density of the order book close to the best bid/ask. Since the density of the order book fluctuates and liquidity varies across assets, $\eta_{i,t}$ could also be taken as an asset-dependent stochastic quantity.

Then the computation of the ES can still be performed in terms of the cost function (9), but now with the T constraints

$$u_\tau + v + \sum_{i=1}^{N} w_i x_{i,\tau} - \sum_i \eta_{i,\tau} w_i^2 \geq 0 \tag{24}$$

in place of Equations (11). In this case, the mapping to a simple $L2$ regularizer that we have laid out in Section 3, is then complicated by the fact that the impact term depends on τ and cannot be absorbed into a τ independent constant. Nevertheless, we do not expect the essential features of the problem to change with respect to the case of a constant η.

Note furthermore that different assumptions for the market impact function lead to different regularizers. For example, considering the instantaneous impact and Equation (23), in the presence of a bid–ask spread, we expect the price to bounce from the bid to the ask, depending on the direction of trading (i.e., on the sign of w_i). This suggests a term proportional to the sign of w_i in the equation for the price, which, in turn, would then introduce an $L1$ regularizer. The choice of the regularizer and the behavior of regularized portfolio optimization under the different choices is a rich subject which deserves a separate treatment. However, this choice is related to market impact and liquidity risk considerations.

Note, finally, that the maximal loss (ML) limit, $\beta \to 1$, is non-trivial. In this limit, the ES reduces to the ML, which reads

$$\mathrm{ML}(\mathbf{w}) = \max_{t=1,\ldots,T} \left[-\sum_i w_i x_{i,t} \right]. \tag{25}$$

If we include the market impact term, i.e., if $x_{i,t} \to x_{i,t} - \eta w_i$ then

$$\mathrm{ML}(\mathbf{w}) = \eta \sum_i w_i^2 + \max_{t=1,\ldots,T} \left[-\sum_i w_i x_{i,t} \right],$$

which is clearly finite, for finite η. However, if the $\beta \to 1$ limit was taken in Equations (17), one would find that $C \to \infty$, suggesting that regularization would disappear. The correct limit is recovered (see the appendix) by keeping $T(1-\beta) = 1$, i.e., by taking $\beta = 1 - 1/T$, and then eventually letting $T \to \infty$. Therefore, $C = T/2\eta$, which implies that for large T and small η, liquidity considerations provide only a weak regularizer in the limit of ML.

6. Conclusion

We have shown that considering an optimal liquidation policy for a portfolio automatically leads to regularized portfolio optimization. Liquidity considerations provide a way to choose the regularizer. When the market impact is assumed to be linear, we obtain the L2-norm as a regularizer.

The typical behavior of large portfolios changes due to the regularization – the otherwise divergent fluctuations in the optimal solution are now tamed. This indicates that regularized portfolio optimization is a better investment strategy for large portfolios than traditional portfolio optimization, which minimizes only the empirical risk.

Acknowledgements

I.K. was supported by the 'Cooperative Center for Communication Networks Data Analysis', sponsored by the Teller program of the National Office of Research and Technology under grant No. KCKHA005. FC was supported by the National Science Foundation under Grant No. 0965673. He is also grateful for the hospitality extended to him at the University of Hawaii at Manoa, Honolulu, during the preparation of this work.

Notes

1. This includes works related to covariance shrinkage (Jagannathan and Ma 2003; Ledoitand Wolf 2003, 2004a,b; DeMiguel et al. 2009). For a discussion see also (Still and Kondor 2009) and references therein.
2. Note the sign convention: in the context of risk measures losses are counted positive.
3. L1 can produce a stable solution only if there is real structure in the data. If there is no structure (say all the items are more or less equivalent), then the solution with the L1 norm will still be sparse, but unstable, as the set of zero weights will vary from sample to sample (N. Gulyas and I. Kondor, unpublished data).
4. Here $x_{i,t}$ are taken as i.i.d. Gaussian variables with zero mean and variance $1/\sqrt{N}$. The latter ensures a meaningful limit $N, T \to \infty$ with $N/T = n$ constant, and is also realistic for typical cases where $N \sim 10^3 - 10^4$.
5. The divergence of $\tilde{\epsilon}$ and $\tilde{q}_0$ is prevented by Equation (21), that admits solutions only if the two variables are finite.
6. It helps to note that Δ is the susceptibility.

References

Acerbi, C. 2002. Spectral measures of risk: A coherent representation of subjective risk aversion. *Journal of Banking and Finance* 26, no. 7: 1505–18.

Acerbi, C. 2004. Coherent representations of subjective risk-aversion. In *Risk measures for the 21st century*, ed. G. Szegö. New York: Wiley.

Acerbi, C., C. Nordio, and C. Sirtori. 2001. Expected shortfall as a tool for financial risk management. Unpublished.

Acerbi, C. and G. Scandolo. 2007. Liquidity risk theory and coherent measures of risk. Available at SSRN: http://ssrn.com/abstract=1048322.

Acerbi, C. and D. Tasche. 2002. On the coherence of expected shortfall. *Journal of Banking and Finance* 26, no. 7: 1487–503.

Artzner, P., F. Delbaen, J.-M. Eber, and D. Heath. 1999. Coherent measures of risk. *Mathematical Finance* 9: 203–28.

Bouchaud, J.-P. and M. Potters. 2000 *Theory of financial risk - from statistical physics to risk management*. Cambridge, UK: Cambridge University Press.

Brodie, J., I. Daubechies, C.D. Mol, D. Giannone, and I. Loris. 2009. Sparse and stable markowitz portfolios. *Proceedings of the National Academy of Sciences, USA* 106, no. 30: 12267–72.

Burda, Z., A. Görlich, A. Jarosz, and J. Jurkiewicz. 2004. Signal and noise in correlation matrix. *Physica* A343: 295–310.

Chen, S., D. Donoho, and M. Saunders, 2001. Atomic decomposition by basis pursuit. *SIAM Review* 43: 129–59.

Ciliberti, S., I. Kondor, and M. Mezard. 2007. On the feasibility of portfolio optimization under expected shortfall. *Quantitative Finance* 7, no. 4: 389–96.

Cortes, C. and V. Vapnik. 1995. Support vector networks. *Machine Learning* 20, no. 3: 273–297.

DeMiguel, V., L. Garlappi, and R. Uppal. 2007. Optimal versus naive diversification: How efficient is the $1/n$ portfolio strategy? *Review of Financial Studies* 22, no. 5: 1915–53.

DeMiguel, V., L. Garlappi, F.J. Nogales, and R. Uppal. 2009. A generalized approach to portfolio optimization: Improving performance by constraining portfolio norms. *Management Science* 55, no. 5: 798–812.

Dietrich, R., M. Opper, and H. Sompolinsky. 1999. Statistical mechanics of support vector networks. *Physical Review Letters* 82, no. 14: 2975–8.

Eisler, Z., J.-P. Bouchaud, and J. Kockelkoren. 2009. The price impact of order book events: Market orders, limit orders and cancellations, preprint arXiv: 0904.0900.

Elton, E.J. and M.J. Gruber. 1995. *Modern portfolio theory and investment analysis*. New York: Wiley.

Embrechts, P. 2000 Extreme value theory: Potential and limitations as an integrated risk measurement tool. *Derivatives Use, Trading and Regulation* 6, no. 1: 449–56.

Fama, E. 1965 The behavior of stock market prices. *Journal of Business* 38, no. 1: 34–105.

Frahm, G. and C. Memmel. 2009. Dominating estimators for the global minimum variance portfolio. Deutsche Bundesbank, Discussion Paper, Series 2: Banking and Financial Studies.

Frost, P. and J. Savarino. 1986. An empirical Bayes approach to efficient portfolio selection. *Journal of Financial and Quantitative Analysis* 21, no. 3: 293–305.

Garlappi, L., R. Uppal, and T. Wang. 2007. Portfolio selection with parameter and model uncertainty: A multi-prior approach. *Review of Financial Studies* 20, no. 1: 41–81.

Golosnoy, V. and Y. Okhrin. 2007. Multivariate shrinkage for optimal portfolio weights. *The European Journal of Finance* 13, no. 5: 441–58.

Hasbrouck, J. 1991. Measuring the information content of stock trades. *Journal of Finance* 46, no. 1: 179–207.

Hols, M. and C.D. Vries. 1991. The limiting distribution of extremal exchange rate returns. *Journal of Applied Econometrics* 6, no. 3: 287–302.

Huber, P.J. 1981. *Robust statistics*. New York: Wiley.

Jagannathan, R. and T. Ma. 2003. Risk reduction in large portfolios: Why imposing the wrong constraints helps. *Journal of Finance* 58, no. 4: 1651–84.

Jobson, J.D., B. Korkie, and V. Ratti. 1979. Improved estimation for Markowitz portfolios using James–Stein type estimators. *Proceedings of the American Statistical Association (Business and Economic Statistics)* 1: 279–84.

Jorion, P. 1986. Bayes–Stein estimation for portfolio analysis. *Journal of Financial and Quantitative Analysis* 21, no. 3: 279–92.

Jorion, P. 2000. *VaR: The new benchmark for managing financial risk*. New York: McGraw-Hill.

JP Morgan and Reuters. 1996. *Riskmetrics*. Technical Document. http://www.riskmetrics.com.

Kan, R. and G. Zhou. 2007. Optimal portfolio choice with parameter uncertainty. *Journal of Financial and Quantitative Analysis* 42, no. 3: 621–56.

Kondor, I., S. Pafka, and G. Nagy. 2007. Noise sensitivity of portfolio selection under various risk measures. *Journal of Banking and Finance* 31, no. 5: 1545–73.

Kondor, I. and I. Varga-Haszonits. 2008. Feasibility of portfolio optimization under coherent risk measures. *Quantitative Finance*, submitted.

Laloux, L., P. Cizeau, J.-P. Bouchaud, and M. Potters. 1999. Noise dressing of financial correlation matrices. *Physical Review Letters* 83, no. 7: 1467–70.

Laloux, L., P. Cizeau, J.-P. Bouchaud, and M. Potters. 2000. Random matrix theory and financial correlations. *International Journal of Theoretical and Applied Finance* 3, no. 3: 391–7.

Ledoit, O. and M. Wolf. 2003. Improved estimation of the covariance matrix of stock returns with an application to portfolio selection. *Journal of Empirical Finance* 10, no. 5: 603–21.

Ledoit, O. and M. Wolf. 2004a. A well-conditioned estimator for large-dimensional covariance matrices. *Journal of Multivariate Analysis* 88, no. 2: 365–411.

Ledoit, O. and M. Wolf. 2004b. Honey, I shrunk the sample covariance matrix. *Journal of Portfolio Management* 30, no. 4: 110–19.

Macrae, R. and C. Watkins. 1999. Safe portfolio optimization. In *Proceedings of the IX international symposium of applied stochastic models and data analysis: quantitative methods in business and industry society, ASMDA-99, 14–17 June 1999, Lisbon, Portugal*, eds. H. Bacelar-Nicolau, F.C. Nicolau, and J. Janssen, 435. Portugal: INE, Statistics National Institute.

Malzahn, D. and M. Opper. 2005. A statistical physics approach for the analysis of machine learning algorithms on real data. *Journal of Statistical Mechanics Theory and Experiment* 2005: P11001.

Mandelbrot, B. 1963. The variation of certain speculative prices. *The Journal of Business of the University of Chicago* 38, no. 4: 394–419.

Mantegna, R. and E. Stanley. 1995. Scaling behavior in the dynamics of an economic index. *Nature* 376: 46–9.

Markowitz, H. 1952. Portfolio selection. *Journal of Finance* 7, no. 1: 77–91.

Merton, R. 1980. On estimating the expected return on the market: An exploratory investigation. *Journal of Financial Economics* 8, no. 4: 323–61.

Muller, U., M. Dacorogna, R. Olsen, O. Picte, M. Schwartz, and C. Morgenegg. 1990. Statistical study of foreign exchange rates, empirical evidence of a price change scaling law, and intraday analysis. *Journal of Banking and Finance* 14, no. 6: 1189–20.

Opper, M. 1995. Statistical mechanics of learning: Generalization. *The handbook of brain theory and neural networks*, 1st ed., 922–5. Cambridge, MA: MIT Press.
Opper, M. and D. Haussler. 1995. Bounds for predictive errors in the statistical mechanics of supervised learning. *Physical Review Letters* 75, no. 20: 3772–5.
Pafka, S. and I. Kondor. 2003. Noisy covariance matrices and portfolio optimization ii. *Physica* A 319: 487–94.
Plerou, V., P. Gopikrishnan, B. Rosenow, L.A.N. Amaral, T. Guhr, and H.E. Stanley. 2002. Random matrix approach to cross-correlations in financial data. *Physical Review E* 65, no. 6: 066126.
Plerou, V., P. Gopikrishnan, B. Rosenow, L. Amaral, and H. Stanley. 1999. Universal and non-universal properties of cross-correlations in financial time series. *Physical Review Letters* 83, no. 7: 1471–4.
Potters, M., J.-P. Bouchaud, and L. Laloux. 2005. Financial applications of random matrix theory: Old laces and new pieces. *Acta Phys. Pol.* B36, no. 9: 2767–84.
Rockafellar, R.T. and S. Uryasev. 2000. Optimization of conditional value-at-risk. *Journal of Risk* 2, no. 3: 21–41.
Schölkopf, B., A.J. Smola, R.C. Williamson, and P.L. Bartlett. 2000. New support vector algorithms. *Neural Computation* 12, no. 5: 1207–45.
Still, S. and I. Kondor. 2009. Regularizing portfolio optimization. *New Journal of Physics*, preprint arXiv: 0911.1694.
Szegö, G. ed. 2004. *Risk measures for the 21st century*. New York: Wiley.
Tibshirani, R. 1996. Regression shrinkage and selection via the lasso. *Journal of Royal Statistical Society B* 58, no. 1: 267–88.
Vapnik, V. 1995. *The nature of statistical learning theory*. New York: Springer.
Vapnik, V. 1998. *Statistical learning theory*. New York: Wiley.
Vapnik, V. and A. Chervonenkis. 1971. On the uniform convergence of relative frequencies of events to their probabilities. *Theory of Probability and its Applications* 16, no. 2: 264–80.
Varga-Haszonits, I. and I. Kondor. 2008. The instability of downside risk measures. *Journal of Statistical Mechanics Theory and Experiment* 2008: P12007.

Appendix 1. The replica calculation

We present here the calculation we use to solve the following optimization problem: find the minimum of the cost function

$$E[\epsilon, \{u_\tau\}] = (1-\beta)T\epsilon + \sum_{\tau=1}^{T} u_\tau + \tilde{\eta}\|w\|^2$$

under the constraints

$$u_\tau \geq 0,$$

$$u_\tau + \epsilon + \sum_{i=1}^{N} x_{i,\tau} w_i \geq 0$$

and

$$\sum_i w_i = wN.$$

The underlying process governing the returns is assumed to be i.i.d normal. We are using the machinery of statistical physics of random systems, and the terminology will be chosen accordingly. The calculation begins with regarding the cost function as a kind of abstract 'Hamiltonian' or energy functional and introducing a fictitious temperature associated with the system. The reason for this is purely technical, and the original problem will be recovered in the zero temperature limit.

Given a realization for the history of returns $\{x_{i,\tau}\}$, the calculation proceeds by considering the partition function or generating functional

$$Z_\gamma(\{x_{i,\tau}\}) = \int_{V(\{x_{i,\tau}\})} \mathrm{d}\vec{Y} \mathrm{e}^{-\gamma E[\vec{Y}]}, \tag{A1}$$

where γ is the inverse temperature, and we have used the notation $\vec{Y}$ to indicate the set of variables, and $V(\{x_{i,\tau}\})$ represents the portion of phase space where all constraints are satisfied. The minimum cost can then be computed as

$$\lim_{N\to\infty}\lim_{\gamma\to\infty} -\frac{\log Z_\gamma(\{x_{i,\tau}\})}{N\gamma}. \tag{A2}$$

In order to compute typical properties of the ensemble, we average over the probability distribution of returns, that is, we compute the average of $\log Z_\gamma(\{x_{i,\tau}\})$. This can be achieved through the replica trick by exploiting the identity

$$\langle \log Z\rangle = \lim_{n\to 0}\frac{\partial Z^n}{\partial n}. \tag{A3}$$

The replicated partition function, corresponding to the partition function of n copies of the system can be computed as (In the following calculation we do not keep track of multiplicative factors which are constant and do not contribute to the final free energy.)

$$Z^n_\gamma[x_{i,\tau}] = \int_{-\infty}^{\infty}\prod_{a=1}^{n}\mathrm{d}\epsilon^a \int_0^{\infty}\prod_{\tau=1}^{T}\prod_{a=1}^{n}\mathrm{d}u^a_\tau \int_{-\infty}^{\infty}\prod_{i=1}^{N}\prod_{a=1}^{n}\mathrm{d}w^a_i \int_{-\infty}^{\infty}\prod_{a=1}^{n}\mathrm{d}\lambda^a \tag{A4}$$

$$\times \int_0^{\infty}\prod_{\tau=1}^{T}\prod_{a=1}^{n}\mathrm{d}\mu^a_\tau \int_{-\infty}^{\infty}\prod_{\tau=1}^{T}\prod_{a=1}^{n}\mathrm{d}\hat{\mu}_\tau \exp\left\{\sum_a \lambda^a(\sum_i w^a_i - wN)\right\} \tag{A5}$$

$$\times \prod_\tau \exp\left\{\sum_a i\hat{\mu}^a_\tau\left(u^a_\tau + \epsilon^a + \sum_i x_{i,\tau}w^a_i - \mu^a_\tau\right)\right\} \tag{A6}$$

$$\times \exp\left\{-\gamma\sum_a(1-\beta)T\epsilon^a - \gamma\sum_{a,\tau}u^a_\tau - \gamma\tilde{\eta}\sum_i w^{a2}_i\right\}. \tag{A7}$$

Averaging over the quenched variables $\{x_{i,\tau}\}$ and introducing the overlap matrix $Q_{a,b} = (1/N)\sum_i w^a_i w^b_i$ one obtains:

$$Z^n_\gamma = \int [D\epsilon][Du][Dw][D\lambda][D\mu][D\hat{\mu}][DQ][D\hat{Q}]\exp\left\{\sum_a \lambda^a\left(\sum_i w^a_i - wN\right)\right\}$$

$$\times \exp\left\{-\gamma\sum_a(1-\beta)T\epsilon^a - \gamma\sum_{a,\tau}u^a_\tau - \gamma\tilde{\eta}\sum_i w^{a2}_i\right\}\prod_\tau \exp\left\{-\frac{1}{2}\sum_{a,b}\hat{\mu}^a_\tau Q_{a,b}\hat{\mu}^b_\tau\right\}$$

$$\times \exp\left\{\sum_{a,b}\hat{Q}_{a,b}\left(NQ_{a,b} - \sum_i w^a_i w^b_i\right)\right\}\prod_\tau \exp\left\{i\sum_a \hat{\mu}^a_\tau\left(u^a_\tau + \epsilon^a - \mu^a_\tau\right)\right\}.$$

Note: The variables $x_{i,\tau}$ are assumed to have zero average and variance $1/N$. Therefore, to leading order in N,

$$\langle e^{x_{i,\tau}\Gamma_{i,\tau}}\rangle \simeq \left\langle 1 + x_{i,\tau}\Gamma_{i,\tau} + \frac{1}{2}(x_{i,\tau}\Gamma_{i,\tau})^2 + \cdots\right\rangle \tag{A8}$$

$$= 1 + \frac{1}{2N}\Gamma^2_{i,\tau} + \cdots \tag{A9}$$

$$= e^{(1/2N)\Gamma^2_{i,\tau}}(1+\cdots), \tag{A10}$$

where $\Gamma_{i,\tau} = i\sum_a \hat{\mu}^a_\tau w^a_i$ and ... stands for higher order terms in expansion in powers of $1/N$. In other words, as long as the variance of $x_{i,\tau}$ is well defined, the results carry through irrespective of the specific distribution of $x_{i,\tau}$ (i.e., no assumption of Gaussian returns is needed). The calculation is performed for the simple case of independent returns. The case of returns with a given correlation matrix can also be dealt with.

We can now perform the Gaussian integral over the variables $\{\hat{\mu}_\tau^a\}$:

$$Z_\gamma^n = \int [D\epsilon][Du][Dw][D\lambda][D\mu][DQ][D\hat{Q}] \exp\left\{\sum_a \lambda^a \left(\sum_i w_i^a - wN\right)\right\}$$
$$\times \exp\left\{-\gamma \sum_a (1-\beta)T\epsilon^a - \gamma \sum_{a,\tau} u_\tau^a - \gamma\tilde{\eta} \sum_i w_i^{a2}\right\} \exp\left\{\sum_{a,b} \hat{Q}_{a,b} \left(NQ_{a,b} - \sum_i w_i^a w_i^b\right)\right\}$$
$$\times \prod_\tau \exp\left\{-\frac{1}{2}\sum_{a,b} \left(u_\tau^a + \epsilon^a - \mu_\tau^a\right) Q_{a,b}^{-1} (u_\tau^b + \epsilon^b - \mu_\tau^b)\right\} \exp\left\{-\frac{T}{2}\mathrm{tr}\log Q\right\}.$$

We are now allowed to perform a Gaussian integration over the variables $\{w_i^a\}$, which is going to bring the inverse of the operator $\hat{Q}_{a,b} + \gamma\tilde{\eta}\delta_{a,b}$ into the game:

$$Z_\gamma^n = \int [D\epsilon][Du][D\lambda][D\mu][DQ][D\hat{Q}] \exp\left\{\sum_a -w\lambda^a N\right\} \exp\left\{-\gamma \sum_a (1-\beta)T\epsilon^a - \gamma \sum_{a,\tau} u_\tau^a\right\}$$
$$\times \prod_\tau \exp\left\{-\frac{1}{2}\sum_{a,b} (u_\tau^a + \epsilon^a - \mu_\tau^a) Q_{a,b}^{-1} (u_\tau^b + \epsilon^b - \mu_\tau^b)\right\} \exp\left\{\sum_{a,b} \hat{Q}_{a,b} N Q_{a,b}\right\} \exp\left\{-\frac{T}{2}\mathrm{tr}\log Q\right\}$$
$$\times \exp\left\{-\frac{nN}{2}\log 2\right\} \exp\left\{-\frac{N}{2}\mathrm{tr}\log(\hat{Q} + \gamma\tilde{\eta}\delta_{a,b})\right\} \exp\left\{\frac{N}{4}\sum_{a,b} \lambda^a (\hat{Q}_{a,b} + \gamma\tilde{\eta}\delta_{a,b})^{-1}\lambda^b\right\}.$$

Integrating now over the $\{\lambda^a\}$ we obtain

$$Z_\gamma^n = \int [D\epsilon[Du][D\mu][DQ][D\hat{Q}] \exp\left\{-\gamma \sum_a (1-\beta)T\epsilon^a - \gamma \sum_{a,\tau} u_\tau^a\right\}$$
$$\times \prod_\tau \exp\left\{-\frac{1}{2}\sum_{a,b} (u_\tau^a + \epsilon^a - \mu_\tau^a) Q_{a,b}^{-1} (u_\tau^b + \epsilon^b - \mu_\tau^b)\right\} \exp\left\{N\sum_{a,b} \hat{Q}_{a,b} Q_{a,b}\right\} \exp\left\{-\frac{T}{2}\mathrm{tr}\log Q\right\}$$
$$\times \exp\left\{-\frac{nN}{2}\log 2\right\} \exp\left\{-\frac{N}{2}\mathrm{tr}\log(\hat{Q} + \gamma\tilde{\eta}\delta_{a,b})\right\} \exp\left\{-Nw^2 \sum_{a,b} (\hat{Q}_{a,b} + \gamma\tilde{\eta}\delta_{a,b})\right\}.$$

Introducing the variables $y_\tau^a = \mu_\tau^a - u_\tau^b$ and $z_\tau^a = \mu_\tau^a + u_\tau^b$ and integrating over the $\{z_\tau^a\}$ one is left with

$$Z_\gamma^n = \int [D\epsilon][DQ][D\hat{Q}] \exp\left\{-Nw^2 \sum_{a,b} (\hat{Q}_{a,b} + \gamma\tilde{\eta}\delta_{a,b}) - \gamma(1-\beta)\sum_a T\epsilon^a + N\sum_{a,b} \hat{Q}_{a,b} Q_{a,b}\right\}$$
$$\times \exp\left\{-Tn\log\gamma - \frac{T}{2}\mathrm{tr}\log Q - \frac{N}{2}\mathrm{tr}\log(\hat{Q} + \gamma\tilde{\eta}\delta_{a,b}) - \frac{nN}{2}\log 2\right\} \exp\{T\log Z_\gamma(\{\epsilon^a, Q\})\},$$

where we have defined

$$Z_\gamma(\{\epsilon^a, Q\}) = \int \prod_a \mathrm{d}y^a \exp\left\{-\frac{1}{2}\sum_{a,b} (y^a - \epsilon^a) Q_{a,b}^{-1} (y^b - \epsilon^b)\right\} \exp\left\{\gamma \sum_a y^a \theta(-y^a)\right\}.$$

We now take the replica symmetric (RS) ansatz

$$Q_{a,b} = \begin{cases} q_1, & a = b, \\ q_0, & a \neq b, \end{cases} \tag{A11}$$

$$\hat{Q}_{a,b} = \begin{cases} \hat{q}_1, & a = b, \\ \hat{q}_0, & a \neq b. \end{cases} \tag{A12}$$

and we define the susceptibility $\Delta q = q_1 - q_0$ as well as $\Delta\hat{q} = \hat{q}_1 - \hat{q}_0$. For Q^{-1}, we then have

$$Q^{-1}_{a,b} = \begin{cases} \dfrac{(\Delta q - q_0)}{(\Delta q)^2} + \mathcal{O}(n), & a = b, \\ \dfrac{-q_0}{(\Delta q)^2} + \mathcal{O}(n), & a \neq b. \end{cases} \tag{A13}$$

The effective partition function $Z_\gamma(\{\epsilon^a, Q\})$ reads

$$Z_\gamma(\{\epsilon^a, R^a, Q\}) = \int \prod_a \mathrm{d}x^a \exp\left\{-\frac{1}{2}\sum_{a,b} x^a Q^{-1}_{a,b} x^b\right\} \exp\left\{\gamma \sum_a (x^a + \epsilon^a)\theta(-x^a - \epsilon^a)\right\},$$

where we have defined $x^a = y^a - \epsilon^a$. By introducing a Gaussian variable s with measure $\mathrm{d}P_{q_0}(s) = (\mathrm{d}s/\sqrt{2\pi q_0})\mathrm{e}^{-s^2/2q_0}$ we obtain, in the limit $n \to 0$,

$$\frac{1}{n}\log(Z_\gamma(\{\epsilon^a, Q\}) = \frac{q_0}{2\Delta q} + \int \mathrm{d}P_{q_0}(s)\log B_\gamma(s, \epsilon, \Delta q),$$

where

$$B_\gamma(s, \epsilon, \Delta q) = \int \mathrm{d}x \exp\left\{-\frac{(x-s)^2}{2\Delta q} + \gamma(x+\epsilon)\theta(-x-\epsilon)\right\}.$$

If we also consider that

$$\operatorname{tr}\log Q = n\left(\log\Delta q + \frac{q0}{\Delta q}\right)$$

and

$$\operatorname{tr}\log(\hat{Q} + \gamma\tilde{\eta}\delta_{a,b}) = n\left(\log(\Delta\hat{q} + \gamma\tilde{\eta}) + \frac{\hat{q}_0}{(\Delta\hat{q} + \gamma\tilde{\eta})}\right),$$

we finally obtain the free energy

$$\begin{aligned} -\frac{\gamma F(q_0, \Delta q, \hat{q}_0, \Delta\hat{q}, \epsilon)}{nN} &= q_0\Delta\hat{q} + \hat{q}_0\Delta q + \Delta q\Delta\hat{q} - w^2(\Delta\hat{q} + \gamma\tilde{\eta}) - \gamma t(1-\beta)\epsilon - t\log\gamma \\ &\quad + t\int \mathrm{d}P_{q_0}(s)\log B_\gamma(\epsilon, s, R, \Delta q) - \frac{t}{2}\log\Delta q - \frac{\log 2}{2} - \frac{1}{2}\left(\log(\Delta\hat{q} + \gamma\tilde{\eta}) + \frac{\hat{q}_0}{\Delta\hat{q} + \gamma\tilde{\eta}}\right), \end{aligned}$$

where we have put $T = tN$. From the saddle point equations for $\hat{q}_0$ and $\Delta\hat{q}$ we get

$$\Delta\hat{q} + \gamma\tilde{\eta} = \frac{1}{2\Delta q},$$

$$\hat{q}_0 = \frac{w^2 - q_0}{2(\Delta q)^2}.$$

Exploiting these relations the free energy becomes

$$-\gamma f(\epsilon, q_0, \Delta q) = -\frac{\gamma F}{nN} = \frac{1}{2} - t\log\gamma - \gamma t(1-\beta)\epsilon + t\int \mathrm{d}P_{q_0}(s)\log B_\gamma(\epsilon, s, R, \Delta q)$$
$$+\frac{1-t}{2}\log\Delta q + \frac{q_0 - w^2}{2\Delta q} - \gamma\tilde{\eta}q_0.$$

Note that

$$\Delta q = \frac{1}{2N}\sum_i (w_i^a - w_i^b)^2 \tag{A14}$$

is the squared distance between two approximate solution of the optimization problem, drawn with a Gibbs measure with energy E. As $\gamma \to \infty$ the Gibbs measure gets more and more peaked on the optimal solution. If the latter is unique, then we expect $\Delta q \to 0$. Indeed, given that the measure is nearly Gaussian, we expect $\Delta q \sim 1/\gamma$. Hence, in the large γ limit, it is natural to rescale $\Delta q = \Delta/\gamma$ keeping ϵ and q_0 independent of γ. In this limit, we obtain the energy function

$$E = t(1-\beta)\epsilon - \frac{q_0 - w^2}{2\Delta} - \int_{-\infty}^{-\Delta}\frac{\mathrm{d}x}{\sqrt{2\pi q_0}}\mathrm{e}^{-(x-\epsilon)^2/(2q_0)}\left(x + \frac{\Delta}{2}\right) + \frac{t}{2\Delta}\int_{-\Delta}^{0}\frac{\mathrm{d}x}{\sqrt{2\pi q_0}}\mathrm{e}^{-(x-\epsilon)^2/(2q_0)}x^2.$$

We now define $\tilde{x} = x/\Delta$, $\tilde{\epsilon} = \epsilon/\Delta$ and $\tilde{q}_0 = q_0/\Delta^2$. The reason for this change of variables is that we want to expose the singular behavior at the phase transition in terms of a single divergent quantity[6] Δ. Hence, we anticipate that $\tilde{\epsilon}$ and $\tilde{q}_0$ are going to attain finite values at the transition. In terms of the rescaled variables, we have

$$E(\tilde{\epsilon}, \tilde{q}_0, \Delta) = \frac{w^2}{2\Delta} + \Delta\left[t(1-\beta)\tilde{\epsilon} - \frac{\tilde{q}_0}{2} + \frac{t}{2\sqrt{\pi}}\int_{-\infty}^{\infty}\mathrm{d}s\mathrm{e}^{-s^2}g(\tilde{\epsilon} + s\sqrt{2\tilde{q}_0})\right] + \tilde{\eta}t\tilde{q}_0\Delta^2,$$

where

$$g(x) = \begin{cases} 0, & x \geq 0, \\ x^2, & -1 \leq x \leq 0, \\ -2x-1, & x < -1 \end{cases} \tag{A15}$$

and $\tilde{q}_0$ and $\tilde{\epsilon}$ are the solutions of the saddle point equations

$$-1 + \frac{t}{\sqrt{2\pi\tilde{q}_0}}\int \mathrm{d}s\mathrm{e}^{-s^2}sg'(\tilde{\epsilon} + s\sqrt{2\tilde{q}_0}) + 2\tilde{\eta}\Delta = 0, \tag{A16}$$

$$1 - \beta + \frac{1}{2\sqrt{\pi}}\int \mathrm{d}s\mathrm{e}^{-s^2}g'(\tilde{\epsilon} + s\sqrt{2\tilde{q}_0}) = 0, \tag{A17}$$

$$-\frac{w^2}{2\Delta^2} + t(1-\beta)\tilde{\epsilon} - \frac{\tilde{q}_0}{2} + \frac{t}{2\sqrt{\pi}}\int \mathrm{d}s\mathrm{e}^{-s^2}g(\tilde{\epsilon} + s\sqrt{2\tilde{q}_0}) + 2\tilde{\eta}\Delta\tilde{q}_0 = 0. \tag{A18}$$

Appendix 2. The maximal loss problem

We show here how to recover the correct $\beta \to 1$ limit leading to the ML problem. The problem of finding the set of weights that minimizes the ML (25) can be cast into that of finding the minimum of the cost function

$$E[u] = u \tag{A19}$$

under the constraints

$$u + \sum_i w_i x_{i,t} \geq 0 \quad \forall t$$

and

$$\sum_i w_i = wN.$$

Let us show how this can be recovered starting from the general problem for the ES

$$E[\epsilon, \{u_\tau\}] = (1-\beta)T\epsilon + \sum_{\tau=1}^{T} u_\tau, \tag{A20}$$

$$u_\tau \geq 0 \quad \forall \tau, \tag{A21}$$

$$u_\tau + \epsilon + \sum_{i=1}^{N} x_{i,\tau} w_i \geq 0 \quad \forall \tau, \tag{A22}$$

$$\sum_i w_i = wN. \tag{A23}$$

The first observation is that, for $\epsilon \geq ML$, (A22) is satisfied for any set of $\{u_{i,\tau}\}$ satisfying Equation (A21). The minimum of the cost function can then be obtained by taking ϵ equal to the ML and $u_{i,\tau} = 0 \; \forall i, \tau$. By comparing the resulting expression for Equation (A20) with Equation (A19), we can see that the two are equivalent if we keep $T(1-\beta) = 1$. If we now introduce the regularization, then the cost function for the ML problem reads

$$E[u, \{w_i\}] = u + \frac{T}{2C} \|\vec{w}\|^2.$$

As in Section 3, an equivalent expression can be obtained by introducing the effect of the price impact. The two approaches are equivalent once we have taken

$$C = \frac{T}{2\eta}. \tag{A24}$$

Note that one can derive Equation (A24) also by taking $1-\beta = 1/T$ in (17), which is indeed the appropriate confidence level for ML, because in a finite time window of T points, the worst possible outcome occurs with probability $1-\beta = 1/T$.

Nonlinear dynamics in economics and finance and unit root testing

Efthymios G. Pavlidis, Ivan Paya, David A. Peel and Costas Siriopoulos

The recent financial crisis exposed the inability of traditional theoretical and empirical models to parsimoniously capture the rich dynamics of the economic environment. This has stimulated the interest of both academics and practitioners in the development and application of more sophisticated models. By allowing for the presence of nonlinearities, complex dynamics, multiple equilibria, structural breaks and spurious trends, these latter models resemble more closely the properties of economic and financial time series. In this article, we illustrate the flexibility of a family of econometric models, namely the exponential smooth transition autoregressive (ESTAR), to encompass several of the above characteristics. We then re-assess the power of the ESTAR unit root test developed by Kapetanios, Shin and Snell (2003) in the presence of nuisance parameters typically encountered in the literature and compare its performance with that of the augmented Dickey-Fuller and the Enders and Granger (1998) tests. Our results show the lack of dominance of any particular test and that the power is not independent to priors about the nuisance parameters. Finally, we examine several asset price deviations from fundamentals and one hyper-inflation series and find contradictory results between the nonlinear fitted models and unit root tests. The findings highlight that new testing procedures with higher power are desirable in order to shed light on the behavior of financial and economic series.

1. Introduction

Asset price misalignments have been at the heart of the debates about the economic development of countries in the last few years. The recent global economic turndown has been characterized by substantial fluctuations in asset prices in the years prior to it as well as in its aftermath. Understanding the variations of prices in asset markets and their information content is crucial in order to assess the factors that were behind the crisis and the policy reactions to them.

Traditional models in economics and finance establish a linear framework in which asset prices are closely tied to fundamentals. For instance, with respect to stock markets, the cost of the carry model predicts that stock futures prices should comove with spot prices (Taylor et al. 2000). While the log-linear present value models imply a linear relationship between log dividends and prices (Campbell and Shiller 1988). Similarly in the housing market, which appears to have triggered the recent financial crisis (for a discussion see Ackermann 2008), as long as the real value of residential property is a constant proportion of the expected value of future real disposable income, the house price to income ratio should be stable (Black, Fraser, and Hoesli 2006). Finally, the purchasing power parity (PPP) predicts a linear relationship between the exchange rate and aggregate price levels.

In most cases, the results of empirical research based on traditional models are discouraging. These models cannot explain the observed large swings in asset prices. Deviations from the predicted fundamental values appear to wander with no tendency to revert to a single equilibrium point. This finding is in sharp contrast to the theory and highlights the risk of employing linear models in economic decision-making, such as risk management, for the efficient operation of capital markets and, hence, the efficient allocation of the economy's resources.

During the last two decades, numerous theoretical and empirical contributions have attempted to shed light on the poor performance of traditional models. Perhaps the most important explanation provided is that the failure to find economically meaningful results is due to the assumption of linearity. In fact, a number of authors have provided evidence supporting the existence of rich dynamics in financial series (see Sollis, Leybourne, and Newbold 2000; Kyrtsou and Vorlow 2009). A family of nonlinear models which is gaining popularity in finance and macroeconomics is the exponential smooth transition autoregressive (ESTAR). The ESTAR functional form has three particularly appealing features.

First, it is in line with the presence of limits to arbitrage in financial and commodity markets due to market frictions, uncertainty regarding equilibrium asset prices and heterogeneous agents. These factors make deviations from equilibrium and arbitrage conditions inherently nonlinear and highly persistent. On this basis, applications of the ESTAR model and ESTAR unit root tests include modeling deviations from the covered interest parity (Peel and Taylor 2002), spot-futures relationship (Sarno and Monoyios 2002), dividend-price ratios (Gallagher and Taylor 2001), optimal money holdings (Sarno, Taylor, and Peel 2003), as well as deviations of nominal exchange rates from the equilibrium value suggested by PPP (Michael, Nobay, and Peel 1997; Taylor, Peel, and Sarno 2001; Kilian and Taylor 2003).

Because factors, such as the degree of market frictions and preferences, may change over time, recent studies have extended the analysis to allow also for structural change (see Lundbergh, Tërasvirta, and van Dijk 2003; Sollis 2005, 2008; Pavlidis, Paya, and Peel 2009). Notably, Sollis (2005), motivated by the work of Papell (2002) on modeling abrupt changes in the deterministic components of linear unit root tests, employs the exponential transition function to allow for non-monotonic gradually changing trends in the real exchange rate process. The author finds that the incorporation of gradual rather than abrupt changes in the trend function leads to substantially stronger evidence in favor of stationarity. While Sollis (2008) derives a unit root test based on a very general time-varying smooth transition model and shows that numerous US dollar real exchange rates exhibit both nonlinearity and structural change.

The second appealing feature of ESTAR models is that they can display multiple equilibria. This property might turn out to be crucial for capturing the salient aspects of series such as real interest rates and inflation. Models of monetary policy rules suggest that once you take into account the zero bound on nominal interest rates, real interest rates might follow a number of equilibria (see e.g. Benhabib, Schmitt-Grohe, and Uribe 2001). In their seminal paper, Sargent and Wallace (1973) show that when authorities print money to finance a real budget deficit, inflation is a nonlinear process with two equilibria, one stable and the other unstable.[1] Moreover, a stylized fact regarding inflation is the high persistence of the series. In numerous empirical and theoretical contributions, inflation is assumed to be a linear integrated of order one, I(1), process. However, this assumption has severe economic and statistical implications. The nominal exchange rate, via PPP, should be an I(2) process, and nominal asset returns would exhibit unit root behavior, which is in sharp contrast with the empirical findings. Clearly, the performance of unit root tests is crucial in this context.

Third, ESTAR models can exhibit complex, possibly chaotic, dynamics. Several authors provide empirical evidence in favor of complex dynamics in economic and financial series (see Bonanno, Lillo, and Mantegna 2001). In addition to the empirical findings, there are several theoretical models that support a complex data generating mechanism. Day (1982) modifies the neoclassical growth model and shows that growth cycles can exhibit an asymmetric saw-toothed pattern. Grandmont (1985) employs overlapping generations models to illustrate how a deterministic equilibrium model can produce regular asymmetric cycles as well as chaotic dynamics. Chapell (1997) shows how a discrete version of the Sargent and Wallace (1973) model of hyper-inflation can exhibit both complex and chaotic dynamics.

Regarding financial markets and their instability, Brock (1988) and De Grauwe, Dewachter, and Embrechts (1993) construct heterogeneous agents models which can generate similar complex behavior, or even chaos, in asset prices. As illustrated by De Grauwe and Grimaldi (2006) and Kaizoji (2004), speculative bubbles can be endogenized in these type of models. Kyrtsou and Malliaris (2009), motivated by the fact that the underlying process of economic series may well be nonlinear, extend the analysis to nonlinear trading rule models. Their findings show that, due to the inherent structural complexity of the system, the arrival of new information can induce high volatility and instability. In a related study, Kyrtsou (2008) demonstrates how conditional heteroskedasticity, a stylized property of financial series at high frequencies, can arise endogenously in agent-based models. Extreme events and large and persistent deviations from fundamentals predicted by these type of models can clearly have contagion effects on other sectors of the economy and lead to financial crises. All the above arguments motivate a nonlinear adjustment mechanism with possible multiple equilibria and complex dynamics such as the one provided by the ESTAR model.

The first contribution of this article is to illustrate and discuss the relevant properties of ESTAR processes to macroeconomic and financial modeling in Section 2. Given the widespread application of integration and cointegration techniques in macroeconomic modeling and decision-making, we also examine the properties of the most widely employed ESTAR unit root test, the Kapetanios, Shin, and Snell (2003) (KSS hereafter) test, and compare it with two more general tests in Section 2.

To be more specific, the Kapetanios, Shin, and Snell (2003) testing procedure formally distinguishes between nonlinear single equilibria globally stationary processes and unit root processes. On the basis of Monte Carlo simulation experiments, KSS conclude that their procedure improves substantially upon existing tests. In particular, their nonlinear unit root test appears to have better power properties that the standard augmented Dickey-Fuller test (ADF hereafter) and the statistic proposed by Enders and Granger (1998) (EG hereafter).

In this article, we extend the analysis of KSS in three directions. First, we employ a different range of parameter values than the ones considered initially by Kapetanios, Shin, and Snell (2003). The new range approximates the range of values typically reported in the empirical literature and corresponds to ESTAR processes which exhibit more closely unit root-like behavior. Second, we examine the impact of uncertainty regarding the presence of deterministic components in the data-generating process (DGP) on the performance of the test. Clearly, researchers are often ignorant and in many cases have no priors about the true DGP so that they have to rely on hypothesis testing to determine the significance of deterministic components. Given that ESTAR models can exhibit spurious constants and trends (Paya and Peel 2003), the examination of the impact of the specification procedure on the performance of nonlinear tests appears important. Finally, we investigate further the impact of multiple equilibria on the performance of the nonlinear test. This exercise is interesting because the test is based on the assumption of a single equilibrium point.

Section 4 examines the performance of the unit root tests on financial and macroeconomic time series that have been suggested to follow nonlinear processes as mentioned above.

2. Modeling nonlinear economic and financial dynamics with the ESTAR model

A typical ESTAR model for a univariate time series y_t is given by

$$y_t = \beta y_{t-1} + \gamma y_{t-1}[1 - \exp(-\theta y_{t-d}^2)] + \epsilon_t,$$

or, equivalently,

$$\Delta y_t = \phi y_{t-1} + \gamma y_{t-1}[1 - \exp(-\theta y_{t-d}^2)] + \epsilon_t, \quad (1)$$

where β, γ and θ are constants, $\phi = \beta - 1$ and $\epsilon_t \sim \text{iid}(0, \sigma^2)$ is the disturbance term.[2] When $\gamma < 0$ and $\phi + \gamma < 0$, the process is globally mean reverting although close to the equilibrium it may exhibit unit root or even explosive behavior. As aforementioned, the fact that ESTAR models allow the speed of mean reversion of the process toward the equilibrium to be a function of the distance from the equilibrium is particularly appealing in modeling several macroeconomic and financial variables. It has been proved that the presence of transactions costs and other market frictions in arbitrage models imply this type of nonlinear adjustment mechanism.

However, for different parameter values, the ESTAR model can display multiple equilibria, complex dynamics and chaotic-like behavior that can lead to misleading conclusions when unit root tests are employed. For instance, consider the following model

$$y_t = 1.1 y_{t-1} \exp(-8.059(y_{t-3} - 0.175)^2) + \epsilon_t \quad (2)$$

which is globally stationary and corresponds to $\beta = 1$. Figure 1, which depicts Δy_t against y_{t-1}, shows that the process has three equilibria which correspond to the cases where the curve intersects with the horizontal axis. The stable equilibria are given by 0 and 0.283. To shed more light on the properties of the process, we simulate Equation (2) without noise and a starting value of 0.1. The first 100 realizations of the series are presented in Figure 2. The process moves from the starting value to the high equilibrium with oscillations. This behavior could be mistakenly interpreted as either explosive or suggestive of a time trend in small samples. Figure 3 shows 100 observations of the same process with the noise switched on. It can be observed that the series exhibits high persistence, which makes it difficult to distinguish it from a process with an intercept

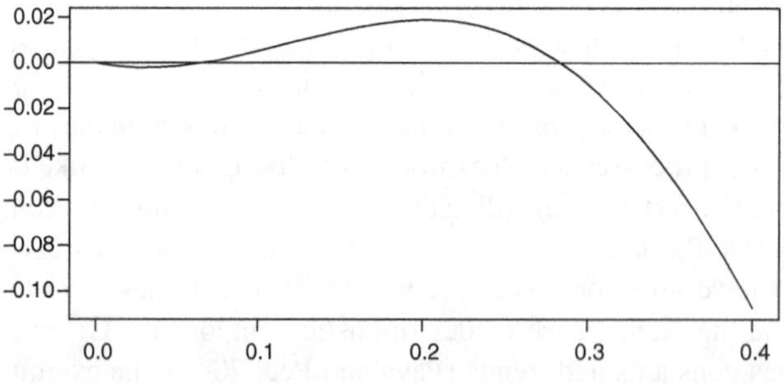

Figure 1. Equilibria of the skeleton of Model (2).

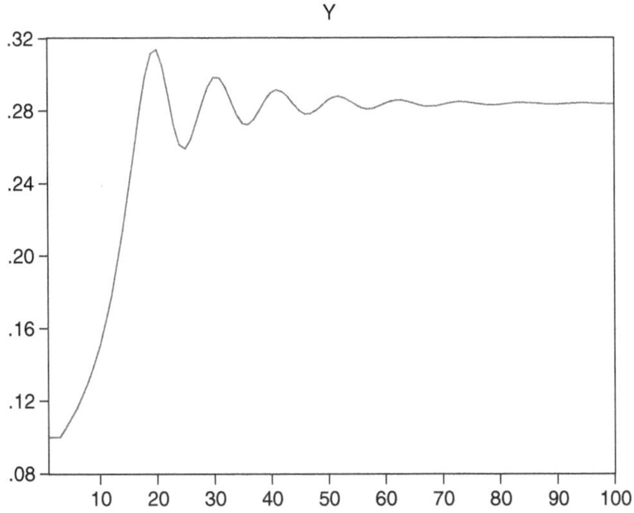

Figure 2. Realization of Model (2) with no noise and starting value of 0.1.

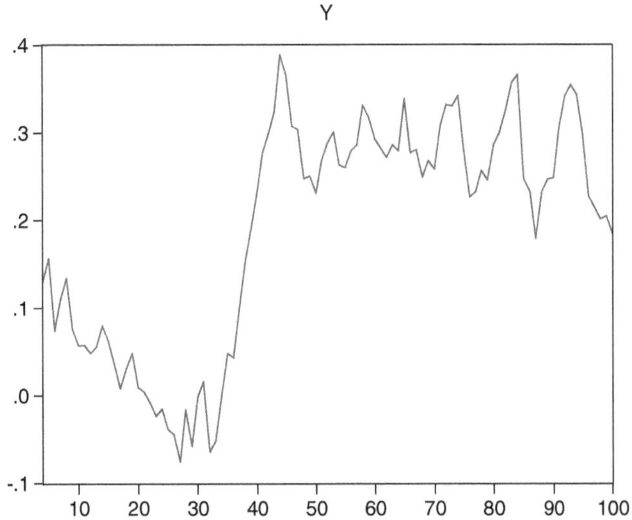

Figure 3. Realization from Model (2) with noise and starting value of 0.1.

and trend, a unit root or even an explosive process.[3] Lundbergh and Teräsvirta (2002) conduct a similar simulation experiment using a stationary logistic smooth transition autoregressive (STAR) process that fluctuates between two local means. Their overall conclusion is that standard unit root tests when applied to these series do not reject the unit root hypothesis.

Macroeconomic and financial series may in fact exhibit this type of behavior. Byers and Peel (2000) motivated by the theoretical literature on inflation dynamics fit ESTAR models to the inflation series of high inflation countries. They examine Brazil and Argentina in the second half of the twentieth century and Germany in the interwar period.[4] Their results support the presence of multiple equilibria. In particular, Brazil has a stable high inflation equilibrium, while for the remaining two countries the high inflation state is characterized by inflation cycles. This finding has potential consequences for asset markets, such as the foreign exchange (FX) and bond markets, through spillover effects. Exchange rates, interests rates and asset returns are linked with prices through, for example, the PPP hypothesis and the Fisher equation.

The ESTAR model is also capable of mimicking the chaotic-type behavior which can arise in asset prices through the interaction of chartists and fundamentalists in the market. Heterogeneous agents models have been derived for the FX market (De Grauwe, Dewachter, and Embrechts 1993), the stock market (Huang and Day 1993) and the housing market. To illustrate this point, we slightly modify Equation (2) by changing the autoregressive parameter from 1.1 to 1.5. Figure 4 illustrates the path of the series in the case of no noise for 200 observations. In this case, the series exhibit cycles of 34 periods. Close inspection of the figure would show that the values of the series do not ever repeat. Figure 5 shows a scatter diagram of y_t on y_{t-34} for the whole 10,000 replications, which corroborates this fact. Clearly, the above could be falsely considered as evidence in favor of chaotic behavior. This example highlights the importance of accurate econometric estimation and inference when dealing with highly complex dynamics. Coefficients values within the 95% confidence interval could in fact have radically different economic implications for the series under consideration.

We have so far demonstrated the flexibility of a simple ESTAR model to nest a number of alternative processes with high persistence, spurious trends, multiple equilibria and chaotic-like behavior suggested by different theoretical models in the financial and economic literature. Given the popularity of the ESTAR model, KSS focus on the issue of persistence and propose a test to discriminate between a linear unit root process and a globally stationary ESTAR. The next section extends the work of KSS in examining its performance in cases of extreme persistence, multiple equilibria and no priors regarding the DGP deterministic components.

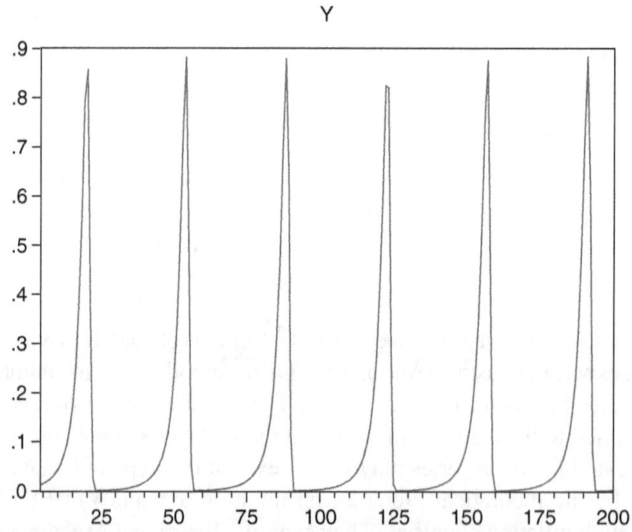

Figure 4. Realization from Model (2) with autoregressive coefficient 1.5, no noise and starting value of 0.1.

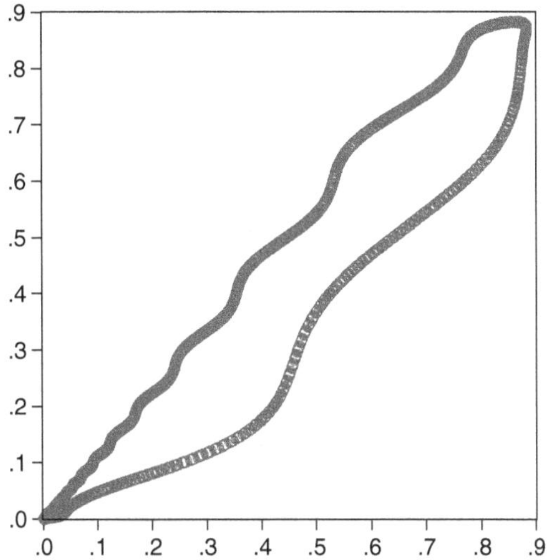

Figure 5. Scatter plot of y_t on y_{t-34} of 10,000 realizations from Model (2) with autoregressive coefficient 1.5, no noise.

3. Nonlinear unit root tests

Consider Equation (1) and let the process exhibit the unit root behavior in the inner regime ($\phi = 0$ or, equivalently, $\beta = 1$) and the delay parameter be equal to unity, $d = 1$. It follows that

$$\Delta y_t = \gamma y_{t-1}[1 - \exp(-\theta y_{t-1}^2)] + \epsilon_t, \tag{3}$$

and by following Luukkonen, Saikkonen, and Tërasvirta (1988) and taking a first-order Taylor series approximation

$$\Delta y_t = \delta y_{t-1}^3 + u_t. \tag{4}$$

Under the null hypothesis of a linear unit root model, $H_0 : \delta = 0$. While under the alternative $H_1 : \delta < 0$. The KSS test statistic is written as

$$t_{\mathrm{NL}} = \frac{\hat{\delta}}{\text{s.e.}(\hat{\delta})} \tag{5}$$

and converges weakly to a functional of Brownian motions.

Contrary to the KSS test, the EG test is based on the assumption that the adjustment mechanism is abrupt. Specifically, y_t is assumed to be a threshold autogressive process such that

$$\Delta y_t = \begin{cases} \rho_1 y_{t-1} + \epsilon_t, & \text{if } y_{t-1} \le 0, \\ \rho_2 y_{t-1} + \epsilon_t, & \text{if } y_{t-1} > 0, \end{cases} \tag{6}$$

or equivalently,

$$\Delta y_t = I_t \rho_1 y_{t-1} + (1 - I_t)\rho_2 y_{t-1} + \epsilon_t, \tag{7}$$

where I_t is the Heaviside function that takes the value of unity if $y_{t-1} \le 0$ and zero otherwise. Note that the above regression allows for asymmetric adjustment of the process. In this setting, testing for a unit root corresponds to testing the null hypothesis $H_0 : \rho_1 = \rho_2 = 0$ with an F-test. Like the t_{NL}, the EG F-type statistic does not follow a standard asymptotic distribution.

In the presence of the serial correlation in the residuals, Equations (4) and (7) are augmented with lags of the dependent variable. Moreover, if the data exhibit an intercept/trend, y must be replaced by the demean/detrended series. Both KSS and EG employ a two-step procedure. In the first stage, the researcher, who has a prior regarding the deterministic component characterizing the DGP, runs an ordinary least squares regression of the raw data on an intercept or an intercept and a trend and obtains the residuals (demeaned or detrended series). In turn, the nonlinear unit root test is applied on the estimated residuals. However, when there is uncertainty about the presence of the deterministic components, the econometrician typically regresses the raw data on an intercept or an intercept and a trend, and the ones that are not significant are omitted. We examine the effect of using hypothesis testing to specify the deterministic components of the DGP on the KSS and the EG tests in the next section. It is also noted that the ADF test is not based on this procedure. The test is always run with the raw data and then specific critical values for different restrictions are tabulated to select the DGP. Next, we follow KSS and compare the power of the t_{NL} statistic with that of the ADF and EG tests.

3.1 *Monte Carlo simulation, new parameter values*

KSS evaluate the power of their test by employing a DGP with speed of adjustment parameter $\theta \in \{0.01, 0.05, 0.1, 1\}$. The findings of recent empirical research (Taylor, Peel, and Sarno 2001; Kilian and Taylor 2003; Paya, Venetis, and Peel 2003) suggest that even lower values of θ are warranted, in particular, values around $\theta = 0.001$ are also reported in empirical work.[5] We employ this value as well as the more extreme case of $\theta = 0.0001$ which is closer to the linear unit root case. Regarding γ and ϕ, we set them equal to -1 and 0, which are the values reported or imposed in most empirical research on PPP or other arbitrage conditions. The nominal significance level is set equal to 5% for all the experiments implemented in this study and the number of replications is set to 10,000.

Table 1 reports rejection rates of the unit root hypothesis corresponding to the KSS, EG and ADF statistics. Cases 1–3 correspond to DGPs with no constant, constant and constant and trend, respectively. The results for the KSS and EG tests presented in Panel A are based on the procedure advocated by KSS, where there are priors regarding the nuisance parameters. Not surprisingly, for relative high values of θ, 0.01, the power of the t_{NL} statistic is always higher or similar to the power of the ADF and the EG. As the value of θ decreases, the power of all three statistics falls and when θ reaches 0.001 the power is reduced up to five times. It is important that the reduction in power is generally more severe for the KSS than the ADF so that in some cases (and always for $\theta = 0.0001$) the latter becomes superior to the former.

We now turn to Panel B where there is no prior regarding the deterministic components. Before we discuss the results, we note that a constant and a trend is often found significant when the DGP has none, which alters the rejection probabilities of the KSS and EG tests.[6] Starting with the no constant DGP, Case 1, and the KSS test, the broad conclusion that emerges is that specifying the deterministic components on the basis of hypothesis testing results in lower power compared with Panel A. This is not always true for the remaining cases and, in particular, for small samples and low values of θ. On the contrary, the EG test exhibits now greater power, especially, in small samples. It is also worth mentioning that now the ADF test outperforms the t_{NL} statistic except in Case 3 for $\theta = 0.01$ and T is equal to 100 and 200.[7]

Table 1. Power of alternative unit root tests.

	$\theta = 0.01$			$\theta = 0.001$			$\theta = 0.0001$		
	t_{NL}	EG	ADF	t_{NL}	EG	ADF	t_{NL}	EG	ADF
				Panel A					
Case 1									
$T = 100$	0.917	0.259	0.866	0.178	NA	0.228	0.063	NA	0.135
$T = 200$	0.997	0.958	0.998	0.612	0.147	0.478	0.094	0.059	0.169
$T = 350$	1.000	0.998	1.000	0.972	0.351	0.861	0.203	0.071	0.232
$T = 1000$	1.000	1.000	1.000	1.000	0.999	1.000	0.951	0.245	0.829
Case 2									
$T = 100$	0.477	0.245	0.481	0.100	0.100	0.252	0.052	0.061	0.141
$T = 200$	0.954	0.908	0.960	0.195	0.146	0.412	0.074	0.070	0.168
$T = 350$	1.000	0.996	1.000	0.498	0.303	0.726	0.106	0.081	0.228
$T = 1000$	1.000	1.000	1.000	0.997	0.997	1.000	0.393	0.261	0.769
Case 3									
$T = 100$	0.267	0.164	0.252	0.089	0.081	0.113	0.055	0.052	0.078
$T = 200$	0.814	0.686	0.761	0.115	0.115	0.161	0.060	0.058	0.091
$T = 350$	0.988	0.967	0.991	0.280	0.216	0.251	0.083	0.079	0.117
$T = 1000$	1.000	1.000	1.000	0.970	0.994	0.993	0.202	0.183	0.181
				Panel B					
Case 1									
$T = 100$	0.534	0.383	0.866	0.122	0.129	0.228	0.071	0.082	0.135
$T = 200$	0.859	0.885	0.998	0.242	0.174	0.478	0.094	0.087	0.169
$T = 350$	0.993	0.995	1.000	0.440	0.341	0.861	0.127	0.107	0.232
$T = 1000$	1.000	1.000	1.000	0.982	0.997	1.000	0.298	0.228	0.829
Case 2									
$T = 100$	0.415	0.368	0.481	0.130	0.135	0.252	0.086	0.093	0.141
$T = 200$	0.864	0.895	0.960	0.199	0.189	0.412	0.093	0.096	0.168
$T = 350$	0.996	0.997	1.000	0.411	0.322	0.726	0.124	0.101	0.228
$T = 1000$	1.000	1.000	1.000	0.982	0.995	1.000	0.297	0.240	0.769
Case 3									
$T = 100$	0.352	0.332	0.252	0.114	0.105	0.113	0.070	0.072	0.078
$T = 200$	0.780	0.745	0.761	0.151	0.145	0.161	0.075	0.078	0.091
$T = 350$	0.982	0.987	0.991	0.296	0.231	0.251	0.095	0.097	0.117
$T = 1000$	1.000	1.000	1.000	0.970	0.994	0.993	0.202	0.183	0.181

Notes: The table reports rejection rates of the null hypothesis of a unit root. The nominal significance level is 5%. NA indicates that the value is not available due to the fact that the computation of the statistic is not feasible.

3.2 *Monte Carlo simulation, multiple equilibria*

In the previous exercise, the ESTAR model (1) has only one real equilibrium value, $\bar{y} = 0$. However, with $\phi = 0.1$ and $\gamma \in \{-1.5, -1, -0.5\}$, which are values employed by KSS, there are three equilibria. Specifically, the values of the equilibria are given by

$$\bar{y} = 0 \quad \text{and} \quad \bar{y} = \pm\sqrt{\frac{-\ln((\phi + \gamma)/\gamma)}{\theta}}.$$

The smaller the θ the further apart are the inner and outer equilibrium values. Figure 6 depicts a single realization of four processes with 10,000 observations generated from model (1) with $\phi =$

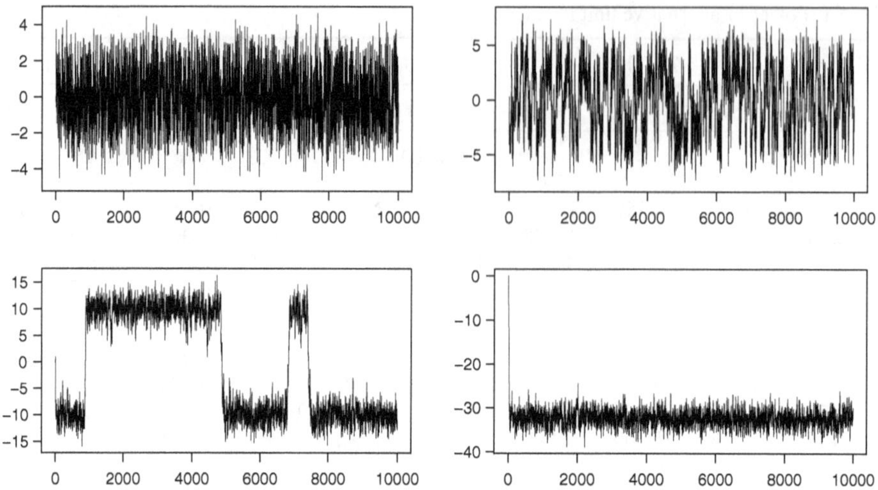

Figure 6. Four simulated ESTAR processes. The parameter values for the DGPs are $\gamma = -1$, $\phi = 0.1$ and θ is set equal to 0.1 (top left), 0.01 (top right), 0.001 (bottom left) and 0.0001 (bottom right).

0.1, $\gamma = -1$ and $\theta \in \{0.1, 0.01, 0.001, 0.0001\}$. We emphasize that the relationship between the parameter θ and the degree of persistence appears to be non-monotonic in the samples considered. As θ decreases, the equilibria move further apart and the degree of persistence increases since shocks make the process bounce between equilibria. However, when the equilibria are *sufficiently* far apart, the process remains in the neighborhood of only one of the equilibria for very long periods until a shock of sufficient magnitude bounces it to the other stable equilibria. Hence the process may appear to be less persistent. Therefore, the relationship between the degree of persistence and the value of θ is not monotonic which motivates the examination of the impact of different values of θ on the power properties of the tests.

The two panels of Table 2 report the power of the unit root tests for $\phi = 0.1$, $\gamma = -1$ and $\theta \in \{0.01, 0.001, 0.0001\}$. Starting with Panel A, which is based on the KSS methodology outlined above, and in the case of a constant and a constant and a trend (Cases 2 and 3), it is interesting that the power of all tests increases as θ decreases. This finding may be attributed to the fact that, in small samples, the series with lower θ hardly ever change their equilibrium value and the persistence in the neighborhood of an equilibrium point is lower for lower values of θ.[8] This is also the reason that the power corresponding to 1000 observations is lower than the power for 350. Note also that for low values of θ, the KSS test performs worst than the competing unit root tests. Turning to Case 1, we observe that while the power of the ADF increases as θ decreases, the power of t_{NL} and EG become virtually zero.[9]

Panel B of Table 2 reports results for the same parameter values as above but with the specification of the deterministic components in the KSS and EG tests being determined by hypothesis testing. Two results for the KSS test are worth mentioning. First, the test never displays the highest power except for Case 3 and $\theta = 0.01$. Second, its power drops with respect to Panel A for $\theta = 0.01$, but improves in the remaining cases.

The overall conclusion of the above results is that the performance of the KSS test is not universally better than the EG and the ADF. Specifically, it depends crucially on, first, the methodology adopted for specifying the deterministic components of the data and, second, the DGP under examination. Regarding the former, new procedures are required which can deal with possible

Table 2. Power of alternative unit root tests for the case of multiple equilibria.

	$\theta = 0.01$			$\theta = 0.001$			$\theta = 0.0001$		
	t_{NL}	EG	ADF	t_{NL}	EG	ADF	t_{NL}	EG	ADF
				Panel A					
Case 1									
$T = 100$	0.888	0.038	0.357	0.004	NA	0.628	0.000	NA	0.751
$T = 200$	0.986	0.201	0.904	0.035	NA	0.915	0.000	NA	0.987
$T = 350$	1.000	0.841	0.989	0.438	NA	0.948	0.000	NA	1.000
$T = 1000$	1.000	1.000	1.000	0.784	NA	0.900	0.000	NA	1.000
Case 2									
$T = 100$	0.306	0.201	0.360	0.422	0.621	0.619	0.510	0.759	0.764
$T = 200$	0.734	0.353	0.580	0.662	0.928	0.907	0.818	0.986	0.991
$T = 350$	0.925	0.833	0.952	0.743	0.968	0.962	0.910	0.999	0.999
$T = 1000$	0.999	1.000	1.000	0.650	0.926	0.904	0.962	1.000	1.000
Case 3									
$T = 100$	0.211	0.144	0.260	0.271	0.463	0.510	0.325	0.623	0.752
$T = 200$	0.489	0.299	0.326	0.549	0.886	0.835	0.705	0.970	0.964
$T = 350$	0.821	0.641	0.489	0.663	0.952	0.940	0.847	0.994	0.995
$T = 1000$	1.000	0.991	0.994	0.629	0.907	0.909	0.934	1.000	1.000
				Panel B					
Case 1									
$T = 100$	0.326	0.261	0.357	0.389	0.628	0.628	0.465	0.750	0.751
$T = 200$	0.593	0.443	0.904	0.665	0.919	0.915	0.797	0.979	0.987
$T = 350$	0.871	0.833	0.989	0.715	0.949	0.948	0.908	0.998	1.000
$T = 1000$	1.000	0.996	1.000	0.673	0.906	0.900	0.964	1.000	1.000
Case 2									
$T = 100$	0.312	0.301	0.360	0.405	0.618	0.619	0.491	0.755	0.764
$T = 200$	0.570	0.412	0.580	0.650	0.910	0.907	0.793	0.987	0.991
$T = 350$	0.895	0.770	0.952	0.742	0.964	0.962	0.899	0.999	0.999
$T = 1000$	1.000	0.993	1.000	0.65	0.903	0.904	0.957	1.000	1.000
Case 3									
$T = 100$	0.229	0.220	0.260	0.317	0.536	0.510	0.387	0.657	0.752
$T = 200$	0.508	0.368	0.326	0.554	0.887	0.835	0.706	0.970	0.964
$T = 350$	0.821	0.641	0.489	0.663	0.952	0.940	0.847	0.994	0.995
$T = 1000$	1.000	0.991	0.994	0.631	0.908	0.909	0.934	1.000	1.000

Notes: The table reports rejection rates of the null hypothesis of a unit root. The nominal significance level is 5%. NA indicates that the value is not available due to the fact that the computation of the statistic is not feasible.

spurious trends in macroeconomic and financial series (e.g. Paya and Peel 2003). These procedures should test jointly for deterministic elements and a unit root. As far as the latter is concerned, in the absence of priors regarding the exact DGP, unit root tests should be general enough to include multiple equilibria and structural change.

Two general tests that incorporate structural change are derived by Sollis (2005 and 2008). The first utilizes the exponential transition function to allow for non-monotonic changes in the deterministic components of the DGP, while the latter allows for both structural change and nonlinearity. Specifically, the Sollis (2008) test facilitates the selection between four competing models: an AR, a time-varying AR, an ESTAR and a time-varying ESTAR. Because these tests nest numerous adjustment mechanisms, they are ideal for investigating the validity of the implications of several theoretical models.[10] For instance, Sollis (2005 and 2008) examine numerous PPP deviations series and find that structural change is an important feature of the data. This finding can be attributed to the presence of changes in monetary policy, productivity and exogenous shocks.

4. Empirical applications

In the introduction, we highlighted the fact that numerous theoretical and empirical contributions suggest that factors such as agent heterogeneity, transactions costs, uncertainty regarding equilibrium values or the sunk costs of international arbitrage can induce smooth transition nonlinearity in the deviation process of asset prices from their fundamental value in different asset markets (Dumas 1992; Gallagher and Taylor 2001; Berka 2005; Kim and Bhattacharya 2009). Many studies have further shown that these processes can be parsimoniously modeled by the ESTAR (Michael, Nobay, and Peel 1997; Taylor, Peel, and Sarno 2001; Sarno and Monoyios 2002; Kilian and Taylor 2003).

However, smooth transition nonlinearity is not constrained to deviations of asset prices from fundamentals. Sargent and Wallace (1973) show that when authorities print money so as to finance a real budget deficit inflation becomes a nonlinear process with multiple equilibria. Evans, Honkapohja, and Marimon (2001) illustrate further that under adaptive learning a stable high inflation state may arise. To this end, Byers and Peel (2000) advocate the use of ESTAR models which allow high persistence of the series as well as multiple equilibria.

Given all this evidence, it seems interesting to test the properties of a number of series representative of those markets. Our data set consists of five real exchange rates, a house price–income ratio, a dividend–price ratio, a stock index basis and an inflation series. The first real exchange rate series is the annual dollar–sterling ($q_{\text{uk,a}}$) analyzed in Lothian and Taylor (1996). The series is extended by using data for the US and UK consumer price indices and the dollar–sterling nominal exchange rate obtained from the International Financial Statistics (IFS) database. The extended data set covers the period from 1791 to 2005. The remaining four are monthly rates for the USA-UK (q_{uk}), USA-Japan (q_{jp}), USA-Canada (q_{can}) and USA-France (q_{fr}) country pairs that cover the period January 1973 to December 2005. The series was constructed by using consumer price indices and nominal exchange rates from the IFS database. We employ the daily spot and futures prices of the FTSE 100 for the period 1 January 1988 to 31 December 1998 to construct the log FTSE 100 basis (b_{ftse}) as analyzed in Sarno and Monoyios (2002). The next two series are the quarterly UK log house price–income ratio ($hp - y$) and the monthly Nasdaq log dividend-price ratio ($d - p$). Data for the former variable span the period 1983–2008 and are obtained from Nationwide and the IFS. Price and dividend data cover the period 1973–2008 and were downloaded from Datastream. The final series is the monthly inflation rate for Brazil (π), which covers the period January 1957 to December 1990. The series is analyzed in Byers and Peel (2000) and Baillie, Chung, and Tieslau (1996) and can be downloaded from http://qed.econ.queensu.ca/jae/. In order to assess the significance of nonlinearities in all series but inflation, we first fit nonlinear ESTAR models of the form proposed by Kilian and Taylor (2003):

$$y_t = \xi_0 + \sum_{i=1}^{p} \xi_i (y_{t-i} - \xi_0) \exp\left(-\frac{\theta}{\text{var}(y_{t-1})}(y_{t-1} - \xi_0)^2\right) + \eta_t, \tag{8}$$

where ξ_i with $i = 1, \ldots, p$ are parameters, p denotes the lag order and $\sum_{i=1}^{p} \xi = 1$.[11] The above parameterization is very appealing for modeling deviations from parity and equilibrium

Table 3. Empirical applications.

Series	$\hat{\theta}$	t_{NL}			EG			ADF		
		NC	C	CT	NC	C	CT	NC	C	CT
$q_{uk,a}$	0.058[a]	−0.871	−3.778[a]	−3.658[a]	NA	7.234[a]	9.854[a]	−0.255	−3.794[a]	−4.327[a]
q_{uk}	0.009[a]	−1.434	−2.671[b]	−2.576	1.543	3.227	3.933	−0.385	−2.488	−2.753
q_{jp}	0.007[a]	−0.630	−2.530	−2.807	NA	2.157	1.6806	−0.457	−2.076	−1.810
q_{can}	0.004[b]	−0.990	−1.513	−1.264	0.413	1.235	1.065	−0.448	−1.556	−1.005
q_{fr}	0.010[a]	−0.446	−1.831	−1.675	NA	2.444	2.540	−0.088	−2.014	−2.090
b_{ftse}	0.0145[a]	−4.162[a]	−4.216[a]	−4.351[a]	29.393[a]	29.393[a]	33.288[a]	−7.661[a]	−7.660[a]	−8.154[a]
$hp - y$	0.011[b]	−0.171	−1.770	−1.914	NA	1.553	1.751	−0.129	−1.645	−1.679
$d - p$	0.009[b]	−0.424	−2.597	−3.186[b]	NA	1.234	3.191	−0.044	−1.533	−1.340
π	0.047[a]	−0.761	−1.136	−1.799	0.389	1.429	1.334	0.837	−0.031	−1.178

Notes: NA indicates that the value is not available due to the fact that the computation of the statistic is not feasible. NC, C and CT correspond to the case of no constant, constant and constant and trend, respectively.
[a]Significance at 5% level.
[b]Significance at 10% significance level.

conditions. Unlike in a linear model, the process moves between a white noise and a unit root depending on the size of the deviation, $|y_{t-1} - \xi_0|$ and the speed of adjustment θ. Intuitively, small deviations that do not cover transactions costs or the sunk costs of international arbitrage are left uncorrected and the process exhibits unit root behavior. On the other hand, large deviations are much less persistent. Given the size of the deviation, the speed of mean reversion increases with θ. As far as the inflation for Brazil is concerned, we employ the estimates provided by Byers and Peel (2000).[12] These estimates indicate that the process moves between multiple equilibria, one of which is high and one low inflation.

The second column of Table 3 shows the estimated θ coefficients. The estimates vary considerably across applications. Moreover, all coefficients are statistically significant at least at the 10% significance level implying that the series are nonlinear and globally stationary. The maximum θ estimate is about 0.058 and corresponds to the annual dollar-sterling real exchange rate data. While the minimum is about 0.004, which lies outside the range examined by KSS but included in the previous section, for the real exchange rate of Canada.

These results have the following economic implications. Regarding real exchange rates, they suggest that prices and exchange rates are related to the adjustment mechanism being nonlinear. Moreover, they are in line with other studies which utilize nonlinear models and explain the documented difficulty of unit root tests typically employed in the 1980s to reject the null hypothesis (Michael, Nobay, and Peel 1997; Sollis 2008). Turning to the dividend-price ratio, the fact that θ is significant for the Nasdaq index complements the analysis of Gallagher and Taylor (2001) and *rules* out the presence of bubbles (the dot-com bubble) suggested by other studies. A similar conclusion can be drawn from the estimate of the speed of adjustment for the house price-income ratio of the UK housing market. The fact that the FTSE futures basis is nonlinearly mean reverting is in accordance with Sarno and Monoyios (2002) and stresses the importance of modeling stock market frictions.

Turning to the results displayed in the remaining columns of Table 3, we observe that the unit root hypothesis cannot be rejected for all the monthly real exchange rates, the house price-income ratio and the dividend-price ratio.[13] On the other hand, the null is rejected for the annual dollar-sterling real exchange rate and the FTSE 100 basis for the constant and constant and trend cases. These two series have the highest estimated θ values. The fact that the number of rejections is substantially lower than the number of statistically significant θ coefficients raises concerns regarding the power of the tests which is consistent with the results of the previous section.

A particularly interesting case is the inflation rate series presented in the last row of the table. As mentioned above, Byers and Peel (2000) show that this process exhibits multiple equilibria, one with low inflation rate and one with high. The country appears to be in its low steady state until the mid-1980s (mean monthly inflation before 1986 was 3.6%) and then to move slowly into the high state (the mean inflation for the period 1986–1990 was 17.3). The change from one equilibrium to the other has clearly severe consequences for unit root tests. The ADF which cannot account for multiple equilibria suggests that the series is explosive for the no constant and constant cases.[14] This has important economic implications since, via PPP, the Brazilian nominal exchange rate should also be explosive. Moreover, asset returns should exhibit a similar behavior. The results for the t_{NL} and EG statistics, although do not imply an explosive behavior, still indicate that non-stationarity cannot be rejected.

Overall, rejections of the null hypothesis for all tests appear to be related with the magnitude of the θ coefficient, the sample size and the existence of multiple equilibria. These results seem to be in line with the simulation experiments.

5. Conclusion

Over the last decades and especially since the recent financial crisis, there has been a steadily increasing interest in the development and application of nonlinear time series models. In this study, we focus on the widely used family of smooth transition autoregressive models, which appear to parsimoniously capture the nonlinear dependence of many economic and financial time series. Specifically, we illustrate the flexibility of the ESTAR model to encompass a number of different characteristics found in empirical work and suggested by the theoretical literature using market frictions and heterogeneous agents. These are multiple equilibria, complex dynamics, chaotic-like behavior and spurious trends.

In turn, we examine the properties of a recently proposed unit root test against smooth transition stationary processes when there are no priors regarding the deterministic components and possible multiple equilibria. We also make comparison with two alternative unit root tests widely employed in the literature. Our results stress that the power of the tests is highly dependent on the properties of the series. Moreover, no test dominates the others.

Finally, we run several applications on the foreign exchange, stock and housing markets as well as a hyper-inflation series. Despite the fact that we can successfully fit nonlinear models implying a stable nonlinear adjustment mechanism which supports arbitrage conditions as well as globally stationary multiple equilibria inflation series, unit root tests fail, in general, to detect the mean reversion. Overall, our findings suggest that the difficulty to reject the unit root property in many financial and macroeconomic data on the basis of unit root testing should not be regarded as conclusive evidence. In particular, the factors examined here can severely contaminate the power of both linear and nonlinear unit root tests.

Acknowledgements

We are grateful to the editors of the special issue and an anonymous referee for constructive comments. Any remaining errors are our own responsibility. Ivan Paya acknowledges financial support from the Spanish Ministerio de Educacion y Ciencia Research Project ECO2008-05721/ECON.

Notes

1. In the case that agents form adaptive expectations, the lower equilibrium is stable but not the higher, ruling out steady states of high inflation. However, Evans, Honkapohja, and Marimon (2001) illustrate that two stable solutions can also occur and, therefore, a stable high inflation state may arise with adaptive learning.
2. The assumption can be relaxed to allow ϵ to be a martingale difference sequence.
3. We use model (2) to simulate 1000 series each of 100 observations and then apply the ADF test with a constant and a trend. The test rejects the null of a unit root, while the process is stationary, only in 7 out of the 1000 cases at the 5% significance level.
4. Model 2 corresponds to the estimates for the case of Brazil. Note that the speed of adjustment coefficient in Equation (2) has been scaled by the variance of the series.
5. In order to make comparisons across models and studies the speed of adjustment parameter must be standardized. That is, it must be divided by the variance of y_{t-d}.
6. For instance, in sample sizes of 100 and 200 around 70% and 65% of the times, respectively, an intercept or a trend are found significant.
7. The results for the ADF test are the same in Panels A and B due to the fact that the deterministic components are always obtain within the test.
8. Note that in Figure 1, the series with $\theta = 0.001$ is more persistent (the autocorrelation coefficient is $\rho_1 = 0.993$) than the series with $\theta = 0.01$ ($\rho_1 = 0.945$) for a sample of 10,000 observations. However, the persistence displayed by the series with $\theta = 0.001$ is actually lower for small sample sizes similar to the ones used in our Monte Carlo ($T = 100, 200, 350, 1000$). This is due to the fact that, in small samples, the series with lower θ hardly ever changes its equilibrium value and the persistence 'within' a regime (with ρ_1 around 0.84) is lower than in the case of $\theta = 0.01$ ($\rho_1 = 0.945$).
9. The power of the EG test is not reported for θ equal to 0.001 and 0.0001 due to the fact that the generated series take only positive (values) values making the computation of the statistic unfeasible.
10. Our focus on the KSS, EG and ADF tests is based on their popularity as well as the fact that they are simple and not computationally intensive. Examining the performance of the test of Sollis (2008) is a promising direction for future research.
11. The lag order p is determined on the basis of the Akaike Information Criterion.
12. Note that the authors adopt a slightly different ESTAR parameterization that the one of Kilian and Taylor (2003) allowing for the sum of the autoregressive coefficients to be different from unity.
13. There are two exceptions, q_{uk} in the KSS constant case and $d - p$ in the KSS constant and trend case.
14. The critical values for the explosive alternative can be found in Fuller (1996).

References

Ackermann, J. 2008. The subprime crisis and its consequences. *Journal of Financial Stability* 4, no. 4: 329–37.

Baillie, R.T., C.-F. Chung, and M.A. Tieslau. 1996. Analysing inflation by the fractionally integrated ARFIMA–GARCH model. *Journal of Applied Econometrics* 11, no. 1: 23–40.

Benhabib, J., S. Schmitt-Grohe, and M. Uribe. 2001. Monetary policy and multiple equilibria. *American Economic Review* 91, no. 1: 167–86.

Berka, M. 2005. General equilibrium model of arbitrage trade and real exchange rate persistence. MPRA Paper 234, University Library of Munich, Munich.

Black, A., P. Fraser, and M. Hoesli. 2006. House prices, fundamentals and bubbles. *Journal of Business Finance & Accounting* 33, nos. 9–10: 1535–55.

Bonanno, G., F. Lillo, and R.N. Mantegna. 2001. Levels of complexity in financial markets. *Physica A* 299, no. 1–2: 16–27.

Brock, W.A. 1988. Nonlinearity and complex dynamics in economics and finance. Working papers, Wisconsin Madison – Social Systems.

Byers, D.J., and D.A. Peel. 2000. Non-linear dynamics of inflation in high inflation economies. *Manchester School* 68, suppl. s1: 23–37.

Campbell, J.Y., and R.J. Shiller. 1988. The dividend–price ratio and expectations of future dividends and discount factors. *Review of Financial Studies* 1, no. 3: 195–228.

Chapell, D. 1997. Chaotic behaviour in a simple model of inflation. *Manchester School* 65, no. 3: 235–43.

Day, R.H. 1982. Irregular growth cycles. *American Economic Review* 72, no. 3: 406–14.

De Grauwe, P., H. Dewachter, and M. Embrechts. 1993. *Exchange rate theory: chaotic models of foreign exchange markets*. Oxford: Blackwell.

De Grauwe, P., and M. Grimaldi. 2006. Exchange rate puzzles: a tale of switching attractors. *European Economic Review* 50, no. 1: 1–33.

Dumas, B. 1992. Dynamic equilibrium and the real exchange rate in a spatially separated world. *Review of Financial Studies* 5, no. 2: 153–80.

Enders, W., and C.W.J. Granger. 1998. Unit-root tests and asymmetric adjustment with an example using the term structure of interest rates. *Journal of Business & Economic Statistics* 16, no. 3: 304–11.

Evans, G.W., S. Honkapohja, and R. Marimon. 2001. Convergence in monetary inflation models with heterogeneous learning rules. *Macroeconomic Dynamics* 5, no. 1: 1–31.

Fuller. 1996. *Introduction to statistical time series*. New York: Wiley.

Gallagher, L.A., and M.P. Taylor. 2001. Risky arbitrage, limits of arbitrage, and nonlinear adjustment in the dividend–price ratio. *Economic Inquiry* 39, no. 4: 524–36.

Grandmont, J.M. 1985. On endogenous competitive cycles. *Econometrica* 53, no. 4: 995–1045.

Huang, W., and R. Day. 1993. Chaotically switching bear and bull markets, the derivation of stock price distributions from behavioral rules. In *Nonlinear dynamics and evolutionary economics*, ed. R. Daya and P. Chen, 169–82. Oxford: Oxford University Press.

Kaizoji, T. 2004. Intermittent chaos in a model of financial markets with heterogeneous agents. *Chaos, Solitons and Fractals* 20, no. 2: 323–7.

Kapetanios, G., Y. Shin, and A. Snell. 2003. Testing for a unit root in the nonlinear STAR framework. *Journal of Econometrics* 112, no. 2: 359–79.

Kilian, L., and M.P. Taylor. 2003. Why is it so difficult to beat the random walk forecast of exchange rates? *Journal of International Economics* 60, no. 1: 85–107.

Kim, S.-W., and R. Bhattacharya. 2009. Regional housing prices in the USA: an empirical investigation of nonlinearity. *The Journal of Real Estate Finance and Economics* 38, no. 4: 443–60.

Kyrtsou, C. 2008. Re-examining the sources of heteroskedasticity: the paradigm of noisy chaotic models. *Physica A* 387, no. 27: 6785–9.

Kyrtsou, C., and A.G. Malliaris. 2009. The impact of information signals on market prices when agents have non-linear trading rules. *Economic Modelling* 26, no. 1: 167–76.

Kyrtsou, C., and C. Vorlow. 2009. Modelling non-linear comovements between time series. *Journal of Macroeconomics* 31, no. 1: 200–11.

Lothian, J.R., and M.P. Taylor. 1996. Real exchange rate behavior: the recent float from the perspective of the past two centuries. *Journal of Political Economy* 104, no. 3: 488–509.

Lundbergh, S., and T. Teräsvirta. 2002. Forecasting with smooth transition autoregressive models. In *A companion to economic forecasting*, ed. M.P. Clements and D.F. Hendry, 485–509. Oxford: Blackwell.

Lundbergh, S., T. Tërasvirta, and D. van Dijk. 2003. Time-varying smooth transition autoregressive models. *Journal of Business & Economic Statistics* 21, no. 1: 104–21.

Luukkonen, R., P. Saikkonen, and T. Tërasvirta. 1988. Testing linearity against smooth transition autoregressive models. *International Economic Review* 75, no. 3: 419–99.

Michael, P., R.A. Nobay, and D.A. Peel. 1997. Transactions costs and nonlinear adjustment in real exchange rates: an empirical investigation. *Journal of Political Economy* 105, no. 4: 862–79.

Papell, D.H. 2002. The great appreciation, the great depreciation, and the purchasing power parity hypothesis. *Journal of International Economics* 57, no. 1: 51–82.

Pavlidis, E.G., I. Paya, and D.A. Peel. 2009. The econometrics of exchange rates. In *Palgrave handbook of econometrics*, ed. T. Mills and K. Patterson, vol. 2, Part 5.4, 1025–86. London: Palgrave.

Paya, I., and D.A. Peel. 2003. Purchasing power parity adjustment speeds in high frequency data when the equilibrium real exchange rate is proxied by a deterministic trend. *Manchester School* 71, Suppl. 1: 39–53.

Paya, I., I.A. Venetis, and D.A. Peel. 2003. Further evidence on PPP adjustment speeds: the case of effective real exchange rates and the EMS. *Oxford Bulletin of Economics and Statistics* 65, no. 4: 421–37.

Peel, D.A., and M.P. Taylor. 2002. Covered interest rate arbitrage in the interwar period and the Keynes–Einzig conjecture. *Journal of Money, Credit and Banking* 34, no. 1: 51–75.

Sargent, T.J., and N. Wallace. 1973. Rational expectations and the dynamics of hyperinflation. *International Economic Review* 14, no. 2: 328–50.

Sarno, L., and Monoyios, M. 2002. Mean reversion in stock index futures markets: a nonlinear analysis. *Journal of Futures Markets* 22, no. 4: 285–314.

Sarno, L., M.P. Taylor, and D.A. Peel. 2003. Nonlinear equilibrium correction in US real money balances, 1869–1997. *Journal of Money, Credit and Banking* 35, no. 5: 787–99.

Sollis, R. 2005. Evidence on purchasing power parity from univariate models: the case of smooth transition trend-stationary. *Journal of Applied Econometrics* 20, no. 1: 79–98.

Sollis, R. 2008. US dollar real exchange rates: nonlinearity revisited. *Journal of International Money and Finance* 27, no. 4: 516–28.

Sollis, R., S. Leybourne, and P. Newbold. 2000. Stochastic unit roots modelling of stock market indices. *Applied Financial Economics* 10, no. 3: 311–5.

Taylor, N., D. van Dijk, P.H. Franses, and A. Lucas. 2000. SETS, arbitrage activity, and stock price dynamics. *Journal of Banking & Finance* 24, no. 8: 1289–306.

Taylor, M.P., D.A. Peel, and L. Sarno. 2001. Nonlinear mean-reversion in real exchange rates: toward a solution to the purchasing power parity puzzles. *International Economic Review* 42, no. 4: 1015–42.

Index

Note: **Bold** page numbers refer to tables, *italic* page numbers refer to figures and page numbers followed by "n" denote endnotes.

For Product Safety Concerns and Information please contact our EU representative GPSR@taylorandfrancis.com
Taylor & Francis Verlag GmbH, Kaufingerstraße 24, 80331 München, Germany

www.ingramcontent.com/pod-product-compliance
Lightning Source LLC
LaVergne TN
LVHW080649011026
849160LV00014B/1366

* 9 7 8 0 3 6 7 6 7 1 0 9 9 *